CLANDESTINE

ENCOUNTERS

CLANDESTINE

PHILOSOPHY IN THE NARRATIVES
OF MAURICE BLANCHOT

ENCOUNTERS

edited by

KEVIN HART

University of Notre Dame Press

Notre Dame, Indiana

Library of Congress Cataloging-in-Publication Data

Clandestine encounters : philosophy in the narratives of Maurice Blanchot /
edited by Kevin Hart.
    p. cm.
Includes bibliographical references and index.
ISBN-13: 978-0-268-03092-6 (pbk. : alk. paper)
ISBN-10: 0-268-03092-8 (pbk. : alk. paper)
1. Blanchot, Maurice—Criticism and interpretation. 2. Blanchot, Maurice—
Philosophy. 3. Philosophy in literature.   I. Hart, Kevin, 1954–
PQ2603.L3343Z572   2010
843'.912—dc22
                                       2010024332

 This book is printed on recycled paper.

for Geoffrey Hartman

Contents

viii   *Contents*

Acknowledgments

I would like to thank Christophe Bident and Jean-Luc Nancy for answering questions about Maurice Blanchot that I put to them while editing this collection of essays. As always, the Comité de Rédaction Espace Maurice Blanchot supplied exact information and sound advice. Marianne Peracchio translated Christophe Bident's essay, and Alain Toumayan helped to bring it to a high polish in English. I am indebted to both of them. Jean-Louis Giovannoni generously gave permission for several lines from his poems to be translated into English and to appear in Christophe Bident's essay on *Au moment voulu*. Claire Lyu kindly answered my questions about some French idioms in Blanchot. From the very beginning, when I proposed this collection of essays to her over lunch, Barbara Hanrahan, director of the University of Notre Dame Press, has been supportive. Her ability to tell what will be a good book from a few words about it, along with her insight into making books and her creativity in publishing them, make her a beacon in the world of university presses in North America. Rebecca DeBoer provided acute and probing copy-editing. Once again, my wife and children allowed me the time to reread those volumes published by Gallimard, Minuit, Fata Morgana, and several little presses, volumes that have given me such intricate pleasure over so many years. To my family I wish "le oui léger, innocent, de la lecture" in anything they read. To my fellow contributors, who know what it is to write on Blanchot, I recall these words in memory of their work, "Toujours cette angoisse au moment d'écrire. . . ." And to the dedicatee, Geoffrey Hartman, I simply say, "Pour l'amitié."

CLANDESTINE

ENCOUNTERS

INTRODUCTION

PHILOSOPHY AND THE PHILOSOPHICAL

Kevin Hart

Speaking at Maurice Blanchot's cremation at Guyancourt, outside Paris, on February 24, 2003, Jacques Derrida evoked his friend's "récits, novels, fictions" that "we are scarcely beginning, it seems to me, to read," and observed that their "future remains pretty much intact," untouched by literary or philosophical criticism.[1] He then went on to mention *L'attente l'oubli* (1962) and *L'écriture du désastre* (1980) as examples of works that "inseparably mix, in a still unprecedented way, philosophical meditation and poetic fiction" (45). Some years earlier, when introducing *Parages* (1986), a book of his essays and lectures on and around Blanchot, Derrida had noted that he had recently rediscovered the narrative part of his friend's oeuvre. All of Blanchot's narratives, not only *L'attente l'oubli* and *L'écriture du désastre,* query the usual distinctions between philosophy and literature, he had found, and he suggested that a whole new redistribution of distinctions was needed before we could talk of them. Doubtless one should not speak without caution of the "literary critical" and "philosophical" works of Blanchot, Derrida wrote, for those labels are woefully inadequate to the singular texts they seek to describe. Yet the books by Blanchot that we conventionally recognize by those terms—from *Faux pas* (1943) to *La communauté inavouable* (1983)—belong to an "essential movement of thought" that Derrida had long acknowledged and had taken into account in his own writing.[2] The "fictions," as he called them, had remained inaccessible to him, however. Reading them, he said, was like being submerged "in a fog from which came to me only fascinating gleams, and sometimes, but at irregular intervals, the light of an invisible beacon on the coast" (11). In 1995, speaking about Blanchot's last narrative, *L'instant de ma mort* (1994), Derrida once again noted the difficulty of classifying the work. "I do not know whether this text belongs, purely and properly and strictly and rigorously speaking, to the space of literature [*l'espace de la littérature*], whether it is a fiction or a testimony, and, above all, to what extent it calls these distinctions into question or causes them to tremble."[3]

Derrida is right: we have yet to read Blanchot's narratives with the openness to their ways of being that is needed, and a part of that intellectual labor is a rethinking of the relations between the philosophical and the literary in them. Derrida has jump-started this process with *Parages* (1986) and *Demeure* (1998), but, as he says, the future of Blanchot's narratives has not yet been compromised, let alone programmed, by past or present criticism.[4] I recall a comment he made to me in New York in 1997: "It will be centuries—*centuries!*—before we can read Blanchot's fictions," quickly adding, "He has rethought so radically what it means to read and write that each page calls forth an immense commentary." The thought of all those decades of close reading of Blanchot seemed to suffuse him with pleasure, and all the contributors to this collection will testify to the strange joy that comes from responding as fully as possible to Blanchot's novels and *récits*. This collection of new essays seeks to take a modest step along the path of reading Blanchot well. All his narratives are commented upon: the early stories "Le dernier mot" (1935) and "L'idylle" (1936); *Thomas l'obscur,* mostly the *récit* (1950) but also the novel (1941); *Aminadab* (1942), *Le Très-Haut* (1948), *L'arrêt de mort* (1948), "La folie du jour" (1949), *Au moment voulu* (1951), *Celui qui ne m'accompagnait pas* (1953), *Le dernier homme* (1957), and *L'instant de ma mort* (1994).[5] Of the "mixed" works, full attention is given to *L'attente l'oubli* (1962), although neither *Le pas au-delà* (1973) nor *L'écriture du désastre* (1980) is considered.[6] To be sure, traces of a narrative can be discerned in each of these fragmentary texts but not enough, or not regularly enough, to call forth sustained commentary under the heading of "Philosophy in the Narratives of Maurice Blanchot." Another work that might be considered "mixed," *L'entretien infini* (1969), begins with a "fictional" dialogue of considerable interest, and a chapter has been devoted to it.[7]

For the title of this collection of essays, I have adapted the title of Blanchot's contribution to François Laurelle's *Textes pour Emmanuel Lévinas* (1980), "Notre compagne clandestine." Blanchot recalls his time with Lévinas at Strasbourg in the 1920s, an encounter not only with a man who would become a lifelong friend but also with philosophy. As soon as he had met Lévinas, Blanchot says, "it was with a sort of testimony that I persuaded myself that philosophy was life itself, youth itself, in its unbridled—yet nonetheless reasonable—passion, renewing itself continually and suddenly by an explosion of new and enigmatic thoughts."[8] Impatient with the sequestering of philosophy exclusively to the world of professors, Blanchot proclaims, "Whether shamefully, gloriously, mistakenly, or by default, we are all philosophers" (41). Yet Blanchot is sympathetic to that side of modern philosophy that declares or prophesies the end of philosophy, whether it be the end of metaphysics (Kant) or the conclusion of philosophy itself in one or more ways (Nietzsche, Hegel, Heidegger). So it comes as a surprise to hear Blanchot embracing philosophy in such an unrestrained way. As it happens, he does not embrace *philosophy* without reserve, and he remains committed to some ideas in that dark strain of modern philosophy. Yet those ideas do not have their roots in Kant, Hegel, Nietzsche, or Heidegger. Those roots go far deeper, all the way back to Greek philosophy and one of its most enduring irritants, skepticism.

Blanchot well knows, as he writes in another essay, that "[w]hat ends, continues."[9] And in order to keep faith with both philosophy's self-critique and its remarkable ability to renew itself from unlikely points and in surprising ways, he does what any good philosopher would do: he draws a distinction. He prefers to talk, he says, of "the philosophical" rather than of "philosophy" as such. The philosophical would be that which prompts "a questioning so radical that the entire tradition would have to be called forth in its support" (41). Later in the essay he returns to the word "philosophical" when giving a precise sense of what he values in Lévinas's writing. One is always struck, he says, by one of his typical procedures: to begin, or to follow out, an analysis (most often, phenomenologically inspired) with such rigor and informed understanding that it seems precisely in this way that everything is said and that truth itself is disclosed—right along, that is, until we get to a minor remark, usually introduced by, e.g., an "*unless*" ["à moins que"] to which we cannot fail to be attentive, which fissures the whole of the preceding text, disturbing the solid order we had been called upon to observe, an order that nonetheless remains important. This is perhaps *the* movement that could properly be called philosophical [*C'est peut-être là le mouvement proprement philosophique*], not by stroke of force or belabored assertion, but a movement that was already Plato's expedient in his dialogues (his probity, and ruse as well). (48)

For Blanchot, then, the philosophical would be that which undoes an apparent order without simply denying its importance or replacing it with something else.

Elsewhere, as we shall see, Blanchot will tell us a lot more about this movement that characterizes the philosophical, but here he notes something significant about it, to which Derrida was alert, and which will become important when we read Blanchot's narratives. "Philosophy would henceforth be our companion day and night," he writes of his student days in Strasbourg, "even by losing its name [*en perdant son nom*], by becoming literature, scholarship, the lack thereof, or by standing aside" (42). Philosophy loses its proper name and the rights accrued to it over the centuries—to sit in judgment over other discourses, to weigh their rationality, their truth claims, and to expand itself by means of the formula "the philosophy of *x*"—and it does so first of all in becoming the philosophical. One way it does that is in becoming literature when literature constitutes itself as a radical questioning, beginning, no doubt, with received notions of "literature" as given by Nicolas Boileau, Charles Augustin Saint-Beuve, and the brothers Edmond and Jules Goncourt, among others. The same would presumably happen with anthropology, history, politics, psychology, sociology, and so forth. So philosophy becomes a clandestine companion—secret, concealed, working underground—hidden in other discourses in order to question everything more thoroughly than any one discipline will allow, even the discipline that philosophy itself has become.

In becoming philosophical we need to be attentive to philosophy without being unduly distracted by the prestige of the proper names we associate with it, big names from Heraclitus to Derrida, and perhaps without our paths being circumscribed by borders between its provinces—epistemology, ethics, logic, metaphysics, political philosophy, and the rest—and without restricting ourselves to the vocabularies that have imposed themselves as foundational at specific times, from the Greeks (*logos* and *nous, ousia* and *morphē*) to the moderns (consciousness and intentionality, the transcendental and the reduction, among others). The vocabulary of intelligibility given by Aristotle in Book Delta of the *Metaphysics* is essential to thought, but it is also essential, Blanchot would remind us, that we remain attuned to what presses against intelligibility. Not that Blanchot was himself inattentive to the formal study of philosophy. No later than 1929 he was working at the Sorbonne on a thesis for a Diplôme d'Études Supérieures. Its title was "La conception du dogmatisme chez les sceptiques."[10] The thesis was submitted in June 1930, about two years before he started writing *Thomas l'obscur,* in which one can feel the pressure of its apparent concerns from time to time.[11] Throughout his life, he read philosophy with care, and, as Derrida would admiringly observe in conversation, had a profound "philosophical culture." His interest in skepticism would color that culture and would be transformed in his writings, both theoretical and literary—if I may rest lightly for a moment on a distinction that gives way in his later writing.

Blanchot's early interest in skepticism returns unexpectedly in "Notre campagne clandestine," prompted by a sentence in one of his friend's books. Toward the end of Lévinas's *Autrement qu'être ou au-delà de l'essence* (1974) we read, "Language is already skepticism" [*Le langage est déjà scepticisme*].[12] As Blanchot rightly suggests, the sentence should be pronounced with the accent on the adverb: "Language is *already* skepticism" (47). The skeptical is not something that contaminates language when it is used imprecisely or something into which it stumbles when it attempts to grasp metaphysical principles outside the realm of the understanding, Lévinas suggests. Not at all: the skeptical is constitutive of language as such. This insight becomes the *point d'appui* of Blanchot's essay. What intrigues him, as it does every student of skepticism, is that, "[w]hile easily refuted, the refutation leaves skepticism intact. Is it really contradicted when it openly uses reasons that it destroys?" (42).[13] He goes on:

> Contradiction is also the essence of skepticism: just as it combats every dogmatism openly, by exposing its unsatisfactory or onerous presuppositions (origin, truth, value, authenticity, the exemplary or proper, etc.), so does it do so in an implicit way, referring itself back to a "dogmatism" so absolute that every assertion is threatened (this is already to be observed in the ancient skeptics and in Sextus Empiricus). (42)

This situation does not allow us to accede to an easily won nihilism, or to a loose and baggy epistemological or moral relativism, which merely teaches us that there is no point in searching for the truth. Instead, as Blanchot's Lévinas realizes, it requires us to recognize that everything we say is "overseen by an indefatigable adversary [*contradicteur infatigable*], one to whom he does not concede but who obliges him to go further, not beyond reason into the facility of the irrational or towards a mystical effusion, but rather towards another reason, towards the other as reason or demand [*mais vers une raison autre, vers l'autre comme raison ou exigence*]" (42).

In *Autrement qu'être,* Lévinas elaborates this theme in terms of a distinction between the Saying and the Said. It is not simply a division between two different functions of language. "Is not the inescapable fate in which being immediately includes the statement of being's *other* not due to the hold the *said* has over the *saying,* to the *oracle* in which the *said* is immobilized?," the philosopher asks in one of the rhetorical questions that contribute to his unique style.[14] Saying is an ethical openness to the other person, and—in its moment of self-exposure, its act of invitation and unstudied receptiveness—is strictly irreducible to the settled being of the Said. And yet there is an inevitable passage from the Saying to the Said. For as Stéphane Mallarmé observed, "everything in the world exists to end up as a book."[15] The master had in mind *Le livre,* his projected great book that would contain the whole world. Yet the remark can also be played in a minor key, and that is what Lévinas wishes to do: the book in question may well be a collection of parliamentary debates or a classroom notebook, not a collection of poems or a novel, and once the Saying has become the Said it presents a closed face to us. Unless, of course, it is unsaid, shaken up, by not attending solely to what is written as a list of so many themes but by being approached from a fresh angle, with a view to indicating that another person is presumed by what has been said, even if only by being addressed or being assumed to read what has been written.

Lévinas's later moral philosophy turns on affirming the Saying without the Said, on accepting a "responsibility for another" that is "bound to an irrecuperable, unrepresentable, past, temporalizing according to a time with separate epochs, in a diachrony" (47). In Saying, I do not speak to you simply in the present, I address you as you come to me from an immemorial past that has never been present, and that frustrates any attempt I might make to figure my responsibility for you in the limited terms of a moral contract made in the past, the present, or even in a time to come. I am always and already responsible for the other person, regardless of any relation or non-relation I may have with him or her, even to the point, Lévinas will say in a moment of hyperbole, of being responsible for the other person's lack of responsibility.[16] Blanchot affirms this idea of Saying without the Said, speaking, in a darker tone, of "the unqualifiable Saying, the glory of a 'narrative voice' that speaks clearly, without ever being obscured by the opacity or the enigma or the terrible horror of what it communicates."[17] It is an instance, one among many, of Blanchot accepting a distinction drawn by a philosopher in the narrow sense of the word and then drawing it into his own terms: a translation, if you like, of philosophy into the philosophical. What is at issue, as we shall see, is what Blanchot means by "narrative voice."

I return to the expression "indefatigable adversary." When reading these words, and not limiting them to a narrowly dialectical context, anyone familiar with Blanchot's narrative writing is likely to think of *Thomas l'obscur*, where an obscure nonbeing sets itself on Thomas in the night. "He was locked in combat with something inaccessible, foreign, something of which he could say: That doesn't exist . . . and which nonetheless filled him with terror as he sensed it wandering about in the region of his solitude."[18] One may think, too, of the terse yet constant questioning in

Celui qui ne m'accompagnait pas, and the dialogues in *L'entretien infini* and hidden even in fragments of *Le pas au-delà* and *L'écriture du désastre.* In another way, the words on the last page of *L'arrêt de mort* come to mind: "As for me, I have not been the unfortunate messenger of a thought [*une pensée*] stronger than I, nor its plaything, nor its victim, because that *thought,* if it has conquered me [*si elle m'a vaincu*], has only conquered through me, and in the end has always been equal to me."[19] Certainly we also think more generally of the "other" evoked by Blanchot, "the other as reason or demand," that impinges on all his narrative writing, as well as on all his critical and philosophical writing. It is tempting to associate skepticism, understood as contestation of any dogmatic attitude, with one of the ways in which this "other" presses on some of Blanchot's narratives. For there is often a moment in these narratives when a settled view, a situation or language itself, turns into questions that are seemingly without end. In *Celui qui ne m'accompagnait pas* we read of a question that "kept opening and closing" so that the narrator "could not even fall into it"; and in *Le dernier homme* we are told, "our words are so light that they keep opening out into questions," while in *L'attente l'oubli* one fragment reads, "When you affirm, you still question."[20]

We can get closer to what this "other" is for Blanchot if we turn to another of his essays on a philosopher, this time his reflections on Maurice Merleau-Ponty, "Le 'discours philosophique'" (1971). The philosopher and the writer are very close to one another, Blanchot says, since each is borne along by a movement of self-effacement. Philosophy does not forever depend on the one who develops it: the *Phenomenology of Mind,* for example, transcends Hegel's signature.[21] And the same is true, Blanchot says, of a novel or a *récit.* On hearing this, we are likely to recoil and insist on the importance of an authorial idiom when reading Rabelais or Flaubert, Proust or Duras. Yet Blanchot looks at the matter through the lens of ontology: "before the work, the writer does not yet exist; after the work, he is no longer there: which means that his existence is open to question."[22] Philosophical discourse is *"without right,"* he says; it does not have the legitimate power to say what it wants to say—the truth—and keeps falling short of itself even when, especially when, it authorizes itself to tell the truth.[23] He turns to *Le visible et l'invisible* (1964) to hear what Merleau-Ponty says on the topic:

It is a question of knowing if philosophy, as the reconquest of brute or wild being [*comme reconquête de l'être brut ou sauvage*], can be accomplished by means of eloquent language, or if it would not be necessary for philosophy to use language in a way that takes its power of immediate or direct signification from it in order to match it with what it wants all the same to say [*pour l'égaler à ce qu'elle veut tout de même dire*].[24]

Philosophy needs an indirect mode of expression in order to be able to say what it wants to say. It has known that ever since Plato wrote dialogues. But what is this something that can only be spoken of indirectly?

The philosopher, Blanchot says (with Merleau-Ponty specifically in mind), is the one who speaks in the name of philosophy, forever questioning what comes before him or her, including his or her received language and style of questioning, and holding open "an empty place" where "a word always other" (2) than the one he or she actually says can indirectly be heard. So the philosopher is the person of "double speech" (2), oriented to two phased counterparts. On the one hand, the philosopher elaborates a discourse, a rigorous critical reflection on being, knowledge, rights, and so on; while, on the other hand, he or she responds to a "*dis-course*," Blanchot's term for a word without any rights, the "other word, word of the Other [*l'Autre*]" (2), which lacks any sense or direction and cannot be heard directly. This "other word" incessantly poses a question to us, disturbing the discourse on being, knowledge, and rights, while nonetheless leaving it intact. We do not doubt that this discourse has its value, but the question that comes to us from the other word makes the philosopher lose this discourse at a certain point. And that loss, for Blanchot, is constitutive of "philosophical discourse" (4). Philosophy loses itself when "the other word" comes to dispute the philosopher's argument, even in its most assured points, thereby forcing him or her to continue the discussion by examining its premises and conclusion ever more radically. Merleau-Ponty writes "philosophical discourse," Blanchot thinks, in being attentive to the indirect call of brute or wild being, while, for his part, Blanchot calls this "other word" the murmur of the Outside [*le Dehors*].[25] We might see ancient skepticism, as Blanchot understands it, as a foreshadowing of this *dis-course* of the Outside.

It is worthwhile to pause a moment to consider this central notion of the Outside, for it comes up time and again in the essays in this collection, and has already been raised in the notion of "narrative voice."

Blanchot approaches the Outside (or as he sometimes calls it, the Neutral or the Imaginary) from several vantage points—from literature and art, from mysticism and the everyday, from Marxism and psychoanalysis, and always from dying. There can be no understanding any of his writings, including his narratives, without grasping what he means by it; and this is no simple matter, partly because of the strangeness of the notion itself and partly because he characterizes it in different ways, depending on the text or question which he is considering. Consider, first, his evocation of it in "La littérature et le droit à la mort" (1947–48):

> The word acts not as an ideal force but as an obscure power, as an incantation that coerces things, makes them *really* present outside of themselves. It is an element, a piece barely detached from its subterranean surroundings: it is no longer a name, but rather one moment in the universal anonymity, a bald statement, the stupor of a confrontation in the depths of obscurity. And in this way language insists on playing its own game without man, who created it. Literature now dispenses with the writer: it is no longer this inspiration at work, this negation asserting itself, this idea inscribed in the world as though it were the absolute perspective of the world in its totality. It is not beyond the world, but neither is it the world itself: it is the presence of things before the *world* exists, their perseverance after the world has disappeared, the stubbornness of what remains when everything vanishes and the dumbfoundedness of what appears when nothing exists. That is why it cannot be confused with consciousness, which illuminates things and makes decisions; it is *my* consciousness *without me*.[26]

The ground against which Blanchot cuts his figure here is Hegel's account of language as creating meaning by negation. When a singular thing is named its simple singularity is abolished, Hegel argues, for it is then incorporated into a general category.[27] Language is not consumed by negativity, however, for it also plays a passive, neutral role simply by itself: it keeps an author, whether alive or dead, held between being and non-being, in an impersonal twilight existence. We hear the murmur of our own words without the minds that wrote them; we hear an "endless resifting of words without content" (332). When we read a story we can hear the narrator's voice, but beneath that voice we can also overhear the "narrative voice," the endless murmur of the Outside.[28]

This eerie sense of the Outside, like a macabre device in a story by Edgar Allen Poe, continues to be explored in *L'espace littéraire* (1955). Here, though, Blanchot associates the Outside more generally with art, not only with language:

> Art—as images, as words, and as rhythm—indicates the menacing proximity of a vague and vacant outside, a neutral existence, nil and limitless: art points into a sordid absence, a suffering condensation where being ceaselessly perpetuates itself as nothingness.
>
> Art is originally linked to this fund of impotence where everything falls back when the possible is attenuated. In the world, decisive affirmation dependably serves truth as a basis and foundation, as the place from which it can arise. By comparison, art originally represents the scandalous intimation of absolute error: the premonition of something not true but whose "not" does not have the decisive character of a limit, for it is, rather, brimming and endless indeterminacy with which the true cannot communicate. Nor does truth by any means have the power to reconquer it [*le pouvoir de reconquérir*]. The true cannot define itself vis-à-vis this "not" except by becoming the violence of the negative.[29]

Here we do not have "wild being" so much as "wild nonbeing." The very nature of art is tied to the image, Blanchot maintains. So we are not dealing with figurative rather than nonfigurative visual art, with a poetry that is rich in visual images (Philippe Jaccottet, say) as distinct from a more discursive poetry (Gérard Macé, for example), but with art *as image*. The artist does not seize the phenomenon before him or her but instead takes the image that is given at the same time (but not in the same way) as the

phenomenon. In the terms that Blanchot puts it, a phenomenon gives itself as being while its image gives itself as nonbeing; and the artist each
time chooses nonbeing over being in order to produce art. If this situation grants the artist an unusual, and hardly pleasurable, experience, it
also yields to him or her direct contact with what Blanchot takes to be
most profound in reality, something beyond or beneath being itself. To
be sure, philosophers and mystics have been on the verge of formulating
a concept of the Outside—Heraclitus and Eckhart, Merleau-Ponty and
Lévinas, among them—but the artist, who works daily with the space of
images, encounters this profundity without the need of an education in
philosophy. Artistic practice seems to confirm phenomenology (the artist
is less bothered with *what* to look at than with *how* to look at it), and yet it
also questions the scope and status of phenomenology: for art, as Blanchot understands it, is constitutively drawn to what remains obscure, not
what manifests itself.

Later, in "L'homme de la rue" (1962), now better known by the new
title it received in *L'entretien infini* (1969), "La parole quotidienne," Blanchot once again considers the nearness of the Outside, though this time
with no reference to literature or art. Now it is the everyday that indicates
the Outside. I quote a very rich passage at some length:

> There must be no doubt about the dangerous essence of the every-
> day, nor about the uneasiness that seizes us each time that, by an un-
> foreseeable leap, we stand back from it and, facing it, discover that
> precisely nothing faces us: "What? Is this my everyday life?" Not only
> must we not doubt it, we must not dread it; we should rather seek to
> recapture the secret destructive capacity in play in it, the corrosive
> force of human anonymity, the infinite wearing away. The hero, while
> still a man of courage, is he who fears the everyday; fears it not be-
> cause he is afraid of living in it with too much ease, but because he
> dreads meeting in it what is most fearful: a power of dissolution. The
> everyday challenges heroic values; but this is because, even more, it
> impugns all values and the very idea of value, ruining always anew
> the unjustifiable differences between authenticity and inauthenticity.
> Day-to-day indifference is situated on a level at which the question of
> value is not posed: there is [*il y a*] the everyday (without subject, with-

out object), and while there is, the everyday "he" does not have to be of account; if value nonetheless claims to step in, then "he" [or "it," *il*] is worth "nothing" and "nothing" is worth anything through contact with him. To experience everydayness is to undergo the radical nihilism that is something like its essence and by which, in the void that animates it, everydayness does not cease to hold the principle of its own critique.[30]

If the everyday was first a sociological category, a way of evoking the rituals, symbols, and social practices of average daily life in a big modern city, and then a metaphor of utopia (as proposed by the Neo-Marxist Henri Lefebvre), it becomes for Blanchot a philosophical notion in his sense of the word "philosophical."

Two very different vanishing points are set in place in "La parole quotidienne." The first is Heidegger's account of everydayness, *Alltäglichkeit*, in *Sein und Zeit* (1927), which brings in its wake a host of related concepts: authenticity and inauthenticity [*Eigentlichkeit* and *Uneigentlichkeit*], chatter [*Gerede*], the "They" [*das Man*], and publicness [*Öffentlichkeit*]. The everyday is what wears away the distinction between acting on one's own and acting so as to follow what "They" say one should do or indeed failing to act because of indifference. It erodes the "as mine" [*je meines*] of *Dasein*. The second vanishing point is Lévinas's notion of the *il y a* or the "there is": not the generosity of being that Heidegger affirms in his talk of the "es gibt," but the impersonal persistence of being even in nonbeing. Even if we imagine a cosmos where there is absolutely nothing, we must imagine that sheer nothingness weighing on the one who imagines it. This sense of the inescapable nature of being is concretely experienced in states of deep boredom, fatigue, and insomnia. For Lévinas, the advent of another person to whom one cannot remain indifferent suffices for us to overcome the *il y a*. It is a passage from being in general to a particular being, and hence a movement going in the exact opposite direction from the one that Heidegger follows in *Sein und Zeit*.[31]

Blanchot is close to Lévinas in many respects, but his Outside and the *il y a* are not quite the same.[32] For him, the other person comes to me in the strangeness of the neutral, and there is no escape from the onset of the Outside in the kingdom of the ethical.[33] Indeed, it is the Outside as it comes endlessly toward us in our everyday life that makes the everyday a site of continuous contestation, and that makes the "man on the street" a dangerous person for the government. (As always in his later political writing, Blanchot is thinking of *les événements* of May 1968.) We are urged to go further in our questioning of political authority, the "I," and even God. Again, we see that skepticism is associated with the Outside, which itself is "untransgressable."[34] I recall what Blanchot said with respect to Lévinas in "Notre compagne clandestine," that skepticism refers back "to a 'dogmatism' so absolute that every assertion is threatened." In the same way, the *dis-course* of the "other word" refers us to the Outside, which is the closest that Blanchot gets to a dogma. This neutral space is certainly not an Absolute (whether in Hegel's, Schelling's, or Bradley's sense), and yet it cannot be transgressed because it is that which enables transgression in the first place.

In putting things in this way, I do not mean to figure the Outside as a curious piece of new metaphysical machinery, or to present the endless questioning that it motivates as a mere academic extension of skepticism. As the discussion of the everyday indicates, the Outside for Blanchot is as much a political concern as it is literary or artistic. Infinite contestation should result not in the formation of a mandarin sensibility, wearily reflecting on the truth as unattainable, but in a transformation of that self, a change that is at once existential (one loses the power to say "I") and political (one becomes a revolutionary of a certain sort). Nor was this a position he reached only years after his meditations on literature. In a critical reflection on Lefebvre's *La somme et le rest* (1959), originally entitled "La fin de la philosophie" (1959), Blanchot contemplates the fate of a dissident Marxist philosopher such as Lefebvre in the world of communist action. Lefebvre was expelled from the Parti Communiste Français (PCF) in 1958, an act that did not surprise many on the far left of French politics, for Lefebvre never represented the official Marxist philosophy of the party, the dialectical materialism that supposedly marked the end of philosophy. On the contrary, his "critique of everyday life" proposed an alternate vision of Marxism, one that inspired the Situationist International.

Marxism seeks to overcome bourgeois philosophy but nonetheless remains a philosophy, Blanchot insists. And not just any philosophy: "the destiny of philosophy has become our destiny," he writes (as a "man of the left" during the Cold War), not only because "philosophy has taken power and exerts it in its very name," but also because "philosophy has transformed the essence of power, which has become the whole of life and accomplishes itself as a whole."[35] Then, once again, he distinguishes the philosophical from philosophy:

> Today the decision is not philosophical because it translates a philosophy; it is philosophical, on the contrary, because philosophy has ceased to exist as a mode of questioning that is autonomous and theoretical, and because, in its place, in the *place* that was specific to it, the overcoming—demanded by the advent of a new power—of what is private and what is public, of thought and action, of society and nature, of discourse and life, of reason satisfied and without power, and of labor discontented and without thought, affirms itself or would like to affirm itself. (87)

With Lefebvre, Marxist philosophy has passed from philosophy to the philosophical; it has become the endless task of contesting sites of power in everyday life, something that will be continued, in a manner less patient with Marxism, by Michel Foucault.[36] In an earlier yet related essay, consecrated to Dionys Mascolo's *Le Communisme, révolution et communication ou la dialectique des valeurs et des besoins* (1953), Blanchot says with sober deliberation, "It is undoubtedly the task of our age to move toward an affirmation that is entirely *other*," an affirmation of human beings abiding in a neutral relation with one another, a relation without relation.[37] This is a political task, one to which "communism recalls us with a rigor that it itself often shirks," and yet it is also "to this task that 'artistic experience' recalls us in the realm that is proper to it" (97). It is, Blanchot acknowledges, a "remarkable coincidence" that politics and art converge in the Outside.

Blanchot's *romans* and *récits* introduce many encounters with philosophy. Some are overt, as when Thomas summons the specter of Descartes in *Thomas l'obscur*, or when Henri Sorge finds that in the absolute state there is also absolute knowledge, that "inside and outside correspond," or

when the Nietzschean figure of the "last man," the person who has nothing to do now that history has ended, is reworked in *Le dernier homme*.[38]
Yet some of these encounters are clandestine, as when philosophy becomes the philosophical and is transmuted into a literary mode that
relentlessly probes a question deeper and deeper, being "tempted by a
splendid thought" that the narrator is "trying in vain to bring to its knees,"
or when—and sometimes it is the same thing—a character feels the Outside impending on him or her.[39]

In *Celui qui ne m'accompagnait pas*, for example, one of the speakers
asks, "Where we are, everything conceals itself, doesn't it?" only to intuit
the advance (and retreat) of the Outside, which is actually mentioned by
name:

> Scarcely was it spoken before this remark sank into the emptiness,
> reverberated there emptily, awoke the infinite distended outside
> [*éveilla le dehors infiniment distendu*], the infinite pain of the affirma-
> tion occupying all of space, where what was said kept passing through
> the same point again, was the same, and, always, at whatever mo-
> ment, said the same thing and eternally remained lacking.[40]

And, later, the narrator again registers the approach of the Outside, this
time in a slightly more heavily marked manner, especially in the English
translation:

> To say that I understand these words would not be to explain to my-
> self the dangerous peculiarity of my relations with them. Do I under-
> stand them? I do not understand them, properly speaking, and they
> too who partake of the depth of concealment remain without under-
> standing. But they don't need that understanding in order to be ut-
> tered, they do not speak, they are not interior, they are, on the contrary,
> without intimacy, being altogether outside [*étant tout au dehors*], and
> what they designate engages me in this "outside" of all speech [*dans
> ce dehors de toute parole*], apparently more secret and more interior
> than the speech of the innermost heart, but, here, the outside is
> empty [*le dehors est vide*], the secret is without depth, what is repeated
> is the emptiness of repetition, it doesn't speak and yet it has always

been said already. I couldn't compare them to an echo, or rather, in this place, the echo repeated in advance: it was prophetic in the absence of time. (72)

The Outside is "older, dreadfully old" (24), an "infinite past" (23), which is Blanchot's way of indicating that it has never been fully present to any consciousness, and is outside time as we know it. Even the slightest word or change of affect can recall this "dead time" (36), as when the narrator is asked, "Someone? Here?" and discerns "the shiver that ran behind them, enveloped them in a fear that he seemed to feel, a fear that drove that instant back towards another sort of time, older, fearfully old" (30).

Never having been wholly present, the Outside never becomes so. Yet it returns eternally, almost brushing against characters in the *récits*—and so we have another clandestine encounter, between Blanchot and Nietzsche—sometimes as an "empty depth" (92), a shadow falling over being, although on occasion it can be figured differently. It can lead a character to affirm "the renunciation of mystery" and to embrace "the ultimate insignificance of lightness" (43). For there is a gaiety in Blanchot that is not always noticed, a sense of gentleness, and sometimes a smile behind the lapidary prose. There is also a dark humor to relish. I think of *L'arrêt de mort*, when the narrator remembers the sister of the young woman who lived at 15, rue —: "What became of her? She lived, as she liked to say, off the kindness of gentlemen. I assume she's dead."[41] And I think, too, of the comic passage in "La folie du jour" when the narrator and the Law have been flirting with one another. "The truth was that I liked her. In these surroundings, overpopulated by men, she was the only feminine element. Once she had made me touch her knee—a strange feeling. I had said as much to her: 'I am not the kind of man who is satisfied with a knee!' Her answer: 'That would be disgusting!'"[42] But such moments are few and far between. In general, no one would confuse the tone of Blanchot's *Death Sentence* with that of David Lodge's *Deaf Sentence* (2008).

More than something that brushes against characters in the narratives, the Outside is also what enables a *récit* to be written in the first place, and what enables us to distinguish a *roman* from a *récit*. A *roman* consists of events that take place in time, that we follow one after the other, interested in how situations develop, get complicated, and are then more or less resolved for characters. A *récit* addresses itself to just the one event that has taken place, if it *has* taken place, and there is no moment in principle when it must end. In "La rencontre de l'imaginaire," the opening piece of *Le livre à venir* (1959), Blanchot identifies the "secret law" of the *récit*. It is, he says, "the movement towards a point—one that is not only unknown, ignored and foreign, but such that it seems, even before and outside of this movement, to have no kind of reality; yet one that is so imperious that it is from that point alone that the narrative draws its attraction, in such a way that it cannot even 'begin' before having reached it."[43] A *récit* begins, then, not by the act of an author expressing himself or herself, being in control of a content and a style, but by being drawn toward the point where being and image pass endlessly into one another, a point that is real only while the narrative is being written or read. From the first word of the narrative, language has been detached from the world and the author; it seems to go on as though by itself—an experience familiar to any writer of prose fiction or poetry, commonly known as "inspiration." The attraction of the Outside is Blanchot's revision of this old idea. Whereas Plato in *Phaedrus* 244 thought that the artist was taken into a higher world when in the throes of creation. Blanchot suggests that in fact he or she descends to what flows beneath being, namely, the Outside.

The *récit*, as Blanchot sees it, is a better medium than the novel for the philosophical, for it needs no conclusion, thereby allowing contestation to continue (at least in theory) without ever coming to an end. Also, the *récit*, as Blanchot practices it, embodies the philosophical *par excellence:* it responds to the lure of the Outside. And yet we should be careful not to draw too continuous and firm a line between the *roman* and the *récit*, as Blanchot thinks of them. In 1941 *Thomas l'obscur* was a *roman*, and then it was edited in 1950 to become what Blanchot called a "nouvelle version" and what his readers regard (with the prompting of the liminal text) as a "récit." Minor characters were omitted to allow a sharp focus on Thomas and Anne, and many passages were removed. Nothing, except quite minor rephrasings, was added to the text. Also, what is at first a *récit* can be transformed, with next to no changes, into something that is either not a *récit*, as Blanchot conceives it, or that does not need its genre to be marked as a *récit*. When Gallimard published *Le dernier homme* in 1957, it bore the designation "récit," yet when the same house reissued it in 1979, with only a few slight changes here and there, the word "récit" had been replaced by "nouvelle version."[44]

If we adopt a long perspective, we can see Blanchot contributing to the French "philosophical novel." It has many variants. In the eighteenth century alone, it is possible to point to three quite different exemplars: Voltaire's *Candide, ou l'optimisme* (1759), Rousseau's *Julie, ou la nouvelle Héloïse* (1761), and Diderot's *Jacques le fataliste et son maître* (1796). In the twentieth century, we find Sartre's *La nausée* (1938) pressing hard on the young Blanchot. Yet, ten years later, he had established himself so firmly as an original and powerful writer, at least within a small circle of admirers, that his friend Georges Bataille pondered writing a book called *Maurice Blanchot et l'existentialisme*.[45] The idea would presumably have been to distinguish Blanchot's thought from the existentialism of Sartre. "La littérature et le droit à la mort" (1947–48) had quietly set itself against Sartre's notion of "committed writing" in *Qu'est-ce que la littérature?* (1947). His narratives introduced a new element, the neutral or the Outside, to the existential fiction characterized by *La nausée* (1938), and undermined the secure "I" on which Sartre's notions of freedom and commitment are based. *Le Très-Haut* offers a dark vision of the end of history, very different from the picture of human freedom given in *L'âge de raison* (1945), and *L'arrêt de mort* (1948) presents a competing vision of France just before the war to the one given in *Le sursis* (1947).

In 1938, several years before he had completed *Thomas l'obscur,* the idea of a book about his work, one offering a contrast with the leading intellectual of the day, must have seemed an eternity away. Reviewing *La nausée* for *Aux Écoutes* shortly after the novel had appeared, he judged the performance "imperfect," yet praised it in terms that revealed something of his own ambitions for his first novel. Sartre "takes the novel to a place where there are no longer any incidents, any plot, any particular person; to the site where the mind sustains itself only by beguiling itself with philosophical notions like existence and being, notions that appear indigestible to art and which are only refractory to it as a result of the arbitrary workings of thought."[46] A novel stripped of extraneous psychological interest in its characters, a novel occupied instead with being and nonbeing, was precisely what Blanchot was writing at the time. More than that, he was drawing on the same philosophical school as Sartre. "This novel," he wrote of *La nausée*, "is visibly inspired by a philosophical movement that is little known in France, but is of the utmost importance: that of Edmund Husserl and especially Martin Heidegger" (34). Phenomenology had made its first French novel, and was about to make its second, though one that (for the faithful) hid a stinging critique of phenomenology and that (for the thoughtful) contained the seeds of a new phenomenology that was aware of its limits and that peered over them into the darkness.

One might call Blanchot a "philosophical novelist" in two senses. First, like Sartre before him and Michel Henry after him, he writes narratives that obliquely investigate what interests him philosophically.[47] *Thomas l'obscur* is about being and nonbeing, about the being that remains in nonbeing, and the central drama of the novel turns on Descartes's "Je pense donc je suis," while *Le Très-Haut* is about the realization of the Hegelian State. Yet philosophical figures, problems, and obsessions, are far less in evidence in the *récits*. And it is in reading these narratives that we might read the expression "philosophical novelist" with a slightly different accent so that we take the adjective in the sense that Blanchot gives to it when reading the work of Lévinas, Merleau-Ponty, or Lefebvre. In these *récits* we find philosophy having gone underground, having passed from the study of canonical works and authors to a style of questioning that started with the Greek skeptics and that was given new life by formulating the idea of the Outside that runs beneath being. In Blanchot's narrative writing, philosophy often loses its proper name; it becomes the philosophical.

Clandestine Encounters tracks Blanchot's narrative writings in chronological order of composition, a passage of almost sixty years, from his first stories written in the mid-1930s to *L'instant de ma mort* (1994). Contributors to the volume were told that they were free to treat its theme, "philosophy in the narratives of Maurice Blanchot," in any way that they wished. Some contributors place an accent on "philosophy"; others, on "the philosophical." Some take their cues from philosophers who have already written on Blanchot's narratives—Derrida, Sarah Kofman, Philippe Lacoue-Labarthe, Lévinas, Jean-Luc Nancy, and Sartre—while others make their own way through this difficult terrain. For some, the philosophical interest is in aesthetics or phenomenology, while for others it is ethics or politics. The result is a wide-ranging introduction to Blanchot's narrative writings, one that opens up the texts in diverse ways and promises to stimulate more discussion among Blanchot's readers and, I hope, excite more people to read him. Contributors to this collection come from the fields of literary criticism, literary theory, philosophy, theology, and the theater. They live in Australia, Belgium, England, France, Scotland, and the United States. These details, banal in themselves, are a testimony to the breadth of scholarly interest in Blanchot's novels and *récits*.

We begin with a jointly written essay by Vivian Liska and Arthur Cools on Blanchot's early stories "Le dernier mot" and "L'idyll." Are these stories to be read by way of questions of aesthetics or issues of political violence? In a meticulously close reading of both *récits*, Liska and Cools examine the question, paying particular care to the shifts between representation and reality in the stories. Along the way they stop to heed philosophers Sarah Kofman, Giorgio Agamben, and Theodor W. Adorno. The stories anticipate Blanchot's major themes developed after World War II, and the authors show that "Le dernier mot" is a very early attempt to talk about the Outside. The Outside that is reached at the end of "Le dernier mot" is, as Liska and Cools say, coordinate with the "space of literature" that Blanchot would elaborate after the war. Yet this Outside does not mark an escape from the world of politics. Even here, it seems, literature and politics converge in the Outside.

Blanchot observes in "Après coup" that the two stories now gathered in *Le ressassement éternel* interrupted the writing of *Thomas l'obscur,* and Liska and Cools point out that a Thomas appears in "Le dernier mot."[48] In my essay on *Thomas l'obscur,* I consider the motif of the double and doubling in the novel and, more particularly, the *récit* that it became in 1950. Thomas is divided into two: a living-dead figure and another obscure being (or, better, nonbeing) that abides in the Outside. As early as *Thomas l'obscur,* Blanchot questions the unity of the human subject, and he does so here in a dramatic argument with Descartes. Where the philosopher affirms "Je pense donc je suis" in the *Discourse on Method* (1633), Thomas cries out, "Je pense, donc je ne suis pas." The philosopher of *la clarté* must enter the lists with the novelist of *l'obscur*. But how can anyone, novelist or philosopher, talk intelligibly of what must *remain* obscure? To be sure, Blanchot as novelist performs the reduction merely in writing fiction. The novelist's gaze is very like the phenomenologist's. However, Blanchot also performs what I call a "neutral reduction" in order to disclose, insofar as it is possible, the obscure Thomas and, with him, the Outside.

The "Thomas" years of Blanchot come to an end with *Aminadab*, a novel first critically examined by Sartre and here read in a quite different way by Christopher Strathman. Converging on the novel from the perspective of the Kantian style of criticism that Blanchot was formulating in the early 1940s, Strathman shows the importance of a certain conception of language for the young novelist. One might say that *Aminadab* is a novel that, among other things, comes into being by way of an intense reflection on Kantian critique and a redirected Romantic view of language, first explored in the Jena circle, that gave rise to what Lacoue-Labarthe and Nancy have memorably called "the literary absolute." Illuminating as it is, the philosophical background to this novel can never quite account for the peculiarity of *Aminadab*. As Strathman indicates, *Aminadab* not only is about a bizarre house that Thomas enters but also is itself a "haunted house of being."

Le Très-Haut, Blanchot's last novel, has usually been read with reference to Hegel's doctrine of absolute knowledge as mediated by Alexandre Kojève, with a sidelong glance to the Heidegger whose analysis of *Sorge* in *Sein und Zeit* perhaps informs the character of Henri Sorge. Attention to a law that absorbs all attempts to resist it is inevitable when reading this novel; however, as Stephen Lewis shows, it is equally important to examine the law of the other person in the novel, a law associated with desire and sexual difference. To this end, Lewis refers us to Jean-Luc Marion's *Le phénomène érotique* (2003), a book he has translated beautifully into English, to understand the peculiar play of desire and love in the novel. "What I ultimately see going on in the novel," Lewis says, "is the presentation of a world in which human erotic interaction not only lacks but is hostile to what Marion calls 'flesh,' the auto-affective faculty that each human being receives from another flesh in love." This essay offers us a fresh philosophical view of *Le Très-Haut* while introducing Marion's philosophy to the world of "literature and philosophy."

The year 1948 was remarkable for Blanchot and must have been an unsettling one for his early readers. Not only did *Le Très-Haut* appear but also a narrative of a quite different sort, *L'arrêt de mort*, which embodied a more concerted questioning of the unity of the artwork. In the United States, at least, many readers of *L'arrêt de mort* first came across it in Derrida's "Living On," a signal text of the "Yale School."[49] There Derrida attends to the structure of survival of a text, partly with an oblique and passing reference to Shelley's unfinished poem "The Triumph of Life," and mainly by way of a reading of the first part of *L'arrêt de mort*. One thing that attracts Derrida is the character J., who dies and then comes back to life at the narrator's bidding; and, since "Living On" first appeared in print, other readers have commented on the narrative of J. Often left in the shade, though, is the elusive second part of *L'arrêt de mort*, and it is this narrative that Alain Toumayan examines with admirable fidelity to the text. This is a narrative neither of being nor nonbeing but of the neuter, Toumayan argues, looking with care at Lévinas's account of the *il y a* in his *De l'existence à l'existant* (1947). We find ourselves faced in this narrative not with death but with an existence haunted by death or worn down by a dying that seems to last forever. Just as *Aminadab* is a haunted house of being, so, too, is the second part of *L'arrêt de mort*.

"La folie du jour" has received close attention from Derrida and Lévinas.[50] Here, Christopher Fynsk brings a new philosophical lens to bear on the text, that of sovereignty. He examines the sovereign refusal of the epistemic, juridical, and political order in this powerful *récit*. Also, however, it contains a sovereign affirmation of life. Fynsk's question is: What relation is there between this "yes" and this "no"? Pursing the question leads him to seek the sovereign traits of the "other relation," the neutral one, and to push past Lévinas's reading of the text. Neutral this relation may be, but it is associated with women. The affirmation of life and death, Blanchot's narrator tells us, is something he has found only in women, "beautiful creatures."

Alain Toumayan asks us to look more closely at the second part of *L'arrêt de mort*, which readers have not emphasized as they have the first part. In an unusual study, Christophe Bident invites us to listen very closely to the opening words of *Au moment voulu*—"In the absence of the friend who lived with her, the door was opened by Judith" [*En l'absence de l'amie qui vivait avec elle, la porte fut ouverte par Judith*]—because it is a way of beginning a phenomenology of recognition. That phenomenology can be explored, Bident believes, by attending to the performance of the sentence; to that end, he directed a theater workshop devoted to the opening of the *récit*. Here is a rare opportunity to find Blanchot's biographer in his other life as a theater director, one who does not forget his philosophical interests. He concerns himself with reference, reflection, and the structure of enunciation in that first sentence, and is attentive to the murmur of the Outside, the "narrative voice," in the background of what Blanchot writes.

In a dense, closely argued essay, Rodolphe Gasché tackles one of the most challenging of Blanchot's *récits, Celui qui ne m'accompagnait pas.* For the assigned task given to the contributors, this *récit* is particularly tough going, for, as Gasché quickly points out, the narrative seems not to solicit any philosophical theme, and it stages itself so that it remains at odds with the usual procedures of philosophical inquiry. Yet Gasché notes that in the words "Je me le demande" the narrative performs a phenomenological reduction, and this gives him the purchase he needs to explore it by way of its phenomenological description, that reflective attitude which is also a reception of what shows itself. Much of the *récit* turns on light, the medium of manifestation. And yet the narrative does not yield completely to a phenomenological reading; it frustrates description as much as it engages in it. The narrator reflects on his inability to describe things, and the light in rooms varies in peculiar ways.

"Blanchot asked me," Bataille wrote in 1943, "why not pursue my inner experience as if I were the *last man?*"[51] Blanchot may have had Nietzsche's "der letzte Mensch" in mind, although if he did, he must have been using the figure ironically. For Nietzsche's "last man" is the exact opposite of the *Übermensch;* he is the weary modern man who avoids risk and no longer has any zest for life, which is far from how Bataille wanted to live. More likely, Blanchot was thinking of the Kojèvian idea of man at the end of history, the man who has nothing to do except play, make love, and produce art. This would involve a radical transformation of "man," for, as Kojève says, "[t]he end of History is the *death* of man, strictly speaking."[52] Yet if this is Blanchot's source, it could only have been anecdotal, drawn from someone, perhaps Bataille, who had attended Kojève's lectures at l'École pratique des Hautes Études (1933–39). Those lectures appeared in print only in 1947. We should not be too quick, though, to assimilate Bataille's remark to Blanchot's *récit* of 1957, *Le dernier homme*. As Caroline Shaeffer-Jones argues, we cannot grasp *Le dernier homme* without following the allusions to Nietzsche's "last man" and indeed to Nietzsche's Oedipus. Like so much of Blanchot's writing, in all its genres, *Le dernier homme* is about death and dying. Yet it is also about life, Shaeffer-Jones insists: not a vitalism, to be sure, but a new understanding of human being without reliance on the "I" in the first-person singular but as a "he" and as plural, "a Who?, a whole crowd of Who?s."[53]

L'attente l'oubli and *Le dernier homme* form a diptych, Michael Holland argues, while also noting that this "mixed" work reaches back to *Aminadab* in its attention to rooms and corridors. *L'attente l'oubli* learns from *Le dernier homme* something about language. "And, therefore, in a single language always to make the double speech [*parole*] heard," reads one of the fragments quite early in the text.[54] We think of the duality of discourse and *dis-course* explored earlier, of philosophical speech and the murmur of the Outside. Holland maintains that in *L'attente l'oubli*, Blanchot carries forward what he has learnt in *Le dernier homme*, namely, the idea of a language that is neither philosophical nor narrative, a "vocative-invocative" mode. This modality of language comes from poetry, not narrative, and Holland subtly points out that in *L'attente l'oubli* Blanchot is not engaging in a dialogue with Heidegger the thinker, as is usually assumed, but with what is poetic in his writing. "By gesturing to Heidegger as a poet rather than as a philosopher in 1958," Holland says, "Blanchot is not just signaling the importance of the poetic in *Awaiting Oblivion*. He is referring back to the work of his in which the relation between poetry and philosophy in Heidegger's thinking is thoroughly explored and radically overturned."

Leslie Hill tells the fascinating story of how a book came to include a *récit*, and how this *récit* came to contain, in a sense, the longest and most philosophically attuned of Blanchot's books. The *récit* is the dialogue that first appeared as "L'entretien infini," discussed by Christopher Fynsk at the end of his essay on *La folie du jour*, and the book is of course *L'entretien infini* (1969), which features the *récit* at its start. At one with Holland, Hill affirms that Blanchot is less concerned to stage an infinite dialogue between literature and philosophy than to point out that the two are infinitely held together and apart. *L'entretien infini*, a "mixed" work, shows that literature and philosophy abide in a relation without relation. The weariness that pervades Blanchot's "L'entretien infini" is not a fundamental attunement of the kind that Heidegger analyzes so brilliantly in *Sein und Zeit* (1927) or in the slightly later lecture course of 1929–30, *Die Grundbegriffe der Metaphysik: Welt—Endlichkeit—Einsamkeit*.[55] Not at all: it undermines even the attunement of deep boredom that interests Heidegger and that allows what Jean-Luc Marion calls "the third reduction."[56] It does not open a rapport between Dasein and being, or between Dasein and what gives itself beyond the horizon of being, but erodes the self so that it cannot even be that structure of open doors and windows that Dasein is.[57] Philosophy can deal with *Angst* and boredom; it cannot get any traction with weariness.

The opening essay of this collection addresses the relation between aesthetics and historical violence in Blanchot's first stories. Exactly the same disjunction is considered in the final essay, Thomas Davis's reading of *L'instant de ma mort*. This last, apparently limpid, yet surprisingly enigmatic narrative of a young *maquisard* who is nearly executed by the Nazis has called forth long commentaries by Derrida and Lacoue-Labarthe; and Davis keeps one eye on them as he reads it for the meaning of "the political." Again, double speech comes into the spotlight: for Davis's Blanchot, it has pertinence in the philosophy of history, with the negative—the dialectical—making history, and with historical disasters, where the negative breaks down, incapacitating language as the bearer of meaning and truth and neutrally keeping watch over us. *L'instant de ma mort* is not related by a self-sufficient "I" but by a voice that has lost the power to say "I," an afflicted voice where the murmur of the Outside can be heard. As Davis is at pains to stress, the neutral and the Outside are not apolitical philosophical notions in *L'instant de ma mort*. The narrative is political in its solidarity with those who have been lost in the disaster of the war. And the political, here, is not a concept of philosophy, from this system or that, but "an incessant questioning." Once more, philosophy has dissolved into the philosophical.

And now the very last word, or, rather, two words: Geoffrey Hartman. In his essay "The Fullness and Nothingness of Literature," published in *Yale French Studies* in the Winter issue of 1955, Hartman first brought English-speaking readers into contact with Blanchot and underscored the importance of Blanchot's narratives as philosophical novels and stories.[58] Several years later, in 1961, we were able to read his "Maurice Blanchot: Philosopher-Novelist" in the *Chicago Review*.[59] Later, on the appearance in the *Georgia Review* of the first part of Lydia Davis's translation of *L'arrêt de mort* in 1976, he guided us on how to think about that dark, mysterious work; and then, in 2004, he joined me in editing a collection of new essays on Blanchot, *The Power of Contestation,* to which he contributed a strong new essay.[60] Geoffrey Hartman is the father of Blanchot studies in the English-speaking world. This collection of essays is dedicated to him.

NOTES

1. Jacques Derrida, "A Witness Forever," trans. Charlotte Mandell, in *Nowhere without No: In Memory of Maurice Blanchot,* ed. Kevin Hart (Sydney: Vagabond Press, 2003), 45.

2. Derrida, "Introduction," in *Parages* (Paris: Galilée, 1986), 11.

3. Derrida, *Demeure: Fiction and Testimony,* bound with Maurice Blanchot, *The Instant of My Death,* trans. Elizabeth Rottenberg (Stanford: Stanford University Press, 2000), 26.

4. The first studies of Blanchot tended to consider his work by way of themes, an approach that of course has continued. An early instance of this approach, the first monograph dedicated to Blanchot, is Françoise Collin, *Maurice Blanchot et la question de l'écriture* (Paris: Gallimard, 1971). Among the more memorable contributions to understanding Blanchot's narrative writing are Bernard Noël's essay "D'une main obscure" on *L'arrêt de mort,* in Roger Laporte and Bernard Noël, *Deux lectures de Maurice Blanchot* (Montpellier: Fata Morgana, 1973); Evelyne Londyn, *Maurice Blanchot, romancier* (Paris: Éditions A.-G. Nizet, 1976); and Brian T. Fitch, *Lire les récits de Maurice Blanchot* (Amsterdam: Rodopi, 1992). Of early articles on the narratives, special mention should be made of Jean Starobinski, "*Thomas l'obscur,* chapitre première," *Critique* 229 (June 1966): 498–513. More attention to the narrative works has been given in the last decade. I list books only. See Chantal Michel's reading of *Au moment voulu* in her *Maurice Blanchot et le déplacement d'Orphée* (Saint-Genouph: Librairie Nizet, 1997). Marie-Laure Hurault touches on several of the narrative works in her *Maurice*

Blanchot: Le principe de fiction (Saint-Denis: Presses Universitaires de Vincennes, 1999), and François Dominique discusses *Le dernier homme* in his *Maurice Blanchot: Premier témoin* (Langres: Éditions Virgile, 2003).

5. Blanchot's "Le dernier mot" was first published in *Fontaine*, no. 60 (May 1947), and "L'idylle" first appeared in *La Licorne*, no. 1 (Spring 1947): 33–58. Both stories were gathered together in *Le ressassement éternel* (Paris: Minuit, 1951). "La folie du jour" first appeared, under the title "Un récit"—perhaps a mistake for "Un récit?"—in *Empédocle*, no. 2 (May 1949), and then as *La folie du jour* (Montpellier: Fata Morgana, 1973). English translations of some of these narratives— "The Idyll," "The Last Word," *Thomas the Obscure* (*récit* version), *Death Sentence*, *The Madness of the Day*, *When the Day Comes*, and *The One Who Was Standing Apart from Me*—may be found in *The Station Hill Blanchot Reader: Fiction and Literary Essays*, ed. George Quasha, trans. Lydia Davis et al. (Barrytown, NY: Station Hill Press, 1999). Some are available as individual volumes: *Vicious Circles: Two Fictions and "After the Fact,"* trans. Paul Auster (Barrytown, NY: Station Hill Press, 1985); *Thomas the Obscure*, trans. Robert Lamberton (Barrytown, NY: Station Hill Press, 1995); *The Madness of the Day*, trans. Lydia Davis (Barrytown, NY: Station Hill Press, 1981); *Death Sentence*, trans. Lydia Davis (Barrytown, NY: Station Hill Press, 1998; reprint of 1978 edition); *When the Time Comes*, trans. Lydia Davis (Barrytown, NY: Station Hill Press, 1985); and *The One Who Was Standing Apart from Me*, trans. Lydia Davis (Barrytown, NY: Station Hill Press, 1993). Also see *Aminadab*, trans. and intro. Jeff Fort (Lincoln: University of Nebraska Press, 2002); *The Most High*, trans. Allan Stoekl (Lincoln: University of Nebraska Press, 1996); *The Last Man*, trans. Lydia Davis (New York: Columbia University Press, 1987); and *The Instant of My Death*, trans. Elizabeth Rottenberg, bound with Jacques Derrida, *Demeure: Fiction and Testimony* (Stanford: Stanford University Press, 2000).

6. For English translations of these works, see *Awaiting Oblivion*, trans. John Gregg (Lincoln: University of Nebraska Press, 1997); *The Step Not Beyond*, trans. Lycette Nelson (Albany: State University of New York Press, 1992); and *The Writing of the Disaster*, trans. Ann Smock (Lincoln: University of Nebraska Press, 1986). I devote a chapter to a reading of the most important narrative passage in *L'écriture du désastre* in my *The Dark Gaze: Maurice Blanchot and the Sacred* (Chicago: University of Chicago Press, 2004), ch. 2.

7. For an English translation, see the opening untitled pages of *The Infinite Conversation*, trans. and foreword Susan Hanson (Minneapolis: University of Minnesota Press, 1993), xiii–xxiii.

8. Blanchot, "Our Clandestine Companion," trans. David B. Allison, in *Face to Face with Levinas*, ed. Richard A. Cohen (Albany: State University of New York Press, 1986), 41.

9. Blanchot, "Slow Obsequies," in *Friendship*, trans. Elizabeth Rottenberg (Stanford: Stanford University Press, 1997), 90. I shall return to this important essay when discussing Henri Lefebvre.

10. See Christophe Bident, *Maurice Blanchot: Partenaire invisible. Essai biographique* (Seyssel: Champ Vallon, 1998), 49.

11. Despite repeated attempts, and with the help of several friends in France, I have not been able to obtain a copy of the thesis. One can only hope that it will turn up in Blanchot's posthumous papers.

12. Emmanuel Lévinas, *Otherwise than Being or Beyond Essence*, trans. Alphonso Lingis (The Hague: Martinus Nijhoff, 1981), 170.

13. See, for example, John Koethe, *Scepticism, Knowledge, and Forms of Reasoning* (Ithaca: Cornell University Press, 2005), ch. 1.

14. Lévinas, *Otherwise than Being*, 5.

15. Stéphane Mallarmé, "The Book as Spiritual Instrument," in *Divagations*, trans. Barbara Johnson (Cambridge, MA: Harvard University Press, 2007), 226.

16. See Lévinas, *Ethics and Infinity: Conversations with Philippe Nemo*, trans. Richard A. Cohen (Pittsburgh: Duquesne University Press, 1985), 99.

17. Blanchot, "After the Fact," in *Vicious Circles*, 68.

18. Blanchot, *Thomas the Obscure*, 27 (trans. Lamberton). Also see *Thomas l'obscur: Première version, 1941*, intro. Pierre Madaule (Paris: Gallimard, 2005), 46, and *Thomas l'obscur, nouvelle version* (Paris: Gallimard, 1950), 30.

19. Blanchot, *Death Sentence*, 80. These lines evoke not only a thought but a female character in the narrative.

20. Blanchot, *The One Who Was Standing Apart from Me*, 41; *The Last Man*, 77; and *Awaiting Oblivion*, 50.

21. Yet see Derrida's remarks on the difference between Hegel and Nietzsche on this issue, in his *The Ear of the Other: Otobiography, Transference, Translation*, ed. Christie V. McDonald (New York: Schocken Books, 1985), 56.

22. Blanchot, "After the Fact," in *Vicious Circles*, 60.

23. Blanchot, "Le 'discours philosophique,'" *L'Arc* 46 (1971): 1. Jean-Luc Lannoy offers a full-length essay on Blanchot and Merleau-Ponty in his *Langage, perception, mouvement: Blanchot et Merleau-Ponty* (Grenoble: Jérôme Millon, 2008). Marlène Zarader offers a more general assessment of Blanchot's engagement with phenomenology. See her *L'être et le neutre: À partir de Maurice Blanchot* (Lagrasse: Verdier, 2001).

24. Maurice Merleau-Ponty, *The Visible and the Invisible*, ed. Claude Lefort, trans. Alphonso Lingis (Evanston, IL: Northwestern University Press, 1968), 102–3. Translation modified.

25. Sometimes Blanchot writes *le Dehors* and sometimes *le dehors*, almost always the latter in his narratives.

26. Blanchot, "Literature and the Right to Death," trans. Lydia Davis, in *The Work of Fire*, trans. Charlotte Mandell (Stanford: Stanford University Press, 1995), 328.

27. See G. W. F. Hegel, *System of Ethical Life and First Philosophy of Spirit*, ed. H. S. Harris and T. M. Knox (Albany: State University of New York Press, 1979), 221.

28. See Blanchot, "The Narrative Voice (the 'he,' the neutral)," in *The Infinite Conversation*, 379–87. Can one speak also of a "poetic voice"? Michael Holland takes up the question in his essay on *L'attente l'oubli* in this collection.

29. Blanchot, *The Space of Literature*, trans. Ann Smock (Lincoln: University of Nebraska Press, 1982), 242–43. Also see "The Experience of Proust," in *The Book to Come*, trans. Charlotte Mandell (Stanford: Stanford University Press, 2003), 14.

30. Blanchot, "Everyday Speech," in *The Infinite Conversation*, 244–45.

31. See Emmanuel Lévinas, *Existence and Existents*, trans. Alphonso Lingis (Dordrecht: Kluwer Academic Publishers, 1988), 57–64, and *Ethics and Infinity*, ch. 3.

32. It should be noted that Blanchot uses the expression "il y a" in his story "Le dernier mot." See "The Last Word," in *Vicious Circles*, 45.

33. See Blanchot, "Keeping to Words," in *The Infinite Conversation*, 59.

34. Blanchot, "Le 'discours philosophique,'" 2.

35. Blanchot, "Slow Obsequies," in *Friendship*, 86. This essay first appeared under the title "La fin de la philosophie" in *Le Nouvelle Revue française* 80 (October 1959): 678–89. It should be noted that Blanchot begins "Notre compagne clandestine" by reflecting on Lévinas's sentence, "Ce siècle aura donc été pour tous la fin de la philosophie!" ["This century will therefore have been for everyone the end of philosophy!"]. The sentence appears in "Le regard du poète," the opening essay of Lévinas's little book *Sur Maurice Blanchot* (Montpellier: Fata Morgana, 1973). It first appeared in *Monde Nouveau*, no. 98 (1956): 6–19.

36. See Blanchot, "Michel Foucault as I Imagine Him," in *A Voice from Elsewhere*, trans. Charlotte Mandell (Albany: State University of New York Press, 2007), 126, 131–32.

37. Blanchot, "On One Approach to Communism," in *Friendship*, 97. Blanchot places this essay directly after his piece on Lefebvre in *Friendship*. For the "relation without relation," see "The Relation of the Third Kind (man without horizon)," in *The Infinite Conversation*, 66–74.

38. Blanchot, *The Most High*, 136; *The Last Man*, 2.

39. Blanchot, *Death Sentence*, 31.

40. Blanchot, *The One Who Was Standing Apart from Me*, 50.

41. Blanchot, *Death Sentence*, 2.

42. Blanchot, *The Madness of the Day*, 17.

43. Blanchot, "Encountering the Imaginary," in *The Book to Come*, 7. For further discussion of the *récit*, including its history, see my *The Dark Gaze*, 61–63.

44. The unsigned note to the 1992 "Imaginaire" edition of the *nouvelle version* of *Thomas l'obscur* says that *Le dernier homme* was Blanchot's "first *récit*"; however, the publication date is mistakenly given as 1947.

45. See Georges Bataille, *Choix de lettres 1917–1962*, ed. Michel Surya (Paris: Gaillimard, 1997), 392.

46. Blanchot, "The Beginnings of a Novel," trans. Michael Holland, in *The Blanchot Reader*, ed. Michael Holland (Oxford: Basil Blackwell, 1995), 33.

47. See Michel Henry, *Le jeune officier* (Paris: Gallimard, 1954); *L'amour les yeux fermés* (Paris: Gallimard, 1976); *Le fils du roi* (Paris: Gallimard, 1981); and *Le cadavre indiscret* (Paris: Albin Michel, 1996).

48. Blanchot says that "Le dernier mot" was an attempt "to short circuit" *Thomas l'obscur*. See "After the Fact," in *Vicious Circles*, 64.

49. See Derrida, "Living On: Borderlines," in *Deconstruction and Criticism* by Harold Bloom et al. (New York: Seabury Press, 1979), 75–176.

50. See Derrida, "Title (to be specified)," trans. Tom Conley, *Sub-Stance* 10, no. 2 (1981): 5–22; and Lévinas, "Exercises on 'The Madness of the Day,'" in *Proper Names*, trans. Michael B. Smith (Stanford: Stanford University Press, 1996).

51. Georges Bataille, *Inner Experience*, trans. Leslie Anne Boldt (Albany: State University of New York Press, 1988), 61.

52. Alexandre Kojève, *Introduction à la lecture de Hegel*, ed. Raymond Queneau (Paris: Gallimard, 1947), 388n.

53. Blanchot, *The Last Man*, 11.

54. Blanchot, *Awaiting Oblivion*, 5.

55. See Heidegger, *Being and Time*, trans. John Macquarrie and Edward Robinson (Oxford: Basil Blackwell, 1973), §40; *The Fundamental Concepts of Metaphysics: World, Finitude, Solitude*, trans. William McNeil and Nicholas Walker (Bloomington: Indiana University Press, 1995), §§16–38.

56. See Jean-Luc Marion, *Reduction and Givenness*, trans. Thomas A. Carlson (Evanston, IL: Northwestern University Press, 1998), 192–98.

57. I borrow the brilliant description of Dasein proposed by Jean-Yves Lacoste in his *Experience and the Absolute: Disputed Questions on the Humanity of Man*, trans. Mark-Raftery-Skehan (New York: Fordham University Press, 2004), 11.

58. Geoffrey Hartman, "The Fullness and Nothingness of Literature," *Yale French Studies* 16 (1955): 63–78.

59. Hartman, "Maurice Blanchot: Philosopher-Novelist," *Chicago Review* 10, no. 2 (1961): 1–17.

60. Hartman, "Introduction," *Georgia Review* 30, no. 2 (1976): 379–82, and Kevin Hart and Geoffrey Hartman, eds., *The Power of Contestation: Perspectives on Maurice Blanchot* (Baltimore: Johns Hopkins University Press, 2004).

ONE

THE GLORY AND THE ABYSS

LE RESSASSEMENT ÉTERNEL

Vivian Liska and Arthur Cools

M aurice Blanchot's first *récits*, "Le dernier mot" and "L'idylle,"[1] have repeatedly been called an "insoluble enigma."[2] They are, both in terms of their dark and oppressive atmosphere and the difficulty of comprehending them, disturbingly obscure tales of irrevocable alienation and apocalyptic destruction. The time and circumstances of their creation and publication add to this inscrutability: Not only were the original versions of these stories lost, but, as Blanchot's biographer Christophe Bident suggests, the experiences to which they testify and the spirit in which they were conceived remain elusive.[3] Written respectively in 1935 and 1936, "Le dernier mot" and "L'idylle" were published for the first time in 1947 in two different reviews, and only in 1951 were they brought together and made available in print in a slim volume entitled *Le ressassement éternel.*[4] Blanchot wrote these fictions when he was about to end the journalistic activities linking him to the French nationalist extreme right, and it is not clear whether the stories are still marked by these political engagements or already anticipate his turning away from them in 1937. It is equally difficult to determine whether their narrative mode lies in a continuum with Blanchot's later oeuvre, or whether they are experiments unrelated to—or even incompatible with—the poetics that Blanchot developed in his fictional and theoretical writings after the war. These uncertainties relate to larger issues about Blanchot's oeuvre as a whole, inviting the question as to whether his poetics of rupture, fragmentation, and depersonalization should be regarded as a primarily aesthetic and philosophical endeavor that he pursued from the beginning, or whether it emerged as a response to the historical violence and destruction that he witnessed in the years that separate these early stories from his later work.

In the historical context of twentieth-century Europe, the interval of more than ten years between the completion of these stories and their publication corresponds to the breakdown of an entire world, that is, the disaster of World War II. This rupture in the fabric of collective experience created an insurmountable discrepancy between the context that originally gave rise to these stories and the spirit in which they could be comprehended by their very first readership. The significance of this deferment is addressed by Blanchot in an important afterword entitled "Après coup," which he added to *Le ressassement éternel* when it was reissued in 1983.[5] In this afterword Blanchot describes his own alienation from these stories: "It is not possible for me to know who wrote them, how they were written, and to what unknown urgency they were responding" (490). Viewed from the vantage point of Blanchot's poetics developed during and after the war, this experience of estrangement from his own earlier writings acquires a meaning that points beyond an understanding of these particular stories. "*Noli me legere*"—don't read me (489). These phrases of "Après coup" capture essential features of Blanchot's idea of literary creation: the absence of the author from his work, the impervious sovereignty of literature, and the irrecoverable alterity of the experience of writing itself.[6] Blanchot's invocation "not to read [him]"—not to attempt a reconstruction of the author's original intention and ultimately of a closed and coherent meaning—becomes, in the context of these first stories, not only particularly concrete but also inherently significant. It sheds light on the junction between Blanchot's historical, political, and autobiographical context and his poetics of impersonality, of the absent author and the disappearance of the narrator and the speaking subject itself.

Bident describes the shortcomings of the two stories in terms of "the structure of accumulation of mythical episodes, reducing [them] to an enigmatic allegory in 'Le dernier mot,' [and] the system of symbolic totalization, imposing a tyranny of meaning in 'L'idylle.'"[7] Despite this, the two stories already point to some of the major motifs and concerns of Blanchot's later writings. "L'idylle" and, to a lesser extent, "Le dernier mot" still largely follow the "conventions of writing," which Blanchot, in "The Narrative Voice," calls "linearity, continuity, readability." Although they already feature "the intrusion of the other . . . in its irreducible strangeness" (466), their status and mode of narration seem not yet fundamentally put into question. While they may, in this sense, appear traditional in comparison with Blanchot's later work, the two stories already anticipate some of its characteristic features—ungraspable figures, confusing temporal and spatial parameters, an uncanny atmosphere—and foreshadow the concern in the later work with strangeness, exile, and violence, with threshold states of consciousness, the ubiquity of death, an instrumentalized language, and, however indirectly, with narration and the process of writing itself.[8] Although each of the stories appears to follow a linear plot and seems rounded off and complete in itself, the two *récits* take on a different dimension in *Le ressassement éternel*, where they are joined in a sequence reversing the temporal order in which they were written. In this constellation, held together by a resounding title evoking a central notion of Blanchot's postwar poetics—the ceaseless mutter of another, nonreferential language—they can be read as a narrative dramatization of the passage from a traditional, self-enclosed narrative mode, associated with the oppressively closed system of "L'idylle," to a mode "outside" of all system and closure, which opens up on the last pages of "Le dernier mot." Leaving behind the representational, symbolic, or—mainly in the case of "Le dernier mot"—allegorical narrative constitutive of the stories themselves, this ending points beyond its own finality toward another mode of narration and another language than the one still largely enacted in the stories. It is a narration and a language in which an incessant, interminable saying outside of discourse, communication, and meaning can be heard. The title under which Blanchot later joined the two stories together indicates the vanishing point toward which *Le ressassement éternel* tends, as it narrates the path leading to the depersonalization of writing and the *dehors* that constitutes the very core of Blanchot's poetics.

Prophecy and Failure

In "Après coup," Blanchot highlights the most unsettling consequence of
the gap between the time "Le dernier mot" and "L'idylle" were written and
their availability to a reading public in the aftermath of the war. Some elements of these stories—a maddening proximity of evil and seemingly
idyllic harmony, the arbitrary punishments of an asylum's inmates, an exiled stranger who is murdered in a camp-like institution without explanation or cause, a burning library, entranced masses gathered by loudspeakers on public places, the cruelty associated with enforced hygiene—seem
to prefigure, in uncanny concreteness and detail, events that occurred
under Nazi rule several years after the stories were written. In his retrospective reflections in "Après coup," Blanchot insists, however, that the
meaning of these concurrences eludes him: "[I knew about] nothing that
could have prepared me to write these innocent stories that resound with
murderous echoes of the future" (491).

Aware of but also wary of possible readings of the two stories in
terms of these coincidences, Blanchot underlines the elusiveness of their
original intention and draws ambivalent, if not contradictory, conclusions
from his own perplexity. He explicitly links to Auschwitz and the Gulag
elements of "L'idylle," such as the murdered stranger, the work of "transport[ing] mountains of stones from one spot to another and then back to
the starting place" (493), and the total *naufrage,* the "universal ruin, which
is completed with the fall of the last Tower" (491) at the end of "Le dernier
mot." He simultaneously emphasizes that the events seemingly foreshad-
owed in these stories do not shed light on them but, on the contrary, add
to their strangeness. About "L'idylle" he writes: "Prophetic also, but for
me (today) in a way that is even more inexplicable, since I can only interpret it in the light of the events that came afterwards and were not known
until much later, in such a way that this later knowledge does not illuminate but withdraws understanding from the story" (492). In these lines
Blanchot conveys a view of the relationship between literature and reality
that will characterize his later critical and fictional work. History, politics,
and lived experience haunt Blanchot's writings in indirect and often uncanny ways, even where—as in these stories—he elides any explicit reference to historical facts. Literature, for Blanchot, stands apart from and

exceeds history. Yet the obscurity and strangeness of these stories transmit the premonition of a world beyond repair. The two stories announce
the perversion of a community into an oppressive, totalitarian system that
eliminates all otherness and the corruption of language into an instrument of power that silences all genuine relation to the world. The total destruction that ends "Le dernier mot" appears as both an annihilating
culmination of these developments and as an opening toward the space
of writing imagined by Blanchot in his subsequent work.

While Blanchot accepts the inevitability of reading "L'idylle" and "Le
dernier mot" in terms of events that occurred later, he also rejects a facile
reading of the stories along such prophetic lines and objects to having
them interpreted as a prefiguration "of an already menacing future" (493).
He emphatically calls "The Idyll" a "story from before Auschwitz" (494)
and, in a dense argumentation recalling Theodor W. Adorno's famous
pronouncement that "all lyrical poetry after Auschwitz is barbaric," un-
ambiguously remarks that since Auschwitz cannot be approached by any
fictional means, "no matter when it is written, every *récit* from now on
will be from before Auschwitz."[9] The *récits* of *Le ressassement éternel* seem
uncannily prophetic in some of their aspects, but Blanchot insists that
they do not begin to be commensurable with the actual experience of
the camps because, *as récits,* as coherent "narrations of events that make
sense,"[10] they fail to account for the interruption in the possibility of
(traditional) narration constituted by Auschwitz. In a further paradoxical
turn, however, Blanchot intimates that it is precisely a retrospective
reading—a reading *après coup* that accounts for the impossibility of narrating Auschwitz and therefore sheds an estranged gaze upon the stories'
largely intact narrative mode—that *can* do justice to the exigencies of
literature. From this perspective, Blanchot says of "L'idylle" that it only
"lay[s] the groundwork for the game of deciphering and interpretation,"
but that it essentially "remains a *stranger* to itself" (493). It is this self-
strangeness that reconciles the story with the demands of literature. What
are these demands and how are we to understand Blanchot's claim that
the *récits* of *Le ressassement éternel* fail to live up to them?

TWO "LOIS DU RÉCIT"

The exigencies of literature can be formulated on the basis of Blanchot's
analysis of the "failure" of the stories to fulfill them. Although he starts

his reflections on *Le ressassement éternel* with remarks about his estrangement from both stories, his explanations as to what it is that makes them
appear so strange in his retrospective reading differ greatly. In "Après
coup" Blanchot remarks about "L'idylle": "Even though it seems to open
up the unhappy possibilities of a life without hope, the story as such remains light, untroubled, and of a clarity that neither weighs down nor obscures the pretension of a hidden or serious meaning" (493). By contrast,
the exigencies of literature described by Blanchot in his theoretical writings after the war defy such a totalizing meaning. Calling "L'idylle" an
"unhappy story," Blanchot remarks that it is nevertheless itself an idyll.
The discrepancy he detects between the "unhappiness" of "L'idylle" and
its narrative mode leads him to formulate what he calls, in "Après coup,"
"la loi du récit," the law of the story: "L'idylle" is itself "the little idol that
is unjust and injurious to the very thing it utters, happy in the misfortune
it portends and that it endlessly threatens to turn into a lure. This is the
law of the story, its happiness and, because of it, its unhappiness" (494).
The "happiness" of "L'idylle" resides in the "glory of a 'narrative voice' that
speaks clearly" (494) above and beyond the plight of the stranger who is
rendered mute. The story's "unhappiness"—its failure to comply with the
exigencies of literature—lies in its inability to "take back," to erase and
thereby to escape the affirmation of being that is constitutive of the very
act of telling a story. In saying that this failure makes of "L'idylle" a "story
from before Auschwitz," Blanchot suggests that the—although ultimately
impossible—erasure of this affirmation, which he formulates as the demand of literature and strives for in his postwar fiction, is in some ways
related to the historical catastrophe.

Unlike his assessment of "L'idylle," Blanchot does not call "Le dernier mot" a *récit* "from before Auschwitz," thus implying that the much
more fragmentary and elusive poetics underlying this story—though written a year before "L'idylle"—corresponds more closely, if not yet fully, to
the demands of literature formulated by Blanchot after the war. In "Le
dernier mot" it is not the unbroken clarity, the "glory of a narrative voice"
that is incommensurable with the "exigencies of literature," but its teleological drive, the fact that it "come[s] so quickly to the end" (491). But
Blanchot retrospectively suggests that this *récit* and its "end" are already
close to the demands of literature in its search for the annihilation of
being and its awareness of the impossibility to do so.[11] Following a synopsis of the story in which he describes the "universal ruin" taking place at

the end of "Le dernier mot," Blanchot gives a double reading of the story: "This kind of synopsis or outline—the paradox of such a story—is chiefly distinguished by recounting the absolute disaster as having taken place, so that the story itself could not have survived either, which makes it impossible or absurd, unless it claims to be a prophetic work, announcing . . . what there still is when there is nothing: *there is,* which holds nothingness and blocks annihilation so that it cannot escape its interminable process whose end is repetition and eternity—the vicious circle" (491–92). As a mere *synopsis* of its content, "Le dernier mot" can indeed be read as a prophecy of a historical disaster. When it is not reduced to this representational mode of a summary, however, but instead is experienced as an actual *récit, it does* live up to the exigencies of literature. Unlike "L'idylle," it already contains the self-engulfing abyss counteracting—or rather eternally suspending—the "glory of the narrative voice." In juxtaposing "L'idylle" and "Le dernier mot" in reverse chronological order, *Le ressassement éternel* conveys the impression of a single story, in which those aspects of "L'idylle" that mark it as a "story from before Auschwitz" are thwarted by the abysmal poetics underlying "Le dernier mot," which *is* "compatible" with the demands of literature after Auschwitz. Blanchot's decision to publish the two stories in this particular constellation in 1951 thereby turns *Le ressassement éternel* into a book not only *after* but in the most indirect way *about* Auschwitz, before making this link explicit—in the most complex possible ways—in his "Après coup" of 1983.

This interpretation, however, already constructs a narrative based on the reversal of the chronological order of the two *récits,* and as such may "miss the point"[12] of the narration that is *Le ressassement éternel.* Like Blanchot's own synopsis, it would merely be the "true account of an exceptional event," one that "has actually taken place" and that one can "try to report": the writing of the two *récits* and their joint publication twelve years later as *Le ressassement éternel.* But it fails to read this work as a narration that is, in the end, "not the account of an event but the event itself."[13] Read as such an "event itself," *Le ressassement éternel* is no longer a realistic, linear story of Blanchot's coming to literature in his specific historical and political context, but an experience of this work *as* literature, understood in terms of the *loi du récit* enunciated by Blanchot in *Le livre à venir.*

This "loi du récit"—that narration is "not the account of an event but," precisely in the abysmal destruction of reality, "the event itself"—seems to contrast sharply with the "loi du récit" enunciated in "Après coup" in relation to "L'idylle" and its "glory of a narrative voice." In the chapter "Le Chant des Sirènes," written twenty years earlier, Blanchot defines the *loi du récit,* the "hidden law of all narration," as a force that unsettles all clarity and—far from soothing anything horrible or terrifying—introduces "an abyss into every word."[14] Far from producing a false idyll, from being a "little idol" that betrays the horrors it communicates, the *récit,* according to this earlier law, is itself the rupture in the falsely idyllic fabric sustained by the glory of the narrative voice. Obviously, the "glorious" law of the story in "Après coup" is intended to mark his retrospective distance, his estrangement from the mode of narration of "L'idylle": its clarity, its closure, its coherence. Are then the two *récits* brought together in *Le ressassement éternel* still the narration of an event—Blanchot's beginnings? Or are they already the—glorious or abysmal—event itself?

"L'IDYLLE"

> *"To welcome him in his quality of stranger"*
> —*L'entretien infini*

The title of "L'idylle," the first of the two stories in *Le ressassement éternel,* denotes both a state of being, in which harmony, simplicity, and peace predominate, and a literary genre, the short poem or prose piece depicting pastoral scenes and a happy, carefree life in accord with nature. The word "idyll"—from the Greek *eidolon,* signifying "form" or "figure"—and the definite pronoun in the title announce the story's metafictional dimension, which invites a reflection on the relationship between the world arising in the story and the literary genre of a unified, harmoniously and "naturally" told narrative. Conflating a form of life suggestive of a utopian mode of existence and a literary term designating an affirmative form, "L'idylle" becomes a site where the correlation between the politics and poetics of Blanchot's beginnings can be probed.

"L'idylle" is the story of a stranger—a wanderer or vagabond—who, upon entering a nameless city, is taken to an innocuous-looking "Home," a camp-like institution resembling a hospice for the homeless that turns out to be a murderous penitentiary, where the stranger is kept in detention, committed to forced labor, and finally flogged to death after a vain attempt to flee. The Home, which looks at first like a bright and pretty house akin to a sanatorium or an asylum, is in reality a closed establishment bearing the traits of a totalitarian society. In an atmosphere of falsely caring hospitality that only adds to the terror of the place, the Home requires absolute integration and represses everything that could disrupt its treacherous harmony. From the first lines to the last, the story deploys a centripetal force that swallows up all that is different and foreign. Erasing every trace of an outside, the world of the Home constitutes an inescapable totality, in which everything that is alien to the precepts of the institution is silenced and ultimately killed off. It is only under the smooth, impenetrable surface and in the darkest hours of the night that fleeting shadows and harrowing screams stemming from the masters' quarters indicate the presence of other forces, hidden beneath the Home's deceitful brightness and transparency.

This "clarity of the day" is embodied most of all by Louise, the mistress of the house. For Sarah Kofman, Louise stands for the perfidious principle of the idyll: "Louise, (from lux? Lex?) the eternally young, the always smiling one, lively, gay, jolly, round, chubby, shining, open and welcoming; Louise, the luminous and radiant, who in her seduction unceasingly revolves around the stranger to attract him and rob him of his strangeness, subjecting him, always with a smile and 'for his own good,' but not without violence, to the good order of the house, the law of property and propriety."[15] Kofman links the laws regulating the Home to the narration of a story and sees in Louise the representative of "the law of the *récit*." Louise is indeed the one who, on the first page of "L'idylle," opens the door to the stranger as he enters the Home and who closes the *récit* as she goes about her business after his death. Like Louise and the very principle of the idyll, the telling of a *récit* subsumes everything that is terrible into the lightness and happiness of narration. Therein lies what Blanchot will later call the "glory of the *récit*," a splendor hiding an all-encompassing abyss. The gravity of this abyss will become the primary orientation of Blanchot's later fiction. In "L'idylle," however, Louise seems to reign unabashed.

This principle and driving force of "L'idylle," namely, the elimination of all strangeness and alterity, can be traced at all levels, from the most concrete to the most metaphorical, from the most obvious themes of the plot to individual scenes and passages and to the narrative mode itself. Upon entering the Home the stranger is shoved into an installation of showers, supposedly for the sake of hygiene.[16] This ritual is meant to wash away all traces of an outside that itself remains nameless, as the stranger refuses or is unable to identify his country of origin. He is given the name Alexander Akim by the mistress of the house. Kofman speculates that "Akim" may stem from the Greek *akinéo*, meaning "no movement," which she links to Louise's attempt to immobilize and fix the vagabond, "the exiled, the outcast, the one in the shadow."[17] More plausibly, the name alludes to its Hebrew origin and meaning: "established [or chosen] by God." That the name Akim is most commonly used in Russian (as an abbreviation of Joachim) is equally significant, since it would fit the Jewish or Russian names of other inmates of the Home: Isaiah Sirotk (joining Jewishness and, anagrammatically, Trotskyism), Piotl, and Nikolas Pavlon. Although in his right-wing journalistic writings Blanchot occasionally conflates communist revolutionaries and Jews,[18] no easy conclusions can be drawn from these fictional figures and their names.[19] As Bident points out, some of these figures carrying Jewish or Russian names are indeed depicted in a negative light and associated with spying and cheating. On the other hand, Akim himself "refuse[s] to take part in the game" (9) and is clearly a victim rather than an accomplice of the masters. Furthermore, it is said that "[t]his strange name suited him as well as any other: he was no more than a kind of beggar here" (9). Without any real origin or name, and despite the attempted Jewish stigmatization, Akim remains an arbitrary stranger, inspiring Louise's concern that he will "never really fit in here" (19). However, her very act of giving him a fictive name, unrelated to his actual origins—albeit a strange-sounding name, evoking "stranger"—is already, and inescapably, an act of appropriation that undoes his strangeness. By extension, the narrative—insofar as it is itself an "arbitrary" naming—conspires with Louise's impassible grip on Alexander Akim and his fate.

The stranger's time in the Home is spent in conversation with the director, Pierre, and his wife, Louise, a couple united in an uncannily

troubled relationship; with inscrutable guardians; and with the other inmates who, like Akim himself, are forced to perform futile work in a
quarry. Amid visits to the neighboring village, bouts of illness, violent
brawls, physical punishments, and brutal confrontations with the over-
seers and the other inmates, the stranger increasingly senses the suffocating atmosphere of the place and the impossibility of breaking out. It
is, however, equally impossible for him to settle down and cast off his
strangeness. To a newcomer to the Home, Akim says: "You'll learn that in
this house it's hard to be a stranger. You'll also learn that it's not easy to
stop being one. If you miss your country, every day you'll find more reasons to miss it. But if you manage to forget it and begin to love your new
place, you'll be sent home, and then, uprooted once more, you'll begin a
new exile" (24). Wavering between resignation and resistance, Akim is finally executed in punishment for his attempt to escape the Home the
night before his arranged wedding to an older inmate's daughter, an alliance which, he is told, would signify the end of his existence as a stranger
and corroborate his final integration. At the funeral following his execution, which replaces the wedding originally planned, we are told that
"[t]he sun . . . was shining now with a lovely radiance" in a "superb and
victorious sky" (33). In harmonious accord with an indifferent nature, the
murderous logic of the idyll is triumphant, and, after a brief moment in
which the director has to face the gaze of the dying man, all traces of the
stranger are effaced. In the last lines of the story, Louise "drummed her
fingers mechanically on her knees" and "rose to attend to her duties as
mistress of the house" (33). With this ending, death itself, the extreme
other, is reappropriated and neutralized by the totalizing system.[20]
"L'idylle," at an individual, social, and cosmic level, finalizes the absorption and elimination of the other and the outside. This ending coincides
with the change in narrative perspective. After having shared the stranger's point of view throughout most of the story, the narrator impassibly
continues his tale beyond the protagonist's death.

   "L'idylle" opens with a paradoxical warning made by the guard as he
leads the stranger to the Home: "You'll hold it against me, but it's the
rule. No one escapes the spectacle of happiness" (7). It is the semblance of
an idyllic happiness that is inescapable and that, along with the effacement of difference, precludes freedom. The "spectacle of happiness" most

directly refers to the relationship between the director and his wife. Just as the Home allows for no difference, the relationship between the couple allows for no distance: "[S]he's denied him the possibility of moving away from her a little, of breathing some other air . . . She doesn't leave him, and in that way she can overwhelm him with her solicitude" (17). No space, no opening is left between them. The couple is the foil for what Kofman, in the spirit of Blanchot, describes as a true relationship that rests on "what separates, what leaves at an insurmountable distance."[21] The erasure of difference between the couple corresponds to the elimination of difference and distance inherent in the social, symbolic, and narrative mode of "L'idylle."

The process of integration involves a double movement, the homogenization of the inside and the elimination of an outside. The stranger is told that "[w]e don't like people to live in exile among us" (16). Just as all sense of strangeness is forced to vanish and all remembrance of earlier allegiances is made to disappear inside the Home, all exteriority is annihilated. As the guard tells the stranger, "Everyone here has his prison, but in that prison each person is free" (13). In these words freedom itself is imprisoned; at the same time, all relations between individuals are cut off. For a while the stranger protests against this cynical definition of freedom and its negation of communality. When he voices his longing to return to "community life," he is told by an orderly: "Community life? . . . Everyone lives all together here, but there's no community life." "'No,' the stranger murmured: 'I'm talking about a free life'" (8). Shortly before the end, however, the stranger seems resigned to assimilating himself to his surroundings. He at first "flatly refuse[s]" (25) the marriage arrangement that would make it possible for him to physically leave the Home, but would also mean that he agrees "to say goodbye to the past" (28) and adopt the values and conditions underlying the system of the Home. But gradually he loses his drive and capacity to see through appearances, and he acknowledges the "spectacle of happiness" presented to him. In view of his impending wedding, he goes so far as accepting the director's cynical simulation of being a loving and caring father. His assimilation seems complete as he prepares himself for the celebration of his "transformation," in which a "stranger would die in the morning, and in the afternoon an old friend would take his place" (28). The reference to becoming "an old friend" suggests that, at this point, the narrator too has become part of the Home. After the stranger's death, the narrator again adopts the impassability of the bystanders, who, with the exception of Akim's intended bride, Elise, accept the interchangeability of wedding and funeral without protest or tears.

The most disturbing aspect of this world lies in the intermingling of friendliness and cruelty, of hospitality and violence. The leveling out of differences is primarily an effect of the language used in the Home. This language, full of duplicity and ambiguity, is a tool of the mastery that dissimulates its primary purpose, the manipulation of those exposed to it.[22] Sarcastic irony reigns in every dialogue and, in a sweeping movement, undoes all relation to reality and every possibility of distinguishing between lies and truth. When the stranger approaches the house about to close in on him, Louise "opened the door," saying, "don't be afraid of anything, the house is open to you," and leads him to be greeted by her husband, a young man with square shoulders and an "open, smiling face" (7). The threefold repetition of "open" on the first pages of the story announces the closing of the trap in which the stranger will suffocate and perish. When he is locked up in a dark cell as a punishment for protesting against his confinement, the guard pretends to comfort him: "'Naturally,' he said, 'it's hard to have your freedom taken away from you. But is anyone ever free? Can we do what we want? And there are so many other reasons for being unhappy'" (12). The stranger senses that this rhetoric robs him of everything, even of his own suffering. The "spectacle of happiness" is complete. The behavior of the masters is called "friendly," "good-natured," "jovial," "amiable," and "cordial," their manners are hospitable and polite. The torturers apologize to the stranger for the cruelty inflicted on him and sigh with fake regret at the sight of his execution, which they themselves had ordained. In a book about the Home, its penal methods are described as a source of pride for the State: "[T]he mixture of severity and gentleness, the combination of freedom and restraint—these were the fruit of long experience and it was difficult to imagine a more just or reasonable system" (16).

Only some slight instants and instances escape this system and its language of power and control. There is the stranger's lump in the throat, his choking silence, the stillness of his stare before he dies. There is the rustling of dry leaves from an arid and empty outside; there is a "flower in a frame, a touching and useless object" (14). The only remaining contestation against the instrumentalization of humans and of language lies in an aimless, purposeless being, a withdrawal from any goal and function. In an enigmatic moment, while working at the quarries, the stranger, in a delirium provoked by the sun and the aridity of the place, "ran towards one of the workers, grabbed his pick, and then banged it against a rock. . . . At the same time, he tasted some unknown freshness under the sun, as if, in the midst of a tormenting despair, among all the jostlings of hatred, some pure and gracious feeling had remained" (25). But this moment, like the choking silence, the rustling leaves, the framed flower, remains without consequences. "[H]e fell back into a despondency that made him indifferent to the passing of time, and soon he found himself with the prisoners in one of the convoys returning to the Home" (25).

In the first lines of the story, the guardian accompanying the stranger to the Home warns him of the treacherous appearance of this place as "a simple and happy dream" (16): "I urge you to follow my advice: don't trust appearances" (7). But even this advice is misleading, in that it suggests the possibility of distinguishing between the "happy" appearance and the underlying horror of this "idyllic" world. Yet it is precisely the capacity to perceive differences that is eliminated in the Home's unified microcosm, which bars all the openings and eliminates all distinctions. The world of the Home can be described in terms of Giorgio Agamben's definition of the "state of exception that has become the rule." Like Walter Benjamin before him, Agamben describes this state as a "negative indistinction," a fatal state of indifference, paradigmatically exemplified by life in the village in Kafka's novel *The Castle*.[23] In this state, in which human existence is reduced to "bare life" at its most vulnerable and exposed, the law permeates everything and has become indistinguishable from the life it ought to organize. All dividing lines between the private and the public realm are eliminated. While remaining invisible, the law invades the most intimate aspects of life. As in Kafka's village, in "L'idylle," conversations about rules and punishments intermingle with speculations about the marital relationship between the master and mistress of the house or the guardian's unhappy love life. At first, the stranger protests: "I can't get mixed up in the private lives of people who are above me" (15). But soon he, too, becomes obsessed with the marital situation of the couple and merges it with his reflections on the state of the Home and his will to freedom. Overstepping all limitations, the rules engulf and contaminate everything. Even the vegetation is putrid, and the stranger feels "the strange effects of the corrupted air" (29).

There is little doubt that the Home depicts the workings of a totalitarian society, but its actual political and ideological underpinnings are far from self-evident. Critics have disagreed about the regime or political system associated with the organization and functioning of the "sad house" (16). Although Kofman insists that one should not see in "L'idylle" "a *récit* anticipating Auschwitz,"[24] she nevertheless clearly connects the world of the Home with the totalitarian regime of National Socialism. The story, written in July 1936, when Blanchot interrupted for several months his participation in the right-wing journal *Combat*,[25] could testify to Blanchot's premonition of the implications and possible consequences of the xenophobia underlying this political movement and its French counterparts.

It is, however, at least equally conceivable that the murderous idyll refers to the communist utopia of total state control. In contrast, Ulrich Haase and William Large discuss the story in terms of Blanchot's allegiances to the extreme right and see in the Home's semblance of openness and hospitality a critique of "our modern liberal democracies."[26] For them, the main thrust of the story is an indictment of democratic systems for their destruction of an earlier, true community based on radical freedom, for their drive to level out and destroy all specificity and singularity, and for their oppressive homogenization hidden under layers of false friendliness, tolerance, and care. However, the possibility arises— and is strengthened by its publication alongside "Le dernier mot" in *Le ressassement éternel*—that "L'idylle" should not be correlated with any particular political system. Perhaps Blanchot's political allegiances in "L'idylle" remain enigmatic because it is far from certain whether its primary concern is to give a diagnosis, a warning, or an anticipation of an impending political development.

As with Agamben, the "state of exception" for Blanchot is a correlate of modernity. On one of the stranger's walks to the city, which is nothing but an extension of the Home, he enters a bookstore and, obviously thinking of escaping, asks for "a detailed map of the city and the surrounding area." The owner of the bookstore replies: "A map of the city, yes" (16). But no map exists of what lies outside. On a second visit to the shop, however, the bookseller hands the stranger a "very old book that gave the history of the entire region" (24), but he does not reply when Akim asks for a more recent work. This exchange suggests that in older times, the area lying outside of the Home and the city was still registered on maps; the obliteration of the outside would then correspond to a newer development. This impression is corroborated by the bookseller's description of the Home's advantages: "To be housed and fed, to enjoy all the modern comforts [*installations modernes*]" (26). In this light, "L'idylle" presents itself as a general critique of modern society. Such a reading suggests that the antimodernist tendencies of Blanchot's engagement with the nationalist extreme right could very well also underlie his early fiction. But the story is more specific. On the stranger's third visit to the bookshop, the owner hands him "a new book," but even this supposedly more recent depiction of the city's surrounding regions fails to conform to the present reality. Planning his escape, the stranger copies parts of the map and memorizes others, but his flight fails because, although "[t]he map he had made that morning was fresh in his mind," it is "the city [that] had changed" (29). The system in which the stranger is caught—a world that knows no outside—seems to be even more recent than its most recent *existing* portrayal. This indication could point to the analogy between the Home and the state of the political world in which Blanchot finds himself at the very moment of writing "L'idylle"—a world not yet depicted in any, not even the newest, book. By extension, this world is what Blanchot attempts to leave behind in—and through—writing "L'idylle." It seems as if the changes in the city that belie its description in the "new book" occur concurrently with Akim's attempt to escape; or, at another level, it seems as if the city closes in on the stranger at the very moment in which these lines are written—and ultimately in the act of writing as such.

The discrepancy between the map and the city, between representation and reality, leads to the stranger's disorientation, to his failure to find an exit, and ultimately to his death. Given that this emerges concurrently with the very writing of the story, it is likely that the stranger's failed escape is an enactment of the writing process itself. The failure of Akim's escape reflects Blanchot's invective against the idea of writing as an act of liberation. What the stranger—and with him the narrator and the author—seem to be unable to escape may, therefore, be less the law of any *cité* or form of state, than the law of the *récit* itself. As the stranger tries to forge his path,

> the houses, built one on top of the other, and made even more jumbled by the darkness, opened awkwardly onto alleyways in which people glided by. It seemed that by entering these streets he was entering the houses themselves; courtyards were mixed up with public squares; bridges went from one building to another and ran above the houses like endless balconies; as soon as you found a little open space, it meant that you were shut up in a garden, and to discover a new exit you had to climb stairs and plunge on through constructions you had no way of knowing would ever lead you outside. (29–30)

This visualization of a nightmarish, absolute closure evokes an entrapment without exit, a situation without hope. It brings to mind the critique of bureaucracy and state power in Kafka's court-buildings and imperial spaces, but it also resembles the drawings of endlessly intricate constructions by Giovanni Battista Piranesi or M. C. Escher, where the intensity of an unceasing movement arises in the midst of the most opaque self-enclosed world. Amid an ultimate experience of closure, whatever faintly opens up in these lines could be the beginning of a ceaseless, inescapable, meaningless reiteration, of a *ressassement éternel*.

When Akim finally reaches what could be "the end of the city" or "the beginning of a new life" (30), he is crushed by fatigue and is taken back to the Home to be executed under a bright and glorious sky that participates in the obliteration of the outside. In "L'idylle," the outside is not to be found. It takes "Le dernier mot," read against the foil of "L'idylle," to make of *Le ressassement éternel* a primary scene of Blanchot's *dehors*.

"LE DERNIER MOT"

To go out, into an outside[27]

Although written one year earlier, "Le dernier mot" in many ways goes beyond the largely traditional and realistic narrative mode of "L'idylle."

In the latter, the classical form—the unity of time, place, and event—
determines the narrative, and it is still possible to read it as a story articu-
lating chronologically the experience of the stranger Alexander Akim,
from the moment of his arrival to the Home to the moment of his execution. The story relates the impossibility for the stranger of finding a
place in the Home *as stranger,* but it does so by means of a conventional
representation of the protagonist's experiences and encounters. The coherence of the narration itself remains intact, and the roles of the various
figures—the director and his wife, the older inmate who is the father of
Elise—are unified, recognizable, and stable. Similarly, the position and
status of the narrator as well as the possibility of narrating a sequence of
events remain unquestioned. This is not the case for "Le dernier mot,"
where the constraints of the classical form are abandoned in favor of a
more disrupted narrative mode. The temporal articulation and the spatial
localization of the events are broken up into a series of seemingly unrelated, enigmatic episodes. The scenes follow each other abruptly and
without any other link than the presence of the first-person narrator, who,
up to a significant moment before the ending, also provides the focalizing
perspective on the events. However, throughout the *récit,* this narrating
"I" lacks consistency. It is difficult to discern a pattern in the narrator's behavior, and his position changes each time he is confronted with a different figure: the stranger in the street, the janitor in the library, the old
woman in the corner of the cell, the children in the classroom, the young
woman, and finally, the owner of the "last tower." These figures seem to
have the possibility of determining the events in which they are involved,
and they ultimately turn out to be nothing but a vanishing presence in a
strangely inconsequential, yet ominously self-erasing, movement leading
from one scene to the next. This movement culminates in the final episode, in which the young woman, the owner of the tower, who is also
called the "All Powerful One," and the narrator himself are thrown "outside," as the tower in which the three figures find themselves collapses.
In contradistinction to "L'idylle," where the narrated event is dominated
by an all-pervasive force of integration—the subjection to the logic of the
Home—"Le dernier mot" is driven by a force of disorientation and dissolution that eventually points to the imminent demise of the representational narrative and, beyond this particular tale, toward a radical transformation of the literary space altogether.

As indicated in the title, "Le dernier mot" stages a radical experience of estrangement originating in a crisis of language. The story opens with the narrator's expression of his sense of alienation from common language: "The words I heard that day rang strangely in my ears" (37). In the story's subsequent scenes it becomes clear that this opening sentence reflects less an individual perception or psychological state than the evidence that language, considered as a means of communication, comprehension, and expression, has been shaken in its foundations. "Le dernier mot" stages this crisis of language as loss of certainty and direction, but also as the demise of the kind of authority and power that is all-pervasive in "L'idylle." It is therefore not surprising that the words "strangely" and "stranger" feature in the first sentence of "Le dernier mot": that which, in "L'idylle," has—if only briefly—"upset the order of the house" (30) is, in "Le dernier mot," the harbinger of the end of this order. Read in the sequence in which it appears in Le ressassement éternel, "Le dernier mot" becomes a response to the world of the Home in "L'idylle." The transformation of language and narration taking place in the former presents itself as a critique of the totalitarian system of the latter. The killing of the stranger at the end of "L'idylle" finds its counterpart at the end of "Le dernier mot," in which the centralized authority embodied in the tower crumbles, along with its all-powerful owner and his accomplices.

After the narrator's initial experience of the strangeness of the words that he "heard that day," he addresses a stranger on the street: "Can you tell me what the watchword is?" The stranger replies, "I'd be happy to tell you . . . but somehow I haven't managed to hear it yet today." The narrator's response is ominous: "Never mind . . . I'll go find Sophonie" (37). This allusion to the biblical prophet Zephaniah (in French, Sophonie), who announces an apocalyptic destruction brought about by the wrath of God against the sinful and the "oppressing city" (Zeph. 3:1), introduces the Bible as a first reference of authoritative language. In the scenes that follow, the library, the school, the legal institutions, and finally the tower—the latter symbolizing not only worldly power but, given its owner (the "All Powerful One"), divine power and ultimately power as such—are shattered in the midst of an atmosphere of upheaval and apocalyptic destruction. The loss of certainty is a correlative of the crisis of language. In the very first lines of the story, the narrator indicates that he continues speaking although he is aware that, from this point on, the use of words lacks all foundation. "Are you sure of your words?" asks the stranger. "No," replies the narrator, "shrugging my shoulders. How can I be sure? That's the risk you run" (37). The resolve to "run the risk," to go on speaking in spite of the absence of the watchword (*mot d'ordre*) and the lack of certainty, is linked to a search for a different language—and, by implication and analogy, for a different mode of narration, in which the absence of any fixed point of reference is taken into account and affirmed.

This affirmation of the consequences resulting from the crisis of language also lies at the core of Blanchot's first novel, *Thomas l'obscur*. According to his own account, he interrupted his work on the novel in order to write "Le dernier mot," which he calls "an attempt to short circuit the other book that was being written, in order to overcome that endlessness and reach a silent decision, reach it through a more linear narrative that was nevertheless painfully complex" (491). While the central theme of "Le dernier mot" thus seems clearly to communicate with the work in progress on *Thomas l'obscur*, the *récit* differs from the novel in the conventionally allegorical mode with which it stages the disappearance of the watchword. In both the novel and the story, the crisis of language is related in a fictional narrative, ending up in a movement of total annihilation in which not only the fictional figures but the very possibility of narration itself disappear. As in *Thomas l'obscur*, the movement of destruction in "Le dernier mot"—a cosmological cataclysm that shakes the earth and shatters everything—is not related to the mode of being of one of the figures, but emerges from an experience of the crisis of language. This destruction is announced at the beginning of the story in the reference to Zephaniah and, up to the final scene, takes place as a narrated event. In *Thomas l'obscur*, by contrast, the destructive force is not represented but is instead enacted by Thomas—more a name than a figure—who is called "le sacrificateur."[28] Thomas's incapacity to use language goes beyond mere passive muteness.[29] "The destruction of words was part of his nature."[30] In "Le dernier mot" the crisis of language is, to a large extent, still narrated in a representational mode, and it is precisely in this divergence from the novel that the importance of the *récit* for an understanding of the development of Blanchot's writing and its transformation of literary space is revealed. Although, up to the final scene, the consequences of this crisis do not yet manifest themselves in "Le dernier mot" as a transformation of the mode of writing or as a destruction of the order of narration, the *récit* tells the story of this transformation and this destruction. In *Thomas l'obscur* the moment of total destruction coincides with the dissolution of Thomas as a fictional figure, in which the narrated event, the narration of the event, and the figuration of a whole poetic world are destroyed. Although "Le dernier mot" does not as yet fully enact such a transformation, it already suggests the aporia that follows from it: "[T]he last word cannot be a word, nor the absence of words, nor anything else but a word" (48).

The narrator in "Le dernier mot" has ambivalent reactions to this dissolution of order because he realizes that its disappearance would also dismantle his own position. His actions and encounters are all situated in representative places of authority: the library, the classroom, the tower. However, these sites of symbolic power are in ruins, and their functioning has fallen "out of order": the library, a monumental building guarded by bronze lions and obviously representing the written word as an institution of power, now features only empty shelves and is about to close; the classroom is filled with noisily playing children who are on "holiday" (42); nothing is left of the justice department but its ferociously barking dogs, and the *récit* as a whole ends on the collapsing of the All Powerful One's tower. Although the signs and symbols of power refer to existing instances of authority, it becomes increasingly clear that the authority of the narrator itself is at stake. Time and again, the narrator becomes aware that he is the ally of the figures of authority. He is, respectively, the judge, the teacher, and the servant of the tower's owner, but in each case these instances of power are invalidated. When the librarian repeats that "there is no watchword anymore" (40), the narrator goes out on the street and meets a woman who tells him, "with a malicious smile: 'Have you heard the news? There's no more library. From now on, people can read any way they like'" (40). The narrator's violent response—"I want to kill you"— is triggered by the awareness of the threat this poses to his own authority as manipulator of the tale and its principal character—and ultimately to his very existence. The experience of his loss of power results in his continuous laments over what he calls "my own torments" (43): "Why am I being humiliated like this? What should I do?" (39); "How am I supposed to live now?" (40); "Where are we going? . . . What am I going to find now?" (41). The words of the woman are later repeated in the context of the classroom scene, but this time they are pronounced by the narrator himself: "'Since the watchword was done away with,' I said, 'reading is free. If you think I talk without knowing what I'm saying, you're within your rights. I'm only one voice among many'" (43). In these words it becomes clear that the narrator in "Le dernier mot" tells the story of his own disappearance. And, in a dizzying *mise en abîme,* he even reflects on this impossible self-erasure: "I was the monument and the hammer that breaks it" (48).

The sequence of the narrator's realization, admission, and renunciation or demise of his position of authority is repeated throughout the story. It is enigmatically introduced in the encounter with the old woman, in which the narrator announces a monumental confession: "Days of shame . . . I stand before you to offer up the spectacle of my mistakes" (38). In a scene in which the justice department is associated with ferocious dogs, the narrator comes to admit: "But I belonged to the justice department as well. That was my shame: I was a judge. Who could condemn me?" (42). The children in the school ask him, "Are you the teacher or God?" and although he at first behaves like a schoolmaster, he replies, "[A]t this special hour, we can help each other. I, too, am a little child in a cradle, and I need to speak with cries and tears" (42). These words evoke a faint promise of redemption through the birth of an infant savior. In the final scene, the narrator is presented as the servant of the All Powerful One, the owner of the tower, who, echoing the Neoplatonic metaphor of the artist as a godlike creator (demiurge), calls him "[m]y accomplice" (49). However, the narrator again rejects this analogy: "You're the owner of the tower. . . . But I don't own anything" (49). In an uncannily explicit reference to Hegel's elaboration on the master-slave relationship, the narrator undoes his relationship to the ultimate instance of power: "I loved him, too, and in loving him I defied him. I bowed down, I humbled myself before him as though before a sovereign; and because I treated him as master, I chained him to his sovereignty" (49). As a result, the sovereign, by his own admission, is revealed as being "no more than a beast" (49). It is at that very moment of defiance of the supreme power that the narrator himself becomes disconnected from the narrating voice and literally turns into "one voice among many," (43) into one of the many figures of the *récit.*

The scene of the encounter with the All Powerful One starts out with the narrator's experience of gradual weakening of his strength: "How could I be so weak and yet still be able to talk? What weakness! What weariness! I knew that I was already too weak to die, and I saw myself as I was—an unlucky man who has no life and yet who struggles to live" (49). The inability to die anticipates Blanchot's notion of an interminable dying of the self in the act of writing, which is enacted here in a scene that culminates in the disruption of the fictional space of the *récit:* following the revelation that the sovereign is nothing but "a sad animal, watched over by a servant," who is none other than the narrator himself, an epiphanic moment enacts the narrator's disappearance in the texture of the narration itself. The narrator's description of his increasing weakening culminates in the vanishing of the first-person pronoun: "A ray of sunlight, erect like a stone, enclosed both of *them* in an illusion of eternity" (49; emphasis added). The narrator's "I" has disappeared; the "je" is turned into an "il" that is now merged with the All Powerful One and will not appear again. With this vanishing of the narrator's subjectivity, the narrative voice performs the renunciation of his own authority and henceforth speaks in an impersonal mode. The demise of the narrator's power, which is directly associated with the figure of divine power, correlates with the collapse of the tower and opens up a void into which the very possibility of a representational narration disappears. As the abyss engulfs everything, including the last word of a language obeying the order of symbolic representation, "Le dernier mot" announces another mode of narration that no longer pretends to represent reality but instead creates "an illusion of eternity," (49) the space of fiction. It is the space described by the narrator to the schoolchildren as a world in which time is suspended and "[y]ou forget the first word and the last word" (43). This other, nonrepresentational space and nonlinear time are correlated with another, nonreferential language.

Throughout "Le dernier mot" there are intimations of an alternative language, one that is not ruled by a *mot d'ordre*: the squawking of the children (37), the narrator's need to "speak with cries and tears" (42), a choking mode of speaking with a "lump of fear in your throat" (43), like the stranger in "L'idylle," the woman's speaking "without having to say a word" (41), the stammering of the narrator before breaking apart (48), the dog's "trembling, muffled howls, which at that hour of the day resounded like the echo of the word *there is*" (42). The words *il y a*, which resonate with the impersonality reached at the level of narration at the end of the story, are, as the narrator muses, "probably the last words," but they are "still able to reveal the things that were in this remote neighbourhood" (42). Suggested here is that "Le dernier mot" is itself the fictional space where, for the last time, words still function in the mode of revelation, but what they reveal is this "lastness." They disclose and make tangible the erasure, within language, of the ordering function of words that takes place at the very edge of language, before it turns mute or transforms into meaningless sounds of presymbolic utterances. At the point where the narrator accepts that he is only "one voice among many," he "broke up [the] meaning [of these sentences] by replacing some of the words with gasps and sighs" (43).

These individual instances of a creaturely language are, in one scene, extended to a collective mode of expression. As the narrator makes his way across a trembling earth and through streets filled with smoke, he is carried along by crowds led by voices coming out of loudspeakers and moving "as one . . . from east to west" (40), in the opposite direction of the biblical site of redemption toward one suggesting doom and destruction. The crowds are heading toward "a chaotic celebration, with torches burning in broad daylight. . . . The great consecration of the *until* [*jusqu'à ce que*]," an endpoint in time that turns, in this intransitive form, into the end of time itself. On its way to this site, where "time . . . becomes its own wreckage" (40), where the time of history comes to an end and the world goes asunder in a monumental wreckage [*naufrage*], the crowd's "trampling feet" crush "all that remained of language": "little scraps of words" drawn out into the "forms of a long sentence," resulting in the singing and shouting of the word *until*. This scene, which in some ways resembles a revolution, stages the end of time as the destruction of a language that has become an instrument of power, and anticipates the transformation of language into the ceaseless mutter designated by the title, *Le ressassement éternel*.

The most explicit and significant instance of another, wordless language is evoked toward the end of the *récit* in the narrator's encounter with the young mute girl, who, naked under a cloth of gold, "opened her coat a little and showed me the marks of fire. They seemed to be forming the first shapes of a vague language" (47). She is also the one who realizes the final disappearance of the foundation holding together the entire fictional world of the story, as she speaks the last words before the final crumbling of the tower: "'Oh no,' . . . 'can't you feel that we're not standing on anything?'" (50). The premonitory signs on the girl's body turn her into the muse of another narration and another language. These marks of fire on a woman's body are not merely an instance of another language, but point to the experience of writing itself.[31] The old woman in the cell of the library—the old muse—stops in midsentence after uttering the word "shipwreck" and says, "I can't go on" (38) and "I can't fulfill my role" (39); the young woman at the end of the story is the new muse, henceforth accompanying the narrator in his demise. In this function she joins him and his alter ego, the All Powerful One, in the tower, from which all three are thrown "outside" in the last lines of the story: "and when the tower collapsed and threw them outside, all three of them fell without saying a word" (50). This last word is a word, it is not the absence of words, nor is it "anything else but a word" (48).

If the outside reached at the end of *Le ressassement éternel* corresponds to Blanchot's description of the space of literature, it is not, however, to be understood as an escape from a world lying in ruins. Although Blanchot turns away from realistic narrations of figures engaged in real life,[32] he also explicitly rejects an escapist literature that turns away from the world and fails to confront the crisis of its times.[33] The priority of this exigency entails the blocking of all escape. In "Le dernier mot," this obstruction surprisingly manifests itself in direct reference to *Thomas l'obscur.* Significantly, a brief passage at the heart of the *récit* mentions the name Thomas in relation to the act of writing:

> I wrote out several sentences on the blackboard. . . . I couldn't stop trembling. I read the sentences and broke up their meaning by replacing some of the words with gasps and sighs. After a few moments the clamoring of the pupils merged with my groans, and I wrote out the passage on the blackboard, so that everyone could become familiar with it. *When the census of population was taken, it happened that an individual by the name of Thomas was not included in the*

general list. He therefore became superfluous, and others began treating him as if, in relation to humanity—which was itself insane—he had lost his mind. (43)

In *Thomas l'obscur,* the act of writing is evoked in terms that echo the description of *Le dernier mot.* In the novel, it is on a "blackboard" that the act of writing makes "readable" for everyone "the equation that can not be resolved."[34] At first, this absence of a solution seems to be negated in the passage of "Le dernier mot" describing the fate of Thomas on the blackboard:

> *The storm ended at the moment when the enemies took the balloon of the only surviving inhabitant and sent it off into the air. How did he [Thomas] manage to get away? By what means did he trick the guards and leave a place that was hemmed in on all sides? No one could say and not even he knew how it was done.* (43)

In this passage, Thomas seems to succeed where the stranger in "L'idylle" fails. But the narrator pierces the fallacy of representation when, in his role of teacher, he disrupts his storytelling and says to the children: "'What I suggest,' I said, 'is to cross out all these words and replace them with the word *not*. For this is my commentary: after his extraordinary escape, no sooner did the inhabitant of the city set foot on free ground than he discovered the walls of his enormous prison all around him'" (44). Thomas in "Le dernier mot" rejoins the vain attempt of the stranger in "L'idylle" to escape the Home and the city. The passage implies that the act of writing does not open up nor reverse anything. The escape itself features as only another episode in the movement of the story. Is the "outside"—this final site of *Le ressassement éternel*—any different? Such a reading is possible; it would entail that the two *récits*, though written independently before the war, are brought together in 1951 into one linear narrative in which, at the political as well as poetic level, the language and literature as imagined in "Le dernier mot" are the revolt against the totalitarian world of "L'idylle." In this narrative interpretation, the closure of "L'idylle" is countered by the fall of the tower and the opening up, in "Le dernier mot," of a new world without power and authority, without judge and master, without God and narrator. But this world evoked beyond the pages of the book is, to speak with Blanchot, "hélas, rien qu'un livre."[35] Since the outside at the end of *Le ressassement éternel* is itself "still a word," and since "there can be no last word," what opens up beyond this ending may be nothing but an endless reiteration, a ceaseless mutter infinitely repeating itself with no escape in sight. In "L'idylle," in the midst of the labyrinthine structure closing in on the fleeing stranger, there is the suggestion of an internal opening: a movement both infinite and futile and glorious in its infinite futility. The obverse is true for "Le dernier mot," where, at the end, the figures are thrown into a vast and empty outside, which, however, only seems to be an exit and a solution. In the end, all we know of them is that they will fall without ever arriving anywhere or reaching anything, plunging endlessly into a void from which there is no escape. It is in this void that Blanchot the writer is born and into which he simultaneously disappears.

NOTES

1. Maurice Blanchot, "L'idylle" and "Le dernier mot," in *Après coup, précédé par "Le ressassement éternel"* (Paris: Minuit, 1983), 9–81. Quoted here from the English translation: Maurice Blanchot, "The Idyll" and "The Last Word," in *The Station Hill Blanchot Reader: Fiction and Literary Essays,* ed. George Quasha, trans. Lydia Davis, Paul Auster, and Robert Lamberton (Barrytown, NY: Station Hill Press, 1999), 5–50. Also quoted in translation: Blanchot's "The Narrative Voice," in *The Station Hill Blanchot Reader,* 459–69. All the page references in the text refer to this volume.

2. See Wacław Rapak, *"Après coup" précédé par "Le ressassement éternel" de Maurice Blanchot: Une lecture* (Krakow: Universitas, 2005), 17: "Enigme irrésolue qu'il faut prendre pour 'irrésoluble'"; see also Christophe Bident, *Maurice Blanchot: Partenaire invisible. Essai biographique* (Seyssel: Champ Vallon, 1998), 130–38.

3. See Bident, *Maurice Blanchot,* 130.

4. Maurice Blanchot, *Le ressassement éternel* (Paris: Minuit, 1951).

5. Blanchot, *"Après coup" précédé par "Le ressassement éternel,"* 93–94. Unless otherwise indicated, "Après coup" is quoted here from the English translation in *The Station Hill Blanchot Reader,* 487–95.

6. See Maurice Blanchot, *L'espace littéraire* (Paris: Gallimard, 1955), 17–18.

7. Bident, *Maurice Blanchot,* 133–34: "la structure d'accumulation des épi-

sodes mythiques, qui confine à l'allégorie énigmatique dans 'Le Dernier mot,' le système de totalisation symbolique, qui surimpose comme une dictature du sens dans 'L'idylle.'"

8. See ibid., 134.

9. For a comparison between Blanchot and Adorno in this respect, see Vivian Liska, "Two Sirens Singing: Literature as Contestation in Maurice Blanchot and Theodor W. Adorno," in *The Power of Contestation: Perspectives on Maurice Blanchot,* ed. Kevin Hart and Geoffrey H. Hartman (Baltimore: Johns Hopkins University Press, 2004), 80–101.

10. Sarah Kofman, *Paroles suffoquées* (Paris: Galilée, 1987), 14.

11. Blanchot situates the writing of this story in the context of his first novel, *Thomas l'obscur,* which he was struggling with at that time and could only bring to a close in 1941, six years after finishing "Le dernier mot."

12. Maurice Blanchot, *Le livre à venir* (Paris: Gallimard, 1959), 14.

13. Ibid.

14. Ibid., 10. See also Liska, "Two Sirens Singing," 90.

15. Kofman, *Paroles suffoquées,* 25–26.

16. Kofman speaks of a "true baptism," a "ritual destined to clean away everything from the outside that sticks to his skin and marks . . . his non-belonging to the land of light." See *Paroles suffoquées,* 26.

17. Ibid., 27.

18. Bident, *Maurice Blanchot,* 86.

19. See Bident, *Maurice Blanchot,* 133: "La considération du Juif reste marginale, étrangère à tout présage comme à toute pensée, limitée à la conception stratégique de la défense passive" (The concern with the Jew remains marginal, devoid of all prediction and reflection. It is limited to the strategic conception of passive defense).

20. The interpretation of the stranger's death by Ullrich Haase and William Large, namely, that "in a strange way, then, he has achieved his freedom in the eyes of the others by way of his death, which expresses the interruption of the unitary society," is not plausible. It does not account for the impassibility with which this death is received by the inhabitants of the Home or for the "victorious sky" that extends imperviously over the final scene of the stranger's funeral and suggests that his death has interrupted nothing. Ullrich Haase and William Large, *Maurice Blanchot* (London and New York: Routledge, 2001), 91.

21. Kofman identifies the couple in "L'idylle" with "an idyllic community that effaces all discord, difference, death, that pretends to repose on a perfect harmony, a fusion implying an immediate unity which is necessarily an illusion or more a beautiful (psychotic) story." *Paroles suffoquées,* 35–36.

22. Kofman describes this language as the effect of fiction understood as aesthetic "naming": "The night reveals to the ear the unhappiness inherent in language, the lie that it dissimulates: the loss of death, of difference, of the

outside, of strangeness which it covers up and masters with beautiful names" [La nuit fait entendre le malheur inherent au language, le mensonge qu'il dissimule: la perte de la mort, de la difference, du dehors, de l'étrangeté qu'il recouvre et maitrise par de beaux noms]. Kofman, *Paroles suffoquées*, 33.

23. Giorgio Agamben, *Homo Sacer: Sovereign Power and Bare Life*, trans. D. Heller-Roazen (Stanford: Stanford University Press, 1998), 55.

24. Kofman, *Paroles suffoquées*, 39.

25. See Bident, *Maurice Blanchot*, 131.

26. Haase and Large, *Maurice Blanchot*, 91.

27. Maurice Blanchot, "Mots de désordre," quoted here from the English translation, "Disorderly Words," in *The Blanchot Reader*, ed. and trans. Michael Holland (Oxford: Blackwell, 1995), 202.

28. Maurice Blanchot, *Thomas l'obscur* (Paris: Gallimard, 1941), 80.

29. Ibid., 49, where Thomas is called an "être muet."

30. Ibid., 99: "la destruction des mots faisait partie de sa nature."

31. For an approach to this presence of the female body as lying at the source of the experience of writing in Blanchot's fictional work, see Arthur Cools, "Le rouge, la nuit: Le retour du féminin comme source de l'écriture," in *L'oeuvre du Féminin dans l'écriture de Maurice Blanchot*, ed. E. Hoppenot (Paris: Éditions Complicités, 2004), 111–31.

32. See Maurice Blanchot, *Faux pas* (Paris: Gallimard, 1943), 209.

33. See Maurice Blanchot, "*Ames et visages du vingtième siècle*, par André Rousseaux," *La Revue universelle* 18 (1932): 742–45, where Blanchot confirms that "[c]e divorce de la littérature et de la vie . . . annonce la crise dont les lettres souffrent aujourd'hui."

34. Blanchot, *Thomas l'obscur*, 205: "vite, un tableau noir, une cornue, que soit écrite lisiblement la formule de l'équation qui n'a pu être résolue."

35. Blanchot, *Le livre à venir*, 16.

TWO

THE NEUTRAL REDUCTION

THOMAS L'OBSCUR

Kevin Hart

> *"Certains êtres ont une signification qui nous manque. Qui sont-ils? Leur secret tient au plus profond du secret même de la vie. Ils s'en approchent. Elle les tue."*[1]
> —René Char

When Blanchot entitled his first novel *Thomas l'obscur,* he immediately released it into what would become an increasingly complex network of literary, philosophical, and religious associations, not all of which would help elucidate it. Some of these associations are borne out in the text itself, which plainly deals in some way or other with the figure of a twin or double, and thus places the book in a series of nineteenth- and twentieth-century narratives having to do with the *Doppelgänger* or double, the twin, and the alter ego, and raises all sorts of issues, directly philosophical or at least of clear interest to philosophers, about what it means to be human.

Other of these associations can tease the reader with plausible significance for reading the 1941 *roman* or, indeed, the *récit* that it became in 1950.[2] For *Thomas l'obscur* is itself a double or twin, existing in two versions, each of which calls forth interpretations based on what is in it and what its title merely attracts. So, for example, one may ask if one is right on opening *Thomas l'obscur,* in either version, to recall the pre-Socratic thinker, Heraclitus "the Obscure," on whom Blanchot was to write much later in *L'entretien infini* (1969).[3] If so, how should he be recalled? What would be the proper "quantity of connection" to seek between his thought and Blanchot's or Blanchot's narrator?[4] Would it be enough of a connection to place the novel under the sign of "philosophy and literature" and perhaps even to make it an example of what is commonly called, though usually in no more than an impressionistic way, a "philosophical novel"?

Heidegger, a privileged thinker for Blanchot since the late 1920s, tells us that Heraclitus was called "the Obscure" [ὁ Σκοτεινός], "even when his writings were preserved intact," although now we can read him only in fragments.[5] "Because we can scarcely surmise what the well-spring is that gives the writing of Heraclitus its unity, and because we find this source so difficult to think, we are justified in calling this thinker 'the Obscure'" (102–3). Here obscurity is understood by way of difficulty, not simply as a hard problem to solve but as something that resists thought itself, thought taken in Heidegger's sense of *Denken,* or reflective meditation, which is contrasted to calculative thinking. "Even the inherent meaning of what this epithet ['the Obscure'] says to us remains obscure," Heidegger adds (103). We cannot delimit why and how Heraclitus was regarded as obscure, we are told; and one index of that inability is that, as Heidegger says, the Greek philosopher is also, and perhaps more fundamentally, "the Lucid," for he "tells of the lighting whose shining he attempts to call forth into the language of thinking" (103). Heidegger was always attracted to the metaphor of light, as in his early reconception of phenomenology as letting "that which shows itself be seen from itself in the very way in which it shows itself from itself."[6] He folds Heraclitus into his itinerary, however, only when he begins to understand the event as the lighting of the world.[7] The ancient Greek is held to think "questioningly into the lighting" (123), much as Heidegger does himself in the years after making the *Kehre.*

As absorbing as Heidegger's elucidation of Heraclitus is, it does nothing to clear a path for understanding *Thomas l'obscur,* at least not as regards Blanchot's original intention with the title. The German thinker first lectured on the ancient Greek in the summer semester of 1943 in the course "Der Anfang des abendländischen Denkens (Heraklit)," two years after *Thomas l'obscur* had been published and over a decade after it had been commenced. Perhaps Heidegger influenced Blanchot's explicit reflections on the obscure in *L'entretien infini* (1969), though one should be reticent in making such claims about a thinker whose intellectual vanishing points were established early in his writing life.[8] At any rate, his own sense of the word *l'obscur* was well and truly in place long before then, and if it was shaded by the epithet associated with Heraclitus, it was from the angle of Blanchot's own reading of the Greek.[9] Yet Blanchot had no need to look as far away as Heraclitus to ponder the obscure. He had Mallarmé close to hand, whose work impinged heavily on him as novelist and critic, and whose unique writing he affirmed in several early reviews, most particularly in "La poésie de Mallarmé est-elle obscur?" published on February 24, 1942, only months after *Thomas l'obscur.*[10] In that column Blanchot reviews Charles Mauron's *Mallarmé l'obscur* (1941), an attempt to explain the poems line by line, and finds it sadly inadequate to the poems themselves. True poetry, such as Mallarmé's, is not an object, he says, but a power of vision that gives "the reader the feeling of himself being explained and contemplated.[11] Poetry is a matter of counter-intentionality, then, and counter-intentionality will figure significantly in much of his own writing in narrative prose, including *Thomas l'obscur,* where it is associated with obscurity. More generally, we should not assimilate too readily what Mauron means by *l'obscur* in *Mallarmé l'obscur* with what Blanchot means by the same word in *Thomas l'obscur.* For one thing, Mauron assumes that Mallarmé's poems can be made clear by paraphrase, and that seems not to be the case with the obscure Thomas.

If little of Heraclitus, and nothing of Heidegger's Heraclitus, satisfies our desire to link him to the character of Thomas in Blanchot's *roman* and *récit,* we are not thereby left completely adrift in attempting to situate the work in history. We are equally likely to recall Thomas Hardy's last novel, *Jude the Obscure* (1895), and here we do indeed have characters, the motif of doubling, and another sense of "obscure" in play.

Thomas l'obscur can be read as the mortally truncated love story of Thomas and Anne, while *Jude the Obscure* insists on being approached as the star-crossed love story of Jude and Sue. Hardy's narrator tells us of Sue's "double nature," and Jude and Sue almost get married at St. Thomas's Church, but the threads that join the two novels are few, far between, and very slight.[12] The narrator sees Sue as "double" only because she eludes traditional categories of female character and appropriate behavior; the word carries no special philosophical weight. Jude and Sue are "poor obscure people" (248), obscurity here meaning that they are indistinctly seen, if seen at all, by those who matter in society, especially those in the university colleges of Christminster, Hardy's imaginary Oxford. In particular, the rigid class system of England has kept Jude, for all his innate talent and ambition, academically undistinguished, and made him forever unknown to literary fame, a "mute inglorious Milton," as Thomas Gray put it so poignantly.[13]

Blanchot's Thomas may not stand out in his society, but *Thomas l'obscur* is not a novel of social criticism as *Jude the Obscure* is. And if Jude and Sue are "shadowed by death" (327), it is not in the same ways that Thomas and Anne are. Only one event in Hardy's novel is remotely akin to anything in Blanchot's narrative. It is the graveyard scene following the devastating discovery of the deaths of their children in their temporary lodgings in Christminster. "A man with a shovel in his hands was attempting to earth in the common grave of the three children, but his arm was held back by an expostulating woman who stood in the half-filled hole. It was Sue" (329). Yet when we place this scene against its supposed counterpart in *Thomas l'obscur,* we find little basis for comparison. "As soon as the grave was finished, when Thomas threw himself into it with a huge stone tied around his neck, he crashed into a body a thousand times harder than the soil, the very body of the gravedigger who had already entered the grave to dig it."[14] Thomas finds himself already in the very grave he has dug for himself. As the narrator goes on to say, Thomas "was really dead and at the same time rejected from the reality of death" [*était réellement mort et en même temps repoussé de la réalité de la mort*] (36, 77–78, 40). And this statement, unlike the narrator's harrowing image of a mother's grief in *Jude the Obscure,* involves philosophy from the very beginning, and not only because of the adverb "réellement" and the noun "réalité." It makes a bold claim about the relations of life and death that invites dialectical inspection.

If the title of Blanchot's novel does not indicate a vantage point from which to approach the narrative, perhaps the motif of the double or twin will aid us. Nineteenth-century literature, especially fiction, brooded on the figure of the double. Alfred de Musset's poem "La nuit de décembre" (1835) turns and turns again on the appearance of "Un pauvre enfant vêtu de noir, / Qui me ressemblait comme un frère," who is finally revealed to be Solitude.[15] Musset's double is benign; not so with others later in the century, beginning with the one described in Edgar Allan Poe's tale "William Wilson" (1840), in which the main character encounters another man exactly like him. "Not a thread in all his raiment—not a line in all the marked and singular lineaments of his face which was not, even in the most absolute identity, *mine own!*"[16] This double shadows the narrator for years until, right at the end, the narrator kills him. "I could have fancied that I myself was speaking," the narrator says, when he hears his double's last words (356). *"You have conquered, and I yield,"* the double says, *"Yet, henceforward art thou also dead—dead to the World, to Heaven and to Hope! In me didst thou exist—and, in my death, see by this image, which is thine own, how utterly thou has murdered thyself"* (357). This is the closest that the literary tradition of the double comes to the strange experience explored in *Thomas l'obscur,* although there are indeed two William Wilsons, not an otherness in the one William Wilson; Poe's story participates more fully in the genre of the grotesque than Blanchot's; and Blanchot's narrative is more philosophical than psychological in its ambitions.

An intensity of psychological focus similar to that found in Poe's tale marks Dostoevsky's *The Double,* itself published in two forms, that of 1846 and 1866. Yakov Petrovich Golyadkin goes home one night and at last fully sees a figure that has been brushing past him in recent times. Sitting on his bed in an overcoat and hat was "none other than himself, Mr Golyadkin himself, another Mr Golyadkin, but exactly like him, in a word, what is called his double in every respect."[17] One of the characters in the story, Anton Antonovich, says, "let me tell you something: the very same thing happened to her aunt on my mother's side. Before she died she also saw her double" (68). The link of doubleness and death is marked again. It will be found also, though in a quite different way, in Robert

Louis Stevenson's *The Strange Case of Dr Jekyll and Mr Hyde* (1886), in which a drug enables the amiable Dr. Henry Jekyll to become his sinister counterpart, the violent Mr. Edward Hyde. At first the character is able to pass back and forth between the two personalities, but in time he cannot control the changes, which require more and more of the potion to work effectively. Eventually, he runs out of the brew and cannot change back from being Edward Hyde. The novel ends with Hyde facing the choice of killing himself or being executed for his crimes. In Stevenson's story, the figure of the double is less a matter of animating the uncanny than of a dramatic presentation of the psychiatric idea of "disassociation" or "split personality," the dark side of Jekyll having been hiding in him and needing only a stimulus to emerge.

Between the two versions of Dostoevsky's *The Double*, Gérard de Nerval wrote *Aurélia* (1854), a signal narrative for Blanchot, one that also evokes a *Doppelgänger* and ponders the same premonition of death.[18] Here, though, the double is not asserted to be flesh and blood but is the product of an overheated imagination. "By a strange effect of vibration it felt as though [*il me semblait*] his voice was echoing in my own chest, and that my soul was, so to speak, assuming a dual existence—distinctly divided between vision and reality. For a second I thought of making an effort to turn towards the person in question; then I shivered as I remembered a well-known German superstition which says that everyone has a *double* and that when you see him death is close at hand."[19] Equally far from the naturalism of Poe and Stevenson, however stretched, is Guy de Maupassant's story "Lui?" (1883). Here the imagined double is directly called a phantom. The narrator comes home to find him in his chair: "I could see him perfectly clearly: his right arm was hanging down, and his legs were crossed; his head, leaning back on the chair, a little to the left, gave an unmistakable impression of a man asleep."[20] An apparently external phantom, however, enters the narrator's mind, dividing him from himself. "He won't show himself again—that's all over. But he is there all the same—in my thoughts. Even though he remains invisible, that does not prevent him from being there" (142).

Of course, a double could be present while also remaining invisible, and this is exactly what happens in Joseph Conrad's story of an alter ego, "The Secret Sharer" (1912). A young, inexperienced captain, his boat anchored at the head of the Gulf of Siam, allows an escaped sailor from another vessel to climb aboard his ship and hide in his cabin. The captain must whisper to him in order to avoid detection. "He was not a bit like me, really; yet, as we stood leaning over my bed-place, whispering side by side, with our dark heads together and our backs to the door, anybody bold enough to open it stealthily would have been treated to the uncanny sight of a double captain busy talking in whispers with his other self."[21] No one has parsed this odd situation better than Walter J. Ong: "The stranger-double is somehow there in the captain's own cabin because the captain himself feels a stranger on his own ship, and this because he is a stranger to himself in his own soul."[22] Ong extends his psychological sense of what is at issue in Conrad's tale in an ontological direction. The captain's entertaining of his double "reveals a rift, a limitation inside our own beings, but a rift which opens its own way to salvation—for it is a rift which comes from our bearing vicariously within ourselves the other with whom we must commune, and who must commune with us, too, and thereby compensate for the rift, the limitation, in our persons" (53).

In passing from psychology to ontology we are getting closer to what is at issue in *Thomas l'obscur,* although we are not quite there yet. Ong, a Jesuit priest, moves very quickly from talk of what it is to be human to talk of salvation. And we may recall that the doubling in our being that he has in mind has a long history in philosophy and the Christian church. In theology there are several versions, all drawing to a greater or lesser degree on the Platonic dualism of body and soul. They are not always driven by an appeal to different substances or properties, however. In an influential formulation, St. Augustine distinguishes between "two kinds of life," one regulated by need and the other oriented to delight.[23] In this life we are perpetually caught in a tension between them, much as we might long for a life composed only of pure delight. A more striking version of doubling in theological anthropology goes back at least as far as Origen's commentary on the Song of Songs, written circa 240, and Origen ingeniously credits it with an even earlier starting point. He claims that in Genesis, Moses records "the making of two men, the first *in the image and likeness of God,* and the second *formed of the slime of the earth.*"[24] St. Paul is interpreting these passages of Genesis, Origen thinks, when he writes, "but though our outward man perish, yet the inward *man* is renewed day by day" (2 Cor. 4:16), and Moses "sees Paul, who understood what Moses wrote much better than we do" (25). For Origen, following Paul, "there are in fact two men in every single man" (25), and we may hope for salvation when we turn from the corruptible man formed of slime to the incorruptible man who is made in the image of God. This means, of course, that we can overcome the doubleness of our mortal being precisely by salvation. Or, to reverse the statement, a view to which Blanchot would be far more sympathetic, there can be no salvation because we cannot overcome our doubleness.

Some of Blanchot's readers have found this a hard lesson to learn and have sought a parallel in a noncanonical religious text, despite the lack of empirical influence from the one to the other. "For there is nothing obscure [or hidden or secret] that will not become shown forth": so reads a passage from one of the Oxyrhynchus Greek fragments discovered in 1897 and 1903, that were later found to belong to the *Gospel of Thomas,* which, for all its departures from what was to become orthodoxy, remains a discourse of salvation.[25] The linking of obscurity and the name Thomas has encouraged some of Blanchot's readers to find a hidden path that runs from this lost Gospel to the novel. "*Thomas the Obscure* has long seemed to us," George Quasha and Charles Stein write, "to echo in some impossible way *The Gospel of Thomas.*"[26] It could not be a possible echo, unless Blanchot had read the Oxyrthynchus fragments or the *Acts of Thomas,* which was found in Syriac and published in 1871. The *Gospel of Thomas* was discovered intact at Nag Hammadi only in 1945, along with the *Book of Thomas the Contender,* four years after the publication of *Thomas l'obscur.* In the Gospel, the Book, and the Acts, "Thomas" is Judas Thomas, the twin of Jesus. Indeed, the "Sinai text" of the *Acts of Thomas,* dated to the fourth or fifth century, speaks solely of Judas, and only the later Syriac text, dated to 936, uses Thomas as a proper name.[27] Over the years, the ordinary Aramaic word for twin, *t'oma* (the Arabic is *tau'am*), has become a proper name, "Thomas."[28] And sometimes, as in the Gospel of John, the Greek word for twin, *Didymus,* has also been mistaken for a proper name. Consider what the disciple says when Jesus proposes to go to Bethany, regarded as a dangerous journey because the Jews had recently tried to stone Jesus: "Then said Thomas, which is called Didymus, unto his fellow disciples, Let us also go, that we may die with him" (John 11:16).

There is no authentic echo of the *Gospel of Thomas* in *Thomas l'obscur,* partly for chronological reasons and partly because the novel rejects the vision of human being appearing properly and fully under the sign of light. Yet Thomas asks in his Gospel, "On the day that you were one, you made two. And when you are two, what will you do?" (*Thomas,* 11), and, as we shall see, this is precisely the situation in which Thomas finds himself at the start of *Thomas l'obscur* and a question that the reader is bound to ask of him. Parallels between texts can always be found if one looks hard enough. The obscurity of the *Gospel of Thomas* can partly be overcome, however, by referring to Hellenistic myths of *exitus-reditus,* which have no purchase on *Thomas l'obscur.* It takes more than a name and the word "l'obscur" to be of help in interpreting the work, but the distance to which Blanchot's readers will go in order to find a "reading head" for *Thomas l'obscur* is a powerful indication of the work's mystery or secret— to use two quite different words that were close to Blanchot at the time of writing the novel.[29]

In order to bypass misleading associations prompted by the title of the *roman* and *récit* and to avoid a temptation, perhaps by succumbing to it for a moment, let us look ahead from 1941 and 1950 to glimpse how Blanchot himself responded to the obscurity of *Thomas l'obscur* after he had written all of his narratives, save *L'instant de ma mort* (1994). In the first of his full-length fragmentary works, *Le pas au-delà* (1973), he returned obliquely to his first novel and asked a question that had perplexed him for decades. "From where does it come, this power of uprooting, of destruction or change, in the first words written facing the sky, in the solitude of the sky, words by themselves without prospect or pretense: 'it—the sea' ['*il—la mer*']?"[30] As any reader of Blanchot will quickly recognize, what is summoned here is the opening sentence of *Thomas l'obscur:* "Thomas sat down and looked at the sea" [*Thomas s'assit et regarda la mer*] (7, 23, 9). Also evoked, if more discreetly, is a duality that runs throughout Blanchot's writing, in narrative and criticism. There is negativity, "this power of uprooting, of destruction or change," particularly as construed by Hegel ("the labor of the negative").[31] And there is also what Blanchot will come to call the Neutral or the Outside, the *il* or it, which is the main concern of *Le pas au-delà*. Without trying to explain the Outside in any detail right now, let us remain with Blanchot's words, and say with him that it "attracts us, were we allowed, having disappeared from ourselves, to write within the secret of the ancient fear" (1).

This Outside is not something wholly exterior to *Thomas l'obscur*; it is not a philosophical concept, developed after writing both versions of the narrative, that could explain both after the fact and perhaps turn the *roman* and *récit* into allegories of Blanchot's metaphysical stance as developed in *L'espace littéraire* (1955) and *L'entretien infini* (1969). It is already indicated, but not named, in the difficult liminal text set in italics that marks the transformation of the *roman* into the *récit*, a paragraph whose second sentence condenses much of Blanchot's "philosophy of literature" into a few words. Both of his narratives are the same, he says, "if one is right in making no distinction between the figure and that which is, or believes itself to be, its center, whenever the complete figure itself expresses no more than the search [*la recherche*] for an imaginary center."[32] Each version of *Thomas l'obscur* is a means, not an end, it would seem: a quest, two among "an infinity of possible variants," for a point that does not exist before the quest begins and that attains reality only in the movement of the narrative toward it. It is in writing that we are drawn to this elusive point, this Outside, where we lose any sense we may have of being unified over time or even at an instant; it is an encounter with death in its aspect of dying, not one's empirical demise. Blanchot addresses himself as well as his reader: "Do not hope, if there lies your hope—and one must suspect it—to unify your existence, to introduce into it, in the past, some coherence by way of the writing that disunifies" (*Step Not Beyond*, 2). One cannot place two pieces of writing, *Thomas l'obscur* and *Le pas au-delà*, beside one another and discern a continuity that gives substantial content to an "I" that signs itself "Maurice Blanchot" and in doing so makes an ontological as well as a legal claim. And that is because writing, in and of itself, disperses unity, including the presumed unity of the author (determined by way of consciousness, soul, spirit, or whatever). This death by writing, this being carried into an endless dying, is one variant of "the ancient fear."

Indeed, what Blanchot holds to be happening to himself in the writing of *Thomas l'obscur* applies to everyone, writer or not, he says in a frag-

ment later in *Le pas au-delà:* "If it is true that there is (in the Chinese
language) a written character that means both 'man' and 'two,' it is easy to
recognize in man he who is always himself and the other, the happy duality of dialogue and the possibility of communication. But it is less easy,
more important perhaps, to think 'man,' that is to say, also 'two,' as separation that lacks unity, the leap from 0 to duality, the I thus giving itself
as the forbidden, the between-the-two" (39). Blanchot is thinking of the
character *ren,* which, as an ideograph, means more than two things. It is
usually translated as "benevolence," but along the lines that Blanchot
suggests it means both "man" and "human belonging."[33] Doubles and
doubling clearly make up a thread that runs throughout Blanchot's writing, and not just in his early novels *Thomas l'obscur* and *Aminadab* (1942).
In the *roman* and *récit,* however, there is reason to think that Thomas becomes two, while in *Le pas au-delà* and other more philosophical works, it
seems that Blanchot holds that human beings are always and already divided. Despite this difference, the coherence that Blanchot is unwilling to
find in the sequence of his writings in case it misleadingly indicates a
unity of self, one that he rigorously doubts at all points, is surely there, if
not at the level of substance then at the levels of theme, style of questioning, and idiom. But that is not to say that he is affirming the same thing
in 1941 and 1950 as he is in 1973. Coherence is a weaker state than identity, self-identity, or unity. And of course it would have been possible for
Blanchot to argue for the coherence of a life's work without also making a
case for personal self-identity or unity.[34]

Blanchot's own reflection on the change of *Thomas l'obscur* from
roman to *récit* has raised several intriguing philosophical questions,
mostly in metaphysics, though also bearing on the philosophy of literature. One is the status of the point that is projected by the writing of a narrative (or perhaps any text). On the one hand, it is not claimed to be real
in the sense of existing irrespective of human consciousness; while, on
the other hand, it serves to disperse any presumed unity in a person and
therefore has real effects. Blanchot seems to be committed to a form of
dualism, more likely one of properties than substances, since the Outside
(or, as he sometimes calls it, the imaginary) does not seem to be anything
like a substance, and yet it bespeaks more than would be involved in
claiming that language requires two sorts of predicates when offering a

full description of the world. And he appears to maintain that there is an interaction between these properties, for the Outside has definite effects in the world: it disperses what might have been taken as unified, and the person concerned experiences this loss of personal unity. Also in question, then, is the nature of experience: given that there is no unity of consciousness for Blanchot, whether transcendental or substantive, who or what is the subject of the experience? Indeed, since Blanchot thinks of experience, especially the experience of writing, as a brushing against death, as the complete loss of selfhood, can we speak properly of it as "experience" in the first place? More generally, how does the distinction between life and death, as Blanchot draws it, fit with "human being"? Plainly, none of these questions can be answered in a few words here and now, but they will continue to press on us as we read *Thomas l'obscur*, as will further questions soon to emerge.

In both versions, *Thomas l'obscur* begins by drawing attention to a permeable line between reality and appearance, and between self and other, whether by way of Thomas's "conviction" [*certitude*] (7, 24, 10) or his "fantasy" [*rêverie*] (14, 33, 17). The surface of the sea into which he goes swimming "was lost in a glow which seemed the only truly real thing [*la seule chose vraiment réelle*]" (7, 24, 9), and Thomas, who gets into trouble while in the water, which he is convinced does not exist, "sought to free himself from the insipid flood which was invading him [*l'envahissait*]" (7, 25, 10), experienced an "intoxication of leaving himself, of slipping into the void [*glisser dans le vide*]" (8, 27, 11), and, even more strangely, felt that he was "dispersing himself [*se disperser*] in the *thought* of water" (8, 27, 11; my emphasis).

Later, back on land and walking through a small wood, he has what at first seems to be an odd fantasy that picks up on the blurring of external reality and thought: "outside himself there was something identical to his own thought which his glance or his hand could touch" (14, 32, 17). In his disordered state, Thomas finds himself repulsed by the correspondence theory of truth, in particular the version of it affirmed by St. Thomas Aquinas: *veritas est adequatio rei et intellectus*, that is, truth is "the conformity of thing and intellect."[35] Then the narrator goes a step further. "Soon the night seemed to him gloomier and more terrible than any night, as if it had in fact issued from a wound of thought which had ceased to think, of thought taken ironically as object by something other than thought" (14, 33, 17). Here, Thomas passes from an epistemological fantasy to an ontological one. He momentarily becomes a subjective idealist of a peculiar kind, taking external reality as a product of his past thought; but he is a frustrated idealist in that this reality is interpreted, against his understanding of it, to exist without reference to his subjectivity. Rational thought slowly begins to reorder what was a fantasy world, restoring its ontological integrity, and then, "[h]is solitude no longer seemed so complete, and he even had the feeling that something real had knocked against him and was trying to slip inside [*se glisser en lui*]" (15, 33, 18). We pass back from ontology to epistemology. The exterior world, now firmly registering itself as abiding outside his consciousness and existing independently of it, is giving itself to him as so many items of knowledge. Yet his experience of it remains vivid: "from all evidence a foreign body [*un corps étranger*] had lodged itself in his pupil and was attempting to go further" (7, 34, 18). It is not just a mite of dust in his eye but the entire scene before him. To which he adds, in what will become a significant speculation after the death of Anne, "Perhaps a man slipped in [*se glissa-t-il*] by the same opening" (15, 34, 18).

Interlaced with these observations we find the narrator's reflections on changes of perception and being perceived that are distinct from his fantasy. In the night, his eye does not merely modify itself to accommodate the darkness; it changes in a qualitative way. "Not only did this eye which saw nothing apprehend something, it apprehended the cause of its vision. It saw as object that which prevented it from seeing. Its own glance entered into it as an image, just when this glance seemed the death of all image" (15, 33, 17–18). Thomas can see the night, and in a moment of auto-affection can see himself seeing the very darkness of the night. And when Thomas reads in his room, in a passage that indicates how you and I should be reading the *roman* or *récit* that we have opened, we find a scene in which the reader's intentionality is matched, in an edgy way, by the counter-intentionality of language itself. "He was reading. He was reading with unsurpassable meticulousness and attention," we are told, and then there comes one of the scenes of metamorphoses into monstrosity that will punctuate the narrative: "In relation to every symbol, he was in the position of the male praying mantis about to be devoured by the female" (25, 44, 27). Thomas "perceived all the strangeness there was in being observed by a word as if by a living being, and not simply by one word, but by all the words that were in that word, by all those that went with it and in turn contained other words, like a procession of angels opening out into the infinite to the very eye of the absolute" (25, 44, 28). Soon he finds himself being explored by "obscure words [*des paroles obscures*], disembodied souls and angels of words" (26, 45, 29).[36] And then his struggle with words is heightened and strangely rendered concrete: "He was locked in combat with something inaccessible, foreign, something of which he could say: That doesn't exist . . . and which nonetheless filled him with terror as he sensed it wandering about in the region of his solitude" (27, 46, 30).

This phenomenon has phenomenality but no physical presence; it impinges on Thomas in space but exists "outside time" (27, 47, 31). He senses that it is replaced by another phenomenon, which has a distinct way of not being present. Doubtless the writing of any literature performs a phenomenological reduction, a conversion of the gaze from that of the natural attitude to another that answers more fully to experience.[37] And certainly Blanchot (or one of his alter egos) came to think that it precipitated an endless reduction that is not quite the same as the one put in motion by Husserl's *epochē*.[38] Here, though, Thomas has made a quite classical phenomenological reduction. Always, the reduction involves a shift from asking "What?" to asking "How?," although usually it takes place within the field of present being (with at least one profile of the phenomenon being present). But here Thomas passes to the question "How?" in an attempt to register the precise shading in which the phenomenon is absent from him. "It was a modulation of that which did not exist, a different mode of being absent, another void in which he was coming to life" (27, 46, 30). Is this an experience of a change from blank nonexistence to the eerie sifting of being and nonbeing that is the Outside? There is insufficient evidence to say for sure. Certainly there follows a struggle between a "sort of Thomas" (27, 47, 32) who leaves him to fight the threatening phenomenon, and the Thomas who finds himself "bitten or struck . . . by what seemed to him to be a word, but resembled rather a giant rat, an all-powerful beast with piercing eyes and pure teeth" (28, 47–48, 32).[39] The border between language and nonlinguistic reality is once again deemed to be equivocal. More disturbing still, the limit between life and death is revealed not to be absolute.

In a passage we have already touched on when considering possible parallels between *Thomas l'obscur* and *Jude the Obscure,* we find a knot in the thread we have been following:

> This grave which was exactly his size, his shape, his thickness, was like his own corpse, and every time he tried to bury himself in it, he was like a ridiculous dead person trying to bury his body in his body. There was, then, henceforth, in all the sepulchers where he might have been able to take his place, in all the feelings which are also tombs for the dead, in this annihilation through which he was dying without permitting himself to be thought dead, there was another dead person who was there first, and who, identical with himself, drove the ambiguity of Thomas's life and death to the extreme limit. (35–36, 76–77, 38–39)

And, to make plain what is happening, and perhaps to link it to the literary tradition of the *Doppelgänger* already noted, the narrator points to "a double [*un sosie*] wrapped in bands, its senses sealed with the seven seals, its spirit absent" that occupies Thomas's place, "this double" [*ce sosie*] being "the unique one with which no compromise was possible, since it was the same as himself" (36, 77, 39). As the biblical allusion to Rev. 5:1 ("And I saw in the right hand of him that sat on the throne a book written within and on the backside, sealed with seven seals") makes clear, this double is completely sealed, unable to be opened except by the very God who has no place in the world of the *roman* and the *récit.* This Thomas, the double of the living Thomas, to use a description that will become dubious, is utterly obscure, and he is obscure because he is already dead, and dead without hope of resurrection whether before the last day or on it. And so the living Thomas knows himself, in an intolerable paradox, "to be dead, absent, completely absent from his death" (36, 77, 40). "He was really dead and at the same time rejected from the reality of death" (36, 77–78, 40).

It should be noted that the claim that one is already dead while apparently alive is a very common one. Christians believe that when one is baptized one is buried with Christ. ("Know ye not, that so many of us as were
baptized into Jesus Christ were baptized into his death?" asks Paul in Romans 6:3.) But plainly this Christian sense of being dead while still being
alive can be put to one side. Blanchot is elaborating a quite different concept. Thomas is pictured as one of the walking dead, an image that is at
once gothic yet quite unlike anything one might find in a story by Horace
Walpole, Mary Shelley, Bram Stoker, or Matthew Lewis. He appears "at the
narrow gate of his sepulcher, not risen [*non pas ressuscité*] but dead, and
with the certainty of being snatched at once from death and from life" (37,
79, 42).[40] At first he is called a "mummy" [*momie*], then Blanchot returns
to a biblical image that he adapts in his own way: "He walked, the only true
Lazarus, whose very death was raised [*la mort même était ressuscitée*]" (38,
79, 42; trans. slightly modified). In French there is no noun that comes
from the verb *ressuciter*—its nominal counterpart is *la résurrection*—and
so care must be taken when distinguishing in French between being re-
suscitated and being resurrected. Blanchot phrases things strictly when
he prefers the verb *ressusciter* to the noun *la résurrection* for the raising of
the biblical Lazarus of Bethany (John 11:1–46). Jesus and Martha use the
word "la résurrection," to be sure, the second while naming the general
resurrection, "la résurrection, au dernier jour" (John 11:24), and the first
when declaring, in one of his powerful "I am" statements, "I am the resurrection" [*Moi, je suis la résurrection*] (John 11:25). Yet when Jesus says to
Martha, "Thy brother shall rise again" [*Ton frère ressuscitera*], he means he
will be revived now, today, and not only at the resurrection at the last day,
which is a qualitatively different sort of event in which mortal bodies will
be definitively transformed into immortal bodies.[41] Irenaeus was right:
the raising of Lazarus and all the other raisings in the New Testament are
signs of the resurrection to come, and are testimonies that the resurrection will be in the flesh.[42]

It is because Jesus *is* the resurrection, divinely powerful and com-
manding, and Martha believes him to be so, that he can revive Lazarus
now, though his friend remains mortal, with death to come again. (The
thirteenth-century compilation *The Golden Legend* has Lazarus and Mary
Magdalene being herded into an unmanned ship, which miraculously ar-

rives in Marseilles, while popular stories have him becoming the first bishop of the city.)[43] Thus John 11:44: "Le mort sortit, les pieds et les mains liés de bandelettes, et son visage était enveloppé d'un suaire. Jésus leur dit: 'Déliez-le et laissez-le aller'" (La Bible de Jérusalem). There is no talk of a transformed body here, such as one finds in John 20:26, when Jesus enters the upper chamber, even though the doors are shut, and talks with Thomas, who does not believe that Jesus has risen from the dead. It is worth noting that in the biblical narrative, the same disciple, Thomas, announces to the other followers of Jesus that, dangerous as it is (because of the attempt to stone Jesus reported in John 10:31), they should all follow Jesus to Bethany. In the fourth Gospel, Thomas silently observes the raising of Lazarus to new life, while later doubting that Jesus has been resurrected; in the *roman* and *récit*, it is Thomas's *death* that is raised. Parallels between the Gospel of John and *Thomas l'obscur* are at best sharply ironic.[44] The same is true of the synoptic Gospels, as Blanchot's treatment of the daughter of Jairus makes plain (89, 289, 100).

That passage introduces the narrator's reflections on Anne's corpse. "She had stopped at the point where she resembled only herself [*elle ne ressemblait qu'à elle-même*], and where her face, having only Anne's expression, was disturbing to look at" (89, 289, 100). The peculiar expression "she resembled only herself" is important in the philosophical economy of the *roman* and the *récit*. It is this self-resemblance that generates a peculiar effect. "At the moment everything was being destroyed she had created that which was most difficult: she had not drawn something out of nothing (a meaningless act), but given to nothing, in its form of nothing, the form of something. The act of not seeing had now its integral eye" (90, 291, 102). In dying, Anne has become her own image, so, for a while, she is both herself and her image. A fissure in being has been discerned that allows us to sense, as it were, the approach of the Outside. Blanchot will return to this in "Two Versions of the Imaginary" (1951), one of his most concise and philosophically powerful reflections on the relations of being and the neutral.[45] And, ironically enough, his friend Emmanuel Lévinas will adapt the insight as the basis of his remarkable critique of art, "La réalité et son ombre" (1948). "Reality would not be only what it is, what it is disclosed to be in truth, but would be also its double [*son double*], its shadow, its image."[46]

I pass from Anne's death over the preceding love story of Thomas and Anne, in which Anne herself is revealed as not quite coinciding with herself and as "already dead" (82, 283, 91), to the crucial depiction of Thomas that will unravel what it means for Thomas's death to have been raised. In doing so, I bypass not only memorable chapters of great human passion but also the narrative's intense reworking of a mythological rather than philosophical scene—the story of the death of Eurydice—and the difficult question of the relation, or perhaps non-relation, of the mythological and the philosophical in both the *roman* and the *récit*. Proclus declared, "For all the Grecian theology is the progeny of the mystic tradition of Orpheus," the word "theology" meaning here partly what the word "metaphysics" covers in its sense of dealing with "the first and most self-sufficient principles of things."[47] Francis Bacon took the story of Orpheus to be "a picture of universal philosophy," the word "philosophy" in his day being broader in scope than it is now.[48] But in *Thomas l'obscur*, at least, philosophy arranges itself in tension with the narrative of Orpheus's descent to the underworld and his ascent from it. Several philosophers are evoked in the narrative, especially in the *roman* (Socrates, Pascal, Descartes, Spinoza), although none is more important than Descartes. The central dispute in the *roman* and the *récit* is not between Orpheus and the King of the Dead but between Thomas and Descartes. Before we get to that passage, though, we need to listen to Thomas speaking after Anne's death.

Before this moment, the narrator has spoken of Thomas being already dead. Now Thomas himself talks of being dead, of subsisting in "the paradox and the impossibility of death" (92, 295, 104). Death, for him, is not "a slight accident" that touches the end of his life, as it is for other people, but "an anthropometric index," for, as he says, "I was real only under the name of death" (92, 296, 105). Here, unlike earlier and later in the *roman* and *récit*, Thomas speaks of his condition as singular, not general, doubtless because it turns entirely on his experience of being dead while apparently still alive.[49] This conception of death requires us to distinguish an anterior death from an empirical death. Thomas knows that he will die one day but takes himself to have already suffered an anterior death, a death that has been "raised" from the grave, and when death finally comes to him it will be "the death of death" (91, 293, 103). At the back of this notion is Hegel's conception of the ego as "the power of the negative."[50] After the death of Anne, Thomas enjoys a deep "serenity" that "made of every instant of [his] life the instant in which [he] was going to leave life" (92, 294, 103–4). Absent from Anne and his love of her, Thomas not only flees the horizon of the world but also flees from his flight; he experiences a "supreme moment of calm" (103, 309, 121). If life is the power of the negative—change, destruction, uprooting—then the refusal to exercise that power, the lapse into radical passivity, is death in life. The "I" remains abstract, it does not fulfill any possibilities; it becomes a "perfect nothingness [*néant*]" (96, 301, 110). Without Anne, Thomas has passed from "you[*toi*]-consciousness (at once existence and life) to you[*toi*]-unconsciousness (at once reality and death)" (98, 303, 114). He is "infinitely more dead than dead" (104, 310, 122), even though alive, because he feels himself to be without relation, without possibilities that can be realized, and without any opposition to overcome. In Hegel's terms, he is universal, without any contradiction between himself and his genus, so that, with his death, "the species died each time, completely" (93, 297, 106).[51]

Thomas l'obscur is not concerned simply to chart the experience of non-experience of a man who is dead to life and, it seems, dead in life; it converges on the non-relation of twins, one of whom is dead in life while the other is the "obscure Thomas." The narrative approaches its climax with the "dead" Thomas, who is "the same as a living person but without life," wondering how to reach the obscure Thomas, who is "the same as a dead person but without death" and who has somehow slipped into him:

> Death was a crude metamorphosis beside the indiscernible nullity which I nevertheless coupled with the name [*nom*] Thomas. Was it then a fantasy, this enigma, the creation of a word [*un mot*] maliciously formed to destroy all words? But if I advanced within myself, hurrying laboriously toward my precise noon, I yet experienced as a tragic certainty, at the center of the living Thomas, the inaccessible proximity of that Thomas which was nothingness [*ce Thomas néant*], and the more the shadow of my thought shrunk, the more I conceived of myself in this faultless clarity as the possible, the willing host of this obscure Thomas [*cet obscur Thomas*]. (97–98, 303, 112–13)[52]

"Thomas" slides from a proper name to a common noun meaning "twin," and the double in this word endangers the operations of language. (Exactly how it does will become apparent only in Blanchot's essays, as we shall see.) The living-dead Thomas is the host of the obscure Thomas: the inaccessible one depends on the living-dead one. One of the twins is "perfect nothingness," while the other is neither nothingness nor being but what Blanchot will come to call the neutral. He is the one who belongs, as it were, to the Outside. "I found myself," the living-dead Thomas says, "with two faces, glued one to the other. I was in constant contact with two shores. With one hand showing that I was indeed there, with the other— what am I saying?—without the other, with this body which, imposed on my real body, depended entirely on a negation of the body, I entered into absolute dispute with myself [*je me donnai la contestation la plus certaine*]" (96–97, 301, 111).

This dispute suddenly takes the form of rethinking a canonical moment in modern philosophy, Descartes's "Je pense donc je suis" in the *Discourse on Method* (1633), later recast in Latin as "ego cogito, ego sum" in his *Principles of Philosophy* (1644). "It was then," Thomas says, "that, deep within a cave, the madness of the taciturn thinker appeared before me and unintelligible words rung in my ears while I wrote on the wall these sweet words: 'I think, therefore I am not' [*Je pense, donc je ne suis pas*]" (99, 304, 114). Is this Plato's cave, or is the cave a figure for Thomas's skull? Either way, there is a sudden illumination. For on saying these words Thomas has a vision of a great lens that captures the rays of the sun and, redirecting them outwards, burns out whatever it aims at. "I think, it said, I am subject and object of an all-powerful radiation; a sun using all its energy to make itself night, as well as to make itself sun" (99, 304, 115). This visionary lens is the Hegelian ego, a pure negativity that expends itself in action in order to make history. The firm establishment of an ego, an "I," Thomas tells us, entails the destruction of that ego or "I" and, with it, all solid ground for thought. Far from seeking epistemological security, Thomas's "goal of [his] understanding" becomes the obscure Thomas, "a sort of being composed of all that which is excluded from being" (105, 311, 124). And, as happened earlier in the *roman* and *récit*, Thomas feels the dark gaze of this obscure Thomas: "it is him who understands me [*c'est lui qui me comprend*]" (105, 312, 124, trans. slightly modified).

Descartes, in the discovery of the *cogitatio*, first performed the phenomenological reduction, as Husserl acknowledged. "It is a most noteworthy fact that the fundamental consideration that inaugurates the entire course of the development of modern philosophy was nothing other than the staging of a phenomenological reduction."[53] Much modern European philosophy, from Descartes to Jean-Luc Marion, has brooded on the *cogitatio*, and phenomenology has elaborated a highly influential and flexible extension of it, namely, the idea that the *cogito* is not isolated and pure but always and already involved with the world. The converted gaze that can be brought about by performing the reduction presents us with a world of things that is meaningful for us because we are involved from the beginning in the construction of its meaning. Consciousness is shown to be always and already in an intentional relationship with the things of the world. Or, to put it more directly, human being is, from the first, a being-in-relation.

With this in mind, let us continue to read Thomas's reflections on the obscure Thomas, a non-relation between the twins that is occluded in the English translation:

> Invisible and outside of being, it perceives me [*me perçoit*] and sustains me in being. Itself, I perceive it [*Lui-même . . . je le discerne*], an unjustifiable chimera if I were not there, I perceive it [*je le discerne*], not in the vision I have of it [*j'ai de lui*], but in the vision and the knowledge it has of me [*il a de moi*]. I am seen. Beneath this glance [*ce regard*], I commit myself to a passivity which, rather than diminishing me, makes me real. I seek neither to distinguish it [*à le distinguer*], nor to attain it [*à l'atteindre*], nor to suppose it [*à le supposer*]. Perfectly negligent, by my distraction I retain for it [*je lui garde*] the quality of inaccessibility which is appropriate to it [*qui lui convient*]. My senses, my imagination, my spirit, all are dead on the side on which it looks at me [*où il me regarde*]. . . . I am seen. (105, 312, 124–25)

If the reduction gives us a richer sense of our relationship with the ten thousand things of the world, including other people (though only as phenomena), and shows that we are intimately involved in the production of their meaning for us, then can we speak coherently of a reduction here? We can—in terms of counter-intentionality. Yet caution is needed, for this is not a description of what it is like to be reduced, to become a phenomenon for someone else. Not at all: the neutral reduction, as I shall call it, shows that the relationship that the obscure Thomas has with his twin brother falls outside relationship, at least of the kinds that phenomenology usually countenances. The obscure Thomas is always and already involved with his twin, though in a manner that is not described for us. The living-dead Thomas cannot find his double in an intentional horizon and therefore cannot unfold the concrete meaning of the other from whom he is divided. To be sure, the obscure Thomas can be indicated in his obscurity: his phenomenality can be experienced as a strangeness, but he cannot be brought into the light of intelligibility. He cannot become a phenomenon and must remain haunting the Thomas whose aching, relentless voice we hear as we read the narrative. The obscure Thomas remains in what the narrator calls—in an expression to which Blanchot was to return many times, investing it with increased significance—"*une autre nuit*" (105, 311, 124), the space where being passes into image and back again without end and without point.

Descartes and Thomas remain phased counterparts in both the *roman* and the *récit*. In a sense, they too form a double.[54] The one inaugurates modern philosophy; the other, by way of his twin, either challenges the scope of that philosophy or extends it in a new direction, one that includes the discussion of what passes under being—the neutral, the Outside—as well as being itself. The one insists on epistemic certainty; the other prizes being convinced, which may take place in a reverie instead of a state of cold, analytic reason. The one proposes a dualism of temporal body and eternal soul; the other is a temporal Thomas and an obscure neutral Thomas who abides beneath being.[55] The one adduces a firm ground; the other opens a space of "error," of eternal wandering between being and the Outside.[56] Whatever else he does in this narrative, Blanchot challenges the much-prized "unity of reason" in the history of philosophy. There is no way in which Thomas and his twin can be brought together in anything that could plausibly be called a unity. "There are three errors to be avoided in the sciences," St. Bonaventure wrote, by way of allergic reaction to the radical Aristotelianism that he believed to have beset and endangered the University of Paris. "One of these is against the cause of being, another is against the ground of the understanding, and the third is against the order of living."[57] *Thomas l'obscur* may not be guilty of radical Aristotelianism but it nonetheless wanders in all three "errors."

Many things in *Thomas l'obscur* remain to be discussed and evaluated: Blanchot's philosophy of the subject, his philosophy of experience, his philosophy of death, the way in which monstrosity and the Outside are related, and the ways in which these philosophical questions lose their sense of entitlement and pass from being philosophy to the philosophical, thereby making *Thomas l'obscur* a "philosophical novel" in a new sense.[58] In conclusion, though, I restrict myself to one point that has been raised: as we have heard, the narrator speaks of the noun "Thomas" as "the creation of a word [*un mot*] maliciously formed to destroy all words" (97, 303, 112). Nowhere is this operation explicitly described or clarified in the *roman* or the *récit*. It is addressed only in the essays, indirectly at first in *Comment la littérature est-elle possible?* (1942), and finally quite directly in "La littérature et le droit à la mort" (1947–48). At the very end of that long and powerful probing of the relations between writing and death, Blanchot once again attends to the figure of the double. This time, though, it is not a character in a novel but a strange power that abides at the heart of language:

> Now nothing can prevent this power—at the very moment it is trying to understand things and, in language, to specify words—nothing can prevent it from continuing to assert itself as continually differing possibility [*une possibilité toujours autre*], and nothing can stop it from perpetuating an irreducible *double meaning* [*un* double sens *irréductible*], a choice whose terms are covered over with an ambiguity that makes them identical to one another even as it makes them opposite.[59]

The double, here, is language as negativity and language as neutral. If we think of language solely by way of its daily work in the world, its ability to

construct meaning, then that very conception of language will be undermined by its ghostly double, the neutral.

Without death, Blanchot says (following Hegel, especially Kojève's
Hegel), there could be no meaning; and this is because meaning relies on
the possibility of separating essence from its empirical shell. Language is
the form of the "essential content" of what is expressed, Hegel argues in
the *Phenomenology of Mind*. When an ego expresses itself in language and
is understood by others, "its existence is itself dying away."[60] Kojève puts
this more dramatically in a well-known passage about a dog and the concept of a dog: "if the dog were not *mortal*—that is, essentially *finite* or limited with respect to its duration—one could not *detach* the Concept from
it—that is, cause the Meaning (Essence) that is embodied in the *real* dog
to pass into the *non* living word."[61] And yet death is not always an end;
sometimes it is encountered passively as an endless dying, and then the
clarity of death, of negativity, of the concept, is lost, and we have only the
neutral vaguely pressing on us. Then the author's consciousness is raised,
like Lazarus, before or after his or her actual demise by the mere act of
reading. Blanchot describes this neutral existence for several pages in "La
littérature et le droit à la mort" before he reaches his conclusion: "The
writer senses that he is in the grasp of an impersonal power that does not
let him either live or die: the irresponsibility he cannot surmount becomes the expression of that death without death which awaits him at the
edge of nothingness; literary immortality is the very movement by which
the nausea of a survival which is not a survival, a death which does not
end anything, insinuates itself into a world, a world sapped by crude existence" (340).

In writing, then, we find ourselves both forming meaning and con-
demning ourselves to a meaningless, neutral existence in the reader's
consciousness. One odd thing about this perception is that what most
other writers in all periods of history have prized above all other things—
being in a position to make the Horatian boast *non omnis moriar*—is recast by Blanchot as something horrific. For him, it has the sort of terror
found in certain stories of Poe but raised to philosophical dignity. To want
literary fame, for Blanchot, amounts to having a desire for a ghostly half-
existence that is to be feared and that cannot be eliminated, even if one
turns out in the end to have been a very minor writer. Even more peculiar,

perhaps, is that this shudder before literary immortality is not a rhetorical flourish in a single essay that could be taken as a defense mechanism against literary failure. It is a position that Blanchot explores relentlessly in later essays and fragmentary writings.[62] And yet the Neutral is said in many ways: it involves more than the survival of endlessly dying authorial consciousness; it also directs us to a doubling in being itself, as we have seen with the death of Anne and as is taken up, and directed to a different end, in Lévinas's philosophy of art. But what is philosophy was once narrative. In 1941, *Thomas l'obscur* marked a particularly powerful literary presentation of this fissure in human being, one that Blanchot would reinforce in the 1950 redaction of the *roman* into the *récit* and would continue to explore until his last published words.

NOTES

1. I take the epigraph from "Le partenaire mortel," a prose poem that René Char dedicated, significantly, to Maurice Blanchot. Susanne Dubroff translates these lines as follows: "Certain beings have a meaning that escapes us. Who are they? Their secret resides within the depths of the very secret of life. They approach it. It destroys them," René Char, *This Smoke that Carried Us: Selected Poems* (Buffalo, NY: White Pine Press, 2004), 97.

2. The 1941 *roman* was not reissued after the appearance of the 1950 *récit* until 2005, two years after Blanchot's death in 2003. It was never disowned, however, and it returned in an eerie manner, quoted without explanation on the back of the *récit* in Gallimard's "Collection L'Imaginaire" edition of 1992.

3. See Maurice Blanchot, "Heraclitus," in *The Infinite Conversation*, trans. and foreword Susan Hanson (Minneapolis: University of Minnesota Press, 1993), 85–92. The piece first appeared in *Nouvelle Revue française* 85 (1960): 93–106, and was reprinted in *L'entretien infini* (Paris: Gallimard, 1969), 119–31. Blanchot alludes to Heraclitus in a short piece on Gaston Bachelard, "Le Feu, l'eau et les rêves" (1942), now collected in *Chroniques littéraires du "Journal des débats": Avril 1941–Août 1944*, ed. Christophe Bident (Paris: Gallimard, 2007), 244. Robert Lamberton raised the possibility of a connection between Blanchot and Heraclitus in his "*Thomas* and the Possibility of Translation," added to the English translation of the *récit* version of *Thomas l'obscur*. See *Thomas the Obscure*, trans. Robert Lamberton (New York: David Lewis, 1973), 119–24.

4. I take the expression "quantity of connection" from Jacques Derrida. See his *The Archeology of the Frivolous: Reading Condillac*, trans. John P. Leavey, Jr. (Pittsburgh: Duquesne University Press, 1980), 72.

5. Martin Heidegger, "Aletheia (Heraclitus, Fragment B 16)," in *Early Greek Thinking: The Dawn of Western Philosophy,* trans. David Farrell Krell and Frank A. Capuzzi (San Francisco: Harper and Row, 1975), 102. Blanchot started to read *Sein und Zeit* in 1927 or 1928, an event that was, he said decades later, "a true intellectual shock." See his "Penser l'apocalypse," in *Écrits politiques 1958–1993: Guerre d'Algérie, Mai 68 etc* (Paris: Éditions Léo Scheer, 2003), 162. Yet also see Blanchot's dismissal of Heidegger in his review of Denis de Rougemont's *Penser avec les mains* in *L'Insurgé* 3, 27 January 1937, 5.

6. Heidegger, *Being and Time,* trans. John Macquarrie and Edward Robinson (Oxford: Basil Blackwell, 1973), 58.

7. H. Heidegger, *The Essence of Human Freedom: An Introduction to Modern Philosophy,* trans. Ted Sadler (London: Continuum, 2002), §11, and "Aletheia," 118. In modern German, *die Lichtung* is a clearing in a forest; however, Heidegger reties the word to its original association with light, *Licht.*

8. Emmanuel Lévinas figures the intellectual relationship between Heidegger and Blanchot by way of convergence, not influence. See his "The Poet's Vision," in *Proper Names,* trans. Michael B. Smith (Stanford: Stanford University Press, 1996), 129.

9. See Blanchot's "Comment découvrir l'obscur?," the second part of a long essay nominally concerned with Yves Bonnefoy, that appeared in *Nouvelle Revue française* 83 (1959), two numbers of the journal before the publication of "Héraclite." It was reproduced in *L'entretien infini,* 57–69. It is easy to imagine the Blanchot of *Thomas l'obscur* resonating with Heraclitus's remarks, "Only the living may be dead" (from Fragment 78) and "I am as I am not" (from Fragment 81). See Heraclitus, *Fragments,* trans. Brooks Haxton, foreword James Hillman (New York: Viking, 2001), 49, 51.

10. Blanchot's review appeared in *Journal des débats,* 24 February 1942, 3, and was reprinted in *Faux pas* (Paris: Gallimard, 1943), 126–31. As with all the reviews that, revised or not, appeared in *Faux pas,* the piece is not reprinted in *Chroniques littéraires.* A translation, "Is Mallarmé's Poetry Obscure?," may be found in *Faux Pas,* trans. Charlotte Mandell (Stanford: Stanford University Press, 2001), 107–11.

11. Blanchot, "Is Mallarmé's Poetry Obscure?" 111. Blanchot's fear of paraphrasing poetry was life-long. See his note of regret that he may have been guilty of turning poems of Louis-René des Forêts into a "prose approximation," in "Rough Draft of a Regret," in *A Voice from Elsewhere,* trans. Charlotte Mandell (Albany: State University of New York Press, 2007), 10.

12. Thomas Hardy, *Jude the Obscure,* ed., intro., and notes Patricia Ingham (Oxford: Oxford University Press, 2002), 200. Also see 221 and 327. That Hardy names the church "St Thomas" perhaps indicates that they would never have become truly one in marriage.

13. Thomas Gray, "Elegy Written in a Country Church-Yard," in *Thomas Gray and William Collins, Poetical Works,* ed. Roger Lonsdale (Oxford: Oxford University Press, 1977), 36.

14. Blanchot, *Thomas the Obscure*, 35, 76, 38. Throughout, I cite this English translation of the *récit* first, followed by the relevant page of the French novel, followed by the relevant page of the French *récit*. See *Thomas l'obscur: Première version, 1941*, intro. Pierre Madaule (Paris: Gallimard, 2005), and *Thomas l'obscur, nouvelle version* (Paris: Gallimard, 1950). Lamberton draws attention to the scene in Hardy's novel in "*Thomas* and the Possibility of Translation," 123. I do not know whether Blanchot ever read *Jude the Obscure*. He makes no mention of Hardy in his early reviews gathered in *Chroniques littéraires du "Journal des débats"* or *Faux pas*. Firmin Roz translated Hardy's novel into French as *Jude l'obscur* (Paris: Ollendorff, 1901).

15. See Alfred de Musset, *Oeuvres complètes*, ed. Philippe van Tieghem (Paris: Éditions du Seuil, 1963), 153–55.

16. Edgar Allan Poe, "William Wilson," in *Poetry and Tales* (New York: Library of America, 1984), 356.

17. Fyodor Dostoevsky, *The Double: Two Versions*, trans. Evelyn Harden (Ann Arbor, MI: Ardis, 1985), 57.

18. See, for example, Blanchot, "Un essai sur Gérard de Nerval," *Journal des débats*, 22 June 1939, 2, and Blanchot's brief review (centered on *Aurélia*) of Albert Béguin's *Gérard de Nerval* in *L'Insurgé* 33, 25 August 1937, 4. The Nerval who wrote under his portrait "Je suis l'autre" would clearly be a sympathetic figure for the Blanchot of *Thomas l'obscur*.

19. Gérard de Nerval, "Aurélia," in *Selected Writings*, trans. and intro. Geoffrey Wagner (Ann Arbor: University of Michigan Press, 1957), 121–22.

20. Guy de Maupassant, "He?" in *The Dark Side: Tales of Terror and the Supernatural*, foreword Ramsey Campbell, intro. Arnold Kellet (New York: Carroll and Graf, 1989), 139.

21. Joseph Conrad, *The Secret Sharer*, ed. Daniel R. Schwarz (Boston: Bedford Books, 1997), 34.

22. Walter J. Ong, "Voice as Summons for Belief: Literature, Faith, and the Divided Self," in *The Barbarian Within and Other Fugitive Essays and Studies* (New York: Macmillan, 1962), 52.

23. See St. Augustine, Sermon 255, in *Sermons III/7: On the Liturgical Seasons* (230–272B), trans. and notes Edmund Hill, ed. John E. Rotelle, The Works of Saint Augustine (New Rochelle, NY: New City Press, 1993), 161, and Sermon 302, in *Sermons III/8: On the Saints* (273–305A), trans. and notes Edmund Hill, ed. John E. Rotelle, The Works of Saint Augustine (Hyde Park, NY: New City Press, 1994), 300. Whether knowingly or not, Blanchot inherits from Augustine in his understanding of different attitudes to communism. See Blanchot, "On One Approach to Communism," in *Friendship*, trans. Elizabeth Rottenberg (Stanford: Stanford University Press, 1997), 95–96.

24. Origen, *The Song of Songs: Commentary and Homilies*, trans. and ed. R. P. Lawson, Ancient Christian Writers (New York: Newman Press, 1956), 25. Origen has in mind Gen. 1:26 and 2:7.

25. The Gospel According to Thomas, 5 (my additions in square brackets), in *The Gnostic Scriptures,* trans., intro., and annotations Bentley Layton (London: SCM Press, 1987), 381.

26. George Quasha and Charles Stein, "Afterword: Publishing Blanchot in America," in *The Station Hill Blanchot Reader: Fiction and Literary Essays,* ed. George Quasha, trans. Lydia Davis et al. (Barrytown, NY: Station Hill Press, 1999), 523. Also see Derrida, *On Touching—Jean-Luc Nancy,* trans. Christine Irizarry (Stanford: Stanford University Press, 2005), 335 n. 23.

27. See A. F. J. Klijn, ed., *The Acts of Thomas: Introduction, Text, and Commentary,* 2nd rev. ed. (Leiden: Brill, 2005), 1–4.

28. Jean-Luc Nancy muddies the waters when he implies that "Thomas" comes from the Greek *thauma,* meaning "wonder." See his "The Name *God* in Blanchot," in *Dis-Enclosure: The Deconstruction of Christianity,* trans. Bettina Bergo et al. (New York: Fordham University Press, 2008), 87.

29. I take the expression "reading head" from Derrida, "Living On: Borderlines," in *Deconstruction and Criticism,* ed. Geoffrey Hartman (London: Routledge, Kegan Paul, 1979), 107.

30. Blanchot, *The Step Not Beyond,* trans. and intro. Lycette Nelson (Albany: State University of New York Press, 1992), 1. There is a thread in *Thomas l'obscur* that is sewn into the latter text: "I am truly in the beyond, if the beyond is that which admits of no beyond [*pas d'au-delà*]" (104–5, 311, 123).

31. G. W. F. Hegel, *The Phenomenology of Mind,* trans. and intro. J. B. Baillie, intro. George Lichtheim (New York: Harper and Row, 1967), 81.

32. Printed on a page preceding the first chapter of *Thomas the Obscure.* Blanchot formulates the same idea as a general account of narrative in "Encountering the Imaginary," in *The Book to Come,* trans. Charlotte Mandell (Stanford: Stanford University Press, 2003), 7. The passage was originally published as "Le chant des sirènes," *Nouvelle Nouvelle Revue française* 19 (June 1954): 104.

33. My thanks to Gloria Davies for explaining the Chinese character *ren* to me.

34. Blanchot speaks of unity rather than identity or self-identity. It is important to note, though, that unity and identity (or self-identity) are not the same, especially when talking of personhood. See, for example, Lynne Rudder Baker, *The Metaphysics of Everyday Life: An Essay in Practical Reason* (Cambridge: Cambridge University Press, 2007), ch. 4.

35. St. Thomas Aquinas, *Truth,* 3 vols., trans. Robert W. Mulligan (1954; rpt. Indianapolis: Hackett Publishing Co., 1994), q. 1, art. 1, *responsio.*

36. The expression "*des paroles obscures*" is added in the *récit* version of the narrative.

37. See Husserl, "Husserl an von Hofmannsthal (12. 1. 1907)," in *Briefwechsel,* 10 vols., vol. 7, *Wissenschaftlerkorrespondenz,* ed. Elisabeth Schuhmann and Karl Schuhmann (Boston: Kluwer Academic Publishers, 1994), 135.

38. See Blanchot, "René Char and the Thought of the Neutral," in *The Infinite Conversation*, 304. The views presented about the reduction are given by one person in a conversation and are not specifically endorsed by Blanchot. Yet see "Our Clandestine Companion," trans. David B. Allison, in *Face to Face with Levinas*, ed. Richard A. Cohen (Albany: State University of New York Press, 1986), 47. Also see Blanchot's assessment of the value of phenomenology in "Atheism and Writing: Humanism and the Cry," in *The Infinite Conversation*, 250–52. Finally, see Alain David, "La réduction," *Magazine littéraire* 424 (October 2003): 64–66.

39. On the fantasy of the rat in *Thomas l'obscur* (1941), see Jacques Lacan, "De la realization du fantasme," *Magazine littéraire* 424 (October 2003): 46–47. Lacan's text was delivered at his seminar on June 27, 1962.

40. In the *roman* the sentence reads "qu'il était arraché en même temps à la vie et à la mort" (79), while in the *récit* the sentence reads "d'être arraché en même temps à la mort et à la vie" (42).

41. The point is likely to be appreciated only by those well versed in Christian theology of the resurrection. Even in French ecclesiastical language, *ressusciter* is sometimes used as a verbal form when one is needed to give the sense of "resurrection." But this usage can lead to theological confusion. Nancy, for one, misses the point of the distinction in his essay "Blanchot's Resurrection" [*Résurrection de Blanchot*], in *Dis-Enclosure*, 89–97. Unfortunately, he is encouraged to make the mistake by, among other sources, the Bible de Jérusalem, which has the subheading, before John 11, "Résurrection de Lazare."

42. See Irenaeus, *Adversus Haereses*, V.13.1.

43. See Jacobus de Voragine, *The Golden Legend: Readings on the Saints*, trans. William Granger Ryan, 2 vols. (Princeton: Princeton University Press, 1993), 1:376.

44. The same is true of Blanchot's use of Lazarus in "Literature and the Right to Death," in his *The Work of Fire*, trans. Charlotte Mandell (Stanford: Stanford University Press, 1995), 327. The Lazarus motif recurs in Blanchot's writing, sometimes named and sometimes unnamed. See, for instance, *Death Sentence*, trans. Lydia Davis (Barrytown, NY: Station Hill Press, 1978), 20. "The dead came back to life dying," observes one of Blanchot's speakers in a later text. See *Awaiting Oblivion*, trans. John Gregg (Lincoln: University of Nebraska Press, 1997), 28.

45. See Blanchot, *The Space of Literature*, trans. Ann Smock (Lincoln: University of Nebraska Press, 1982), 258.

46. Emmanuel Lévinas, "Reality and Its Shadow," in *Collected Philosophical Papers*, trans. Alphonso Lingis (The Hague: Martinus Nijhoff, 1987), 6.

47. Proclus, *The Platonic Theology*, trans. Thomas Taylor, preface R. Baine Harris, 6 vols. (Kew Gardens, NY: Selene Books, 1985), Book I, ch. 5 and 3, respectively. Also see Aristotle, *Metaphysics* 1026a.

48. Francis Bacon, "Orpheus, or Philosophy," in *The Wisdom of the Ancients and Miscellaneous Essays* (New York: Walter J. Black, 1932), 250. It should be noted that in the *Symposium* 179d, Plato allows Orpheus to be characterized by Phaedrus as a weak creature, something of a coward for not dying for his wife. In classical philosophy, then, he is not a figure of philosophical dignity.

49. The later episode I have in mind is when Thomas sits beside a girl on a bench and says, "I was her tragic double" (100, 306, 117), an insight that seems to be shared by the girl.

50. Hegel, *The Phenomenology of Mind*, 94.

51. See Hegel, *Philosophy of Mind: Being Part Three of the "Encyclopedia of the Philosophical Sciences" (1830)*, trans. William Wallace and A. V. Miller, foreword J. N. Findlay (Oxford: Clarendon Press, 1971), 11.

52. In the *roman* Blanchot writes "ce Thomas-néant," a stronger formulation than "ce Thomas néant" in the *récit*. Also, see "Thomas" regarded as a word rather than as a name in 116, 322, 135. The *roman* has "le mot de Thomas," while the *récit* has "le mot vide de Thomas." The English translation has "Thomas's empty word," which misses what Blanchot actually writes.

53. See Husserl, *The Basic Problems of Phenomenology: From the Lectures*, trans. Ingo Farin and James G. Hart (Dordrecht: Springer, 2006), §16. Husserl observes with dismay that Descartes relinquished the reduction on discovering it.

54. See Mark C. Taylor, *Altarity* (Chicago: University of Chicago Press, 1987), 222.

55. See Descartes, "The Passions of the Soul," in Elizabeth S. Haldane and G. R. T. Ross, ed. and trans., *The Philosophical Works of Descartes*, 2 vols. (Cambridge: Cambridge University Press, 1972), 1:345.

56. Blanchot explores this idea in *The Space of Literature*, 237–38.

57. St. Bonaventure, *Collations on the Seven Gifts of the Holy Spirit*, intro. and trans. Zachary Hayes, notes Robert J. Karris, Works of St Bonventure 14 (St. Bonaventure, NY: Franciscan Institute Publications, 2008), 176.

58. For the distinction between philosophy and the philosophical, see the introduction to this volume.

59. Blanchot, "Literature and the Right to Death," 343–44.

60. Hegel, *Phenomenology of Mind*, 530.

61. Alexandre Kojève, *Introduction to the Reading of Hegel: Lectures on the "Phenomenology of Spirit,"* ed. Raymond Queneau, ed. Allan Bloom, trans. James H. Nichols (Ithaca: Cornell University Press, 1969), 141. I discuss this issue with slightly different emphases in my *The Dark Gaze: Maurice Blanchot and the Sacred* (Chicago: University of Chicago Press, 2004), ch. 4.

62. See, for example, *The Infinite Conversation*, 48; *The Step Not Beyond*, 75; and *The Writing of the Disaster*, trans. Ann Smock (Lincoln: University of Nebraska Press, 1986), 20, 37.

THREE

AMINADAB

QUEST FOR THE ORIGIN OF THE WORK OF ART

Christopher A. Strathman

> *We sail within a vast sphere, ever drifting in uncertainty, driven from end*
> *to end. When we think to attach ourselves to any point and to fasten to it,*
> *it wavers and leaves us; and if we follow it, it eludes our grasp, slips past us,*
> *and vanishes forever. Nothing stays for us. This is our natural condition,*
> *and yet most contrary to our inclination; we burn with desire to find solid*
> *ground and an ultimate sure foundation whereon to build a tower reaching*
> *to the Infinite. But our whole groundwork cracks, and the earth opens to*
> *abysses.*
>
> —Blaise Pascal

In a 1951 essay, "Maurice Blanchot as Novelist," Georges Poulet notes that for Blanchot, "the goal of the novel is not the fictional existence of characters or the portrayal of an imaginary world, even less is it that kind of supplementary reality which the naturalists attempted to weave into the compact pattern of an uncontested and preestablished world. Such novels, in Blanchot's opinion, are impure and imperfect, as insignificant as poems without poetry. What he tries to attain is a novel of which every element ought to be returned to a doubtful status, a novel which would be obliged to invent and authenticate, as it was being written, its own existence and its own universe."[1] As a description of Blanchot's literary theory and practice, this passage is remarkably prescient, for Poulet already sees that even at this juncture the novel is for Blanchot neither a romantic sublimation nor a naturalistic debasement of the world, but rather, somewhat after the example of Heidegger, an opening for the writer to embark upon a journey to the unsettling origin of the work of art, upon which the existence of the world depends. And in all of Blanchot's writings there is perhaps no better example of the novel understood in this sense—as a quest for the origin of the work of art—than his early novel *Aminadab*.

Often overlooked by English-speaking readers, *Aminadab* (1942) is Blanchot's second novel. However, as with everything having to do with Blanchot, this claim needs some qualification. Written after the far better-known *Thomas l'obscur* (1941) and published the following year, the volume bears the generic subtitle *roman,* or "novel," but only on its faded yellow cover and not on the title page. While the publisher may simply have added *roman* to the cover of the volume to inform potential readers, the author's hesitation to call it that surely suggests some ambiguity regarding the book's genre. The term fits the text loosely at best, and Blanchot abandons the designation altogether when referring to subsequent works, choosing instead to employ the more neutral-sounding *récit* or "narrative." The switch is telling: over time, Blanchot's narratives undergo a systematic simplification, a stripping away of everything nonessential until they reach a point where they are seemingly borne along by nothing but the exigency of language itself. Of course, such ambivalence with regard to genre is nothing new; Blanchot has important precursors in the early German romantics and their efforts to rethink the novel in terms of dialogue rather than plot.[2] More specifically, it is consistent with the romantic appropriation of Kant's efforts in the *Critique of Pure Reason* (1781) to secure reason against the threat of skepticism, inherent in both Cartesian idealism and British empiricism, by clarifying the conditions under

which knowledge is possible. Under what precise conditions, Kant famously wanted to know, is knowledge possible? In order to answer this
question, Kant proceeded to set aside, or bracket, everything in human
experience that was not absolutely necessary for philosophical investigation. "I have to deal with nothing," he wrote in the preface to the first edition of the *Critique,* "save reason itself and its pure thinking."[3] Just as
Kant wanted to establish firmer ground for reason so that it might be free
of skepticism, so, too, the romantics sought in poetry a more authentic
foundation for the work of art. More than this, they sought to locate in poetry the ground of the world itself. Following their lead, Blanchot in his
early writings explores the possibility of a discourse that cannot be contained within the traditional boundaries of the novel understood as a
genre. On this understanding, pieced together from several essays and reviews, Blanchot's view of the novel engages in a dialogue with Heidegger
concerning the latter's conception of the role of language in establishing
and maintaining the being of existence. This, of course, is the conception
that informs the well-known assertion in Heidegger's "Letter on Humanism" (1947) that language is "the house of Being."[4]

Inspired by these efforts to translate certain features of Kant's thought
into the idiom of romantic poetics, Blanchot raises the question of the
conditions under which literature, as opposed to knowledge, is possible.
In many ways, this question informs his lifelong understanding of literature. To take only the most salient example, the 1941 review-essay "How
Is Literature Possible?" carries in its title an unmistakable indication of its
alignment with Kant's philosophical ambitions, although such ambitions
are now redirected toward the question of literature.[5] In gesturing toward
an answer to this somewhat unusual question, Blanchot makes the comparison with Kant explicit:

> Now we are ready to give an answer to the question, How is lit-
> erature possible? It is actually through virtue of a double illusion—
> illusion of some who struggle against commonplaces and language
> by the very means that engender language and commonplaces; illu-
> sion of others who, renouncing literary conventions or, as we say, lit-
> erature, cause it to be reborn in a form (metaphysics, religion, etc.)
> that is not its own. It is from this illusion and from the awareness of

this illusion that Jean Paulhan, through a revolution that can be called Copernican, like that of Kant, proposes to draw the most precise and rigorous literary reign. (82; 104)[6]

Just so: in his subsequent writings, the question of literature's possibility—the question not simply of its content or its long-term cultural survival but of the conditions under which it is possible for it to exist in the first place—emerges, along with death, ethics, and politics, as one of the central concerns of Blanchot's work. In addition to evidence of the influence of Kant's critique, one can also detect echoes of Heidegger's effort to retrieve the question of the meaning of Being out from under the shadow of the assumption that thinking should address the question of beings as entities, that is, things as "real" or material objects, an effort, moreover, in which language and poetry are profoundly implicated. For Blanchot, as for Heidegger, language serves as the foundation—even when it calls itself into question, perhaps most profoundly when it calls itself into question—of the human world.

My modest goal in what follows is to extend and complicate this characterization of Blanchot by positing a correspondence of sorts between the kind of text he advocates in his essays and reviews and the existentially and linguistically recoded romantic tradition that echoes throughout the body of his narratives. More specifically, a romantic-existentialist concern with the origins of language and its relation to the reciprocal interplay of being and nothingness is on exemplary display in *Aminadab*. Such a concern surfaces initially in the haunted, and haunting, novelistic discourse that facilitates the zombie-like circulation of numerous ghostly, anonymous, shape-shifting figures, domestics, guardians, tenants, and body-doubles, whose status, together with the doubling—or is it the self-tormenting?—of the main character Thomas, calls into question some basic assumptions about the nature of human existence.[7] It culminates, I argue, in the gradual emergence of the ubiquitous and yet elusive boardinghouse, in which the novel's action takes place, as not merely the work's physical setting but also its central character, its abiding theme, and, indeed—anticipating Heidegger's critique of Sartre's existential humanism in the celebrated "Letter on Humanism"—its very raison d'être.

Transcendental Poetry

Scholars commonly locate the origin of the ancient quarrel between phi-losophy and poetry in Plato's banishment of the poets in the *Republic*—although Socrates describes the "antagonism" as already "long-standing" (607b–d).[8] Taken up with renewed urgency during the romantic period by the Schlegel circle, transformed by Nietzsche's use of the opposition between the forces of Apollo and Dionysus, and further radicalized by Heidegger's reflections on the relationship between thinking [*Denken*] and poetizing [*Dichten*], this quarrel between philosophy and poetry is given a decisive and fateful turn toward the question of the possibility (or impossibility) of literature, by Blanchot. In this section I emphasize the origins of this notion of literature in German romanticism's conception of "romantische Poesie," in its transformation of poetry into something like the novel or, more accurately, novelistic discourse. As novelistic discourse, romantic poetry inhabits a space beyond, or just outside of, genre as it is commonly understood and instead gestures toward the space be-tween philosophy and poetry, speech and silence, being and nothingness.

One can trace the emergence of this view of poetry to a series of re-markable texts produced around the close of the eighteenth century by Friedrich Schlegel, his brother August and sister-in-law Caroline, and their small circle of friends living in the German university town of Jena. In the *Athenäum Fragments* (1798), Friedrich Schlegel rethinks the cele-bration of classical perfection he had espoused in his essay "On the Study of Greek Poetry" (1797) and begins to acknowledge important differences between the poetry of antiquity and the more irregular aesthetic embod-ied in the works of moderns such as Dante, Cervantes, Shakespeare, Swift, Sterne, and Goethe. In one of his best-known fragments, he ex-presses the difference between them as follows:

> 238. There is a kind of poesy whose one and all is the relation-ship between the ideal and the real, and which, according to the anal-ogy of philosophical terminology, should be called transcendental poesy. . . . In the same way, the poesy that unites the transcendental materials and preliminary exercises of a poetic theory of writing

common to modern poets with the artistic reflection and beautiful self-mirroring that is found in Pindar, in the lyric fragments of the Greeks, in the ancient elegy, and among the moderns in Goethe—this poesy should also represent itself as a part of each of its representations, and should always be simultaneously poesy and the poesy of poesy.[9]

So, while Kant searches for a transcendental foundation upon which reason can function without nagging questions about its own legitimacy, Schlegel indicates the possibility of a "transcendental" poetic ground upon which rational certainty and inevitable doubt can not only tentatively coexist but meet one another and productively, fruitfully, interact.

In the following year, Schlegel, not content with this formulation, raises the stakes. Without the "first, originary poesy," he claims in the *Dialogue on Poesy* (1799), "there would surely be no poesy of words" (180; 166).[10] In addition to providing some of the inspiration for the description by Poulet cited above, this distinction between what he is now calling "originary [*ursprüngliche*] poesy" and the "poesy of words" marks the emergence of a radically new conception of poetry (if indeed that is what it is), and it indicates a turning point in the history of European poetics. But what exactly does it mean? In the "Letter on the Novel" from the same *Dialogue,* Schlegel tries to clarify the idea by dissolving the distinction between ancient and modern, classical and romantic, and by moving toward a consideration of the romantic kind of poetry as a universal impulse that inheres in all of the greatest works, no matter what their historical epoch or cultural point of origin. That is to say, it remains in the greatest works of art in the form of a trace of the originating force of poetry itself or, as it were, poetry-as-such. He explains this as follows: "There was but one difference [between ancient Greek and modern "romantic" poetry], namely, that the romantic is not so much a genre as an element of poesy that may predominate and recede to a greater or lesser extent but may never be completely absent. In my opinion, it must be obvious to you that I demand that all poetry be romantic but loathe the novel insofar as it is a particular genre, and why I do so" (193, my interpolation; 209).[11] Here Schlegel dispenses with genre theory entirely and instead strives to explain romantic poetry as a force, even a limit concept, or at any rate an impulse that exists to a varying degree in all sorts of verse, ancient and modern, classical and romantic, traditional and avant-garde. But it also exists in other forms as well, including, but not limited to, the novel. Most revealing in this regard is his insistence on the importance of romantic poetry, or novelistic discourse, as the *sine qua non* of modern literature and his simultaneous disdain for the novel as a distinct literary genre. This transformation of the concept of literature from an aggregate of genres to something like a limit concept, consisting of radical self-interrogation in relation to, and at times even at odds with, philosophy, is a move that will interest Blanchot greatly.

A brief glance at one last text from the romantic canon may provide additional perspective on the question of transcendental poetry as Blanchot inherits it from Schlegel. In a famous, and famously cheeky, farewell essay to the readers of the *Athenäum*, which appeared under the title "On Incomprehensibility" (1800), Schlegel strikes a defiant tone in order to defend his practice of writing fragments. Toward the conclusion of the essay, he takes the opportunity to poke fun at the very idea of a system of genres that would be able to subdue the destabilizing force of irony:

> In order to facilitate this overview of the entire system of irony, we would like to present some of its most exemplary kinds. The first and most distinguished of all is unrefined irony. It is most often found in the real nature of things and is one of its most universally widespread substances; unrefined irony is quite at home [*zu Hause*] in the history of humankind. Then there is fine or delicate irony, the extra fine. This is the way in which Scaramouch works, when he seems to be conversing with someone in a friendly and serious manner, awaiting only the moment when he will be able to effectively administer a kick in the behind. This sort of irony is also found among poets, as is sincere irony, which, in its purest and most unspoiled form [*ursprünglichsten*], is most appropriate in old gardens, where wonderful pleasant grottoes lure the nature lover, brimming with feeling, into their cool laps, only in order to spray him thoroughly from all sides with water and in this way to dispel his tender mood. Then there is dramatic irony, when the author who has written three acts unexpectedly becomes a different person and must now write

the last two. Then there is double irony, when two lines of irony run parallel to one another without disturbing each other, one sort of irony for the gallery and the other for the boxes, though small sparks can still fly into the curtains. Finally, there is the irony of irony. (124–25; 369)[12]

This classic passage parodies the hubris of a classical literary theory that operated more or less under the auspices of Aristotelian metaphysics and, to a lesser extent, classical rhetoric and its penchant for cultivating the neat (and not infrequently tedious) classification and division of genres—as if that explains anything about the truth of poetry. Among other things, it suggests that for Schlegel the irony, or better the anarchism, of poetic language cannot be mastered from an analytical or theoretical distance; rather, one must engage it on its own terms, live with it, talk through it, and labor over it with diligence and delight. In short, there are no short-cuts, only unpredictable, and often deeply unsettling, detours through the linguistic "house of Being."

One additional thought: the gist of the above passage—that romantic poetry draws its power from and has its ultimate origins in a quasi-mystical poetic source that rests on the hither side of genre—is further re-inforced by Philippe Lacoue-Labarthe and Jean-Luc Nancy in their study *The Literary Absolute* (1978). In the preface they state:

> This [desire to produce a modern poetic work that will rival the greatest works of the ancients] is the reason romanticism implies something entirely new, the *production* of something entirely new. The romantics never really succeed in naming this something: they speak of poetry, of the work, of the novel, or . . . of romanticism. In the end, they decide to call it—all things considered—*literature*. This term, which was not their own invention, will be adopted by posterity . . . to designate a concept. . . . They, in any case, will approach it explicitly as a new *genre*, beyond the divisions of classical (or modern) poetics and capable of resolving the inherent ("generic") divisions of the written thing. Beyond divisions and all de-finition [sic], this *genre* is thus programmed in romanticism as *the* genre of *literature*: the genericity, so to speak, and the generativity of literature,

grasping and producing themselves in an entirely new, infinitely new
Work. The *absolute,* therefore, of literature.[13]

Leaving aside for now the question of whether or not literature in this
sense ought to be determined as a "concept," Lacoue-Labarthe and Nancy
here point to the romantic work as one informed not by genre but by *lit-*
erature itself. Such a work is infinitely progressive but nonetheless always
unfinished, nurtured by the groundless ground of poetry.

FROM ANGUISH TO LANGUAGE

Blanchot's affinity for romanticism's rethinking of poetry as literature is
mediated by his encounter with the symbolist poet Stéphane Mallarmé,
an encounter that introduces a decisive wrinkle into his thought. In a
number of reviews written for the pro-Pétain paper *Journal des débats*
around the time of his earliest narratives, Mallarmé serves as a tutelary
spirit of sorts for Blanchot. These reviews—especially those later reprinted in his first book of essays, *Faux pas* (1943)—provide a useful point
of entry into Blanchot's thinking about the novel at roughly the same time
that he was composing *Aminadab.* In these brief meditations the poet's
name turns up repeatedly, as if Mallarmé's work represents an exemplary
instance of how romantic-poetry-as-novelistic-discourse, now embodied
in the work of the symbolist poet, might be useful in providing a way forward for the moribund modern novel. The value of beginning with these
provocative, if often slight, pieces is that they move one closer to an understanding of *Aminadab* not just as an allegory of writing, textuality, or
reading in the usual sense, which it almost certainly is, but also as a
haunting and haunted work that replays endlessly—with each repeated
reading, as it were—the game of existential hide-and-go-seek that insinuates itself into the relation between language and the ground of being.

   Some of the highlights of Blanchot's engagement with the romantic
rethinking of poetry, particularly with regard to Mallarmé's role in trans-
mitting it to the twentieth century (and beyond), include "[The Author's
Introduction]" to the first section of the book, subtitled "From Anguish to
Language"; two reviews, "The Silence of Mallarmé" and "Is Mallarmé's

Poetry Obscure?" from the second section, subtitled "Digressions on Poetry"; and the review "Mallarmé and the Art of the Novel" from the third
section, "Digressions on the Novel." Such a catalogue, however, barely
scratches the surface. Even in less substantial pieces that have little to do
with either Mallarmé or romantic poetry, Blanchot appears to be mulling
over the question of the novel. "The Enigma of the Novel," for instance,
opens with the following observation: "The little book that René Lalou has
devoted to the *Roman français depuis 1900* [French novel since 1900] draws
attention to difficulties in grasping the novel as a literary genre and in
discerning its conventions and laws" (187; 221).[14] "The Birth of a Myth"
raises a similar question: "What adds to the interest of [Henri's novel
Hyacinthe] is that it is the sketch of a form that forces the novel to break
with its conventions" (192, my interpolation; 227).[15] Another essay,
"Mythological Novels," is even more explicit about the role played by the
novel in the overall destiny of literature: "Raymond Queneau's novel *Les
Temps mêlés* will likely make evident the questions that the fate of the
French novel and even the existence of the novel in general pose for literature. . . . We have certainly perceived that for quite a long time the novel,
as a literary work, has undergone a crisis whose meaning remains obscure" (196; 232).[16] One can see from this brief glance that the future of
the novel and its consequences for literature is a question that for Blanchot verges on an obsession.

More narrowly, Blanchot is interested in the question of what might
happen to literature and to the theory and practice of literary study if the
novel were conceived as a question *for* philosophy, and not as just another
one of the sites where philosophical problems turn up. So in "[The Author's Introduction]" to *Faux Pas*, Blanchot directly confronts the challenge of existentialism, linking its penchant for lingering near the abyss
of the nothing intimately, even inescapably, to the question of writing.[17]
In a famous passage from this introduction, Blanchot describes the
daunting situation facing the writer who sits before a blank sheet of
paper: "The writer finds himself in the increasingly ludicrous condition
of having nothing to write, of having no means with which to write it,
and of being constrained by the utter necessity of always writing it. Having nothing to express must be taken in the most literal way. Whatever
he would like to say, it is nothing. The world, things, knowledge are to

him only landmarks across the void" (3; 11).[18] At first glance a rather
straightforward account of the writer's dilemma, this passage also resonates with echoes of Heidegger's and Sartre's emphases in their thought
on the concrete fact of human existence and its defining encounter with
nothingness. Although Heidegger rejected the label of existentialism
and Sartre's existential humanism remains controversial, both thinkers
reflected extensively on the relationship between being and nothingness,
and both took seriously the contribution that literature can make to the
individual's search for meaning in a world where the anguished encounter with the nothing cannot simply be folded into, or subsumed within,
larger metaphysical narratives of being. For Blanchot, too, writing is not
simply an occupation or a profession but rather a human condition, perhaps the exemplary instance of *the* human condition. "The writer," Blanchot speculates, "sometimes seems strangely *as if anguish were part of his
occupation* and, even more, as if the fact of writing so deepens anguish
that it attaches itself to him rather than to any other sort of person" (4, my
emphasis; 12).[19] With this description of writing as an encounter with
the nothing, Blanchot inflects existentialist phenomenology with the
question of writing in a way that has had an immense impact on twentieth century literary theory and cultural studies.

Some of this becomes more explicit in what is arguably the thematic
center of the collection, the essay "Mallarmé and the Art of the Novel."[20]
Revisiting his earlier review of Henri Mondor's biography of Mallarmé,
Blanchot hints in this essay at an underlying connection between romanticism's attempt to appropriate Kant's philosophy and Heidegger's insistence on poetry as the ultimate foundation for being. Blanchot, most
probably with some such thoughts in mind, cautiously approaches his
point:

It is curious that no novelist has discovered in Mallarmé's remarks
[in the letter in which we find expressed the hope of the poet prepar-
ing *Un coup de dés*] a definition of the art of the novel or an allusion
charged with glory to the work he is called to do. Yet there is in this
page such a profound conception of language, such a wide breadth of
vision of the calling of words [*la vocation des mots*], such a universal
explanation of literature that no genre of creation can find itself

excluded from it. The writer who, thanks to his anxious mission, sees himself forced to construct the rigors of fiction using the facilities of prose is no less directly summoned than the poet. (166, my interpolations; 198)[21]

For Blanchot, the poet's remarks in his letter hold out the possibility of a radically new understanding of the novel, one whereby the novelist will be compelled to work with language much in the way that the poet has historically conjured reality with words, in order to raise literature above the modest confines of the novel construed as a genre and to transform it into something approaching the status of scripture. The crux of his interpretation of Mallarmé vis-à-vis romantic literary theory follows, and it bears directly on a reading of *Aminadab:*

> Mallarmé, more profoundly than any other, conceived of language not as a system of expression, a useful and handy intermediary for a mind that wants to understand and make itself understood, but rather as *a power of transformation and creation, made to create enigmas rather than to clarify them.* The consequences of this conception forced Mallarmé to go very far. Language is what founds human reality and the universe. The man who reveals himself in a dialogue where he finds his fundamental deed, the world that puts itself into words by an act that is its profound origin—these express the nature and dignity of language. The mistake is to believe that language is an instrument that man uses in order to act or in order to manifest himself in the world; language, in reality, uses man in that it guarantees the existence of the world and his existence in the world. (167, my emphasis; 199)[22]

Language, in the sense in which it is conceived here, echoes the "originary poesy" of Schlegel's *Dialogue.* Only now, it is given a more central role in the life of the artist—and the world. If Kant insists on bracketing the contingencies of experience in order to train his eye on "reason itself and its pure thinking," Blanchot envisions Mallarmé as a poet who brackets the contingencies that impinge upon the inner workings of the literary text. Blanchot sees the poet, and by extension the novelist, as one committed by his sacred vocation to the task of exploring the very linguistic essence or origin of literature.

QUEST FOR THE ORIGIN OF THE WORK OF ART

In an illuminating 1947 review, Jean-Paul Sartre constructs a reading of *Aminadab* on what he believes to be "the extraordinary resemblance between [Blanchot's] book and the novels of Kafka. There is the same minute and courtly style, the same nightmare politeness, the same preposterous and studied ceremoniousness, the same vain quests that lead nowhere, the same exhaustive and useless discussions, the same sterile initiations that initiate into nothing."[23] The parallel with Kafka, especially with his posthumous novel *The Castle* (1926), is provocative, especially when one considers that at the time Blanchot was writing his novel, he claims not yet to have read Kafka. This odd, even bizarre, claim notwithstanding, the comparison is an intriguing one, for it suggests a template for the quasi-mystical journey to the apparently infinite linguistic recesses of the world that resonates throughout *Aminadab*. On its surface the story of a man's whimsical decision to enter a boardinghouse in order to discover the origin of a message that he believes was meant for him, on another level Blanchot's novel is a complex, mystifying, and even maddening allegory of the inspiration behind writing, textuality, and interpretation. But, far from being a standard allegory of reading, it is a novel that also turns allegory inside out, inverting the hierarchical economy of literal and figurative discursive registers so that the reader struggles to focus on the excruciating banality of the plot and the continually shifting descriptions of the setting and characters in order to follow exactly what is going on. Nothing in the novel, whether it be setting, character, plot, or even language, is ever quite itself. The discourse of the novel, far from exhibiting the verbal pyrotechnics of a Joyce or Stein, is always shifting just slightly out of focus but is never unintelligible. In fact, it is maddeningly ordinary. As I have already indicated, the following reflections on *Aminadab* are governed by two main thoughts: first, that the novel embodies precisely the kind of book imagined by Mallarmé, a book dedicated to the insight that, as Blanchot writes, language "reveals itself as the foundation both of things and of human reality";[24] and, second, that this self-revelation on the part of language is simultaneously entangled in the interplay of being and nothingness that is one of the legacies not only of existentialist phenomenology but of modern cosmology and of contemporary appropriations of mystical or "negative" theology.

The second of three novels written early in Blanchot's career, *Aminadab* is in some ways one of his most conventional works. It features a recognizable protagonist, Thomas, who is nearly identical to the title character of Blanchot's first novel, *Thomas the Obscure* (Jean Paulhan goes so far as to call *Aminadab* "a second *Thomas*");[25] minor characters who engage, and also fail to engage, Thomas in polite conversation; a boardinghouse where the action, such as it is, takes place; a vocabulary and a syntax that create the impression that the language of the text is a transparent medium; and a narrative structure that can only be deemed classic: that of the quest romance, however fantastically reimagined.[26] Geoffrey Hartman's catalogue of the *matériel* to be found in Blanchot's narratives, from a largely forgotten 1955 essay, fits *Aminadab* pretty well: "The universe of Blanchot's narrations is very restrained: streets, houses, open doors, closed doors, staircases where the *minuterie* [clocks] always fail at some point, dark corridors the cause of sudden pain, a kitchen, a glass of water, windows, one or two companions or strangers and, finally, the reduction of the world of things to a room, and that room to a few apparently vital pieces of furniture, paralleling the reduction of consciousness to a few apparently commonplace sets of question and reply."[27] Given this description, one might be led to expect a work that, for all its "dark corridors" and cryptic reductions, more or less obeys the laws of conventional realism. Yet after reading only a few pages one quickly realizes that *Aminadab* is, as translator Jeff Fort has rightly remarked, a deeply "strange" book.[28] Although the premise of the plot can easily be summarized—Thomas, after noticing what he believes to be a young woman gesturing from the upper balcony of an apartment building, enters in order to find her and to learn what she wants—the content it aims to disclose to its reader remains stubbornly, even maddeningly, elusive. Hartman, for his part, rather cryptically concludes his essay: "Yet in this simple décor is revealed a mystery analogous to that contained in the great myths of antiquity."[29] To some extent, this remains so.

To approach the "mystery" or, better, the (nonrevelatory) revelation embodied in this novel, it is useful to start by looking carefully at its opening words.[30] *Aminadab* begins with an unnamed narrator briefly establishing the setting: "It was broad daylight [*Il faisait grand jour*]" (1; 7).[31] This—in all its banality—is the full extent of the introduction. Without further ado, the novel depicts Thomas observing a man sweeping in the doorway of his shop. Thomas pauses to investigate. The man extends an invitation, but Thomas declines: "Thomas had no such thing in mind" (1; 7). Instead, for some unknown reason, his attention is drawn to a dirty and disorderly but otherwise nondescript house just across the street. What, if anything, is Blanchot trying to signal to the reader by means of such an opening? In an attempt to appreciate its significance, it may be useful to juxtapose it with the first few lines of Blanchot's 1943 review of his friend Georges Bataille's book *Inner Experience* (1943).[32] Blanchot opens his review with a quotation from Nietzsche's *Thus Spoke Zarathustra* (1883–91):

> We come to hear Nietzsche's words, "Now is the time of the Great Noon, of the most formidable clarity," in ourselves when after having destroyed the truth that sheltered us we see ourselves exposed to a sun that burns us, a sun that is yet only the reflection of our destitution and our coldness. . . . The time of the Great Noon is the one that brings us the strongest light; the whole atmosphere is overheated; the day has turned to fire; for the man hungry to see, it is the time when, looking, he risks becoming blinder than a blind man, a kind of seer who remembers the sun as a grey spot, a burden. (37; 51)[33]

In connection with the novel's opening, this is a suggestive passage. Two things are worth noting: first, the theme of "the Great Noon" can be found not only in *Zarathustra* but throughout Nietzsche's writings. Typically it suggests a moment of truth, a crisis or a threshold opening onto a transition, metamorphosis, or transformation. It marks a period of time when humankind stands in the middle of its journey toward its destiny, between beast and superman; it signifies that the human is neither one thing nor another but rather a plurality or multiplicity. This is in many ways an accurate description of the main character of *Aminadab* as he makes his way through the hallways, doorways, rooms, and stairs of the boardinghouse, often chained to his "partenaire invisible," his (mostly) invisible partner Dom. Second, in this passage Blanchot touches on a theme that will become almost ubiquitous in his later writings, the idea of a quasi-mystical or "negative" way by means of which the writer fails, falls, or passively (darkly) "sees" a way beyond the binary oppositions of waking and sleeping, reason and madness, daylight and nighttime, and slips into something akin to a parallel dimension. He begins to "experience" the unsettling neutrality of a foundation without foundation. Perhaps it is not too much to say that already by 1942 Blanchot is trying to represent this sense of inertia [*désoeuvrement*] in his fiction. In the end, reading the opening sentence in the light of such a passage intimates a novel that, Siren-like, lures the reader from the traditional creature comforts of plot, character, and diction into a nebulous world where the subject is mutable and the most banal of phrases is nonetheless haunted by murmurs from who knows where.

The novel has hardly begun when Thomas is caught up in the consequences of a choice he is barely aware of having made. Gazing absently at an art object in the window of a boutique, which consists of a simple portrait painted over another still barely visible image, his eye is nonetheless drawn back across the street to the sight of two figures standing discretely in an upstairs window. As he watches their shadowy forms, those of a woman and a young man, he becomes transfixed, mesmerized, losing himself in the image they project. For his part, the young man exhibits a neutral sort of smile, neither inviting Thomas inside not discouraging him from watching, while the woman appears to communicate something discretely—is it a message?—to him:

> The girl, as if suddenly becoming aware of this expectation, made a quick sign with her hand, like an invitation; then she quickly closed the window, and the room was submerged again into darkness.
>
> Thomas was quite perplexed. Could he consider this gesture truly as a call to him? It was rather a sign of friendship than an invitation. It was also a sort of dismissal. He hesitated. Looking again in the direction of the shop, he realized that the man who was sweeping had gone back inside as well. This reminded him of his first plan. But then he decided that he would always have time to carry it out later, and he decided to cross the street and enter the house. (2; 9)[34]

As confusing as the gesture appears to be at the outset, it has momentous consequences—at least in terms of the novel. Once inside the house, nothing is as it seems for Thomas (or for the reader, for that matter). He spends the bulk of his time as if newly arrived in an exotic land, trying to absorb the lingua franca that, however illogical or impractical it may first appear to him as a stranger, the house's natives take for granted. But rather than becoming acclimated to his new surroundings, Thomas struggles to find himself at home and retains the sense that something is not right.

This pervasive discomfort, it turns out, is mutual. A woman named Mlle Barbe, who serves as a sort of guide for Thomas, leading him to the upper floors of the house, nevertheless expresses a long-standing frustration with his view of language:

> "You behave like a child," she said. "You place too much meaning on certain words, while you completely neglect others for reasons no one can guess. I was already struck by that when I saw you for the first time, and that is what must have made me postpone my remarks. Who knows what great significance you might have seen in them! *Such a fuss over a few words!* At the same time, in other cases one can spell everything out, and you refuse to pay any attention." (138, my emphasis; 159)[35]

He has never quite been able to attune himself to the language as used, or as lived in, by the inhabitants of the house, and as a result he can make little sense of the world around him. The remainder of the narrative concerns his search for the elusive girl who waved to him, which leads him to attempt to ascend the stairs to the highest floor of the house in order to locate her, and then to the realization that he has failed in his search and that the basement may contain even greater secrets.

Again playing the role of spiritual guide, Mlle Barbe scolds Thomas for undertaking his quest in such a narrowly strategic fashion:

> "What I had asked of you—and this demand had its price, but you did not want to see that—was to wait for me without any useless exertions, without trying to search on your own for something you could never attain. Was that so difficult? You had only to remain in your corner. But that was probably too much for your strength. Impatient

as you are, you preferred to follow me into the rooms, at the risk of becoming absorbed in what you saw, and you let me walk away so as to pursue your path as you wished." (138; 159–60)[36]

An image of the mysterious nature of poetic inspiration, the decision to enter the house takes Thomas on a labyrinthine quest for an understanding of the many forms of social life—papers, records, contracts, laws, hierarchies, customs, and practices—that apparently govern the house, its staff, and its guests. But Thomas is, at least initially, unable to appreciate the upside-down logic of the house, governed by the upside-down logic of language, and so he presses on with the mindset of a subject intent on knowing, on getting to the bottom of, the "message" he has received.[37] In the end, the trajectory of his quest is best understood as a search for the secret of the house itself, as well as for his place in it.

Let me return for a moment to an earlier thought. An interpretive assumption that surfaces repeatedly in critical discussions of *Aminadab* is that, whatever else it is, it is an allegory, as Sartre was perhaps the first to propose. But if so, of what is it an allegory? Although it is impossible to establish a firm correspondence between any of the characters in the novel and the ideas or intellectual currents that they presumably represent, the text recalls literary conventions such as the medieval quest romance and the more interiorized quest of the modern period. Jeff Fort is on the mark when he observes that "it is difficult not to see the novelistic world conjured up in *Aminadab* as an allegory that is strangely coextensive with the adventure of writing that it would allegorize."[38] This interpretation dovetails nicely with the assumption, discussed earlier, that Blanchot wishes to explore the inner workings of literature via the novel. Returning to the passage from Blanchot's review of Bataille's book cited a moment ago, perhaps it is possible to think of Thomas's journey as a third type of quest, a quest for some sort of spiritual or quasi-mystical experience that is only possible once the self has been divested of its capacity to have such an experience. On such a reading, Thomas embarks on a post-romantic quest: the journey he undertakes leads not deeper into the Cartesian subject or the Freudian psyche but, by means of what Bataille calls "l'expérience intérieure," into the unsettling mystery of language that continually interrupts the subject's self-sufficiency.[39] In other words, only when the self or the subject has been displaced by language can this sort of "inner experience" take place. Only now, since the subject has been turned upside down or inside out, as Sartre says, what is at stake is not so much inner subjective experience but rather the inner experience of language itself. But how exactly might one prepare oneself to have an "experience" of this particular sort? Does such a thought even make sense? Perhaps, when all is said and done (and it never is with Blanchot), *Aminadab* is the story of such an effort.

THE ABSENT OTHER, UPON WHOM ALL THINGS REST

Such questions can perhaps be formulated in a more accessible way by considering the novel as a work primarily informed by a single question: "Who are you? [*Qui êtes-vous?*]" (13; 20). This is a question that gets repeated at various points throughout the novel; it is also alluded to again and again in many other contexts. In fact, it is the last thing that Thomas says (199; 227). In many ways it serves as a fitting emblem for the novel's interrogation of subjectivity and for its parallel questioning of the meaning-making-and-unmaking powers of literary language. "'It is not always clear to me,' [Thomas says to Mlle Barbe,] 'whether your remarks are meant to reveal to me the fate that awaits me or to help me turn away from it.' Then he added in a low voice: 'May I ask you to speak more slowly? It's not always easy for me to follow you'" (142; 162).[40] Any reader who reaches this point in the novel will nod wildly in agreement, for the request is a wicked parody of what one imagines to be the average reader's response to the novel's relentless discursive indifference. It is as if the book were deliberately written in a language that is all but useless as an expressive instrument. It is a language, in other words, designed to fail, to allow things to slip away, and in that failure to reveal something rather profound: the essence of literature. It is language expressing itself. It is as if, in response to some demand for a massive revaluation of all values, the very question that has appeared to drive the plot (such as it is) has itself now been turned inside out or upside down. Here one is in agreement with Sartre. The subject-noun of the sentence "who are you?"—"Qui êtes-vous?"—has now become more intelligible than the murky object-referent of "you." It is as if one were condemned to experience one's native tongue as a stranger, to be excluded from conversation by one's own words, to hear its rustle only from the outside.[41]

An inscrutable mystery is embodied in the title character: although "Aminadab" is mentioned in the novel that bears his name, he never actually appears. Nevertheless, he is conspicuous by his absence, and his absence occurs at a critical moment. After being rebuked by Mlle Barbe for misunderstanding the original gesture—"'What could you have seen at the window?' she said. . . . 'No, you have been the victim of an illusion; you thought someone was calling you, but *no one was there*, and the call came from you [*l'appel venait de vous*]'" (154, my emphasis; 177)[42]—Thomas falls ill, abandons his climb to the top floor, gradually recovers, and then meets another woman. But their relationship does not develop as one might expect. With Lucie he negotiates a rather bizarre contract that is henceforth to govern their relationship: he must speak as little as possible; he must not look at her; and he must not think of her (174–76; 199–202). At this point his former companion Dom returns to serve as a sort of referee or mediator or guide and "to verify that everything is happening according to the rules" (179; 205). Oddly, however, it is now Dom, the body double and go-between, who censures Thomas: "I was placed with you," he says somewhat sternly, "in order to enlighten you whenever you wished. I was like another you [*J'étais comme un autre vous-même*]. I knew all the pathways of the house, and I knew which one you ought to have followed. All you had to do was ask me" (184; 211).[43] Possibly this is language understood as "the house of being"; it will always rest more or less on a stubborn blind spot—in fact, it may be by virtue of this very spot that, as Blanchot seems to think in his review of Bataille's *Inner Experience*, one may see. In this role, Dom helps Thomas to comprehend the limitations of his supposed "success" (184; 211) and to move beyond the simple binary opposition of success and/or failure toward another dimension of experience. As with Mlle Barbe earlier, moreover, Dom laments that Thomas has rejected an ostensibly easier, softer, negative way, what he optimistically calls "a gentle slope requiring neither effort nor consultation" (185; 212).

Celebrating the charms of life lived under the earth, Dom mentions to Thomas the doorway under the house and the sinister figure who guards it: "Aminadab" (186; 213). In Hebrew the name means "my people are generous" or "wandering people." While appearing at several places in the Hebrew Bible, the name occurs most conspicuously in Canticles 6:12: "Or ever I was aware, my soul made me like the chariots of Aminadab." Against the background of a discussion of the difference between inner experience and more traditional mystical union, Kevin Hart offers a possible reading of the passage in theological terms: "In this verse Aminadab . . . has been taken to stand for both Christ and Antichrist, and in the reading that is of the most interest to us, that of Saint John of the Cross, it is plainly the latter."[44] So, as far as the prospect of spiritual union is concerned, "Aminadab does not and can not appear in the mystical marriage. What we see in the final scenes of Blanchot's novel is not a perfect union of spiritual Bride and Bridegroom but inner experience" (70). This would be an experience of nothing, such as that described by Georges Bataille: pure exteriority, a mystical experience of nothing in particular. According to Hart, Blanchot navigates a way between ascent and descent, oneness and multiplicity, identity and difference, domesticity and strangeness, and, at least to some degree, Judeo-Christian and pagan-atheist. What makes his text so compelling is that, rather than simply choosing one or the other, Blanchot situates the two alongside one another as "phased counterparts" (68). Such a reading has much to commend it.

In terms of a context already noted, Thomas's desire to learn the secret of the woman's gesture and the meandering path that that quest takes as it unfolds—approaching both the highest and lowest architectural points of the boardinghouse—seems to repeat and deepen (if such a thing is possible) K.'s quest in The Castle,[45] suggesting a mixture of philosophical and theological motives and, possibly, a more mundane source. That source would be the effort, ongoing since the dawn of modernity, to locate, using a combination of reason and revelation, the origins and ends of the world itself and to secure ourselves somewhere safely in between. In terms of this effort, Thomas's bewildering journey to the top and to the bottom of the boardinghouse corresponds to past endeavors to establish once and for all the metaphysical effects and causes of the world in which we find ourselves. But, somewhat like Pascal in the epigraph chosen for this chapter, Thomas finds himself perpetually unsettled in the in-between; he wants to build a metaphorical tower of words that will enable him to reach the infinite source of poetic inspiration, but instead is led to the realization that all his groundwork will eventually crack and open onto an abyss. In the end, that abyss is signified by none other than a giant—God or monster?—whose absent presence haunts the boarding-house and its inhabitants. Everything that is seems to depend on the absent other, whose name conjures up biblical figures but also gestures, as has recently been suggested by some scholars, toward the memory of a certain no-one in particular: Aminadab, the youngest of Emmanuel Lévinas's two younger brothers, both of whom were murdered by the Nazis.[46]

Where do such thoughts leave one? In his translator's introduction to the novel, Jeff Fort draws out some of the implications of the title and connects them to the more disparate threads of Blanchot's deeply unsettling work:

> Within the parameters of a novelistic fiction, *Aminadab* attempts to approach and to explore this place that is not a place. Like *The Castle*—whose author may well have had similar reflections in his mind—it is a novel of wandering and speech, endless error and passionate commentary. Thomas is an exile with no abode who finds himself, however, in the promised land of speech. In this sense, *Aminadab* remains true to the exigency of exteriority and strangeness that Blanchot attributes to literary space, in which all movement is wandering and where speech bears the weight of the law—not as a legal corpus but as an ontological principle—the impossible but always shimmering mirage of a destiny and a destination. The task of literature . . . is to maintain this passionate movement toward an intimate strangeness opened by language at the heart of the ordinary and familiar and to speak the language that would keep it open. (xvii)

One might add to this that in the end, the novel *Aminadab* seems to suggest that the place of all places can only be accessed, if at all, through the mystery of poetic language. And the way of language is always a nonproductive or negative way, offering the writer and reader only "a place that is not a place," bringing the seeker close, but never quite close enough, to the possibility of union with the other.

NOTES

1. Georges Poulet, "Maurice Blanchot as Novelist," *Yale French Studies,* no. 8 (1951): 77–81, quotation at 77.

2. For Blanchot's view of romanticism, see "The Athenaeum," in Blanchot, *The Infinite Conversation,* trans. Susan Hanson (Minneapolis: University of Minnesota Press, 1993), 351–59; "L'Athenaeum," in *L'entretien infini* (Paris: Gallimard, 1969), 515–27.

3. *Immanuel Kant's Critique of Pure Reason,* trans. Norman Kemp Smith (1929; New York: St. Martin's, 1965), 10.

4. Heidegger, "Letter on Humanism," trans. Frank A. Capuzzi, in *Pathmarks,* ed. William McNeill (Cambridge: Cambridge University Press, 1998), 236; "Brief über den Humanismus," in *Wegmarken (Gesamtausgabe* I, vol. 9), ed. Friedrich-Wilhelm von Herrmann (Frankfurt am Main: Vittorio Klostermann, 1976), 313.

5. Blanchot, "How Is Literature Possible?" in *Faux Pas,* trans. Charlotte Mandell (Stanford: Stanford University Press, 2001), 76–84; "Comment la littérature est-elle possible?" in *Faux pas* (Paris: Gallimard, 1943), 97–107. Hereafter in main text I provide the page number of the English translation of Blanchot, followed by the page number of the French edition, for the respective editions identified in notes.

6. "Nous voilà donc prêts à donner une réponse à la question: comment la littérature est-elle possible? En vérité, par la vertu d'une double illusion—illusion des unsé qui luttent contre les lieux communs et le langage par les moyens mêmes qui engendrent le langage et les lieux communs; illusion des autres qui, en renonçant aux conventions littéraires, ou comme on dit, à la literature, la font renaître, sous une forme (métaphysique, religion, etc.) qui n'est pas la sienne. Or, c'est de cette illusion et de la conscience de cette illusion que Jean Paulhan, par une revolution qu'on peut dire copernicienne, comme celle de Kant, se propose de tirer un régne littéraire plus précis et plus rigoureux."

7. On this point, see Kevin Hart's essay in this volume, "The Neutral Reduction: *Thomas l'obscur.*"

8. Plato, *The Republic,* trans. Tom Griffith (Cambridge: Cambridge University Press, 2000), 329. Robin Waterfield translates it more conventionally as "ancient quarrel." See Plato, *Republic,* trans. Robin Waterfield (Oxford: Oxford University Press, 1994), 361.

9. "Es gibt eine Poesie, deren eins und alles das Verhältnis des Idealen und des Realen ist, und die also nach der Analogie der philosophischen Kuntssprache Transzendentalpoesie heißen müßte. . . . so sollte wohl auch jene Poesie die in modernen Dichtern nicht seltnen transzendentalen Materialien und Vorübungen zu einer poetischen Theorie des Dichtungsvermögens mit der künstlerischen Reflexion und schönen Selbstbespiegelung, die sich im Pindar, den

lyrischen Fragmenten der Griechen, und der alten Elegie, unter den Neuern aber in Goethe findet, vereinigen, und in jeder ihrer Darstellungen sich selbst mit darstellen, und überall zugleich Poesie und Poesie der Poesie sein." Schlegel, from *Athenäum Fragments,* in *Theory as Practice: A Critical Anthology of Early German Romantic Writings,* ed. and trans. Jochen Schulte-Sasse et. al. (Minneapolis: University of Minnesota Press, 1996), 323; *Kritische und theoretische Schriften* (Stuttgart: Philipp Reclam, 1978), 105. Hereafter in quoting Schlegel, I provide the page number in *Theory as Practice* for the English translation, followed by the page number of the respective German edition.

10. The complete translation of the sentence from Schlegel's *Dialogue on Poetry* in the anthology *Theory as Practice* reads as follows: "But this is the first, originary poesy without which there would surely be no poesy of words." An earlier translation, in *Dialogue on Poetry and Literary Aphorisms,* trans. Ernest Behler and Roman Struc (University Park: Pennsylvania State University Press, 1968), 54, reads: "This, however, is the primeval poetry without which there would be no poetry of words." The original reads: "Diese aber ist die erste, ursprüngliche, ohne die es gewiß keine Poesie der Worte geben würde."

11. "Nur mit dem Unterschiede, daß das Romantische nicht sowohl eine Gattung ist als ein Element der Poesie, das mehr oder minder herrschen und zurücktreten, aber nie ganz fehlen darf. Es muß Ihnen nach meiner Ansicht einleuchtend sein, daß und warum ich fodre, alle Poesie solle romantische sein; den Roman aber, insofern er eine besondre Gattung sein will, verabscheue."

12. "Um die Übersicht vom ganzen System der Ironie zu erleichtern, wollen wir einige der vorzüglichsten Arten anführen. Die erste und vornehmste von allen ist die grobe Ironie; findet sich am moisten in der wirklichen Natur der Dinge und ist einer ihrer allgemein verbreitetsten Stoffe; in der Geschichte der Menschheit ist sie recht eigentlich zu Hause. Dann kommt die feine oder die delikate Ironie; dann die extrafeine; in dieser Manier arbiter Skaramuz, wenn er sich freundlich und ernsthaft mit jemand zu besprechen scheint, indem er nur den Augenblick erwartet, wo er wird mit einer guten Art einen Tritt in den Hintern geben können. Diese Sorte wird auch wohl bei Dicthern gefunden, wie ebenfalls die redliche Ironie, welche am reinsten und ursprünglichsten in alten Gärten angebracht ist, wo wunderbar liebliche Grotten den gefühlvollen Freund der Natur in ihrer kühlen Schoß locken, um ihn dann von allen Seiten mit Wasser richly zu besprützen und ihm so die Zartheit zu vertreiben. Ferner die dramatische Ironie, wenn der Dichter drei Akte geschreiben hat, dann wider Vermuten ein andrer Mensch wird, und nun die beiden letzten Akte Schreiber muß. Die doppelte Ironie, wenn zwei Linien von Ironie parallel nebeneinander laufen ohne sich zu stören, eine fürs Parterre, die andre für die Logen, wobei noch kleine Funken in die Coulissen fahren können. Endlich die Ironie der Ironie." German from Schlegel, "Über die Unverständlichkeit," in *Kritische Friedrich-Schlegel-Ausgabe,* ed. Hans Eichner et. al. (Munich: Schöningh, 1967).

13. Philippe Lacoue-Labarthe and Jean-Luc Nancy, *The Literary Absolute: The Theory of Literature in German Romanticism,* trans. Philip Barnard and Cheryl Lester (Albany: State University of New York Press, 1988), 11.

14. "Le petit livre que M. René Lalou a consacré au *Roman français depuis 1900* attire l'attention sur les difficultés qu'il y a à saisir le roman comme genre littéraire et à en discerner les conventions et les lois."

15. "Ce qui ajoute à l'intérêt du livre, c'est qu'il est l'ébauche d'une forme qui oblige le roman à romper avec ses conventions." The interpolation in brackets is mine.

16. "Le roman de M. Raymond Queneau, *Les Temps mêlés,* est trés proper à rendre les questions que posent à la littérature le sort du roman français et même l'existence du roman en général. . . . On s'aperçoit assurément que depuis fort longtemps le roman, en tant qu'oeuvre littéraire, subit une crise don't le sens reste obscur."

17. About this introduction, Christophe Bident comments: "Le texte inaugural, 'De l'angoisse au langage', imprégné de l'expérience et du vocabulaire de Bataille, est inédit. C'est lui qui tente d'assurer la cohérence de l'ensemble, qui profile l'ordonnancement des articles." Bident, *Maurice Blanchot: Partenaire invisible. Essai biographique* (Seyssel: Champ Vallon, 1998), 226.

18. "L'écrivain se trouve dans cette condition de plus en plus comique de n'avoir rien à écrire, de n'avoir aucun moyen de l'écrire et d'être contraint par une nécessité extrême de toujours l'écrire. N'avoir rien à exprimer doit, ce n'est rien. Quoi qu'il veuille dire, ce n'est rien. Le monde, les choses, la savoir ne lui sont que des points de repère à travers le vide."

19. "L'écrivain apparaît parfois étrangement comme si l'angoisse était proper à sa fonction, plus encore comme si le fait d'écrire approfondissait l'angoisse au point de la rattacher à lui-même plutôt qu'à toute autre espèce d'homme."

20. Blanchot, "Mallarmé and the Art of the Novel," in *Faux Pas,* 165–71; "Mallarmé et l'art du roman," in *Faux pas,* 197–204.

21. "Il est curieux qu'aucun romancier n'ait découvert dans les remarques de Mallarmé une définition de l'art du roman et une allusion chargée de gloire à ce qu'il est appelé à faire. Pourtant, il y a, dans cette page, une conception si profonde du langage, une vue tellement étendue de la vocation des mots, une explication si universelle de la littérature que nul genre de création ne peut s'en trouver exclu. L'écrivain qui par une mission inquiétante se voit obligé de construire les rigueur de la fiction avec les facilités de la prose, n'est pas moin divestment interpellé que le poète." In brackets I have introduced a portion of the essay's opening sentence in order to give the passage greater clarity. The sentence in its entirety reads as follows: "Les livres de M. Mondor sur Mallarmé nous ont donné l'occasion de relire laminable lettre où s'exprime l'espoir du poète préparant le *Coup de dés* [sic]."

22. "Mallarmé, plus profondément qu'aucun autre, a conçu le langage non pas comme un système d'expression, intermédiaire utile et commode pour l'espirit qui veut comprendre et se faire comprendre, mais comme une puissance de transformation et de création, faite pour créer des énigmas plutôt que pour les éclaircir. Les conséquences de cette pensée ont obligé Mallarmé à aller trés loin. Le langage est ce qui fonde la réalité humaine et l'universe. L'homme qui se révèle dans un dialogue où il trouve son événement fondimental, le monde qui se met en paroles par un acte qui est sa profonde origine, expriment la nature et la dignité du langage. L'erreur est de croire que le langage soit un instrument dont l'homme dispose pour agir ou pour se manifester dans le monde; le langage, en réalité, dispose de l'homme en ce qu'il lui garantit l'existence du monde et son existence dans le monde."

23. Sartre, "*Aminadab:* Or the Fantastic Considered as a Language," in *Literary and Philosophical Essays*, trans. Annette Michelson (New York: Criterion Books, 1955), 56–72, 57; "'Aminadab' ou du fantastique considéré comme un language," in *Situations* I: *Essais critiques* (Paris: Gallimard, 1947), 122–42, 123.

24. ". . . il se révèle comme fondement des choses et de la réalité humanie." "Is Mallarme's Poetry Obscure?" in *Faux Pas*, 109; "La Poésie de Mallarmé est-elle obscure?" in *Faux pas*, 137.

25. According to Bident, "Paulhan appelle le livre 'un second *Thomas'*" (*Maurice Blanchot*, 204). Confirming this view, Leslie Hill writes, in *Blanchot: Extreme Contemporary* (New York: Routledge, 1997), that "*Aminadab* presents what seems to be the next stage in Thomas's story" (55).

26. Here I am thinking of Sartre's reading. See his "*Aminadab:* Or the Fantastic Considered as a Language," passim.

27. Geoffrey H. Hartman, "The Fulness and Nothingness of Literature," *Yale French Studies*, no. 16: *Foray through Existentialism* (1955): 63–78, 77–78.

28. The opening sentences of Fort's translator's introduction strike just the right chord: "This is a strange book. For readers familiar with Blanchot's narrative works, such a statement goes without saying. Strangeness is the very element in which these works move and unfold; it is their single most constant 'effect' and has the status of a deliberate, if elusive, method" (vii). See Maurice Blanchot, *Aminadab*, trans. Jeff Fort (Lincoln: University of Nebraska Press, 2002), vii–xx.

29. Hartman, "The Fulness and Nothingness of Literature," 78.

30. Here I have relied on Leslie Hill's discussion of the opening pages of *Aminadab*. See Hill, *Blanchot: Extreme Contemporary*, 53–69, esp. 55–58.

31. All English translations of *Aminadab* are from the Fort translation cited above; French is cited from Blanchot, *Aminadab* (Paris: Gallimard, 1942).

32. Blanchot's review, first appearing as "L'Expérience intérieure," *Journal des débats*, 5 May 1943, 3, was subsequently included in *Faux pas*, 51–56; "Inner Experience," in *Faux Pas*, 37–41.

33. "Les paroles de Nietzsche: 'Voici l'heure du Grand Midi, de la clarté la plus redoubtable', il nous arrive de les entendre en nous-mêmes, lorsqu'après avoir ruiné la vérité qui nous abritait nous nous voyons exposés à un soleil qui nous brûle, soleil qui n'est pourtant que le reflet de notre dénuement et de notre froid. . . . L'heure du Grand Midi est celle qui nous apporte la plus forte lumière; l'air entire est échauffé; le jour est devenu feu; pour l'homme avide de voir, c'est le moment où, regardant, il risque de devenir plus aveugle qu'un aveugle, une sorte de voyant qui se souvient du soleil comme d'une tache grise, importune."

34. "La jeune fille, comme si elle se fût rendu compte de cette attente, fit de la main un petit signe qui était comme une invitation et, aussitôt après, elle ferma la fenêtre et la pièce retomba dans l'obscurité.

Thomas fut très perplexe. Pouvait-il considérer ce geste comme un appel véritable? C'était un signe d'amité plutôt qu'une invitation. C'était aussi une sorte de congédiement. Il resta hésitant. En regardant de côté de la boutique, il constata que l'homme, chargé de balayer, était rentré lui aussi. Cela lui rappela son premier projet. Mais il pensa qu'il aurait toujours le temps de l'exécuter plus tard, et il se décida à franchir la rue pour entrer dans la maison."

35. "— Vous vous conduisez comme un enfant, dit-elle; vous donnez trop de sens à certains mots et d'autres, vous les négligez, on ne sait pourquoi. C'est déjà ce qui m'avait frappée, lorsque je vous ai vu pour la première fois, et c'est ce qui a dû me faire ajourner mes remarques. Quelle signification n'allez-vous pas leur prêter! que d'histoires autour de quelques mots! En revanche, on a beau, dans d'autres cas, mettre les points sur les i, vous vous refusez à être attentif."

36. "Ce que je vous avais demandé, et cette demande avait son prix mais vous n'avez pas voulu vous en apercevoir, c'était de m'attendre sans vous agiter vainement, sans chercher par vous-même ce que vous ne pouviez atteindre. Était-ce si difficile? Vous n'aviez qu'à rester dans votre coin. Mais cela a probablement dépassé vos forces. Impatient comme vous l'êtes, vous avez préféré me suivre dans les chambres au risque de vous laisser absorber par ce que vous voyiez, et vous m'avez laissé partir en poursuivant votre chemin à votre guise."

37. Sartre's discussion of the "topsy-turvy" (60) world of the novel is instructive. He summarizes what for him is the novel's governing trope thusly: "The fantastic is the revolt of means against ends" (61). See "*Aminadab:* Or the Fantastic Considered as a Language," esp. 56–66.

38. Fort, translator's introduction, in *Aminadab,* x.

39. See Georges Bataille, *Inner Experience,* trans. Leslie Anne Boldt (Albany: State University Press of New York, 1988); *L'expérience intérieure* (Paris: Gallimard, 1943).

40. "— Je ne distingue pas toujours très clairement, dit-il, si vos remarkes sont destinées à m'apprendre le sort qui m'attend ou à m'aider à m'en détourner. Il ajouta à voix basse: puis-je vous demander de parler moin vite? Il ne m'est pas toujours facile de vous suivre."

41. For a discussion of these issues, see Michael Holland, "Qui est l'Aminadab de Blanchot?" *Revue des sciences humaines* 253 (January–March 1999): 21–42].

42. "— Qu'auriez-vous donc vu à la fenêtre? disait-elle. . . . Non, vous avez été victime d'un illusion; vous avez cru qu'on vous appelait mais personne n'était là et l'appel venait de vous."

43. "J'avais été placé auprès de vous pour vous éclairer, chaque fois que vous en auriez désir. J'étais comme un autre vous-même. Je connaissais tous les itinéraires de la maison et je savais quel était celui que vous deviez suivre. Il suffisait que vous m'interrogiez."

44. Kevin Hart, *The Dark Gaze: Maurice Blanchot and the Sacred* (Chicago: University of Chicago Press, 2004), 69.

45. For a discussion of Kafka's influence on Blanchot that addresses Sartre's reading of *Aminadab,* see Paul Davies, "Kafka's Lesson, Blanchot's Itinerary," *Parallax* 12, no. 2 (2006): 23–39.

46. See Leslie Hill's discussion, in *Blanchot: Extreme Contemporary,* 10–11.

FOUR

A Law without Flesh

Reading Erotic Phenomena in *Le Très-Haut*

Stephen E. Lewis

Maurice Blanchot's 1948 novel *Le Très-Haut* is abundantly engaged with a variety of philosophical themes and issues, making it in some respects the work of fiction in Blanchot's oeuvre most frequently read from a philosophical viewpoint. The novel's engagement with philosophy occurs within several frames of reference: within the frame of the fiction itself (sometimes in a comic mode),[1] in the novel's relationship with philosophical works outside of it, and in a frame formed by the novel's post-publication impact, where Blanchot's use of aspects of *Le Très-Haut*, especially its title, in later writings—particularly those devoted to the thought of Emmanuel Lévinas—raises a range of retrospective interpretive questions about the novel.

Many fruitful readings of the novel have focused on political or politico-philosophical ideas articulated by certain characters and the position of these ideas in relation to the thought of Hegel, as interpreted by Alexandre Kojève, and of Heidegger.[2] Building on these insights, several commentators have been able to shed light on the novel's political and legal aspects, including the relations the novel explores between writing, the law, and history.[3]

This primary focus on the philosophical dimensions of the narrator Henri Sorge's relationship to the State and to the novel's rebel figure, Pierre Bouxx, nevertheless leaves out of account a good deal of detail in the novel. Christophe Bident was the first to address this critical lacuna in his remarkable reading of the novel, contained in the third part of his 1998 biography of Blanchot, *Maurice Blanchot: Partenaire invisible* (to which I shall return).[4] Bident's work opened up the aspects of the novel that are seemingly nonpolitical and decidedly more strange, because less easily theorized, namely, Sorge's relations with his family, especially his quasi-incestuous relationship with his sister; his encounters with the two principal female characters in the novel, his neighbor, Marie Scadran, and his nurse, Jeanne Galgat; and the complex of hallucinatory details—the spreading black stain, the surging and receding black waters, the thick, heavy, sticky substances that suddenly adhere to Sorge's skin, weighing him down and stealing away his breath—that appear throughout the novel and that act increasingly with motivation and, one is tempted to say, with consciousness within the narrator's perceptions during the last third of the novel.

Convincing attempts to interpret the novel as a whole, accounting for the political and legal detail *and* what we might call the novel's surfeit of "erotic phenomena" (more on this choice of terminology in a moment), have gradually emerged; one particularly suggestive attempt was made by Leslie Hill in his 2001 book, *Bataille, Klossowski, Blanchot: Writing at the Limit*. There, Hill argues that Sorge's interactions with Marie and with Jeanne, respectively, introduce a doubleness within the law that operates within the novel's world; more precisely, these encounters introduce a tension between, on the one hand, the law of the State, which is associated with the dialectical recuperation of crime and rebellion as contestations of the law that confirm its perfection, and, on the other hand, the law of the other, associated with desire and sexual difference.[5]

Hill's argument that the novel is structured by a tension caused by the law's doubleness is promising, not only because it allows for a single approach to both primary aspects of the novel—political and erotic—but also because it participates in another of the novel's philosophical dimensions: the role Blanchot has given the novel in his subsequent thinking about the relation with the other, through the many instances, in both

L'entretien infini and *L'écriture du désastre,* where he has referred to the novel's title and, in some instances, specific details of its plot. Hill does not explore as one of his explicit themes the relevance Blanchot has given the novel as a context for his later work, but when he describes Sorge's physical embrace of his neighbor Marie Scadran as illustrative of the "possibility or, better, impossibility of relation with that which admits of no relation," we see Hill implicitly reading the novel in light of later Blanchot texts, for instance, "Le rapport du troisième genre (homme sans horizon)" from *L'entretien infini.*[6]

It is worth noting, however, that these later writings of Blanchot's rarely have much to say about love or eros—in particular, Blanchot's writing about eros in subsequent books never approaches the violent strangeness that characterizes the erotic in *Le Très-Haut.* The sheer quantity and the strange quality of intercorporal phenomena found in the novel clearly exceed the accounts of intersubjective relations that Blanchot subsequently develops in his ethical writings.[7] Sorge's narrative, with its combination of philosophical reflection, sudden outbursts of affect, and wild "phantasmagoria" (*MH,* 44; *TH,* 49), is simply too messy to be easily matched to philosophical or ethical schema, even those that are elusive and that forestall closure. Regarding the novel, Christophe Bident writes, "Every effort at reasoned commentary, universal or particular, singular or totalizing, finds itself immediately limited if it does not begin by pointing out what gives the story its *force:* its permanent capacity to open new spaces of perception and of dialogue, the rapidity with which the narration invents new lights, new floors, new steps, new objects, new debates, with an infinitely meticulous and time-conscious attention."[8] Sorge himself states that his work as narrator consists largely in the attempt to "slow down this flow of reflections passing through me with incredible speed. Everything's going too fast, it's running, it's as if I always had to walk faster, and not only me but also other people, things, dust; everything is so clear; these are the reflections that never get confused, the thousands of infinitely small and distinct shocks" (*MH,* 77; *TH,* 78).[9] Positions that seem philosophically coherent one moment are quickly undercut or questioned by Sorge himself soon after he articulates them; as a result, the tone of the novel and Sorge's ultimate position on various issues can be difficult to determine. Thus it strikes me that, before an argument like

Hill's—that is, one that is comprehensive—can become fully convincing, we need to make sense of more of the strange erotic phenomena in the novel.

Blanchot himself seems to agree about the importance of the novel's erotic detail. In the text he wrote for the back cover of the 1988 reissue of *Le Très-Haut*, Blanchot even seems to suggest that the reader must first attend to matters of desire and love in the novel if he or she is ultimately to understand the novel's political and legal resonances. Roughly three-fourths of Blanchot's back-cover page of text—which is spoken by Blanchot in the guise of the novel's narrator, Henri Sorge—interprets the novel as a story that dramatizes the paradoxical self-contesting movements of a "négativité sans emploi" [unemployed negativity] within the context of a political regime that, through its achievement of Absolute Knowledge, has brought History, characterized up until then by dialectical struggle, to its static endpoint.[10] But then, in a final paragraph, Blanchot instructs the reader to "forget all of that" and proceeds to speak of what the novel puts forward as an even more ruinous event than the appearance of the self-negating "Most High": the entry into the story of a transgressive, abject "love." The back cover of the novel reads,

> Here rules "Absolute Knowledge." Each man is satisfied. There is nothing left to do. The unsurpassable is reality.
>
> A citizen of the universal and homogeneous State, I am in this sense just anybody, the other and the same, subject to the supreme law that I embody, invisible and faceless, uncontestable because everything that contests me confirms me.
>
> But now someone—a woman, of course—singles me out from what I am and recognizes in this dissolving self the Most High.
>
> The Most High can only be his own negation. In a perfect society, where the plague is declared, such that the plague victims become the only rebels, where AIDS places the supreme law in peril, the Most High, beyond all divinity, is no longer but a sick man who dies without dying, unless he were to become the "Thing" itself, the terrifying nothing, the truth that always fools and fools itself, the final word that only immortal death allows, at last, to be heard.
>
> But reader, forget all of that, for it is just as well Antigone, the pure virgin, joining together with her dead brother, so that the incest taboo,

having now been suspended, might ruin not only the ideal law but the natural law, too. Abjection is love, just as absolute freedom is absolute servitude.[11]

The final two sentences signal, with an imprecision that points up the difficulty of conceptualization, the necessity to resort to myth to assign even the beginnings of a meaning to the novel's ungainly details of bodies of "separation" (*MH*, 39; *TH*, 44), spreading stains, and surging liquid filth: "Oubliez tout cela, car c'est aussi bien Antigone." The wording of this abrupt shift is puzzling: What, exactly, is *it* ("c'est")—the riddle of Sorge's designation as the Most High? The reasoning that explains the relation among a "Most High, beyond all divinity," the law, and death? The novel itself?—and how, precisely, is "*it* . . . just as well Antigone" (my emphasis)? The answers are left unclear, purposely, it would seem: the novel's excess cannot be adequately "dealt with" through what has come to be a customary explanation of the paradoxes of "unemployed negativity"; instead, a forgetting of "all of that," of the philosophical discourse, is necessary, a forgetting that, perhaps, will be brought about by the ruinous effects of what Blanchot implies will be a readerly fascination with the abject love that Sorge's sister, Louise, bears for Sorge.

But Blanchot's decision to name as *love* what we see in the relation between Louise and Henri Sorge seems, at least at first glance, rather tendentious. Sorge bears on his forehead a scar from a brick that Louise threw at him when they were young, and now, as an adult, she continues to display toward him considerable hostility (*MH*, 68, 87; *TH*, 70, 87); also, Sorge is frequently troubled by and critical of her filthy appearance (*MH*, 14–15, 87, 121; *TH*, 22, 87, 119) and is always conflicted about being in her company (e.g., *MH*, 13, 117–19; *TH*, 21, 116–17). Sorge expresses the alternating movement of love and hate that characterizes their relationship when he tells Bouxx, "I'm very attached to [Louise]: she's a terrible girl, she does exactly as she pleases, she's passionate, headstrong. . . . [S]he despises me; she's nasty and hateful" (*MH*, 86; *TH*, 87).[12] Sorge's relations with other figures in the novel have been characterized by students of the novel in terms of "care," following from the German and Heideggerian meaning of Sorge's last name.[13] But for every expression of "care" he shows for the beings around him, one could point to other moments of excessive anger and violent nastiness—Sorge's face is decidedly not only or solely (in Bident's words) a "visage de souci" [face of care].[14] The incident where Sorge refers to the waitress as a "scullery slave" ["torchon de cuisine," literally, "dish-rag"], and shoves her violently when she attempts to prevent him from leaving without paying (MH, 31; TH, 37), is a telling counterpoint to the opening scene of the novel, and even invites one to examine it more closely. In that opening scene, Sorge accidentally bumps into a man while going down into the metro, and is then verbally and physically assaulted by him as Sorge shouts defiances. Sorge tells us that afterward, at the police station, he confronted his "snickering" assailant and said, "Now you're sorry, because you know that I'm a man like you." Sorge continues: "I got right in front of him. 'If I'm not like you, then why don't you crush me under your heel?'" (MH, 1; TH, 9, 10).[15] This is perhaps the best example in the novel of Sorge's incapacity to behave impassively, because here he reproaches, as if with a weapon, his assailant with a dignity of self, and from a height that, according to later ethical writings of Lévinas and of Blanchot himself, ought instead to be self-evident, issuing forth as a commandment from the Other's passive face.[16] Sorge cannot help saying too much, and with too much feeling (as Bouxx points out to him [MH, 40; TH, 45]), to those with whom he interacts.[17]

Before using Blanchot's suggested term "love" to approach the novel, it might be better to begin by characterizing Sorge's inability to approach others with calm neutrality as evidence of his "erotic disposition," a characterization I draw from philosopher Jean-Luc Marion's phenomenology of love in The Erotic Phenomenon (2003). The erotic disposition is the fundamental disposition of a human life, writes Marion, preceding and encompassing any approach to reality in terms of subject-object relations or being:

> Man, as ego cogito, thinks, but he does not love, at least from the outset. Yet the most incontestable evidence—that which includes all other evidence, governs our time and our life from beginning to end and penetrates us in every intervening instant—attests that, on the contrary, we are, insofar as we come to know ourselves, always already caught within the tonality of an erotic disposition—love or hate, unhappiness or happiness, enjoyment or suffering, hope or despair,

solitude or communion—and that we can never, without lying to our-selves, claim to arrive at a fundamental erotic neutrality.[18]

We might wonder whether Marion's description here truly fits Sorge, who claims often, throughout the novel, that he occupies a subject position of total knowledge regarding the objects in the world around him—even in the final pages, between episodes of finding himself horrifically swallowed up by the detritus around him, we find Sorge saying, "I remembered that nothing could happen and I remembered that I knew it. I knew it. This thought was extraordinarily comforting, in one fell swoop it restored everything" (MH, 242; TH, 231). Yet such moments are like islands amid howling storms of erotic affect. Indeed, it is Sorge's tendency to shuttle back and forth between erotic and epistemological or ontic (to use Marion's terms) viewpoints on his world that makes it interesting to read certain key scenes of the novel in relation to Marion's phenomenology of love. In other words, by investigating the variety of intersubjective phenomena in the novel in terms of their "erotic" content, in Marion's sense, I aim toward an understanding of what Blanchot, at least in this novel, thinks of love, without prematurely narrowing our sense of what counts in the novel as a manifestation of love. What I ultimately see going on in the novel is the presentation of a world in which human erotic interaction not only lacks but is hostile to what Marion calls "flesh," the auto-affective faculty that each human being receives from another flesh in love.

Before we proceed, an obvious question of method appears: in reading the fiction of Maurice Blanchot, why resort to Marion on the erotic, rather than Emmanuel Lévinas, whose relationship with Blanchot's work is clearer? My answer, quite simply, is that Marion's work strikes me as more readily useful as a point of reference when approaching the issue of love in Le Très-Haut, especially if one's aim, as here, is to consider as much of the novel's erotic detail as possible. Neither Blanchot's nor Marion's approach to love fits into or is encompassed by the other, and my goal is in no way to force some sort of fit; rather, the decision to bring about the encounter of the two approaches is guided by the fact that there are resemblances, at least at first view, between the kinds of phenomena they each describe. It is also the case, of course, that Marion draws deeply from Lévinas's thought. Marion in The Erotic Phenomenon has developed and, in a number of cases, transformed several key features of the fourth section of Lévinas's *Totality and Infinity*. A reader of *The Erotic Phenomenon* will immediately see Marion engaging with Lévinas's descriptions of the caress, of the tender, and of fecundity; however, Marion develops these figures to a much greater extent than does Lévinas, at least in *Totality and Infinity*, and in many cases he departs from Lévinas's interpretations of these phenomena.[19] Ultimately, an investigation more complete than the one I provide here, of *Le Très-Haut* in light of the philosophy of love carried on from Lévinas through Marion, would take into account what Blanchot might have known of Lévinas's writing and lecturing in the period 1946–47 (beyond the material contained in *De l'existence à l'existant*). We know that during these two years Lévinas produced material that eventually found its way into the fourth section of *Totality and Infinity*.[20] The tone intended by Blanchot for many parts of *Le Très-Haut*—in particular, the extent to which the novel ought to be read as satire—could be better surmised, for instance, if we were able to determine whether Blanchot had an inkling during the composition of the novel that Lévinas would one day write the following sentence: "Alongside of the night as anonymous rustling of the *there is* [*il y a*] extends the night of the erotic, behind the night of insomnia the night of the hidden, the clandestine, the mysterious, the land of the virgin, simultaneously uncovered by *Eros* and refusing *Eros*."[21] My hope is that this essay will serve as a starting point toward a full understanding of Blanchot's engagement with this particular philosophical understanding of the phenomenon of love.

JEAN-LUC MARION ON THE LOVER'S ADVANCE AND THE PHENOMENON OF THE FLESH

Jean-Luc Marion's account of love focuses upon the movement of the "I" from an encounter with reality framed by epistemological and ontic concerns, respectively, to an encounter framed by what Marion terms "the erotic reduction." The account is subtle and detailed; for the purposes of our discussion of love in Blanchot's novel, we will focus primarily on what Marion calls the "giving of flesh" between lovers.

In order to grasp Marion's discussion of the flesh, a brief summary of the dynamics that lead the "I" or *ego*—in the sense of Descartes's *ego*, rather than Freud's—into the erotic reduction is necessary. The entry into the erotic reduction begins when the *ego* discovers that the certainty regarding its own existence, which it gained by dint of certifying the clarity and distinctness of objects of knowledge, is not terribly satisfying. The specter of vanity, which points its finger at such a poor certainty—namely, the *ego*'s disappointing discovery that it is certain of itself only as an object of thought, nothing more—causes the *ego* to ask "What's the use?" This unsettling question nudges the *ego* into the erotic reduction where, its self-assurance now sapped by vanity, the *ego* looks outside itself—"elsewhere"—for assurance, attempting to *make* itself *be* loved, and thereby answer the charge of vanity, first by trying to love itself, and then by trying to make an other outside of itself love it. The result of this attempt to make love happen, to "be loved," is a disaster: the *ego* discovers that this use of the will to make itself be loved leads only to self-hatred and the hatred of all for all.[22] The problem here, as Marion goes on to show in the book's third meditation, is the willful "demand to make ourselves loved." This demand assumes as proper to love—as the guarantee of a just or "happy love" (*EP*, 69, *PE*, 115)—a reciprocal exchange: before I will love you, I need first to be assured that you will love me. But reciprocal exchange requires objects, and it is precisely the construal of oneself and others in terms of objective certainty and certified objects that the *ego* left behind when it left the epistemological and the ontic reductions, respectively, for the field of the erotic reduction (*EP*, 69–70; *PE*, 115). The way forward past this impasse involves a reorientation of the will, away from reciprocity and into a free decision to love first. This decisive movement to love first, without any consideration of reciprocity, which is to say, without any prepayment or guarantee, is termed by Marion the lover's "advance."

The lover's advance is central to our concern with the role of "the flesh" in Marion's account, because it is in and through flesh, that of the lover and of the beloved alike, that the advance advances. Eroticized flesh is both the "medium" and the "gift," so to speak, of the advance. We begin, then, with the most significant feature of the lover's advance: its progressive movement forward attests to the lover's *capacity* (in the sense of a roominess rather than an ability) for the infinite. Of the lover's advance toward the beloved other, Marion writes:

> the [erotic] reduction starts off in an advance that is definitive and without return, an advance that will never cancel itself out, and never catch up with itself; I start off out of balance and I only avoid the fall by lengthening my stride, by going faster, in other words by adding to my lack of balance. The more I do to avoid falling, the more I advance without any hope of return. For even if I reach the other, this does not give me possession, precisely because I only touch her and open an access to her by the impact that I provoke, and therefore according to the measure of the impetus that I take and that I must maintain; the other does not stop me like a wall or an inert and delimited lump, but offers herself to me like a path that opens, always continuing in proportion to my entry forward; the advance thus requires a permanent fresh start, wherein I remain in the race and alive only by repeating my imbalance; each accomplishment asks for and becomes a new beginning. In conformity to the definition of the phenomenological reduction in general, the erotic reduction (radicalized under the form 'Can I be the first to love?') is only definitively accomplished in never ceasing to repeat itself. (EP, 83–84; PE, 135–36)

The infinity of the lover's advance[23] is met by a likewise infinite opening of the other. Marion writes that in the "definitive advance"—the "radicalized" erotic reduction, as opposed to the "provisional" advance known as seduction—the other reveals himself or herself as unique because infinite, with an infinity that never ceases to open out before the lover for as long as the lover remains within the erotic reduction: "the other only becomes unique for me on the condition that she is confirmed to be infinite—that she is able, by herself, not only to support, but to provoke an ever repeatable start of the initial advance, of my initiative to love first" (EP, 84; PE, 136). And of course, when two lovers meet in love, each engages in both the active advance and the passive or receptive opening, simultaneously and constantly, for as long as they can continue.

This brings us, finally, to Marion's account of the flesh and its difference from the body; an understanding of this distinction will offer us a valuable point of reference in our reading of the desires of the characters and the interactions of their bodies in the (for lack of a better word) "love scenes" in Blanchot's *Le Très-Haut*.

Marion describes the phenomenon of the flesh as a sort of passivity that is unlike the passivity found in relations between bodies in the world, where passivity is defined by inertness or nonreactivity. The lover's advance originates in a decision of the will, but results in the lover's total exposure to the possibility of being loved or not loved by another: thus there is a passivity bound up with this act of the will, the passivity that characterizes the phenomenon of the flesh (*EP*, 112; *PE*, 178). Flesh is characterized by auto-affection, and as such it constitutes human individuality, the radical difference between a living human body and every other body, human or not, in the world. My own flesh, and thus my own individuality, is a gift given to me by another. Marion writes,

> [T]he flesh, or rather *my* flesh—I do not have flesh, I am my flesh and it coincides absolutely with me—assigns me to myself and delivers me as such in my radically received individuality. . . . As flesh, I take on a body in the world; I become sufficiently exposed so that the things of the world have an advantage over me, such that they make me feel, experience, and even suffer their dominance and their presence. Not that I take a place among the things of the world, taking my position there as just one more thing, wedged in among others and simply part of the crowd; I do not insert myself among the army of things, I expose myself, since I face them; I do not become so much a thing of the world as I allow the things of the world the right to affect me and to reduce me to my passivity. But which passivity? Certainly not that of things. . . . In fact, the things of the world quite simply do not affect me such as they are, nor do they make me feel anything about them in themselves—for the simple and radical reason that they do not feel themselves or experience anything as their action. . . . [M]y body, which it is quite necessary to call physical because it is nakedly exposed to the things of nature, enjoys above all the exceptional privilege of feeling them, while they never feel anything at all, especially themselves. (*EP*, 112–13; *PE*, 178–79, 180)

In the phenomenon of love, the uniqueness of this flesh that takes on a body in the world meets another unique flesh, "wherein the other feels, because he feels himself there" (*EP,* 115; *PE,* 182). I know, writes Marion, that I am encountering another flesh when what I feel "behave[s] the opposite of physical bodies, which is to say, like my own flesh behaves as opposed to them—by not resisting, by withdrawing, by allowing itself to be stripped of its impenetrability, by suffering being penetrated. There where I feel that something *puts up no resistance to me,* and that, far from turning me back into myself and thus reducing me, this something withdraws, effaces itself and makes room for me, in short that this something opens itself, I know that I am dealing with flesh—or better, with a flesh other than my own, the flesh of another" (*EP,* 118; *PE,* 186–87). In love, the lover and the beloved receive from one another their own flesh, because each flesh makes room, a "place," for the flesh of the other "within itself," and it is in this given, expansive place that the individuality of each grows and is invisibly revealed (*EP,* 118; *PE,* 187). "By entering into the flesh of the other, I exit the world and I become flesh in her flesh, flesh *of* her flesh" (*EP,* 119; *PE,* 188). In other words, "My very own flesh (it makes me become myself, which I was unaware of before then) comes upon me and augments in the measure in which the flesh of the other provokes it. Each discovers him- or herself the depository of what is most intimate of the other" (*EP,* 120–21; *PE,* 191).

The experience of the vanity of life lived under the poor assurances of subject-object relations or of being; the failure to love oneself from elsewhere; the advance; the phenomenon of the flesh and its giving and receiving: these are the features of Marion's account of the erotic phenomenon that will accompany us as we investigate the love scenes in *Le Très-Haut.*

GIVING BODY TO SEPARATION

The first series of erotic phenomena to discuss in the novel occurs within the context of Sorge's relationship with his neighbor, the photograph shop employee Marie Scadran (though Sorge does not actually learn her name until late in their relationship). The day after he apparently meets her for the first time, Sorge makes several attempts to tell his neighbor something "very important" (*MH,* 22; *TH,* 28); then, finally having done so, he offers to take her out to lunch. In the restaurant, as he looks at his neighbor, he is suddenly struck by two different thoughts in quick succession, each regarding the possible meaning for him of this woman seated in front of him. This lengthy quotation captures effectively the two turns in Sorge's thought that I wish to address:

> When I saw her sitting at my side, ready to eat the same things as me, to gesture in the same way, to look at the same people, I was amazed. It was more than surprise. I had always sensed what was going on there; I knew that we all lived together, that each of us reflects the others in himself; but with her this existence in common became a vertiginous and frenzied certainty. First I had proof of it, I could talk to her. What I said thus conformed perfectly with public opinion, with the wisdom of the newspapers that sometimes passed before my gaze like stories from another time. *But then a very different idea grabbed hold of me.* The law was always in movement, it passed ceaselessly from one person to another, it was present everywhere, with its even, transparent, and absolute light, illuminating everyone and everything in an always different and yet identical way. Ordinarily everything made me aware of it and, sensing it, sometimes I got carried away, felt drunk, and sometimes I asked myself if I weren't already dead. But at present, in other words right now, when I looked at her hand—a fairly pretty hand, with well-done nails, big and strong like the rest of her—when I looked at it I couldn't imagine that it was like mine, and I didn't believe it was unique, either. *What bothered me* [*Ce qui me troublait*] was that by taking hold of it, by touching it in a certain way, yes, if I managed to touch this flesh, this skin, this moist swelling, along with it I would touch the law, which was there, it was obvious, and which, perhaps, would linger there for a moment in a mysterious way, held back for me from the world. (*MH,* 28–29, emphasis added; *TH,* 34–35)[24]

According to Leslie Hill, Sorge, as he contemplates the possible meaning of touching his neighbor's hand, imagines an encounter with a figure of the law that is quite different from the dialectical law of the State. Here, says Hill, Sorge thinks that by touching Marie's hand he might encounter what Hill calls the "law of the other."[25] Hill writes, "rather than referring Sorge yet again to the infinite circularity of the dialectical law of the State, [the strange inaccessibility of his guest's hand] has the opposite effect of opening up a modest corner of experience that has the potential to place the rest of the world within parentheses" (202).[26] The idea that the touching of flesh takes one to a place in a space that is not exactly a space, that is to say, to a place outside the world of objects, is resonant with Marion's description of the erotic encounter between two flesh, as we have seen. But is this in fact what Sorge is imagining here?

Attention to the context of Sorge's thoughts suggests that Sorge is not so much imagining the possible discovery of a new or different law as he is fantasizing that he could move beyond his self-described "sterile" (MH, 24; TH, 30), intellectual appreciation of the law (or what he calls a few pages later a "contemplation," as opposed to a "grasp," of the law [MH, 31; TH, 37]), to an intimate, fleshly experience of it—of that same law, not another. In other words, what suddenly occurs to Sorge as he looks at the hand of Marie and shifts from his first idea, characterized by the intellectual contemplation of the law, to the "very different idea" that "grab[s] hold" of him, is the possibility of realizing what he had tried to tell her earlier, before they went to lunch. At that earlier moment in the day, Sorge expressed to Marie his desire that she become for him a "flesh and blood" (MH, 27; TH, 33) human presence that could alleviate his fear of being alone and confirm for him the truth of the "kind of revelation" (MH, 23; TH, 29) about himself that he had recently gained during his illness— namely, his status as the supreme subject of the State, whose every individual act or thought is in fact an act or thought that belongs to or *is* that of the whole of society, such that his very existence as an individual is put into question.[27] Sorge desires that his barely individual existence within the realm of the law could somehow come alive for him in a more satisfying way (he describes his current experience of "common" life as "not enough"), through the individuating effect of another person's response to his words. This is the "very important" thing Sorge eventually tells Marie:

At night, sometimes I feel really alone. I wake up and remember everything: my family, my friends at the office, some face I've seen. I recognize my room, beyond it there's the street, other houses, everything is in its place, everywhere someone is with me, and still it's not enough. At that moment I would like a person in flesh and blood to be at my side or in the other room, and to answer if I talk—yes, that's it, I'd like to know that I've also spoken for her. But if there's no answer, if I raise my voice and realize that I'm speaking all alone, I suddenly almost start trembling—it's worse than anything. It's an insult, a real offense. I feel as if I've committed a crime, I've lived outside the common good. And besides, am I alive? Life is elsewhere, amid these thousands of people packed together, who live like that, who get along, who have attained law and liberty. (*MH,* 27; *TH,* 33)[28]

Sorge's dissatisfaction with the law's assurances as he experiences them bears a certain resemblance to the *ego*'s dissatisfaction under the impact of the experience of vanity within what Marion calls the epistemological reduction: Sorge himself feels at certain moments that "life is elsewhere." And yet, Sorge's situation differs in at least two important ways from the scenario sketched by Marion. In response to the experience of vanity, says Marion, the *ego* can make the decision to turn "elsewhere" for assurance, to something outside of the authority of its own ability to certify objects; this turn is expressed by the question, "Does anyone out there love me?" Assurance from elsewhere is of a different sort from the (poor) assurance gained through objective certification (*EP,* 23; *PE,* 43). Sorge, by contrast, wishes to have the touch of "someone out there," namely Marie, confirm in him the *same* objective assurance he has gained through his intellectual "révélation" (*MH,* 23; *TH,* 29)—a revelation of the law. Sorge desires to find assurance from the same law in two different places: within himself and in another outside of himself. This is the first significant difference between Sorge's situation and that of the *ego* entering the erotic reduction, described in *The Erotic Phenomenon.*

The second difference has to do with Sorge's manifest feelings of guilt over his very desire for further assurance. As Sorge recounts his meditation upon touching Marie's hand, he uses the French verb *troubler* to describe his feeling—he was bothered, in the sense of troubled or stirred, at the prospect: "What bothered me was that by taking hold of [her hand], by touching it in a certain way, . . . along with it I would touch the law." Sorge's "trouble" here, when read in light of his previous conversations with Marie, signals his sense of guilt at admitting his need for flesh and blood assurance. As we just saw, "I feel as if I've committed a crime" [*C'est . . . une véritable faute*] (*MH*, 27; *TH*, 33). To wish that the law would "care" for him, so to speak, by mysteriously taking flesh and abiding with him "for a moment," thus individuating him no longer as just "anybody" (repeated frequently throughout the novel, beginning with the first line and extending almost to the very end of the novel [*MH*, 233; *TH*, 223]), but as himself, in person, is not just an impossible dream—it is also "an insult" to the law. Marion describes the *ego*'s entry into the erotic reduction under the impact of vanity as potentially painful due to the experience of groundlessness, uncertainty, and risk that it entails; however, there is no guilt involved in asking for assurance from "elsewhere." Thus far, then, two points of difference stand out in our comparison: (1) Sorge wants to be individuated by touching flesh, but, contrary to what Marion's account would require, Sorge assumes that the assurance provided by touching flesh will come from the same source as epistemic assurance— namely, the law; and (2) Sorge feels guilt—unmerited, Marion would seem to want to say—at this need for a second, fleshly mode of assurance, additional to what the law has thus far provided him.

Sorge's guilt explains the rapid shifts he exhibits between, on the one hand, tight-lipped satisfaction with existence under the law (e.g., his statement to Bouxx, repeated twice: "I see everyone willingly, I have no preferences, particular relationships seem useless to me" [*MH* 7, 40]), and, on the other, the fact that he can't keep himself away from this "particular relationship" with his neighbor, whose name at this point he still has not sought to learn. After the lunch, Sorge returns to his office and has trouble working. He leaves work again and gives evidence of more dissatisfaction regarding his relationship to the law, undergoing violent, nausea-inducing mental shifts between conviction and doubt regarding the power, ubiquity, and fittingness of the law, shifts which directly influence his movements toward, away from, and then again toward Marie (see *MH*, 34–35; *TH*, 39–40). He eventually returns to her shop and asks to know her name (*MH*, 36), only to take the first opportunity that presents itself to intoxicate himself once more in an experience of indifferentiation by running his hands through a drawer filled with monotonously similar identification photos—"They were the same, but the same in an infinite number. I stuck my fingers in, I pawed them, I got drunk on them" (*MH,* 37; *TH,* 43).[29] Finally, unable to resist any longer, Sorge finds himself again looking at Marie's hand, and attempts to touch and to be touched by the law:

> She got up, then I did too; I grasped her hands. I held her, roughly. She was rigid with a rigidity that called for a hammer. Suddenly the cloth of her dress came to life [*prit corps*] under my fingers. It was strange—an irritating smooth surface, a kind of black skin [*une sorte de chair noire*] that slid, adhered and didn't adhere, billowed up. It was then that she was transformed—I swear, she became different. And I myself became someone else. Her breathing grew deeper. There was a change in every part of her body. It sounds strange, but up to this point we had had the same body, a true common body, impalpable and light. With a shattering suddenness this body broke in two, dissolved, and in its place a burning layer formed, a moist and strange greed that was blind, urgent. Yes, I swear it: I had become a stranger, and the more I held her the more I felt her become a stranger, determined to show me someone and something different. No one will believe me, but, at that moment, we became separated, we felt and breathed the separation, we gave it a body. That was obvious; finally we were no longer touching. (*MH,* 39; *TH,* 44)[30]

Sorge's paradoxical desire was for an experience of individuation assured by the law acting through another's flesh; here he discovers that, even at an intimate level, this law does not recognize the individual except as a moment in the law's own self-assertion. Looking closely at the description, we see that a certain individuation does occur here, but the assurance it produces is quite different from that imagined by Sorge when he fantasized about a flesh-and-blood person listening to his cries in the night. By touching each other, Sorge and Marie each gain difference from a heretofore "common body" that they had been sharing. But this new body is paradoxical, in more ways than one. To begin with, it is described as singular, "a burning layer . . . , a moist and strange greed that was blind, urgent," formed as the "common body" breaks in two and "dissolves." At first glance, then, its singularity would seem to indicate that one shared body has simply been replaced by another (I interpret the "burning layer" and the "body" of "separation" as the same thing). Yet this new body is termed a body of "separation," implying that it cannot be shared, in the sense of mutually inhabited, except as a space of common absence. But then a further twist appears, again suggesting a common participation in this new body: Sorge and Marie each feel and breathe the separation, and thus produce it, somehow, as body. The relation produced by the embrace thus seems equivocal, because paradoxical. As such, it seems to figure the movement of the law on an intimate level. Like the State that allows crime to take place so that the law can then make its power evident (expertly described at several different points in the novel by Sorge, e.g., *MH*, 28,177–79; *TH*, 34,172–74), the law makes use of the bodies of two lovers in order ultimately to show that these bodies and the otherness and individuation they seem to promise are nothing more than a "trap" [*un leurre*] or a "temptation" [*une tentation*], as Sorge will later point out to Bouxx (*MH*, 47; *TH*, 52).[31]

We will gain further insights into the paradigmatic aspects of this scene by reading it in relation to the cemetery scene between Sorge and Louise in the next chapter; but first, Marion's account of love, especially the exchange of flesh between lovers, might help us to see more deeply into the phenomena described here. It is important to keep in mind, as we saw earlier, that for Marion, the phenomenon of the flesh is first and foremost governed by giving and receiving—one only receives one's flesh from another. What, then, if anything, are Sorge and Marie giving to one another in their embrace? We can begin by looking more closely at Sorge's "strange" claim that "up to this point we had had the same body, a true common body, impalpable and light." This suggests that the act of touching actually transforms Marie and Sorge, rather than, for instance, merely uncovering a preexisting facet of their bodily existence. This transformative power of Sorge's touch seems confirmed by the effect it has on Marie's dress: it literally causes the fabric to "take on a body" under his fingers, and become a kind of "black flesh." Sorge's touch, then, gives something the text calls "flesh" to fabric and "breaks," like a "hammer," the "rigidity" of Marie's body, causing it to dissolve and form a wet, "burning layer" that exhibits a nonhuman will ("a moist and strange greed that was blind, urgent"), separating rather than uniting the two lovers. So Sorge's touch gives an estrangement or separation to both human and nonhuman substance. Again, what is striking here are the ways in which Sorge's descriptions resemble, yet ultimately differ from, what Marion describes.

What exactly is at stake in this "gift" of estrangement or separation? At first glance, Sorge and Marie seem to have entered into what could be called an erotic reduction when they embrace: the breaking of the common body would signal this movement out of a world assured by certified subject-object relations (the world of the law in *Le Très-Haut*), into a different experience of reality governed by a different assurance, achieved through a touch that separates. However, the assurance afforded Sorge and Marie by the experience of the embrace is not characterized by an individuation given to each by the other, as in the exchange of flesh in Marion; this fact, in turn, puts into question the initial supposition that something akin to an erotic reduction has been entered into. Instead, the touch that gives the change to the dress and the "common" body turns out not to be a true giving at all, in Marion's sense, but the action of the law's power at an intimate, corporal level. We note that the nonhuman things touched in the embrace—for instance, the dress—take on a human attribute (albeit one associated with a dead human body: black flesh), while the human bodies are transformed into something foreign to what is human: a blind and urgent greed. This seems simply to show that the law's power of objectification recognizes no distinctions between objects and the human. This becomes clearer when we consider the "blind and urgent" "greed" that characterizes the body of separation. It makes sense to ask, greed for what? In Marion's account of the exchange of flesh, each flesh augments as its advance is welcomed by the other's (given) flesh, and in principle this mutually given augmentation could advance infinitely. In the case of Blanchot's "burning layer," movement seems not to move outward in giving, but instead inward, into a void, where consumption of the broken "common" body is figured not only by the "burning" and the "greed" but also by the void-embodying "feeling" and "breathing" of separation accomplished by the transformed Sorge and Marie. This centripetal movement would in principle, it seems, continue until what was once common became thoroughly felt and breathed into the void of separation and foreignness.[32] The body of separation, then, cannot mark individuation or establish the otherness of the two lovers with regard to one another,[33] because individuation, as Marion shows, must be given. A deepening, blind, and greedy void, however, gives out no gifts.

Thus, Sorge's desire for what we might call an intimate assurance from the law is fulfilled, though not in the cuddly form[34] he had guiltily hoped for. What he discovers is that any individuation gained through the touch of another's flesh reveals itself as merely a step in the law's greedy movement toward greater de-individuation of its subjects at a more intimate level. Essentially, under the law there is no "flesh" in Marion's sense of the word, because the law does not give but instead hungrily consumes all that has human appearance, liquidating it within its blind movement.

Having looked in great detail at the erotic phenomena depicted in the important scenes between Sorge and Marie, we can now move at a greater pace through two other significant scenes, between Sorge and Louise and Sorge and Jeanne, respectively. These scenes ultimately add to the sense we gained in our reading of the scene with Marie that the "abject love" (back-cover text, 1988 reissue) that Blanchot depicts in Le Très-Haut is this void-embodying movement of the law as it operates at an intimate level, eliciting and then denying the need for human individuation through a consuming, nongiving alternation between moments of individuation and resemblance.

ALTERNATION AS ABSORPTION INTO THE BODY OF SEPARATION: SORGE, LOUISE, AND JEANNE

For Sorge, his sister Louise is most importantly a power of absorption: she absorbs all punishment and suffering into an abjection that renders it unfit for building or making anything. Bident has masterfully demonstrated how Sorge's narrative creates links between, on the one hand, the formless, spreading stain and the inundating black waters he eventually sees or encounters in every room he inhabits, and, on the other, the mortifying presence—black eyes, dirty black dress—of his sister Louise.[35] But the color red, too, is associated with Louise throughout the novel, and this color represents the sister's absorptive powers, which gather the water and filth that are the ever-flowing source of the stains and black floods, which are increasingly operative as the narrative proceeds. Fairly early in the novel, during his visit to the home in which he grew up, Sorge is suddenly struck by a memory of a scene from many years earlier: one afternoon, he came upon his five year-old sister being reprimanded by their enraged mother. "I saw Louise, her face somber [*noire*], pitifully thin and implacable, with an ageless and timeless impassivity, and in front of her my mother with her fist in the air, the majesty of my mother reduced to this threat. She [the mother] was pitiful, more powerless in front of this patch of red cloth [*morceau d'étoffe rouge*] than she was before the mask of her own crime" (*MH*, 57; *TH*, 60).[36] Louise's absorptive power creates a separation, but not, it is accurate to say, an individuation: the mother's "majesty" is reduced to useless shame, and Sorge, whom the mother has seen watching this confrontation, from that point forward cannot look his mother directly in the face, just as she cannot look at him (*MH*, 57; *TH*, 60).

At the dramatic height of the cemetery scene, Louise whispers in Sorge's ear a kind of prophecy that formulates in words what I have been calling the greedy movement of consuming alternation that characterizes the intimate operation of the law in the novel: "As long as I live, you will live, and death will live. As long as I breathe, you will breathe, and justice will breathe. As long as I can think, there will be a spirit of resentment and revenge. And now, I've sworn it: where there was unjust death, there will be just death; where blood has become crime in iniquity, blood will become crime in punishment; and the best will become darkness so that the worst will lose light" (*MH*, 71; *TH*, 74).[37] Louise's prophecy, addressed to a "vous" that seems to extend to the world beyond her brother (whom she of course always addresses elsewhere as "tu"), describes the now familiar manner in which the law brings about justice—namely, its own glorification—by using crime as a disclosing agent. But just prior to this account of Louise's words, Sorge details for us what we might call the law's erotic or intimate work on their own bodies. Louise looks upon Sorge with eyes that gaze "in such a strange, frozen way, that I didn't feel that it was her eyes but rather that behind them there was someone—and perhaps nothing—doing the looking" (*MH,* 71; *TH,* 74).[38] And when she commands him to kneel in the vault, he reports that "in this void I felt a kind of hatred for my breath, I rejected it, I pushed it away. I stopped breathing, and the void itself made me breathe. I was suffocating and, suffocating, the void filled me with a substance that was heavier, fuller, more crushing than me" (ibid.).[39] Finally, just before she speaks, Sorge looks at Louise: "my eyes were trained on her and looked at her, and not my eyes but rather someone was looking at her behind them, someone and perhaps nothing" (ibid.).[40] No touching takes place here—instead, there are intense gazes—but several of the aspects of the embrace between Sorge and Marie are repeated: we see Louise and Sorge each become someone other to one another, and the form of this otherness is inhuman, rather than individuating in the manner of the phenomenon of the flesh—Sorge states that, paradoxically, what animated their otherness was "perhaps nothing" (ibid.). When Sorge then describes his experience of being passively breathed by the void, we see again the kind of inverse of the lover's advance and the exchange of flesh described by Marion: here, as with the body of separation earlier, a void opens both within and between Sorge and his sister (we assume that Louise undergoes the same experience as does Sorge here), taking from their bodies and their life and giving no flesh but, like the "burning layer" before, instead leaving a "void" that paradoxically "fills" Sorge with "a substance that was heavier, fuller, more crushing than me" (ibid.).

Sorge will encounter the impossibly absorbent "morceau d'étoffe rouge" again at the beginning of the novel's final chapter, in the company of his nurse, Jeanne (*MH,* 235; *TH,* 225). This impossibly absorbent red rag taunts Sorge with its seeming animation, "intoxicating my fingers with the thought that they need only suddenly grab this piece of visible and tidy cloth in order to squeeze out its latent intimacy, to spurt that out and display it forever as an indelible, thick, black stain" (*MH,* 236; *TH,* 226–27).[41] In what I find to be the most comical moment in the novel, Jeanne, observing Sorge's obsessive gaze upon the rag, grabs it, squeezes it, and removes it from his room, "looking like someone who has just won a victory and gotten her revenge" (*MH,* 237; *TH,* 227).[42]

But Jeanne's apparent victory—over Sorge, who had raped her earlier in a fruitless attempt to strip her of her maddening singularity (*MH,* 202;

TH, 194–95), and, symbolically, over Louise, whose synechdochic presence in the red rag had enraged her with its ability to keep her patient's attention rapt (*MH,* 237; *TH,* 228)—is short-lived. Within moments, after verbally attacking Sorge for failure to submit his last shreds of difference to her control, Jeanne and Sorge, bodies interlaced, are submerged in a "black, abject tide" as they struggle with one another in the novel's final scene that is characterized by erotic phenomena (*MH,* 239; *TH,* 228).[43] We again see the law operating at the level of intimacy, through its (by now) typical movement of intimate alternation between individuation and resemblance. At first, Sorge experiences Jeanne's difference, both through touch ("I felt her stuck against me, a foreign flesh, a dead, liquifying flesh; and the more I pushed it away, the more it collapsed and curled around me") and through her voice ("my whole body was expiring, but she too spat in my eyes, on my cheeks, wordlessly, and I sensed the triumph in the incredible scream coming from her throat") (*MH,* 239; *TH,* 229).[44] This difference is disgusting and suffocating, rather than assuring. But then the triumphal difference expressed in her scream, is, as it were, silenced by the law in its public mode, figured by the "strong and authoritarian voice of a loudspeaker" resounding in the world outside the room (ibid.). This voice of the law addresses itself to difference, seeking any listener who is so other, so "anonymous" to it as to have never heard it, so as then to drag it into sameness (ibid.). We read that Jeanne's scream "sat up and listened" as the loudspeaker's voice "loomed up, still desperate and immutable, still addressing anyone from the depths of death, searching for an undiscoverable and anonymous someone incapable of hearing or understanding it" (ibid.). Finally, hounded by the noise of this voice of the law, Jeanne runs from it, until it "gather[s] up everything" and "throw[s] itself" upon Sorge, "with the weight of an enormous, solid mass, which was also a staggering and cavernous void" (ibid.). Jeanne's triumphant difference that initially resulted from the touch of the two bodies has been crushed, replaced with the "staggering and cavernous void" that, in this scene, plays the role of the body of separation.[45]

For now the centripetal force of the void is engaged, greedily sucking the life out of Sorge and Jeanne alike. The relation between Jeanne and Sorge is characterized in the last two chapters of the novel by a rivalry for recognition of their respective authority or "height," as at least one critic has noted.[46] This rivalry becomes clearly evident when Sorge rapes Jeanne (*MH*, 202; *TH*, 195), several pages prior to the "alliance, or pact" that Jeanne then forces him to sign, a pact that she feels individualizes her (*MH*, 209; *TH*, 201). The pact is her first act of "revenge," or "justice"; but any apparent power one gains over the other is ridiculously momentary in this world, as we see here. Jeanne's efforts to differentiate herself from Sorge's condition will, the novel seems to say, ultimately be destroyed by the void, upon which she paradoxically depends for animation, like a puppet.

> [D]uring this time her voice kept groping to find me, as if she had latched on to the memory of a former state of things and, in the midst of this unknown debris, was trying to force her way through. And she herself, when she came forward, seemed to extricate herself with difficulty from an unsteady location, which she really wasn't escaping, which accompanied her with its imbalance. . . . She kept on wobbling and moved like a livid and cadaverous odor whose contact frightened me, or she disappeared in a swirl, floating behind me in order to grab me without warning. This odor was totally threatening. She stayed there, lying down, as heavy as a corpse, contourless, overflowing, everywhere present and waiting with insidious patience to get herself breathed. And I felt that, by dint of patience, waiting, and trickery, she would end up finding a complicitous respiration; . . . when she spoke, saying Now it's over, they didn't get us, it's over, she wasn't really speaking, she was tagging along behind her words, carrying with her a latent life, a life of earth and water; and she was patiently on the lookout for a breathing that was still to come, and that would take her in. She stayed there stubbornly, sometimes smothering and inundating me, as if she were mud destined to swallow me up, sometimes leaving, and letting herself be sought and smelled out in a distance that had become the vague depths of a hollow filled with water. (*MH*, 240; *TH*, 229–30)[47]

In the final sentence of this quotation (which also concludes the scene), the alternation between distance and proximity becomes quite rapid, and the distinction between them increasingly unimportant. Human existence is reduced to struggle for breath, as if any higher struggle—for recognition, for singularity or individuation—were mere play-acting, a "latch[ing] on to the memory of a former state of things." In this novel, another cannot give one the "flesh" necessary to breathe— breath when it comes results only from the law's void, never as a gift but instead as the rushing produced by a "blind" and "greedy" movement from difference to resemblance to difference, and so on, until all has been transformed into the body of separation. When, at the end of the novel, Jeanne fires the pistol at Sorge, the reader has little reason to believe that she has suddenly become free to enter a different experience of life from the one she has been living. The law will eventually crush her little "victories" of individuation, too—she will never gain the flesh she needs to breathe on her own.

ALONGSIDE THE NIGHT OF THE *IL Y A*, THE NIGHT OF EROS

The end of *Le Très-Haut* is a narrative aporia, as virtually all commentators admit. Attending briefly to this ending will allow us the opportunity for a concluding reflection upon the nongiving nature of love that we have seen at work in Blanchot's novel.

Although Sorge refers in the course of the narrative to writings that he is producing, he never accounts for the writing of this particular narrative that constitutes the book; as a result, it is difficult, if not impossible, to determine the significance of his final words, "Now, now I'm speaking" (*MH,* 254; *TH,* 243).[48] To my mind, the most convincing reading of the end has been made by Leslie Hill, who admits unequivocally that "it is not possible to say what happens in the final paragraph of the novel."[49] Looking at what to some readers may appear to be an artistic failure, Hill instead sees an intentional "interruption," an ingenious way Blanchot has found to communicate, through the novel's formal impossibility, its larger political message ("if there is one," writes Hill).[50] According to Hill, the impossibility of the narrative's ending and beginning would silently signal the presence of something generative, a powerless power positioned somewhere secretly outside the recuperative power of the law as it is represented in the narrative, and which has made the narrative's "endless murmur that is everywhere circumference and nowhere centre" a possibility.

This is, of course, a very Blanchotian account of the novel's end, one that could very well describe the way Blanchot himself would wish us to read it. And even if readers have found convincing my rejection of Hill's claim that Sorge's erotic encounters disclose the existence of a "law of the other" that "doubles" the law and thus loosens the State's grip, Hill's reading of the final scene would not necessarily be invalidated. Indeed, with the doubling of the law removed as an indicator within the text of Blanchot's intentions to transgress the law, this reading of the ending could gain even more force.[51] But by using certain features of Jean-Luc Marion's description of the erotic phenomenon as a point of reference while reading key scenes of erotic activity in the novel, we have noted the absence from the world of the novel of what Marion calls "the phenomenon of the flesh." Flesh, as Marion describes it, can only be given outside an ontic or epistemological reduction, which is to say, outside the realm of the law as figured in the novel; it could, then, be another "impossible"[52] generative source for a narrative that seeks to figure or gesture toward a life beyond or other than what is implicated in and recuperable by the law.

I do not claim that Blanchot gestures toward a human flesh, as described by Marion, that breathes somewhere outside the text of *Le Très-Haut* and moves as its impossible generator. Such a claim would crash up against Blanchot's doctrines of language and of the image—his conviction that, as Kevin Hart has put it, "the sheer presence of being is excarnated and turned into a hollow image of itself," or, as Blanchot himself wrote in "La littérature et le droit à la mort," "le langage est *la vie qui porte la mort et se maintient en elle.*"[53] Nevertheless, the possibility that flesh *could* be an "outside," one different from the one Blanchot celebrated and variously named (*il y a, le dehors, le neutre*), yet one that is at least as effective in contesting the dissatisfactions of the law, ought to give us pause. For, then, nothing less than the comprehensiveness of the Blanchotian account of reality would be at stake.

NOTES

1. An instance occurs when the narrator, Henri Sorge, tells his boss, Iche, of his recent "revelation," while he was ill, about man's stature in a godless universe, to which Iche replies, "What's wrong with you? . . . You're talking phi-

losophy!" ["Qu'avez-vous? . . . Mais c'est de la philosophie!"]. Maurice Blanchot, *Le Très-Haut* (Paris: Gallimard, 1948), 30; *The Most High,* trans. Allan Stoekl (Lincoln: University of Nebraska Press, 1996), 24. Subsequent references to the novel will be given in the text parenthetically, using the abbreviations *TH* and *MH,* respectively. Unattributed translations throughout this essay are my own.

2. Pioneering works focusing, explicitly or implicitly, on the novel's politics in relation to Kojévian Hegelianism include Georges Préli, *La force du dehors: Extériorité, limite et non-pouvoir à partir de Maurice Blanchot* (Paris: Recherches, 1977), 93–109, and John Gregg, *Maurice Blanchot and the Literature of Transgression* (Princeton: Princeton University Press, 1994), 72–126. Critical works that have addressed the novel's engagement with Heidegger's thought include Leslie Hill, *Maurice Blanchot: Extreme Contemporary* (New York, London: Routledge, 1997); Robert Savage, "Between Hölderlin and Heidegger: The 'Sacred' Speech of Maurice Blanchot," in *After Blanchot: Literature, Criticism, Philosophy,* ed. Leslie Hill, Brian Nelson, and Dimitris Vardoulakis (Newark: University of Delaware Press, 2005), 149–67; and, indirectly via discussion of Blanchot on Hölderlin and Heidegger, Kevin Hart, *The Dark Gaze: Maurice Blanchot and the Sacred* (Chicago: University of Chicago Press, 2004), 84–87, 92–99.

3. See Gregg, *Maurice Blanchot and the Literature of Transgression;* and Leslie Hill, *Bataille, Klossowski, Blanchot: Writing at the Limit* (Oxford: Oxford University Press, 2001), 181–206.

4. Christophe Bident, *Maurice Blanchot: Partenaire invisible. Essai biographique* (Seyssel: Champ Vallon, 1998), 259–71.

5. Hill, *Bataille, Klossowski, Blanchot,* 203.

6. Ibid., 204. Michael Holland suggests that Blanchot makes polemical use of *Le Très-Haut* in "Connaissance de l'inconnu" ["Knowledge of the Unknown"], one of the other dialogue pieces on Lévinas's *Totality and Infinity* contained in *L'entretien infini.* Holland sees Blanchot linking Lévinas's thought of the other to the experience of physical abjection as depicted in the novel. See Maurice Blanchot, *L'entretien infini* (Paris: Gallimard, 1969), 77; *The Infinite Conversation,* trans. Susan Hanson (Minneapolis: University of Minnesota Press, 1993), 54. Subsequent references to these texts will be given parenthetically, using the abbreviations *EI* and *IC,* respectively. For Holland's brief comment, see Michael Holland, "'Let's Leave God Out of This': Maurice Blanchot's Reading of *Totality and Infinity,*" in *Facing the Other: The Ethics of Emmanuel Levinas,* ed. Seán Hand (Richmond: Curzon Press, 1996), 102–3.

7. In "Connaissance de l'inconnu" ["Knowledge of the Unknown"] (*EI,* 70–83; *IC,* 49–58), for instance, the erotic and bodily dimension of the relation to the other is stereotyped as a "nostalgic" desire for a relation of "union" and dismissed as having nothing to do with the relation to the other: section 4 of *Totalité et infini* is thus passed over in silence (*EI,* 76, 77; *IC,* 53, 54). *L'ecriture du désastre* (Paris: Gallimard, 1980) contains one direct (34) and several oblique (e.g., 18, 36)

references to the novel, and some of its central issues—care: 84–85; the end of history: 115, 118–20; the law: 7, 110, 213, 217—are addressed as well. But inter-corporal phenomena and their relation to love remain out of direct consideration (the body and love, primarily through friendship, are reflected upon to a degree, cf. 47, 71, 77, 186–88, but the connection to the sorts of phenomena explored in the novel is far from obvious). Blanchot's essay "La communauté des amants," which constitutes the second part of *La communauté inavouable* (Paris: Minuit, 1983), suggestively addresses some of the characteristics of the treatment of the erotic relation found in *Le Très-Haut,* but in a manner, as I will show, that should be considered revisionist vis-à-vis the novel (see notes 26 and 31 below). Two conference presentations, available on-line at the "Espace Maurice Blanchot" and the "Site Maurice Blanchot et ses contemporains" websites, respectively, offer preliminary, suggestive surveys of what I am calling erotic phenomena in Blanchot's fiction; both efforts show convincingly that *Le Très-Haut* stands out among Blanchot's fictional texts as the most concerned with the body and erotic violence. See Karl Pollin, "Erotisme et neutralité dans les récits de Blanchot," http://www.blanchot.info/blanchot/index.php?option=content&task=view&id= 70&Itemid=41 (accessed February 3, 2010); and Monika Murawska, "Levinas-Blanchot: corps et désir" (Colloque "Levinas-Blanchot: penser la différence," UNESCO, November 2006), http://www.mauriceblanchot.net/blog/index.php/ 2007/09/30/185-monika-murawska-levinas-blanchot-corps-et-desir-colloque-levinas-blanchot-penser-la-difference-unesco-novembre-2006 (accessed February 3, 2010).

8. "Tout souci de commentaire raisonné, universel ou particulier, unaire ou totalisant, se voit aussitôt limité s'il ne signale d'abord ce qui fait la *force* du récit: sa capacité permanente à ouvrir de nouveaux espaces de perception et de dialogue, la rapidité avec laquelle la narration invente de nouvelles lumières, de nouveaux planchers, de nouveaux pas, de nouveaux objets, de nouveaux débats, avec une attention infiniment minutieuse et minutée" (Bident, *Maurice Blanchot*, 260).

9. "ralentir ce flux de réflexions qui à travers moi passe avec une rapidité inouïe: tout va trop vite, cela court, c'est comme si je devais marcher toujours plus vite, et non seulement moi, mais les autres, les choses et même la poussière; tout est tellement clair; ce sont des réflexions qui ne se brouillent jamais, des milliers de secousses infiniment petites et distinctes."

10. In a letter to Alexandre Kojève, whose seminar on Hegel he had been attending, Georges Bataille referred to his desire to expend himself uselessly in sexual excess and self-lacerating meditation as "négativité sans emploi," energy that has not been, and, Bataille believes (or hopes), that cannot be recuperated into a progressive dialectic (Georges Bataille, "Lettre à X., chargé d'un cours sur Hegel . . . ," in Denis Hollier, ed., *Le Collège de Sociologie, 1937–1939* [Paris: Gallimard, 1979, 1995], 76). Leslie Hill, pointing out that "it is Hegel's philosophy of

history and theory of the modern State [as interpreted by Kojève] that most visibly provides Blanchot with the canvas for his novel" (Hill, *Bataille, Klossowski, Blanchot,* 187), offers a good summary account of some of the ways in which the novel engages with this dominant philosophical strain (186–88).

11. Blanchot, *Le Très-Haut,* back cover of the 1988 Gallimard "Collection L'Imaginaire" reprint, my translation. The original reads:

> Ici règne le 'Savoir absolu'. Chacun est satisfait. Il n'y a plus rien à faire. L'indépassable est réalité.
>
> En ce sens, citoyen de l'État universel et homogène, je suis un homme quelconque, autre et le même, soumis à la loi suprême que j'incarne, invisible et sans visage, incontestable puisque tout ce qui me conteste me confirme.
>
> Mais voici que quelqu'un—une femme sans doute—m'excepte de ce que je suis et reconnaît en ce moi qui se dissout le Très-Haut.
>
> Le Très-Haut ne peut être que sa propre négation. Dans une société parfaite, où la peste se déclare, de telle sorte que les pestiférés deviennent les seuls rebelles, où le Sida met en péril la loi suprême, le Très-Haut, par-delà toute divinité, n'est plus qu'un malade qui meurt sans mourir, à moins qu'il ne devienne la 'Chose' même, le rien terrifiant, la vérité qui toujours trompe et se trompe, la parole ultime que seule la mort immortelle laisse enfin entendre.
>
> Mais, vous lecteur, oubliez tout cela, car c'est aussi bien Antigone, la pure vierge, s'unissant à son frère mort pour que le tabou de l'inceste, dès lors suspendu, ruine aussi bien la loi idéale que la loi naturelle. L'abjection est amour, comme la liberté absolue est servitude absolue.

12. "Je lui suis très attaché: c'est une fille terrible, qui n'en fait qu'à sa tête, passionnée, volontaire. . . . [E]lle me méprise; elle est méchante et haineuse."

13. Pierre Klossowski was the first to discuss this meaning of Sorge's name, within the context of a reading of the novel as a detailed, hypothetical phenomenology of the withdrawal of God the Creator from creation, according to Blanchot's theory of language as it is put forward in his essay "La littérature et le droit à la mort," composed contemporaneously with *Le Très-Haut.* On Sorge's name, see Pierre Klossowski, "Sur Maurice Blanchot," *Les Temps modernes* 40 (1949): 306–7.

14. Bident associates Sorge as "care" with his status as "Most High": "Sorge prend sur lui la mort des autres, la culpabilité du monde. Le temps où son visage de souci attire les regards, c'est pour en recevoir l'affront" [Sorge takes the death of others and the guilt of the world upon himself. His face of care attracts the gaze of others, only to receive insults and injury] (Bident, *Maurice Blanchot,* 266).

15. "'Maintenant, vous le regrettez, parce que vous savez que je suis un homme comme vous.' . . . Je m'avançai sous son nez. 'Si je ne suis pas comme vous, pourquoi ne m'écrasez-vous pas sous votre talon?'"

16. In a late (pub. 1993) text on friendship, Blanchot writes, "La *philia* grecque est réciprocité, échange du Même avec le Même, mais jamais ouverture à l'*Autre*, découverte d'Autrui en tant que responsable de lui, reconnaissance de sa pré-excellence, éveil et dégrisement par cet Autrui qui ne me laisse jamais tranquille, jouissance (sans concupiscence, comme dit Pascal) de sa Hauteur, de ce qui le rend toujours plus près du Bien que 'moi.'" [Greek *philia* is reciprocity, exchange of the Same with the Same, never opening to the *Other*, discovery of the Other as responsible for him, recognition of his pre-excellence, awakening and sobering by this Other who never leaves me in peace, enjoyment (without concupiscence, as Pascal says) of his Height, of that which renders him ever closer to the Good than 'I.'] Maurice Blanchot, "Pré-texte," in Dionys Mascolo, *À la recherche d'un communisme de pensée* (Paris: Fourbis, 1993), 16. Quoted in Hélène Merlin-Kajman, "Réflexions d'une dix-septièmiste à propos de l'amitié selon Blanchot," in *Maurice Blanchot: Récits critiques*, ed. Christophe Bident and Pierre Vilar (Tours: Editions Farrago/Editions Léo Scheer, 2003), 325. Sorge demands treatment as "the Other" from his assailant in a manner that introduces reciprocity into the scenario.

17. See, for instance, *MH*, 6, 85; *TH*, 14, 85.

18. Jean-Luc Marion, *Le phénomène érotique: Six méditations* (Paris: Grasset, 2003), 18; *The Erotic Phenomenon*, trans. Stephen E. Lewis (Chicago: University of Chicago Press, 2007), 7. Subsequent citations will be given parenthetically, using the abbreviations *PE* and *EP*, respectively.

19. Marion's investigation of "the flesh" in *EP* §7 and §§22–28 clearly relates to Lévinas's notion of "the tender," and Marion's account of the lover's advance bears some relationship to "voluptuousness" in *Totality and Infinity*, part 4, section B. On the "caress," see *EP*, 119–20; in relation to "fecundity," see the final meditation in EP, "Concerning the Third Party, and Its Arrival." Marion's engagement with Lévinas's thought figures significantly in Marion's phenomenology of the icon and of the saturated phenomenon; a full-length study of the relation has yet to be made. Marion has engaged with Lévinas's thought at length in at least three important places. In chapter 4 of *Prolegomena to Charity*, in an essay from 1983, Marion sought to adapt and expand Lévinas's thought of the "just any other" to account for the phenomenon of love for a "particular" other ("The Intentionality of Love," in *Prolegomena to Charity*, trans. Stephen E. Lewis [New York: Fordham University Press, 2002], 71–101). Later, he developed this thought further through a notable engagement with, in part, Lévinas's starting point amidst the anonymity of the *il y a* in "D'Autrui à l'individu"; see Emmanuel Lévinas, *Positivité et transcendance, suivi de Lévinas et la phénoménologie, sous la direction de J.-L. Marion* (Paris: Presses Universitaires de France, 2000), 287–308.

Most recently, in "Substitution and Solicitude: How Lévinas Re-reads Heidegger" (forthcoming in Jean-Luc Marion, *The Reason of the Gift*, trans. Stephen E. Lewis [Charlottesville: University of Virginia Press]), Marion pushes further his analysis of the issue of human particularity in Lévinas's thought via an investigation of the philosopher's development of the notion of substitution in and through his recuperation and correction of Heidegger's *Selbstheit*, as elaborated in section 26 of *Sein und Zeit*. An effort to develop a triangulated understanding of Blanchot, Lévinas, and Marion in relation to one another could especially benefit from consideration of these last two items.

20. See Adriaan Peperzak, *To the Other: An Introduction to the Philosophy of Emmanuel Levinas* (West Lafayette, IN: Purdue University Press, 1993), 197–98. The beginnings of Lévinas's thinking about love and fecundity are, of course, already identifiably present in the final pages of the section entitled "L'hypostase," which concludes *De l'existence à l'existant:* Emmanuel Lévinas, *De l'existence à l'existant,* 2nd ed. (Paris: Vrin, 1993),163–65.

21. Emmanuel Lévinas, *Totality and Infinity: An Essay on Exteriority,* trans. Alphonso Lingis (Pittsburgh: Duquesne University Press; The Hague: Martinus Nijhoff, 1969), 258–59. The French reads: "A côté de la nuit comme bruissement anonyme de l'*il y a,* s'étend la nuit de l'érotique; derrière la nuit de l'insomnie, la nuit du caché, du clandestin, du mystérieux, patrie du vierge, simultanément découvert par l'*Eros* et se refusant à l'*Eros*." Emmanuel Lévinas, *Totalité et infini: Essai sur l'extériorité* (Paris: Kluwer Academic/Livre de Poche, 1971), 289.

22. Marion sums up the position of the *ego* at this dead-end as follows: "I cannot require that the other love me, any more than I can promise myself to love myself—as if I could offer an authentic elsewhere for myself, or as if I, in my incontestable finitude, could assure myself infinitely. But above all, who can seriously believe himself unscathed by all self-hatred, transparent, equal, benevolent toward himself, free of ressentiment and of the insolvent debt of a past that is out of reach? . . . If someone can show me how the other *must* love me, let him show it. If someone can show how I *am able* to love myself (from elsewhere, and infinitely), let him show it. And if, as I believe, no one could ever do these things, then all that remains is seriously to consider the aporiae at which we've ended" (*EP,* 65; *PE,* 107–8).

23. See Marion's description of "the properly infinite excess of the lover, as he loves without the condition of reciprocity" (*EP,* 87; *PE,* 140).

24. "Lorsque je la vis assise à mes côtés, prête à manger les mêmes choses que moi, à faire les mêmes gestes, à regarder les mêmes gens, je fus stupéfait. C'était plus que de la surprise. J'avais toujours pressenti ce qui arrivait là; je savais que nous vivions tous ensemble, que nous nous reflétions les uns dans les autres, mais avec elle cette existence en commun devenait une certitude vertigineuse et frénétique. D'abord, j'en avais eu la preuve, je pouvais lui parler: ce que je disais était donc bien conforme à l'avis général, à cette sagesse des journaux

qui parfois passait devant mes yeux comme le récit d'un autre temps. Mais j'étais saisi encore par une impression bien différente. Que la loi fût toujours en mouvement, qu'elle passât indéfiniment de l'un à l'autre, présente partout, avec sa lumière égale, transparente et absolue, éclairant chacun et chaque objet d'une manière toujours diverse et pourtant identique, d'ordinaire tout me le faisait sentir et, sentant cela, tantôt j'étais transporté et ivre, tantôt je me demandais si je n'étais pas mort. Mais à présent, c'est-à-dire maintenant, lorsque je regardais sa main, une main assez jolie, aux ongles bien faits, grande et forte comme toute sa personne, cette main, je ne pouvais imaginer qu'elle fût semblable à la mienne, et je ne croyais pas non plus qu'elle fût unique. Ce qui me troublait, c'est que la saisir, la toucher d'une certaine façon, oui, si je réussissais à toucher cette chair, cette peau, ce gonflement humide, avec elle je toucherais la loi, qui était là, c'était manifeste, qui, peut-être, s'y attarderait alors d'une manière mystérieuse, retenue, pour moi, un moment à l'écart du monde."

25. Hill, *Bataille, Klossowski, Blanchot*, 203.

26. This distinction between a "dialectical law of the State" and a "law of the other" seems present in Blanchot's work in *L'entretien infini* and after, but, as I shall show in a moment, does not describe accurately what takes place in *Le Très-Haut*. In his reading of this scene from the novel, Leslie Hill could very well be seen to be applying a parallel that Blanchot pursues in "La communauté des amants" (1983) between "passion" (his substitute term for love) and Lévinas's notion of responsibility or "obligation" for the other, as developed in the doctrine of substitution. For Blanchot in this 1983 text, passion, like obligation, brings one into a relation with the other that is anterior to legal relations: "Obligation qui n'est pas un engagement au nom de la Loi, mais comme antérieure à l'être et à la liberté, lorsque celle-ci se confond avec la spontanéité. 'Je' ne suis pas libre envers autrui si je suis toujours libre de décliner l'exigence qui me déporte de moi-même et m'exclut à la limite de moi. Mais n'en est-il pas ainsi de la passion? Celle-ci nous engage fatalement, et comme malgré nous, pour un autre qui nous attire d'autant plus qu'il nous semble hors de la possibilité d'être rejoint, tellement il est au-delà de tout ce qui nous importe" ["an obligation which is not an agreement in the name of the Law, but is as if anterior to being and to freedom, where the latter is indistinguishable from spontaneity. 'I' am not free towards the other if I am always free to decline the exigency that sets me off from myself and excludes me at the limit of myself. But doesn't that apply to passion? The latter pledges us fatally and, as if in spite of ourselves, to another who attracts us all the more in that he seems beyond the possibility of ever being rejoined, being so far beyond everything that matters to us"] (*La communauté inavouable*, 74, hereafter abbreviated *CI; The Unavowable Community*, trans. Pierre Joris [Barrytown, NY: Station Hill Press, 1988], 44, hereafter abbreviated *UC*). See also *CI*, 73, note 1; *UC*, 60, note 13, where this anteriority to the Law is described as an "application de la Loi qui toujours précède la Loi" ["application of the Law which always precedes the Law"]: a formulation of the doubleness of the law in Hill's sense.

27. As Sorge puts it to his boss, Iche, a few hours before he communicates the "very important" thing to Marie, "whatever I do, I work usefully. When I speak, when I reflect, I'm working. . . . Because there's a man there who sees things as they should be seen—he exists, and all the notions for which we've been struggling for so many centuries exist with him. I'm perfectly aware that if I changed, or if I went off my head, history would collapse" ["quoi que je fasse, je travaille utilement. Lorsque je parle, lorsque je réflichis, je travaille. . . . [I]l y a là un homme qui voit les choses comme il faut les voir, il existe et, avec lui, existent toutes les notions pour lesquelles nous avons lutté pendant tant de siècles. Je sens partfaitement que, si je changeais ou si je perdais la tête, l'histoire s'écroulerait"] (*MH*, 24; *TH*, 30).

28. "La nuit, il m'arrive de me sentir vraiment seul. Je m'éveille et je me rappelle tout: ma famille, mes camarades de bureau, tel visage que j'ai aperçu; je reconnais ma chambre, au delà il y a l'avenue, d'autres maisons, chaque chose est à sa place, partout quelqu'un est avec moi, et pourtant, cela ne me suffit pas. Je voudrais à cet instant qu'une personne en chair et en os se tienne à mes côtés ou dans l'autre chambre et me réponde, si je parle: oui, c'est cela, que je sache que j'ai aussi parlé pour elle. Tandis que, s'il n'y a pas de réponse, si j'élève la voix en comprenant que je parle tout seul, je me mets presque à trembler; c'est pis que tout. C'est un affront, une véritable faute. J'ai le sentiment d'avoir commis un crime, j'ai vécu en dehors du bien commun. Et du reste, est-ce que j'existe? L'existence est ailleurs, au milieu de ces milliers de gens agglomérés, qui vivent ensemble, qui s'entendent, qui ont réalisé la loi et la liberté."

29. Sorge frequently uses the word "drunk" to describe the feeling he gets when he delivers himself over to an activity that makes him feel like "anybody" or "common," rather than an individual. Cf. *MH*, 18, 29, 232; *TH*, 26, 35, 223.

30. "Elle se leva et, me levant aussi, je lui saisis les mains. Je la serrai violemment. Elle était raide, d'une raideur qui appelait le marteau. Tout à coup, l'étoffe de sa robe prit corps sous mes doigts. C'était quelque chose d'étrange, une surface irritante et lisse, une sorte de chair noire qui glissait, adhérait et n'adhérait pas, se soulevait. C'est alors qu'elle se tranforma: je le jure, elle devint autre. Et moi-même, je devins un autre. Sa respiration se gonfla. Il y eut dans chaque partie de son corps un changement. Jusqu'à présent, chose bizarre à dire, nous avions eu le même corps, un véritable corps commun, impalpable et clair. Avec une rapidité bouleversante, ce corps se cassa en deux, se résorba et à sa place se forma une épaisseur brûlante, une étrangeté moite et avide qui ne pouvait rien voir et rien reconnaître. Oui, je le jure, je suis devenu un étranger, et plus je la pressais, plus je la sentais devenir étrangère, acharnée à me rendre présent quelqu'un d'autre et quelque chose d'autre. Personne ne me croira, mais, à cet instant, nous avons été séparés, nous avons senti et respiré cette séparation, nous lui avons donné un corps. C'était une évidence, enfin nous ne nous touchions plus."

31. The menacing power of the "body" of "separation" found in this scene again distinguishes Blanchot's depiction of the erotic relation here from later, seemingly gentler accounts of the separation that constitutes the relation of passion. Consider the following, from the 1983 text "La communauté inavouable": "la passion échappe à la possibilité, échappant, pour ceux qui en sont saisis, à leurs propres pouvoirs, à leur décision et même à leur 'désir,' en cela l'étrangeté même, n'ayant égard ni à ce qu'ils peuvent ni à ce qu'ils veulent, mais les attirants dans l'étrange où ils deviennent étrangers à eux-mêmes, dans une intimité qui les rend, aussi, étrangers l'un à l'autre. Ainsi, donc, éternellement séparés, comme si la mort était en eux, entre eux? Non pas séparés, ni divisés: inaccessibles et, dans l'inaccessible, sous un rapport infini" ["passion eludes possibility, eluding, for those caught by it, their own power, their own decision and even their 'desire,' in that it is strangeness itself, having consideration neither for what they can do nor for what they want, but luring them into a strangeness where they become estranged from themselves, into an intimacy which also estranges them from each other. And thus, eternally separated, as if death was in them, between them? Not separated, not divided: inaccessible and, in the inaccessible, in an infinite relationship"] (CI, 72; UC, 43). To be sure, a bit later in this text Blanchot will speak of the possibility that the passionate relation without relation "peut aller jusqu'à la destruction" ["can go all the way to destruction"], and that "la violence et la mort nocturne ne puissent être exclues de l'exigence d'aimer" ["violence and nocturnal death cannot be excluded from the exigency to love"] (CI, 76; UC, 45). But these threatening outcomes are envisaged within a relation that is figured as anterior to the Law (see note 26 above); the novel, by contrast, revels in displaying the power of the Law to exercise its menacing grasp at the levels of the State and of interpersonal intimacy, alike.

32. Commentators on this scene like to say that it denies a supposedly stereotypical understanding of sexual intimacy in terms of fusion (see Hill, *Bataille, Klossowski, Blanchot*, 204; likewise Pollin, "Erotisme et neutralité," and Muraskawa, "Levinas-Blanchot"). Bident is more accurate: there clearly *is* a fusion taking place, but it is figured as movement, rather than the achievement of something static, and it is subtractive rather than additive—defined by pure consumption or expenditure, to use a word dear to Georges Bataille. See Bident, *Maurice Blanchot*, 265.

33. My point—that the body of separation in no way signals a moment of escape from the law's grasp—puts me at odds with Christophe Bident's reading of the role of woman in the novel (Bident writes, "La femme . . . libère de la semblance: elle libère la différence," *Maurice Blanchot*, 269). But a careful reading of Bident's deployment of evidence as he leads up to his conclusion reveals an uncharacteristic lack of fidelity to the text on his part. Bident makes it sound as if the scene in which Sorge points out Marie's resemblance to him (MH, 100; TH, 100) takes place *before* the body of separation scene: "C'est pourtant auprès de

Marie, après cette accumulation de semblances, que la différence va surgir. . . . La femme est ce qui manque et échappe au monde de la justice" (*Maurice Blanchot*, 268). In fact, however, Sorge points out Marie's resemblance to him *after* the embrace scene—signaling his recognition, I would say, of what the body of separation really means. Chapter 5 of *Le Très-Haut* in fact contains two attempts by Sorge to make Marie once again "be separated from herself, be separated from me" (*MH*, 98; *TH*, 98; the first attempt occurs two pages earlier: *MH*, 96; *TH*, 96). They fail, however, because the body of separation does not truly individuate: Sorge sums up the paradox of the embrace that we have just explored when he says to Marie, "With you I don't exist—I exist twice," and, after showing her their similar reflections in the mirror, states: "from now on she'd be endlessly haunted by [the resemblance], as by the inescapable proximity of the law" (*MH*, 100; *TH*, 100). Bident also attributes to Sorge the dream of the judge that is in fact dreamed and recounted by Bouxx, to which Sorge replies with the lines about the apparent otherness of a woman being nothing more than a "trap" and a "temptation." See Bident, *Maurice Blanchot*, 268–69.

34. Blanchot seems to take subtle comic delight in the dashing of Sorge's hopes as he, the Most High, botches his attempt to "overshadow" Marie; Bident is alone in recognizing Sorge's "bouffonerie." See Bident, *Maurice Blanchot*, 266.

35. Ibid., 264.

36. "je voyais Louise, la figure noire, pitoyablement maigre et impassible, d'une impassibilité sans âge, hors du temps et, en face, le poing levé de ma mère, la majesté de ma mère réduite à cette menace, pitoyable elle aussi, plus impuissante devant ce morceau d'étoffe rouge que devant le masque de son propre crime."

37. "Tant que je vivrai, vous vivrez, et la mort vivra. Tant que j'aurai un souffle, vous respirerez, et la justice respirera. Tant que j'aurai une pensée, l'esprit sera ressentiment et vengeance. Et maintenant, je l'ai juré: là où il y a eu une mort injuste, il va y avoir une mort juste; là où le sang s'est fait crime dans l'iniquité, le sang va se faire crime dans le châtiment; et le meilleur devient ténèbres pour que le jour manque au pire."

38. "d'une manière si insolite, si glacée que je sentais que non pas eux, mais derrière eux, quelqu'un me regardait, quelqu'un et peut-être, —rien."

39. "Dans ce vide, j'éprouvais pour mon souffle une sorte de haine, je le rejetais, je le repoussais, je ne respirais plus, et le vide lui-même me faisait respirer; j'étouffais et, étouffant, le vide m'emplissait d'une substance plus lourde, plus pleine, plus écrasante que moi."

40. "mes yeux étaient fixés sur elle et la regardaient, et non pas eux, mais derrière eux quelqu'un la regardait, quelqu'un et peut-être, —rien."

41. "donnait à mes doigts une véritable ivresse, à la pensée qu'il leur suffirait de se resserrer soudain sur cette pièce d'étoffe si visible et si nette pour en

exprimer l'intimité latente, la faire jaillir au dehors et l'étaler à jamais en une tache ineffaçable, épaisse et noire."

42. "ayant l'air de quelqu'un qui vient de remporter une victoire et d'assurer sa vengeance."

43. "la marée noire, abjecte."

44. "Je la sentais collée contre moi par une chair étrangère, une chair morte qui se liquéfiait; et plus je la repoussais, plus elle s'effondrait, se ramassait autour de moi. . . . tout mon corps expirait, mais elle aussi me crachait dans les yeux, sur les joues, sans rien dire, et je devinais son triomphe à l'invraisemblable cri de sa gorge."

45. "elle se redressa et prêta l'oreille" . . . ; "surgit toujours désespérée et immuable, continuant du fond de la mort à s'adresser à n'importe qui, cherchant quelqu'un d'introuvable et d'anonyme qui ne pouvait ni l'entendre ni la comprendre"; "le bruit se détacha d'elle, revint à sa rencontre avec une rapidité foudroyante, enveloppa tout, ramassa tout, pour finalement tout jeter au point où je me trouvais et se jeter lui-même sur moi, avec le poids d'une énorme masse solide, qui était aussi un vide titubant et caverneux."

46. Savage, "Between Hölderlin and Heidegger," 162–63.

47. "pendant ce temps sa voix continua à me chercher à tâtons, comme si elle se cramponnait au souvenir d'un ancien état de choses et essayait, au mileu de débris inconnus, de se frayer un chemin. Et elle-même, quand elle s'avança, parut se dégager difficilement d'un endroit vacillant, d'où en vérité elle ne sortait pas, qui l'accompagnait de son déséquilibre. . . . Elle continuait à vaciller, se déplaçait à la manière d'une odeur, livide, cadavérique, qui me faisait craindre son contact, ou bien disparaissait dans un remous, flottait derrière moi pour me presser à l'improviste. Cette odeur était pleine de menaces. Elle restait là, couchée, aussi lourde qu'un corps, sans contour, débordant, partout présente et attendant avec une patience insidieuse de se faire respirer. Et je sentais qu'à force de patience, d'attente et de ruse, elle finirait par trouver une respiration complice; . . . quand elle parlait, disant, maintenant c'est passé, ils ne nous ont pas eus, c'est fini, elle ne parlait pas vraiment, mais elle se glissait à la remorque de ses paroles, apportant avec elle une vie latente, une vie de terre et d'eau et guettant patiemment le souffle encore à venir qui la recueillerait. Elle resta là opiniâtrement, tantôt me suffoquant et m'inondant, comme si elle eût été de la boue destinée à m'engloutir, tantôt s'absentant et se faisant chercher et flairer dans un lointain devenu le fond vague d'un creux rempli d'eau."

48. "—Maintenant, c'est maintenant que je parle."

49. Hill, *Bataille, Klossowski, Blanchot*, 205.

50. Hill writes, "For the fictional duplicity of the novel's ending, the mute gesture it makes towards the unspeakable, the apocalyptic power with which it cancels its own apocalyptic finale: all this introduces into thinking—philosophy, politics, and literature—an interruption that cannot be recuperated by any di-

alectic of the work. Such an interruption, however, does not just interrupt. . . . [It] serves to bracket off the work and treat it as an immense citation, an endless murmur that is everywhere circumference and nowhere centre, which belongs to possibility, but only in so far as the impossible, in the form of the beginning, or the end, has already taken place" (ibid.).

51. An account of the possibly satirical features of the novel, especially a reading of the buffoonery of Sorge's character, could likewise aid this way of reading the novel. The utter lack of verisimilitude, for instance, in Sorge's interactions with the women in the scenes discussed in this essay suggests satirical authorial intention.

52. Hill, *Bataille, Klossowski, Blanchot*, 205.

53. Hart, *The Dark Gaze*, 102; Maurice Blanchot, *La part du feu* (Paris: Gallimard, 1949), 324.

FIVE

THE HAUNTED HOUSE OF BEING

PART II OF *L'ARRÊT DE MORT*

Alain Toumayan

There is no doubt that in the canon of French modernism, Blanchot's fiction occupies a privileged and unique place. Among the most perplexing and challenging works in French fiction, these texts, like their literary models and antecedents by such writers as Sade, Lautréamont, Kafka, and Bataille, defy interpretation and often resist description. The idea or figure of enigma, which is examined systematically in various contexts by both Lévinas and Blanchot, seems to be an apt image to characterize Blanchot's stories in terms of their theme, character development, narrative form, and structure.[1] And within the corpus of Blanchot's fiction, *L'arrêt de mort* (*Death Sentence*) ranks among the most fascinating and enigmatic. It is, with *Thomas the Obscure*, one of Blanchot's best known and most examined texts,[2] and, like *Thomas the Obscure*, it deals forcefully and centrally with a theme that traverses all of Blanchot's fictional and critical work: the problem of death in Western philosophy.[3]

In this essay, I examine *Death Sentence* with particular attention to the second part of the narrative. Two reasons explain the focus of the present study: on the one hand, the first part of the narrative is more straightforward (its narrative structure unfolds in a relatively linear fashion) and, perhaps consequently, has been commented on and analyzed much more extensively than the second part; on the other hand, the narrative's second part, like the eleventh chapter of *Thomas the Obscure*, examines systematically the effects of the death of a character, Anne in the latter case, J. in the former, on the world of those who witness, attend to, or find themselves in the general vicinity of a character's demise. In other words, in both narratives, after the central thematic event of a character's death, the emphasis shifts to the sustained examination of the manner in which death's effects, in the manner of seismic disturbances, reverberate throughout the surrounding area and give particular inflection to time, space, subjectivity, intersubjective relations, and language, to name only the principal axes affected. Various anomalies, often perceived or observable only indirectly, will manifest the particular character of the modification effected by death. The principles of such effects can afford some insight into the particular "work" of death recorded in the story.

Before turning to the second part of *Death Sentence*, a few considerations of a general nature are perhaps in order. The publication of *Death Sentence* corresponded to a particularly fertile period in Blanchot's thinking in which, notably, Blanchot was deeply engaged in rethinking the problem of death.[4] His reflection on death is synthesized, both concisely and extensively, in his essay "Literature and the Right to Death," which, with its system of cross-referencing with Lévinas's concept of the *il y a,* gives perhaps the best measure of the manner in which Blanchot formulates the problem of death in the 1940s.[5] What is distinctive about Blanchot's analysis of death in this period is a transition, characterized by his departure from the morbid predilection and fascination that such writers as Lautréamont, Sade, and Bataille evince with images of violence, decay, dismemberment, and death. This transition is also a departure from the anthropological Hegelianism of Bataille's *L'erotisme,* where the consciousness of death, expressed empirically in the cultural practices of burial, funereal monuments, and rituals, marks a qualitative leap forward in the evolution of humanity toward the spheres of productive endeavor, rationality, labor, and technical progress, even though, in Bataille's analysis, such a step remains—as a complication to the neat Hegelianism he sometimes invokes to explain it—tied to the formless irrationality and violence of its primitive consciousness.[6] "Literature and the Right to Death" articulates clearly and chronicles effectively Blanchot's turn toward an analysis of death that explicitly engages, reworks, and revises both negativity and nothingness, as Hegel and Heidegger in particular have refined these concepts, and for which Blanchot will find both inspiration and guidance in Lévinas. Indeed, in the second half of "Literature and the Right to Death," Lévinas's *il y a* is invoked several times, generally very strategically, to invalidate negativity as a principle describing death (as Hegel has formulated it) and to explicitly challenge the concept of nothingness, as Hegel, Heidegger, and others have employed it.[7] Both negativity and nothingness afford an *instrumental* interpretation of death in the thought of Hegel and Heidegger, and it is this instrumentality of death that is invalidated, even reversed, by Blanchot. Interestingly, in the 1940s (and well beyond for Blanchot), both Blanchot and Lévinas rely extensively on art and fiction more than on philosophy to examine this notion.

The corruption or contamination of life by death, and, more curiously, of death by a persistence of being or of life; death's inability to "end" life; life's inability to rid itself of death's contagion; death's inability to complete the process of dying, never succeeding in dying, never being dead "enough"—such formulas inform a large part of Blanchot's critical and fictional writings and organize, in particular, many of his readings of Franz Kafka. As Blanchot observes, "In 'The Hunter Gracchus' and in 'The Guest from the Dead,' Kafka expressed directly the strange condition of the dead who do not die."[8] Commenting on "The Hunter Gracchus" in his essay "Reading Kafka," Blanchot assesses the curious situation of Gracchus, who, having been killed in a fall, never quite managed to cross to the "other shore": "once killed, he awaited his death in joy; he lay stretched out, and he lay in wait. 'Then,' he said, 'the disaster happened.'"[9] Blanchot summarizes Gracchus's misfortune as follows: "This disaster is the impossibility of death, it is the mockery thrown on all humankind's great subterfuges, night, nothingness, silence. There is no end, there is no possibility of being done with the day, with the meaning of things, with hope: such is the truth that Western man has made a symbol of felicity, and has tried to make bearable by focusing on its positive side, that of immortality, of an afterlife that would compensate for life."[10]

In this passage we have, distilled, the basic argument of the second part of "Literature and the Right to Death": the concept of a death not adequately or completely accommodated by the concepts of nothingness and negativity, one that is expressed by Lévinas's *il y a*. Such a death is figured ambiguously throughout world culture, presenting itself in the guise of various forms of immortality (literary or religious), reincarnation, and darker versions such as those found in works by Baudelaire, Poe, and Kafka, among others. Blanchot juxtaposes—and thereby associates—these two conceptions of death by means of an allusion to Baudelaire's "Le squelette laboureur" and to the celebrated verse on death from 1 Corinthians 15:55, when he writes: "Where is death's rest? O Death, where is thy victory?"[11] And, ending a commentary on Kafka with a long rumination on the status of the symbol in Kafka's narratives, Blanchot assesses it in the following manner: "it vanishes if it awakens; it perishes if it comes to light. Its condition is to be *buried alive*, and in that it is indeed its own symbol, symbolized by what it symbolizes: death that is life, that is death as soon as it survives."[12] In this particular example, the image that Blanchot uses to express the excess of life and death, being and nothingness, over a relation of negativity is the uncanny imagery of being buried alive.[13]

These problems and such images coincide with many that Lévinas examines in the same period: in *Time and the Other*, where he explicitly challenges Heidegger's concept of death as nothingness and as possibility; in *Existence and Existents*, where Lévinas develops the concept of the *il y a;* and in "Reality and Its Shadow," in which Lévinas relates the artwork to the *il y a* and to its temporal correlate, the *entretemps*.[14] As noted above, Lévinas, too, relies extensively on literary and artistic examples to examine the concept of the *il y a*. In the initial essay "Il y a," subsequently incorporated in, and composing the central thesis of *Existence and Existents*, Lévinas seeks to approach, however carefully, the notion of *il y a* by means of a short critical examination of Edgar Allan Poe, which identifies at the heart of Poe's fiction the horror of incomplete death, figured as premature burial. Since the following passages from the essay were omitted in *Existence and Existents*, they are worth citing extensively here:

> Without seeking in a work of art the exact equivalent of a philosophical concept and an interpretation of specific examples applicable to all the instances of a certain notion, we find in the following text of Edgar Allan Poe, which deals with death, a very acute sense of

what we have called the *il y a*. . . . The horror of being buried alive, that is the persistent sense that death is not dead enough, that within death one *is*, appears to be the fundamental emotion in the works of Edgar Allan Poe. In several cases he treats this theme explicitly in his tales. The situation that repeats itself almost identically in his work and which constitutes, no doubt, the essence of the fantastic in his tales, is the imminence of an event of which one follows, helplessly, the approach, second by second and with no possibility of escape; the character finds himself enclosed in a tomb, annihilated, but in this annihilation still within the grips of existence. This situation is transposed into death itself, as if death were still *to be* within the heart of nothingness.[15]

Although this development is not included in *Existence and Existents*, the example of Poe remains in the book's exposition of the *il y a*. In "Reality and Its Shadow" the example of Poe, once again, is evoked to express the situation specifically figured by Kafka's Gracchus—the impossibility of reaching the other "shore" of death, a temporal articulation of the *il y a* or the *entretemps*:

The time of *dying* cannot give itself the other shore. What is unique and poignant in this instant is due to the fact that it cannot pass. In *dying*, the horizon of the future is given, but the future as a promise of a new present is refused; one is in the interval, forever an interval. The characters of certain tales of Edgar Allan Poe must have found themselves in this empty interval. A threat appears to them in the approach of such an empty interval; no move can be made to retreat from its approach, but this approach can never end. This is the anxiety which in other tales is prolonged like a fear of being buried alive. It is as though death were never dead enough, as though parallel with the duration of the living ran the eternal duration of the interval—the *meanwhile*.[16]

Given that Blanchot emphasizes Kafka and Lévinas emphasizes Poe to express the same concept of the inadequacy of traditional concepts of death, it is notable, especially in view of the close intellectual and personal relations of Blanchot and Lévinas during this period, that Blanchot would situate *Death Sentence,* one of his most enigmatic narratives, explicitly in relation to Poe. The paperback cover of the original edition of *L'arrêt de mort* carried the following comment on the story, which I cite in its entirety:

> This tale is perhaps strange, but it recounts with total clarity events about which everything leads one to believe that they truly took place and that they continue still to occur. In a famous tale, Poe recounts the dark story of a person who could not resign herself to die. Yet Poe, obsessed with the memory of his mother, who had died young and whom he identified in all of the women he loved, has expressed in the admirable resurrection of Lady Ligeia only the obsessive character of his own dream and of his own encounter with death.
>
> But what would happen if the one who dies did not completely yield to death? What is it that occurred, in truth, on the day when, for the most profound and the most serious of reasons, one who had already entered death, suddenly, *stopped* death? This story is not a dream, it does not take place in the world of the dream; it began a few years ago, Wednesday, the 13th of October; it unfolded in our midst, and it is likely that it is not yet over, for, no doubt, it can no longer reach an end. For that too, is death.[17]

This cover commentary hardly solves the enigmas the text poses, but it usefully indicates several interpretive parameters. Most apparent, of course, is the explicit acknowledgment of the story's enigmatic character, despite the purported clarity of both the recorded events and the mode of their expression. Second, part of this commentary is essentially devoted to situating the narrative both in relation to and against Edgar Allan Poe's "Ligeia." Thus, while the narrative would appear to examine the unsettling and uncanny persistence of a character's being within or beyond death, like Poe's "Ligeia," Blanchot also, paraphrasing Marie Bonaparte's influential psychoanalytical study of Poe, situates his narrative *against* Poe, emphasizing that his own is not imagined, not a fantasy, a phantasm, or a dream. Indeed, Blanchot explicitly situates the story in relation to lived events, recent dates, and the present time, and he indicates that its drama is ongoing. Thus, the possibility of relating life and death in ways that go beyond the models and concepts of Western culture and philosophy—the possibility of exploring new and unusual patterns of articulation of being and nothingness—is explicitly indicated by Blanchot as a central concern of his story.[18]

Much has been made of the story's title, particularly by Jacques Derrida in *Parages,* and several meanings of the title can usefully be distinguished in relation to the various parts of the narrative.[19] The most obvious and concrete meaning of "arrêt de mort" is in the context of jurisprudence, that is, a death sentence. This meaning could apply to various characters, including the narrator, on whom fatal medical conditions seem to weigh, as well as to the political and historical situation that is evoked in the story, whether it be Munich, the war, the bombardment of Paris, or the Occupation. A second meaning of the title—as a stoppage, temporary cessation, or suspension of death—seems to characterize the central theme and the climax of the first part of the narrative, when the character J. appears to die, to recover for a moment, and then to slip definitively into death (the "partial resurrection" that Luc Decaunes identifies). Such an event, anomalous and unusual, and certainly not normally accessible to consciousness or available for critical or philosophical scrutiny, can serve to illustrate the process of hypostasis that is analyzed by Lévinas in *Existence and Existents,* whereby a subjectivity emerges from the formless anonymity of the *il y a* and constitutes itself as a subject. As Lévinas notes in *Existence and Existents,* the appearance of the subject is a process in which the pure verbality of anonymous being congeals, as it were, into a subject or noun. In this process, the subject "wrests itself from the anonymity of the *il y a*"; the hypostasis "signifies the suspension of the anonymous *there is*";[20] or again, "Identification is in fact the very positing of an entity in the heart of the anonymous and all-invading being."[21] Since the process of death is the reversal of this movement, the momentary interruption or stoppage of death can afford a fleeting glimpse of this action. Thus, the various temporal and spatial dislocations evinced by J.'s questions and comments to the narrator as she emerges from her state of semiconsciousness, and her awareness of words spoken while she lies unconscious, illustrate stages, elements, and characteristics of the impersonal vigilance, the delay in relation to oneself, and the experience of the generality of being and timelessness in what appears to be a temporary or momentary emergence from the *il y a*.

Given that the theme of a momentary malfunction in the natural process of death seems to describe in a general way the first part of the story and, in particular, the narrator's attending to the character J. as she dies, the second part of the story seems to illustrate a third possible interpretation of the title, which would raise it to a higher level of abstraction and would underscore those themes illustrated by Kafka, Baudelaire, and others, and signaled by Blanchot on the book's cover by reference to Poe. In this context, the notion of "arrêt" as stoppage, cessation, or suspension would refer to the specific philosophical interpretation of death *qua* negativity and nothingness. In other words, in a double negation whose process would not be a dialectic, the meanings of death as negativity and nothingness are specifically interrupted, suspended, or arrested. This is what I take Derrida to mean when he argues, "L'arrêt arrête l'arrêt" (*Parages,* 159)—"the stoppage arrests the stoppage"—or, in a fleshed-out, longer version: "En tant que l'arrêt arrête l'arrêt, en tant que l'arrêt suspensif arrête l'arrêt décisif, et que l'arrêt décisif arrête l'arrêt suspensif, l'arrêt de mort arrête l'arrêt de mort" (*Parages,* 160). Throughout many works, Blanchot explores such articulations of a nondialectical relation of life and death, being and nothingness, presence and absence, for example, in the following phrase in both *Awaiting Oblivion* and *Thomas the Obscure:* "the dead came back to life dying."[22] Such an operation yields the *neutre* or, in Lévinas's words, the *il y a,* which spreads throughout the space of the narrative, propagating itself as seismic waves, inflecting space, distorting time, and tracing its effects on language, subjectivity, and intersubjectivity.

The second half of Blanchot's narrative in *Death Sentence* seems to chronicle the propagation of this "neutrality" throughout the space and time of the story. It records the manner in which "neutrality" inflects the narrator, various subjects and their intersubjective relations, the parameters of space and time, and the medium of language with its particular characteristics, which are often perceivable only indirectly. In other words, it is through the recording of various "atmospheric" disturbances that the *neutre* becomes manifest and that it can be characterized as an element within which events occur. An analogy with Lévinas might illustrate this principle. At the end of *Totality and Infinity,* Lévinas uses an image from Einstein's theory of general relativity—its description of gravity as a "curvature of space"—to account for the manner in which the intersubjective space is inflected by the ethical relation.[23] He also calls this distortion a "refraction" and suggests that this modification of space may be the manner through which we perceive God; "this 'curvature of space' is, perhaps, the very presence of God."[24] Similar effects are recorded by the narrator in the second half of *Death Sentence,* although in this case it is death or the *neutre,* not the intersubjective relation, that has modified or distorted the space. Hence the narrator comments occasionally on the experience of an atmospheric refraction that he calls "l'effet de la vitre," whereby persons, things, or even his own experiences are perceived as through a window, that is, as though the element through which they are perceived were of a different composition or density. The resulting dislocation appears to limit ordinary access to the thing, person, experience, or event, and this limiting is felt through an effect of distancing that has both a spatial and a temporal dimension: "Likewise, if I encountered a person who was pleasing to me, everything pleasant that occurred with her was as if it were situated beneath a pane of glass and, thus, unavailable to me but also *at a distance and in an eternal past.*"[25]

These examples suggest the principal hypothesis that informs my understanding of the second half of the narrative: that the narrator, following the death of J., now occupies a dimension characterized by the *neutre,* and that the effects of dislocation, alienation, and distance he experiences with regard to other characters, as well as numerous other experiences that he records, both attest to its distinctness from the normal ontological order and reveal several of its characteristics. More generally, what the text will chronicle, often in considerable detail, is the relation of two spaces of different ontological composition or density, and the manners through which the ontic field of the real is disrupted by the *neutre.* The rather ordinary nature of the events of the second half of the narrative often highlights the "atmosphere" or element within which these events occur, the nature of subjectivity and intersubjectivity within each one, and the relations of proximity, separation, and occasional interference or intersection of these two ontological spaces.[26] Among the characteristics of the space of the *neutre* now inhabited by the narrator are a proximity to death and the description of an existence that seems invested or haunted by death, or is experienced as a dying that seems to go on indefinitely (suggesting, again, the themes of Poe).[27] Numerous observations made by the narrator, occasionally in passing, attest to these characteristics and seem to position him squarely within a space of death or to situate him as a character whose life partakes of death in strange and unsettling ways. He uses the expression, for example, "every time my grave opens,"[28] and repeatedly situates himself as if he were in a tomb, "as if, at that very time, I had not spent my nights in an open grave."[29] He notes atmospheric conditions like those of a tomb: "a sort of strange musty smell came down to me, a cold smell of earth and stone which I was perfectly familiar with because in the room it was my very life."[30] Indeed, this orientation of the narrator with regard to death is something of a leitmotif in the second half of the narrative.[31] For example, Christ's phrase *noli me tangere* is pronounced by J. in the first part of the narrative as she emerges from unconsciousness in the scenario that I observed above: "I took her hand gently, by the wrist (she was sleeping), and scarcely had I touched it when she sat up with her eyes open, looked at me furiously and pushed me away, saying, 'Never touch me again.'"[32] In the second half of the narrative, it is the narrator who locates himself in J.'s position when, in describing his relation to the character N. or Nathalie, he notes that contact with Nathalie is potentially fatal for her: "I could do nothing to help her; by approaching her, by talking to her, I was disobeying the law; by touching her, I could have killed her."[33] As in the example of Lévinas's interpretation of curved space, and indeed in numerous other examples, we see here Blanchot's secular adaptation of religious imagery or biblical stories, with the *neutre* here associated with the transcendent order.[34] The case at hand chronicles the potentially disruptive and dangerous contact of distinct ontological orders, like the divine and human in the case of Mary Magdalene in John 20:17. In the context of the second half of *Death Sentence,* this observation of the narrator opposes two ontological orders, emphasizing their potentially dangerous incompatibility; underscores the narrator's location within the order of the *neutre;* and highlights the transition he has effected from the first to the second half of the story, a transition best understood as occurring as a consequence of J.'s death. A doctor's comment with regard to the narrator—"it's about time we raised a cross over him"—reproduces this ambiguity of divine and secular orders; the "croix dessus" may suggest both Christological imagery (as Derrida claims [*Parages*, 211]) and the proximity or imminence of death.[35] As I note below, I believe that this location of the narrator within the ontological field of the *neutre* is crucial in considering the last scene of the story and the enigmatic "viens" pronounced by the narrator.

The modes of subjectivity within the *neutre* are numerous, and the distortions that they undergo yield some complicated situations. The basic plot structure of the second part involves the narrator's interactions with a series of characters: his neighbor, C. or Colette, N. or Nathalie, S. or Simone D., and Nathalie's daughter, named Christiana. A few other characters are mentioned, for example, his landlady's daughter, the doctor who treats the narrator, and other acquaintances. For the most part, these interactions involve both inadvertent and intentional encounters in various settings, some dialogues concerning intimacy and marriage, the narrator's illness (which is aggravated by the treatment he receives in the form of an injection from his doctor and which, in an echo of part I, proves very nearly fatal), a few acts of physical violence, and, enigmatically, Nathalie's intention to have a mortuary mask and hand print made (in another echo of part I of the story). Many of the episodes, including those involving a key and a business card, as well as several personal encounters, suggest modes of invasion of privacy. The narrator also records, though very succinctly and enigmatically, his role in an anticipated duel involving an acquaintance—a scene in which the narrator's involvement seems to assure a fatal outcome of an imbroglio that is never specified. The last scene of the story is again a scene of encounter, in which the narrator calls to, and seems to be beckoning, Nathalie. I will return to this scene. The actions of the second part of the narrative occur in the context of the exodus from Paris to Free France, air-raids, and the bombing of Paris.

Even such a brief synopsis of the events of the second half of the narrative suggests the prominence of intersubjective encounters and interactions of various types. None is straightforward, and each attests to specific complications that manifest some disturbance of the space, element, or ontic field of its occurrence. In general terms however, these interactions consistently manifest many of those characteristics that Blanchot, elsewhere in his critical and fictional work, associates with the *neutre:* anonymous vigilance, insomnia, impersonality, various modalities of silence, forgetfulness, and untruth or error. Indeed, many of these characteristics will be in evidence throughout the second half of the narrative, and, in the absence of psychological or personal motivations for the behaviors of the characters, these factors seem to account for their actions. For example, when the narrator inquires regarding Nathalie's motivation for entering his room, in one of the first actions of the second half, she answers, "I've forgotten."[36] The innocuousness of this response perhaps hides a deeper meaning, which the narrator subsequently implies,[37] namely, that such forgetfulness is the positive form of memory or knowledge that one may have of an encounter with alterity, as in, for example, the following relation of memory and forgetfulness elaborated in *Awaiting Oblivion:* "Could it be that to forget death is actually to remember it? Would forgetting be the only remembrance commensurate with death?"[38] This observation, too, underscores the fact that in entering the narrator's room, Nathalie has entered an alien element, one whose space is "bent" in such a way as to suggest the irreversibility of her action. This is noted by the narrator, who surreptitiously sees her entering his room in the dark and observes that, as she does so, her demeanor changes; she seems to undergo a fascination and a paralyzing fear, which render her statue-like. He compares her reaction to that of a squirrel when, without suffering any physical harm, it nonetheless expresses by its body language the realization that it has sprung a trap and now finds itself confined.[39]

Subjectivity is prone to distortions, dislocations, and modifications involving modes of presence and absence. The narrator, for example, comments on the manner in which subjectivity seems to overflow itself, leaving echoes, vestiges, or traces of its passage, as in "the bother, when people come, of having to see them and hear them long after they have left."[40] He confirms this experience in the case of N., whose perfume lingers in the room following her departure: "the night had not dispelled N.'s perfume: I could still smell it very clearly."[41] This configuration of subjectivity involves the narrator as well. He is subject to the indiscreet gaze of his landlady's daughter, who, in a reversal of the effect of refraction observed above, gazes through a transom at him. Although he accommodates himself readily to her spying on him while he is present in the room, he is much more sensitive to the indiscretion committed by the young girl, on whom his room exerts a particular fascination when he is absent (55; 89)—a situation that recalls the curious complaint of his neighbor Colette, who is bothered by the fact that the narrator doesn't make enough noise (34; 59). Such dislocations are occasionally evinced by effects of refraction, as described above, such as when N. gazes at the narrator but seems to be staring at a point behind him: "with all my strength, I stared at her, and she too seemed to stare at me, but infinitely far behind me";[42] or, conversely, when the narrator, in his weakened state, perceives Nathalie as from a great distance: "since I was as weak as I have described, I saw her from infinitely far away."[43] Such a context explains various instances of subjectivity described in the abstract form of "pensée."[44] Indeed, on several occasions in the second part of the narrative, the narrator refers to other subjects in this manner, indicating another medium, one in which abstract and concrete forms coincide and where the narrator's medium is one of greater density, one in which time and space are of a greater resistance and heavier composition.[45]

The final scene of the story is enigmatic and has elicited, along with the scenes that pertain to the death of J. in the first part of the narrative, the most commentary.[46] The reading of the scene I propose is based on the premise that it records, in a sense, a reversal of the Orphic scenario that Blanchot so frequently examines and an inversion of the basic thematic movement of the first part of the narrative. In other words, the scene is based on a configuration in which the narrator's location, as he beckons the character N., is from within the space of the *neutre;* in essence, he calls her toward her death, into the very space within which he has been trapped. It is as if Eurydice has called to Orpheus, seeking to draw him into her ontological element.

There are many charged expressions, among them "attendre," "errer," "avenir," and "à venir," in the critical and fictional works of Blanchot. They are often used to designate one of the modes whereby a temporal event withdraws from the parameters of the present and thus from the strategies and modalities of consciousness. The narrative of *Death Sentence* seems to build toward the utterance of the word "viens" by the narrator, addressing N. in the final scene. Of course, at the most basic level, it figures the type of intersubjective approach and encounter that is examined in a whole series of complex scenes in *Awaiting Oblivion*.[47] But the word "venir" also commonly figures, for both Blanchot and Lévinas, the proximity or intersection of different ontological orders and the linguistic articulation of this proximity. A few examples suffice to illustrate this, though many others could be adduced. Perhaps the most striking example in Blanchot is the *Lazare veni foras* meditated on by Blanchot in "Literature and the Right to Death"[48] and related to the oeuvre and the book in *The Space of Literature*.[49] Similarly, in *The Writing of the Disaster*, Blanchot examines the word "viens" as the specific mode of the language of messianism.[50] In other words, both the approach and the call are integral features of the relation with the Messiah. Again, in the following fragment from *The Step Not Beyond*, one notes how the imperative of the word "venir" articulates the relation to a transcendent other: "Viens, viens, venez, vous auquel ne saurait convenir l'injonction, la prière, l'attente."[51] Lévinas similarly underscores the verb "venir" in his analysis of death in *Time and the Other*. In examining the collapse of the Heideggerian "élan" toward death and the inevitably foundering attempts to secure death, attempts which yield to the passivity of death's "à venir" as eternal imminence, Lévinas opposes the attempt to meet or assume death with its "coming" or "venue": "Death is never assumed, it comes."[52]

The "viens" uttered by the narrator to N. occurs in three scenes as the narrative closes. While there are detailed and significant disparities in the locations and situations of the two characters in the first scene, the temporal dimension of the relation is specified. Although it is described in a relatively paradoxical manner, the narrator's utterance remains situated in a temporal instant or moment: "Perhaps this lasted several minutes, perhaps an hour. . . . But *a moment came* when I saw that she was still mortally cold, and I drew closer and said to her: 'Come.'"[53] The second scene simply evokes the first in the form of a reminiscence (73, 117). In the final scene, the "viens" is explicitly situated beyond a temporal framework: "to that thought (à elle), I say eternally, 'Come,' and eternally it is there."[54] In other words, the narrative "ends" with a perpetual approach of N. to the narrator, with the narrator appearing to draw N. into a field where time has ceased to operate. Recorded from the point of view of a

narrator situated within the *neutre* itself, "viens" thus figures N.'s movement toward and entry into a sphere without time. Just as it assigns the
narrator to the space occupied by Eurydice and assigns N. the perspective
of Orpheus, this scene also configures a reversal of Blanchot's elaborate
analysis of Ulysses' approach to the Sirens. As Blanchot attempts to formulate what occurs in Ulysses' encounter of the sirens, Ulysses enters
an "opening" in time, an "ouverture" or a gap within time and space, an
empty interval that, in Lévinas's analysis of the *entretemps*, lies within the
instant and which Lévinas represents by means of Poe. Another articulation of such an "event" would be the "instant en instance" that Blanchot
mentions in several narratives.[55]

   This analysis of *Death Sentence* will not resolve all of the enigmas that
the text poses, and such, in any event, has not been its claim. Rather, I
have sought to establish some baselines of thematic coherence and to advance, and verify to some extent, an interpretive hypothesis for the events
of the narrative. These events can be generalized as the attempt by Blanchot to figure the *neutre* as a sphere of distinct ontic density that produces
subtle effects in its vicinity, analogous to the way that seismological, magnetic, or gravitational forces bend, curve, distort, or otherwise inflect
objects, relations, and the very element or field, the axes of space and
time—to return to Lévinas's metaphor. The second half of the narrative
locates its narrator within this ontic space, a space in which death is replaced by a dying. If this hypothesis is correct, *Death Sentence* has a high
degree of coherence with many of Blanchot's other meditations on death
written in roughly the same period, such as "Literature and the Right to
Death" and *Thomas the Obscure*. Yet in locating a character within the
space of the *neutre* and attempting to give voice to this *neutre*, it would
seem to present a significant variation on the idea. Those questions that
compose the nexus of Blanchot's examinations of death and specifically
his formulations of the *neutre* almost invariably reveal the influence of
Lévinas and of his analyses of the *il y a*: first, the recasting of the temporality of death as suspension, deferral, and delay; second, the disabling of
negativity or, more specifically, its location within a broader framework
where it occurs as a discrete moment or temporary effect of a deeper relation of mutuality and complicity; finally, the revision of the principle of
nothingness and thus the loading of this nothingness with attributes of

being—hence the paradoxical "density" of the *neutre* or the substantiality of the void, some effects of which have been identified and examined in *Death Sentence*. In representing these moments, *Death Sentence* can be read as one of the most sustained fictional and philosophical case studies of Blanchot's complex investigation of death.

NOTES

1. See the manner in which Blanchot discusses the enigma in relation to the image in *The Infinite Conversation,* trans. Susan Hanson (Minneapolis: University of Minnesota Press, 1993), 321, 324. *L'entretien infini* (Paris: Gallimard, 1969), 471, 476. In his afterword to Lévinas's *La mort et le temps,* Jacques Rolland has noted how Lévinas will come to privilege the figure of enigma, as opposed to "mystery," in the relation to death. Emmanuel Lévinas, *La mort et le temps,* ed. Jacques Rolland (Paris: Editions de l'Herne, 1991), 142.

2. Leslie Hill, *Blanchot: Extreme Contemporary* (London: Routledge, 1997), 144.

3. Françoise Collin, *Maurice Blanchot et la question de l'écriture* (Paris: Gallimard, 1971), 49; Steven Shaviro, *Passion and Excess: Blanchot, Bataille, and Literary Theory* (Tallahassee: Florida State University Press, 1990), 153.

4. Joseph Libertson, *Proximity: Lévinas, Blanchot, Bataille and Communication* (The Hague: Martinus Nijhoff, 1982), 70–74.

5. I am referring specifically to the important and strategic references to Lévinas in Blanchot's "Literature and the Right to Death" and to the references to Blanchot in Lévinas's *Existence and Existents*. The system of cross-referencing and commentary of Lévinas and Blanchot is, of course, much more extensive than this, but this example provides an index of the complementarity of their reflections on death in this period.

6. Jacques Derrida, "De l'économie restreinte à l'économie générale," in *L'ecriture et la différence* (Paris: Seuil, 1967), 369–407.

7. Libertson succinctly shows how "Literature and the Right to Death" is "the scene of Blanchot's extrication of his thinking from that of Hegel," and he notes that "this movement involves Lévinas" (*Proximity,* 206–7); see also Hill, *Blanchot,* 110, 112.

8. Maurice Blanchot, *The Work of Fire,* trans. Charlotte Mandell (Stanford: Stanford University Press, 1995), 82; *La part du feu* (Paris: Gallimard, 1949), 87.

9. Blanchot, *The Work of Fire,* 7; "une fois tué, il attendait sa mort dans la joie: il était étendu et il attendait. 'Alors, dit-il, arriva le malheur'" (*La part du feu,* 15). See also Gerald Bruns, *Maurice Blanchot: The Refusal of Philosophy* (Baltimore: Johns Hopkins University Press, 1997), 69.

10. *The Work of Fire*, 8. "Ce malheur c'est l'impossibilité de la mort, c'est la dérision jetée sur les grands subterfuges humains, la nuit, le néant, le silence. Il n'y a pas de fin, il n'y a pas de possibilité d'en finir avec le jour, avec le sens des choses, avec l'espoir: telle est la vérité dont l'homme d'Occident a fait un symbole de félicité, qu'il a cherché à rendre supportable en en dégageant la pente heureuse, celle de l'immortalité, d'une survivance qui compenserait la vie" (*La part du feu*, 15).

11. *The Work of Fire*, 83. "Où est le repos de la mort? O mort où est ta victoire?" (*La part du feu*, 88). Both Blanchot and Lévinas will identify in Baudelaire's poems, specifically "The Mask" and "Skeletons Digging" ("Le Masque" and "Le Squelette Laboureur"), figurations of the *il y a* or the *neutre*. See Blanchot's "Baudelaire's Failure," in *The Work of Fire*, 132–52; *La part du feu*, 133–51; and Lévinas's *Existence and Existents*, trans. Alphonso Lingis (The Hague: Martinus Nijhoff, 1978), 49, 102; *De l'existence à l'existant* (Paris: Vrin, 1981), 34, 63.

12. *The Work of Fire*, 84; "il se dissipe s'il s'éveille; il périt s'il vient au jour. Sa condition est d'être *enterré vif*, et en cela il est bien son propre symbole, figuré par ce qu'il figure: la mort qui est vie, qui est mort dès qu'elle survit" (*La part du feu*, 89).

13. See Freud's comment on this image in "The Uncanny," in *On Creativity and the Unconscious* (New York: Harper Colophon, 1958), 151.

14. Howard Caygill, *Lévinas and the Political* (London, Routledge, 2002), 50–54.

15. My translation. "Sans chercher dans une oeuvre d'art l'équivalent rigoureux d'un concept philosophique et une interprétation de détails s'appliquant à toutes les articulations d'une notion, nous trouvons, dans le texte qui suit d'Edgar Poe relatif à la mort, un sentiment très aigu de ce que nous appelons l'*il y a*. . . . L'horreur d'être enterré vivant, c'est-à-dire le soupçon persistant que la mort n'est pas assez mort, que dans la mort on *est*, apparaît comme l'émotion fondamentale d'Edgar Poe. A plusieurs reprises il reprend explicitement ce thème dans ses contes. La situation qui se répète presque identique dans son oeuvre et qui constitue, peut-être, le secret du fantastique de Poe, c'est l'imminence d'un événement, dont on suit, impuissant, l'approche, seconde après seconde, toute issue étant fermée; le personnage se trouve enfermé dans un tombeau, anéanti; mais dans cet anéantissement, aux prises avec l'existence. Situation que le personnage transpose dans la mort elle-même, comme si mourir était encore *être* au sein du néant." Lévinas, "Il y a," in *L'intrigue de l'infini*, ed. Marie-Anne Lescourret (Paris: Flammarion, 1994), 107–8.

16. *The Lévinas Reader*, ed. Seán Hand (Oxford: Blackwell, 1989), 140–41. "Le temps même du 'mourir' ne peut pas se donner l'autre rive. Ce que cet instant a d'unique et de poignant tient au fait de ne pas pouvoir passer. Dans le 'mourir,' l'horizon de l'avenir est donné, mais l'avenir en tant que promesse d'un présent nouveau est refusé – on est dans l'intervalle, à jamais intervalle. Inter-

valle vide où doivent se trouver les personnages d'Edgar Poe auxquels la menace apparaît dans son approche, aucun geste n'étant possible pour se soustraire à cette approche, mais cette approche elle-même ne pouvant jamais finir. Angoisse qui se prolonge, dans d'autres contes, comme crainte d'être enterré vivant: comme si la mort n'était jamais assez mort, comme si parallèlement à la durée des vivants courait l'éternelle durée de l'intervalle, – *l'entretemps*" (Emmanuel Lévinas, "La Réalité et son Ombre," *Les Temps modernes* 38 [November 1948]: 786). In *Existence and Existents,* Lévinas retains the example of "The Raven" so powerfully analyzed by Baudelaire ("un glas de la mélancolie," "le poème de l'insomnie du désespoir," *L'art romantique* [Paris: Flammarion, 1968], 194) to portray death's excess over nothingness, the persistence of regret (*Existence and Existents,* 78, 133–34). In *Time and the Other,* Lévinas opposes this fear to Heidegger's anguish before nothingness (*Time and the Other,* trans. Richard A. Cohen [Pittsburgh: Duquesne University Press, 1987], 51; *Le temps et l'autre* [Paris: Presses Universitaires de France, 1983], 29). In *Sur Maurice Blanchot,* Lévinas associates Blanchot's narratives on this question ("La mort, ce n'est pas la fin, c'est le *n'en pas finir de finir*") with Edgar Allan Poe (*Sur Maurice Blanchot* [Montpellier: Fata Morgana, 1975], 16–17).

17. My translation. "Ce récit est peut-être étrange, mais il rapporte, en toute clareté, des événements dont tout laisse croire qu'ils ont eu lieu réellement, qu'ils continuent, maintenant encore, à avoir lieu. Poe raconte, dans un récit célèbre, la sombre histoire d'un être qui n'avait pu se résigner à mourir. Mais Poe, obsédé par le souvenir de sa mère, morte toute jeune, et qu'il voyait revivre en toutes celles qu'il aimait, n'a exprimé dans l'admirable résurrection de lady Ligeia que la hantise de son rêve et de son propre face à face avec la mort. Qu'arriverait-il si celui qui meurt ne s'abandonnait pas entièrement à la mort? Qu'est-il arrivé, en vérité, le jour où, pour la plus grande et la plus grave des raisons quelqu'un qui déjà était entré dans la mort, soudain, *arrêta* la mort? Cette histoire n'est pas un rêve, elle n'a pas eu lieu dans un monde de rêve; elle a commencé il y a peu d'années, le mercredi 13 octobre; elle s'est déroulée parmi nous; et il se peut qu'elle ne soit pas encore finie, mais c'est que, peut-être, elle ne peut plus trouver de fin. Car c'est cela aussi, la mort." I owe this text to the excellent website devoted to Blanchot maintained by Eric Hoppenot, "Galerie Maurice Blanchot," at www.mauriceblanchot.net.

18. In an early review of the work, Luc Decaunes situates *Death Sentence* "halfway between Edgar Allan Poe and André Breton" ("A égale distance d'Edgar Poe et d'André Breton"). His comments on the events of *Death Sentence* are interesting. According to Decaunes, the partial resurrection (of J., presumably) "is a never-ending horror, for it sets death in the very center of daily life" ("une horreur qui ne finit pas, car elle enracine la mort au coeur même de la vie quotidienne"). "*L'Arrêt de Mort,*" *Cahiers du Sud* 291 (1948): 377.

19. James Hillis-Miller, "Death Mask: Blanchot's *L'Arrêt de Mort*," in *Versions of Pygmalion* (Cambridge, MA: Harvard University Press, 1990), 187; Jacques Derrida, *Parages* (Paris: Gallimard, Galilée, 1986), 154–60. Derrida tries out such formulas as the "erasure" of death, "la raie de mort" (187).

20. "Le sujet . . . s'arrache à la vigilance anonyme de l'*il y a*" and "l'hypostase . . . signifie la suspension de l'*il y a* anonyme." Lévinas, *Existence and Existents*, 82–83; *De l'existence à l'existant*, 140–41.

21. "L'identification est précisément la position même d'un étant au sein de l'être anonyme et envahissant" (*Existence and Existents*, 87; *De l'existence à l'existant*, 149).

22. Blanchot, *Awaiting Oblivion*, trans. John Gregg (Lincoln: University of Nebraska Press, 1997), 28; *L'attente l'oubli* (Paris: Gallimard, 1962), 56; *Thomas the Obscure* trans. Robert Lamberton (Barrytown, NY: Station Hill Press, 1973), 38; *Thomas l'obscur, nouvelle version* (Paris: Gallimard, 1950), 42. As observed, Blanchot's work is rife with such articulations and such examinations. The opposition he often makes of "la mort" and "le mourir" is one common locus of this examination. See, for notable examples, *The Writing of the Disaster*, trans. Ann Smock (Lincoln: University of Nebraska Press, 1986), 47; *L'écriture du désastre* (Paris: Gallimard, 1980), 81; or *Awaiting Oblivion*, 73; *L'attente l'oubli*, 140. See also John Gregg, *Maurice Blanchot and the Literature of Transgression* (Princeton: Princeton University Press, 1994), 35–45; Bruns, *Maurice Blanchot: The Refusal of Philosophy*, 68–70; Collin, *Maurice Blanchot et la question de l'écriture*, 53. Another major figure of this articulation is the "instant en instance" in *L'instant de ma mort* (Montpellier: Fata Morgana, 1994), 20; *The Instant of my Death*, bound with *Demeure: Fiction and Testimony* by Jacques Derrida, trans. Elisabeth Rottenberg (Stanford: Stanford University Press, 2000), 11; see also *Awaiting Oblivion*, 34, 43; *L'attente l'oubli*, 67, 85.

23. Lévinas, *Totality and Infinity*, trans. Alphonso Lingis (Pittsburgh: Duquesne University Press, 1995), 291. *Totalité et infini* (Paris: Librairie générale française, 1987), 323, 324.

24. *Totality and Infinity*, 291. "Cette 'courbure de l'espace' est, peut-être la présence de Dieu." *Totalité et Infini*, 324. In his commentary on *Totality and Infinity* in *The Infinite Conversation*, Blanchot notes this expression: *L'entretien infini*, 80; *The Infinite Conversation*, 56.

25. My translation and my emphasis. The full French text is: "L'étrangeté consistait en ceci que le phénomène de la vitre, dont j'ai parlé, s'appliquait à tout, mais principalement aux êtres et aux objets d'un certain intérêt. Par exemple, si je lisais un livre qui m'intéressait, je le lisais avec un vif plaisir, mais mon plaisir lui-même était sous une vitre, je pouvais le voir, l'apprécier, mais non l'user. De même, si je rencontrais une personne qui me plaisait, tout ce qui m'arrivait avec elle d'agréable était sous verre et, à cause de cela, inusable, mais, aussi, lointain et dans un éternel passé" (Blanchot, *L'arrêt de mort* [Paris: Gallimard, 1948],

79–80). Part of the last sentence has been omitted in Lydia Davis's translated text, which reads as follows: "The strangeness lay in the fact that although the shop window experience I have talked about held true for everything, it was most true for people and objects that particularly interested me. For instance, if I read a book that interested me, I read it with vivid pleasure, but my very pleasure was behind a pane of glass and unavailable to me because of that, but also far away and in an eternal past" (Blanchot, *Death Sentence,* trans. Lydia Davis [Barrytown, NY: Station Hill Press, 1978], 48). The narrator records many instances of such perception and will take note of others who perceive him as through the medium of a window. (*L'arrêt de mort,* 72–73, 89, 97–98; *Death Sentence,* 43, 55, 60). See also *When the Time Comes,* trans. Lydia Davis (Barrytown, NY: Station Hill Press, 1985), 41; *Au moment voulu* (Paris: Gallimard, 1979), 95–96; *The One Who Was Standing Apart from Me,* trans. Lydia Davis (Barrytown, NY: Station Hill Press, 1993), 15–16, 44, 53–54; *Celui qui ne m'accompagnait pas* (Paris: Gallimard, 1953), 33–34, 84, 100–101. Parenthetical references in the main text to *Death Sentence* give the page of the English edition, followed by the page of the French.

26. It is obvious that one can speak of the ontological order or field of the *neutre* only by considerably expanding the term (perhaps beyond its true meaning), since the *neutre,* like Lévinas's *il y a,* describes a space, element, or field within which being and nothingness paradoxically coincide. Furthermore, due to the nature and character of the *neutre,* the terms "ontic" and "ontological" are equally appropriate or inappropriate.

27. "Death is the irony of that which annihilates without annihilating. It is negation and negation's cruel inefficiency." Libertson, *Proximity,* 69.

28. *Death Sentence,* 52; "chaque fois que ma tombe s'ouvre" (*L'arrêt de mort,* 86).

29. *Death Sentence,* 56; "comme si, au moment même, je n'avais pas passé mes nuits dans une tombe ouverte" (*L'arrêt de mort,* 91).

30. *Death Sentence,* 66; "une sorte de relent étrange descendait vers moi, une odeur froide de terre et de pierre que je connaissais à merveille parce que dans la chambre elle était ma vie même" (*L'arrêt de mort,* 106).

31. See *L'arrêt de mort,* 55, 78; *Death Sentence,* 32, 47.

32. *Death Sentence,* 25; "je pris doucement la main, le poignet de J. (qui dormait), et à peine l'eus-je touchée, elle se redressa, les yeux ouverts, me regardant d'un air furibond et me repoussa en disant: 'ne me touchez plus jamais'" (*L'arrêt de mort,* 44–45).

33. *Death Sentence,* 53; "Je ne pouvais l'aider en rien; en m'approchant, en lui parlant, j'agissais contre la loi; en la touchant, je pouvais la tuer" (*L'arrêt de mort,* 86–87).

34. See Kevin Hart, "The Gospel of *L'Arrêt de Mort,*" *Journal of Philosophy and Scripture* 1.2 (Spring 2004): 10, 14–15.

35. *Death Sentence*, 47; "Mon pauvre monsieur, il faut faire une croix dessus" (*L'arrêt de mort*, 78).

36. *Death Sentence*, 41; "J'ai oublié" (*L'arrêt de mort*, 69).

37. *Death Sentence*, 52; *L'arrêt de mort*, 85.

38. *Awaiting Oblivion*, 46; *L'attente l'oubli*, 89. See, in particular, Blanchot's meditation in *The Space of Literature* on the necessity of Orpheus' forgetfulness in his quest to retrieve Eurydice. *The Space of Literature*, trans. Ann Smock (Lincoln: University of Nebraska Press, 1982), 171. *L'espace littéraire* (Paris, Gallimard, 1955), 227–28.

39. *Death Sentence*, 38–39; *L'arrêt de mort*, 65–66.

40. *Death Sentence*, 38; "l'ennui, si des gens viennent, d'être obligé de les voir et de les entendre longtemps après qu'ils sont partis" (*L'arrêt de mort*, 64).

41. *Death Sentence*, 54; "Je sentais encore très bien le parfum de N. que la nuit n'effaçait pas" (*L'arrêt de mort*, 88).

42. *Death Sentence*, 69–70; "De toutes mes forces, je la fixai et elle paraissait me fixer, mais à l'infini derrière moi" (*L'arrêt de mort*, 111–12). The same dislocation is recorded in a previous scene (68, 109).

43. *Death Sentence*, 50; "Etant dans cette faiblesse que j'ai décrite, je la voyais d'extrêmement loin" (*L'arrêt de mort*, 82).

44. As an expression designating subjectivity, "pensée" is somewhat unusual, though there are many interesting instances in nineteenth-century texts. Baudelaire indicates the abstract sensuality of the lovers Hippolyta and Delphine by means of the expression "ma pensée," used by Hippolyta. *Les Fleurs du Mal* (Paris: Garnier-Flammarion, 1964), 163. Another interesting example can be found in Auguste Villiers de L'Isle Adam, who, as is well known, was heavily influenced by Hegel. As the characters Axël and Sara prepare for their suicide, the former addresses the latter as "chère pensée." *Axël* (Paris: Le Courrier du Livre, 1969), 250.

45. Both Blanchot and Lévinas often emphasize the mask-like and statue-like demeanor that death, or the proximity of death, confers on characters. See *Thomas the Obscure*, 81; *Thomas l'obscur*, 90; *Death Sentence*, 20, 38; *L'arrêt de mort*, 35, 65. In *La mort et le temps*, Lévinas puts it succinctly: "Quelqu'un qui meurt: visage qui devient masque" (14). For both Blanchot and Lévinas, the statue-like form expresses the time of the *neutre* or the *entretemps*.

46. Hillis-Miller, "Death Mask," 191; Derrida, *Parages*, 80; Hill, *Blanchot: Extreme Contemporary*, 157.

47. *Awaiting Oblivion*, 30, 32, 35, 63, 78, 85. *L'attente l'oubli*, 60, 63, 70–71, 120, 148, 162.

48. *La part du feu*, 316; *The Work of Fire*, 326.

49. *The Space of Literature*, 194–95, *L'espace littéraire*, 258–59; Hill, *Blanchot: Extreme Contemporary*, 13; Gregg, *Maurice Blanchot and the Literature of Transgression*, 58–60, 63.

50. *The Writing of the Disaster*, 142; *L'écriture du désastre*, 214.

51. *Le pas au-delà* (Paris: Gallimard, 1973), 185. "Come, come, come, you whom the injunction, the prayer, the wait could not suit." *The Step Not Beyond*, trans. Lycette Nelson (Albany: State University of New York Press, 1992), 135.

52. Lévinas, *Time and the Other*, 73; "La mort n'est donc jamais assumée; elle vient," *Le temps et l'autre*, 61.

53. *Death Sentence*, 69 (my emphasis); "Cela dura peut-être quelques minutes, peut-être une heure. . . . Mais un moment arriva où, la voyant toujours mortellement froide, je m'approchai encore et je lui dis: 'Viens'" (*L'arrêt de mort*, 111).

54. *Death Sentence*, 80; "à elle, je dis éternellement: 'Viens' et éternellement elle est là" (*L'arrêt de mort*, 127).

55. See discussion of "instant en instance" in note 22 above.

SIX

WRITING AND SOVEREIGNTY

LA FOLIE DU JOUR

Christopher Fynsk

La folie du jour (*The Madness of the Day*) concludes with a statement of refusal, a "no" that counterbalances a prior acquiescence from which derives a large portion of the text that we read before those final words.[1] From the present of this concluding refusal, the narrator's avowed silence and the text's own infinite recession are sealed: "A story? No. No stories, never again."

This refusal will suffer no compromise. Playful, almost irresponsible evasion has given way to the decision of an assumed will whose act *interrupts,* remarking and transmuting an interruption at the core of the text. The statement follows an admission of incapacity (shortly before, we read: "I had to acknowledge that I was not capable of forming a story out of these events. I had lost the sense of the story" [199]), but it is sovereign in its refusal.

The future of this declarative act is to be read throughout the works that follow *The Madness of the Day* in Blanchot's corpus, and special attention should be given to its echoes in the political texts, beginning, in particular, with the short essay of 1958 later included in *L'amitié,* entitled "Le refus."[2] The statement's emergence from a situation of confinement, in response to a demand whose ground proves to be juridical, makes the political reference almost inevitable. But before leaping forward in Blanchot's oeuvre to consider the insistence of such forms of refusal, it is worthwhile to pause over the question of the *sovereign* character of this particular statement. For it emerges in a text that appears to bear a meditation on sovereignty and invites us to grasp refusal, a sovereign no, together with at least one form of sovereign yes. We hear this latter affirmation taking form in the opening words of the story as the narrator asserts his boundless contentment with life and his unlimited satisfaction at the prospect of dying. A yes to life, and a yes to death. They are doubled shortly thereafter with the following ecstatic statement:

> I am not blind, I see the world—what extraordinary happiness! I see this day, and outside it there is nothing. Who could take that away from me? And when this day fades, I will fade along with it [*ce jour s'effaçant, je m'effacerai avec lui*]—a thought, a certainty, that enraptures me. (191)

How do we understand the relation between the sovereign refusal and the no less sovereign affirmation that it appears to seal? And what may this text bring to us in terms of a thought of sovereignty?

"Sovereignty," I emphasize, must not be taken here as some form of interpretive key or philosophical operator that could give overall access to the text's elusive meaning. *The Madness of the Day* disqualifies any such assumption, as we will see. Nor does the theme of sovereignty encapsulate the text in any sense. It should serve, rather, to help distinguish in the text four forms of relation to what we might call the "order of the day," or simply the law. The fact that at least one of these four forms summons its name by reason of its powerful evocation of the thought of Georges Bataille will suggest why attention to this motif should carry more than thematic interest. But let us start from the text's first explicit reference to this term, since it brings us quickly to a salutary warning that must be heeded and offers us a valuable point of entry.

THE SOVEREIGNTY OF REASON

Relatively early in a biographical account that seems constantly under a kind of mythopoeic pull and is not without traces of a "madness," perhaps a psychosis, which may help account for the narrator's incarceration—regarding his relation to others, the narrator remarks: "if I have to, I deliberately sacrifice them . . . (sometimes I kill them)" (192)—we learn that this "narrator" is a city-dweller who was, at one point, a public man:

> For a while I led a public life. I was attracted to the law, I liked crowds. Among other people I was unknown. As nobody, I was sovereign. But one day I grew tired of being the stone that beats solitary men to death. To tempt the law, I called softly to her, "Come here; let me see you face to face." (For a moment I wanted to take her aside.) It was a foolhardy appeal. What would I have done if she had answered? (193)

The furtive separation that appears here prefigures, of course, the erotic relation with the personified "law" that will follow in the second half of the text—it speaks already to the trace of another kind of sovereignty. But, in this context, "sovereign" describes a form of participation in a general will (the sovereignty described by Rousseau). This form of sovereignty, which the narrator appears to enjoy for only a limited time (soon he will fall into misery and become a "solitary" man), and for which he will subsequently yearn before falling back again,[3] will also manifest itself in the shared appeal to reason in the second half of the story, by those who demand of the protagonist a full account of the events that led to his near-blinding. Behind the suspicions motivating the nurses who care for him and the doctors who attend him and have incarcerated him, there is always the presumption that "a writer, a man who speaks and who reasons with distinction, is always capable of recounting facts that he remembers" (199). At the foundations of the modern techno-political order, the text suggests, there lies the shared appeal to this principle of reason. Its juridical instantiation will appear in the figure of a "third" standing behind the assembled medical expertise:

> Then I noticed for the first time that there were two of them and that this distortion of the traditional method, even though it was explained by the fact that one of them was an eye doctor, the other a

specialist in mental illness, constantly gave our conversation the character of an authoritarian interrogation, overseen and controlled by a strict set of rules. Of course, neither of them was the chief of police. But because there were two of them, there were three . . . (199)

The narrator underscores the intolerant, invasive, and coercive form of this authority; the doctors, he tells us, comport themselves like kings in the impatient expectation of the cognitive evidence they consider their *due*. Thus, in their appeal to the narrator's presumed rational capacity (his capacity to furnish a cause for his suffering in the form of rationally ordered facts), we glimpse the violent edge of modern technical reason in the era of biopower. We may thus understand the epistemic and juridical order presented in this text as the harsh modern avatar of that "space of sovereignty and tranquil human reign" to which Western thought has been devoted since its beginnings.[4]

The sovereign "no" delivered in the last line of *The Madness of the Day* draws up against this epistemic and juridical order in its refusal of the demand to render an account. It confronts, in the same movement, the complacent commentator—that representative of the modern academy, for example, who will have been trapped in the text's folding movement as he discovers his figuration in the medical authorities and his implication in a narrative that has been offered in a situation of interrogation.

But the rational and legal authority we have identified in this "third," who figures between the two clinical representatives of the medical establishment, does not quite exhaust what lies at the foundations of the order the latter represent. For another figure has been identified in this place, through the protagonist's second reference to a personified law. Earlier, as we have seen, the protagonist envisioned meeting the law face to face; in the second half of his narrative, he claims to have glimpsed her silhouette behind the backs of the doctors. Her relation to the protagonist points to at least one more form of sovereignty—a relation that haunts the technical order embodied by the doctors in a manner that might suggest that this latter order has not fully achieved the secularization it assumes (by which would be meant here a human and rational assumption of the legislative authority that was once divinely sanctioned).

SOVEREIGN IMPURITY

The form of sovereignty indicated here is not immediately the one suggested by the fact that the law treats the protagonist as a fallen bearer of a
form of sacral authority[5]—though we should probably pause before de-
veloping this point, since there is obviously a trace of sovereignty in the
strange powers she attributes to him. Indeed, the narrator's abjection is
all the more disturbing for the law by reason of this prior majesty; fallen,
though still menacing in his very passivity, he is a being apart, who drives
her to extremity and finally to erotic transport.

For whom does she take him? The narrator's story is not without its
playful hints. Early in this story, tinged, as I have noted, with mythopoeic
resonance, we hear a passing colloquialism that is revived in the law's
transports. Evoking an earlier experience of madness associated with the
loss of a loved one, the narrator appears to link his state of mind with that
of the world itself. The event narrated in this sequence, the object of a
later text by Blanchot,[6] is of considerable importance and I will return to
it shortly. But for the moment, I draw attention simply to the protagonist's passing self-address:

> Shortly afterward, the madness of the world broke out. I was made to
> stand against the wall like many others. Why? For no reason. The
> guns did not go off. I said to myself, God, what are you doing? At that
> point I stopped being insane. The world hesitated, then regained its
> equilibrium. (191–92)

The protagonist's reference to himself as "God" will normally pass unno-
ticed until the law calls upon his glory in her erotic games (of which, it
seems, there are more than one)—at which point, the protagonist's earlier quip in response to her statement that she is the angel of destruction
("that's more than enough to get us both locked up") starts to bear a ring
of truth.

> This was one of her games. She would show me a part of space, be-
> tween the top of the window and the ceiling. "You are there," she
> said. I looked hard at that point. "Are you there?" I looked at it with

all my might. "Well?" I felt the scars fly off my eyes, my sight was a wound, my head a hole, a bull disembowelled. Suddenly she cried out, "Oh, I see the day, oh God," etc. I protested that this game was tiring me out enormously, but she was insatiably intent upon my glory. (198)

Again, for whom does she take him? The sacral power she lends to him—or discovers in him—is such that she can play at a kind of primal scene and enjoy, repeatedly, her birth to the day ("je vois le jour"). Is she an Athena to his Zeus? Perhaps; but the play involved and above all the narrator's weariness quickly suspend these attributions of divinity. It would seem that we are prompted to entertain in this text an allegory of the death of god. But the text directs us more specifically to what this "death" reveals. For what the law demands of the narrator in her mad ecstasy is nothing other than a repetition of his confrontation with the madness of the day. The glory to which she is attracted is what the protagonist bears of the day's furious assault upon him; she seeks the day's unmeasured opening to him as a kind of groundless origin. Of that assault, we read:

I had to hold my own against the light of seven days—a fine conflagration! Yes, seven days at once, the seven deadly lights, become the spark of a single moment, were calling me to account. Who would have imagined that? At times I said to myself, "This is death. In spite of everything, it's really worth it, it's impressive." But often I lay dying without saying anything. In the end, I grew convinced that I was face to face with the madness of the day. That was the truth: the light was going mad, the brightness had lost all reason; it assailed me irrationally, without control, without purpose. That discovery bit straight through my life. (195)

It is significant, of course, that another figure of divine law appears here in the reference to a final judgment. But the latter reference is immediately undermined with the narrator's identification of this passage as an experience of dying (which we must call "mere" by reason of the very fact that the experience is "impressive" and even "worth it"). The conclusion, however, carries the narrator beyond his speculative pleasure in the sublime traits of his own death, or even the silence he will henceforth bear with him. He attains the very un-Cartesian and non-Platonic certainty that he has known the truth (of Being) in his brutal exposure to a light gone mad.

Schematizing in the language of psychoanalysis, we might be tempted to symbolize the madness (of the day), to which the narrator accedes, with the Lacanian symbol S($\cancel{A}$). The narrator has experienced the defaulting ground of the law in the course of that near-blinding that follows immediately after his account of a primal fantasy.[7] As for the law and her transports, one might be inclined to see these, from this psychoanalytic perspective, as grounded in a death drive.

But another perspective on the law's dissolute behaviour appears more compelling, and this perspective leads us to our third figure of sovereignty. Putting aside all questions of morality (including her own curious prudishness), it seems appropriate to give her repetitive play an affirmative accent and stress the law's desire to return to the *opening* of the day ("her" day). In her ecstatic relation to the "death" of the other that she summons repeatedly, she knows an infinite that is, for her, like a new origin. Whether we focus on the "sovereign impurity" of her transgression (in her manner of finding her birth through the other outside the law) or stress the affirmative movement in her ecstasy, it is difficult to avoid the conclusion that her conduct involves the pursuit of a distinctly Bataillan sovereignty. Erotism and sacrifice signal this reference ("my sight was a wound, my head a hole, a bull disembowelled"), but Blanchot's own commentary on Bataille's thought in *The Infinite Conversation* provides what is essential for our purposes.[8]

I note immediately that this reference to Bataille should not be understood as exclusive. The phrase "sovereign impurity" comes not from Bataille, as it happens, but from Blanchot himself—specifically, from a later discussion of Sophocles' *Oedipus the King*.[9] The discussion is important in reference to *The Madness of the Day* because it leads us to understand the "other" of a "secularized" law not as something sacred or divine, but as something akin to what Blanchot describes as that share of existence that Oedipus draws into himself in his arrogant blindness (a blind arrogance shown also by the representatives of the technical order who incarcerate the narrator in *The Madness of the Day*): "that part that he cannot recognize as true, because its status is, equally, the non-true, the unworking rupture, radical infidelity in the double withdrawal of the divine and the human, non-presence itself."[10] The incarcerated narrator of *The Madness of the Day* bears an unworking power that is neither divine in origin nor human (as understood in the metaphysics of humanism). This "non-presence" is not immediately comparable to the ambiguity of the presence of the Sphinx, to be sure. Instead, the narrator's unworking passivity, his inability to summon the capacities attributed to him, and the insubstantial, abyssal character of the avowal he presents to his doctors all have distinctively *literary* traits. Is not the combination of menacing power and irresponsible vacuity reminiscent of Blanchot's description of literary language itself, in his magnificent essay, "Literature and the Right to Death"? (There, twice, we read a line that recalls the law's relation to our narrator: "Whoever sees God dies.")[11] To put it a bit irreverently: Is the law, in *The Madness of the Day*, not guilty of fooling with literature?

The Bataillan aspect of the law's sovereign excesses, in short, should not narrow our interpretive approach. But however we describe the singular character of the relations between the narrator and the law, we must recognize that the "sovereign impurity" to which the personified law is seduced in *The Madness of the Day* represents no escape for the narrator. On the contrary, the law's erotic games are wearying for him, as we are told in his last reference to her ("I protested that this game was tiring me out enormously" [198]). She may find something like a new birth in transgression with this *other* who both disturbs her (driving her to demand from him the justice she is due) and offers her relation with an impossible that is something like her non-ground. But the narrator's "discovery" of the madness of the day and the *désoeuvrement* that follows constitute no freedom for him, however playful his resistance vis-à-vis the doctors might appear and however much the law pleases him and finds a form of *jouissance* through him. The narrator's discovery of and repetitious engagement with a lack of limits in the ground of the law is in no way liberating. Let us recall that when Emmanuel Lévinas read *The Madness of the Day*, he saw only fatality.[12] As far as the forms of sovereignty we have considered thus far go, Lévinas's response would seem just.

But if the latter suggestion gives us the Bataillan figure of sovereignty as somehow bound or trapped (fated never to exceed its need for reenactment), then the question of the relation between this form of sovereignty and the one we identified earlier in the opening lines of the text becomes all the more interesting. Is it possible that the third form of sovereignty we will approach now somehow exceeds or circumscribes the transgressive relations that the narrator knows with the law in the second half of our text? Does the affirmation borne by these lines embody a different relation to the day and perhaps constitute a step (not) beyond?

SOVEREIGN EXCEPTION

Let us return to the opening lines of *The Madness of the Day* and note not only their affirmative character, but also the form of engagement they record:

> I am not learned; I am not ignorant. I have known joys. That is saying too little: I am alive, and this life gives me the greatest pleasure. And what about death? When I die (perhaps any minute now), I will feel immense pleasure. I am not talking about the foretaste of death, which is stale and often disagreeable. Suffering dulls the senses. But this is the remarkable truth, and I am sure of it: I experience boundless pleasure in living, and I will take boundless satisfaction in dying. . . .
>
> Is my life better than other people's lives? Perhaps. I have a roof over my head and many do not. I do not have leprosy, I am not blind, I see the world—what extraordinary happiness! I see this day, and outside it there is nothing. Who could take that away from me? And when this day fades, I will fade along with it—a thought, a certainty, that enraptures me. (191)

How has the narrator passed from an experience of truth as groundless, even irrational, to the *certain* assumption of his relation to the day? Not only is the narrator certain of his affect; he is certain of his fate (perhaps even of a kind of capacity), and this very thought brings a surplus of affect, a transport. Leaving aside the playful echo of Descartes (who grounded truth in the certainty of his capacity to represent), we must account for this transmuted relation to the day. But how are we to understand it? How does the narrator come to claim a relation to life and to death that he has usually only found in women, "beautiful creatures" (192)?[13]

The narrator's deceptively simple statement of the grounds of the joy that he has discovered contains an assertion that might prompt us to speak of a kind of finite, quasi-, or immanent transcendence (to draw from a few recent philosophical formulations). It is an extraordinary statement from one whose existence has been defined by an incident of near-blinding and who now lives in a state of incarceration: "I see this day, and outside it there is nothing. Who could take that away from me?" But if his sight of the day is inalienable, it is because it is not wholly dependent on vision. The narrator does not just see the world or what the day illumines; he "sees" the day as such, and thus the visibility of the world—he sees what gives the world to be seen. Not even death, it seems, can take from him this knowledge (or thought)—or at least the joy it brings him: "I see this day, and outside it there is nothing." From the limits of the day—which is to say, from a vertiginous "knowledge" of the nothing—the only death that now matters to the narrator is one of his own act: "ce jour s'effaçant, je m'effacerai avec lui."[14] In the supplemental trace of activity in the second reflexive construction, we have, perhaps, the grounds of the last two forms of sovereignty I seek to describe in *The Madness of the Day*.

Two subsequent texts by Blanchot help bring to the fore the *distance* that is drawn between the "Bataillian" transport enjoyed by the narrator with the law and the form of transcendence anticipated, and already enjoyed, by the narrator. A reference to the first of these (though this is the latest in order of publication) is summoned by the narrator's sense of a kind of immortality. The assertion that the death that may be impending—"When I die (perhaps any minute now)" (191)—is one that he will enjoy strongly recalls the sovereign experience of deliverance to which Blanchot refers in *L'instant de ma mort,* the late publication in which he returns again to the event that is first recounted on the page from which I have just quoted in *The Madness of the Day*.[15] Reading the latter text from the perspective of the former (and armed with the biographical evidence offered by Derrida), it is difficult to avoid the hypothesis that the narrator's free relation to life and death, as it is described in the opening pages of *The Madness of the Day,* owes at least as much to the experience recounted allusively there as it does to the "knowledge" gained in the narrator's near-blinding (involving exposure to the day and a form of silent dying).[16] And even without the perspective it brings to the event in question it throws into relief significant elements of the opening part of the narrative, obliging us to consider more attentively their strangeness. Is the *remembrance* recovered by the protagonist (in the return of reason and memory after the world regains its equilibrium) not incommensurable with that reason to which the doctors and nurses appeal later in the narrative? Again, is the "discovery" of happiness it brings of any less consequence for the sovereign relation to life and death that the narrator enjoys than the discovery of the madness of the day that "bites through his life"? The latter, we might hazard, gives our narrator a relation to the day as such; the former, it seems, has something to do with the capacity to assume this relation, his manner of surviving in the instant of what is an ever-impending death.[17]

Of an instance of "survival" comparable to the one known by our narrator, we read, in *The Writing of the Disaster:* "The always suspended question: being dead of the 'power to die' that brings him joy and ravishment, did he survive? Or rather, what is 'survive' to mean, if not living by way of *an acquiescence to the refusal* [my emphasis]."[18] The refusal, in this case, is of the knowledge ("affirmed and dissolved") of what is given in the experience recounted in one of the "primal scenes" in *The Writing of the Disaster:* "the vertiginous knowledge that nothing is what there is, and first of all nothing beyond."[19] The correlate in *The Madness of the Day* to the acquiescence to which these lines refer is the narrator's nonresistance and his peculiar relation of *Gelassenheit* vis-à-vis life and death. His capacity to *assume* his mortality is grounded in such a prior yes to loss and the gift of transcendence it brings.

In lines immediately preceding the figuration of the death of the *infans* to which the remarks on survival refer in *The Writing of the Disaster,* Blanchot comments on this never-accomplished death with an assertion that seems particularly pertinent:

"A child is being killed." Let us make no mistake about this present: it signifies that the deed cannot be done once and for all, that the operation is completed at no privileged moment in time—that, inoperable, it operates and that thus it tends to be none but the very time which destroys (effaces) time. This is the effacement or destruction, or gift, which has always already been exposed in the precession of Saying outside the said, a speech of writing by which this effacement, far from effacing itself in its turn, perpetuates itself without end, even in the interruption that is its mark.[20]

Is not such an "effacement" what the narrator awaits, ecstatically, in *The Madness of the Day*? Twice he has known the day's interruption, and in this repetition he has come to await not an apocalypse, but an end of the day that he feels empowered to embrace. A biblical tone suffuses the narrator's words, but this end of days is to be understood from the basis of an event, a gift wherein time marks its effacement. Assuming this gift, our protagonist is awaiting, while waiting in, the instant of his death. The strange power of his words derives, in part, from the echo of the saying of this gift. Late in *The Writing of the Disaster*, a voice asks of the "primal scene": "But who recounts?" To which the answer comes: "The story.— The pre-story, the 'flashing circumstance' whereby the dazzled child sees—he has the spectacle of it—the happy murder of himself which gives him words' silence."[21] In *The Madness of the Day*, we can identify a first-person narrator in response to the question of who recounts. But, as in *The Writing of the Disaster*, the narrator speaks in a *narrative voice* whose inner distance constitutes the enigmatic space from which the narrator declares a willed transcendence that cannot be heard by those interrogating him and that will finally be coupled with the final refusal, the concluding no.

We might well say of the one who speaks in *The Madness of the Day* simply that he *writes*. In the pages shortly before the passage concerning the saying of effacement ("a speech of writing whereby this effacement, far from effacing itself in its turn, perpetuates itself without end even in the *interruption* that constitutes its mark"), Blanchot gives precisely this epithet to the acquiescence that we have identified and the claim it makes upon one who assumes it:

> Dying means: you are dead already, in an immemorial past, of a death which was not yours, which you have thus neither known nor lived, but under the threat of which you believe you are called upon to live;

you await it henceforth in the future, constructing a future to make it possible at last—possible as something that will take place and will belong to the realm of experience.

To write is no longer to situate death in the future—the death which is always already past; to write is to accept that one has to die without making death present and without making oneself present to it. To write is to know that death has taken place even though it has not been experienced, and to recognize it in the forgetfulness that it leaves—in the traces which, effacing themselves, call upon one to *exclude oneself from the cosmic order [s'excepter de l'ordre cosmique]* and to abide where the disaster makes the real impossible and desire undesirable.[22]

Is not the narrator of *The Madness of the Day* prepared to "except" himself from the order of the day, in and with the "effacement" of the day? And of equal importance, perhaps: is the "no" with which the text concludes not linked to this self-exception? Are the yes and no perhaps two sides of the same act of writing to which *The Madness of the Day* gives testimony?

I turn, finally, to one other text by Blanchot that offers, if not an answer to this question, at least a reflection of the enigmatic passage that is involved. I refer to the concluding moments of the dialogue that opens *The Infinite Conversation*, specifically to the narrator's wonderment at an act of effacement. The passage immediately preceding this section of the dialogue stages the question of the suspended relation between the event of effacement, as we have seen it described in *The Writing of the Disaster*, and the order of the logos—the Law. To what extent can there be a breach in the latter order—can we think a pure time of exception (interdiction), a writing, beyond the Law? The narration concludes with the following haunting statement about one of the two interlocutors, apparently the one who is in advance of the other in withdrawing from the day:

How had he come to will the interruption of the discourse? . . . And not the legitimate pause, the one permitting the give and take of conversation, the benevolent, intelligent pause, nor that beautifully poised waiting with which two interlocutors, from one shore to another, measure their right to communicate. No, not that, and no more so the austere silence, the tacit speech of visible things, the reserve of those invisible. What he had wanted was entirely different, a cold interruption, the rupture of the circle. And at once this had happened: the heart ceasing to beat, the eternal speaking drive stopping.[23]

We might easily conclude that this passage describes a form of suicide. But *The Madness of the Day*, as we have seen, points to a very different answer, even without the condemnation of suicide it contains. It invites us to understand the willed interruption in question in relation to the refusal that it carries in its own ending. At the same time, it suggests that the protagonist of the dialogue to which this paragraph refers has made the step of "self-effacement."

THE SOVEREIGN NO, THE SOVEREIGN YES

What, then, of the relation between the no and the yes? Does the concluding refusal of *The Madness of the Day* communicate somehow with the in-finite act described at the start? Does the same will sound in its concluding decision as the one that carries the ecstatic engagement of the narrator, pronounced in the phrase on which we have focused: *ce jour s'effaçant, je m'effacerai avec lui?*

Let us acknowledge, first, the exceptional character of this "no". It is spoken from a position of enunciation that is not present in the narrator's recognition of his incapacity to form a narrative, and it bears a quite different "edge" in its decision. It bears and conveys a *knowledge* of interruption that is not evident in the narrator's previous statements, and it seems almost to issue from a space other than that of the incarceration described in the lines that precede it, or from a different time. It speaks to the law and the sovereignty of reason, to be sure, but it now draws a line in relation to this latter demand. We might even be tempted to speak of a kind of freedom in this declaration of self-exception. But it also draws a line in relation to the narrative contained in the body of the text.

The step (not) beyond of which the narrator describes himself capable in the opening of the text (is this necessarily the *same* narrator?) points to a *passage* in exception—a crossing of the line, so to speak. It announces a "freedom," if this word may be hazarded here, that would seem to be of a very different order from the one claimed in the refusal—a rarer and ultimately more enigmatic transcendence. But does the concluding "no" suspend it, after the fact, or does it condition or even preserve it somehow?

In conceptual terms, and from the basis of this text, there would appear to be no way to establish the relation between this sovereign act of exception (an act of taking exception from the demand for an ordered account—ethico-political in its manner of delimiting the order of the day) and the sovereign will to self-effacement. Both forms of sovereignty proceed from an experience of interruption, but the bridge between them, if it exists, escapes discursive articulation. Nothing assures us that the "no" is carried or inspired by the "yes" (in the sense that refusal would find its force in a different relation), or that it could ever carry beyond the knowledge of interruption—it carries, in effect, no further than the engagement embedded in its statement. It does not seal or negate the preceding, infinitely receding yes (what preceded it was hardly a story), any more than it actively guards it or prepares its advent in a rigorous commitment to waiting. It refuses surrender; but it does not look explicitly beyond the demand from which it turns.

We can say of this relation, then, no more than that it is a neutral or interrupted one, and we can surmise that in this relation—between a declarative act of sociopolitical import and the trace of an unworking freedom—we have all the ambiguity of "le pas au-delà." This is not to abandon, with the claims of conceptual reason, all hope of thinking this relation (without relation). It is to surmise that its thought requires something on the order of a sovereign writing.

NOTES

1. Two paragraphs before the end of the text, we read: "I had been asked: Tell us 'just exactly' what happened. A story? I began: I am not learned; I am not ignorant. I have known joys. That is saying too little" (199). What the narrator recounts here, of course, are the opening words of the story we have been reading. Thus, once the narrator's agreement to recount the story is recounted, the text we have been reading slips from the present of narration and the end of his ac-

count cannot be determined. The reader is confronted with the perspective of an endlessly self-enfolding movement. Jacques Derrida gives long and careful attention to this structure in several essays in *Parages* (Paris: Galilée, 1986). Only the final statement of refusal appears to stand clearly apart, and it begins with the same words as the recounted acquiescence to the doctors: "A story?"

All quotations from *The Madness of the Day* are from the translation by Lydia Davis in *The Station Hill Blanchot Reader: Fiction and Literary Essays,* ed. George Quasha, trans. Lydia Davis et al. (Barrytown, NY: Station Hill Press, 1999).

2. Maurice Blanchot, *L'amitié* (Paris: Gallimard, 1971), 130–31.

3. I refer here to the narrator's desire for the light of day in the second half of his narrative, a desire that drives him into the street, despite the difficulty he experiences (though he has declared himself "cured" and claims that his vision has "hardly weakened"): "I walked through the streets like a crab, holding tightly onto the walls, and whenever I let go of them dizziness surrounded my steps. I often saw the same poster on these walls; it was a simple poster with rather large letters: *You want this too.* Of course I wanted it, and every time I came upon these prominent words, I wanted it. Yet something in me quickly stopped wanting" (195–96).

4. I quote here from a text in *The Infinite Conversation,* trans. Susan Hanson (Minneapolis: University of Minnesota Press, 1993), to which I will return below: "The Most Profound Question," 18.

5. Already we have a figure of sovereignty in this power, though it seems most appropriate—or "reasonable"—to treat it in conjunction with the claims and behavior of the personified law (thereby leaving aside the possible implications of the narrator's attribution of this power to himself). Thus, I will focus only on the "sovereignty" acted out in her relation to him. But it will be evident that we are dealing, in this second form of sovereignty, with a complex of traditional notions to which Georges Bataille was always attentive.

6. Blanchot, *L'instant de ma mort* (Montpellier: Fata Morgana, 1994).

7. I refer to the narrator's "brief vision" of a woman with a baby carriage (194). The narrator describes the affect accompanying this vision as follows: "This brief scene excited me to the point of delirium. I was undoubtedly not able to explain it to myself fully, and yet I was sure of it, that I had seized the moment when the day, having stumbled against a real event, would begin hurrying to its end. Here it comes, I said to myself, the end is coming, something is happening, the end is beginning. I was seized by joy."

8. See "The Limit-Experience," in *The Infinite Conversation,* 202–17. We also find in these pages what might well be a means of recognizing Blanchot's implicit "delimitation" of the law's excesses. In discussing the affirmative character of the Bataillan experience of the negative, Blanchot seeks to push Bataille's thought beyond any substantialization of the notion of the "nothing" or any final hold of the dialectic: "Are we to see here a last dialectical reversal, the

last degree (but a degree pertaining to no scale) on the basis of which man, this intellect accomplished in proportion to the universe, would send the entire edifice back into the night and, doing away with this universal intellect, still receive from this ultimate negation a light, a supplementary affirmation that would add to the whole the truth of the sacrifice of the whole? Despite the nature of such a movement—so immoderate that one cannot pretend to refuse it (assign to it a meaning precise enough to enable one to reject it, it not being deniable)—I would like to say that the limit-experience is still more extreme. For this act of supreme negation we have just supposed (and that for Georges Bataille was no doubt for a time represented by the research of *Acéphale*) still belongs to the possible. Power, the power that is capable of everything, is able even to do away with itself as a power (the explosion of the nucleus itself being one of the extremes of nihilism). Such an act will in no way make us accomplish the decisive step, the step that would deliver us over—in a sense without ourselves—to the surprise of impossibility by allowing us to belong to *this nonpower that is not simply the negation of power*. For thought, the limit-experience represents something *like* a new origin. What it offers to thought is the essential gift, the prodigality of affirmation; an affirmation, for the first time, that is not a product (the result of a double negation), and that thereby escapes all the movements, oppositions and reversals of dialectical reason" (*The Infinite Conversation*, 208–9). Is the law, in short, possibly caught at the stage Blanchot identifies with *Acéphale* in her description of herself as the angel of destruction?

9. In *The Infinite Conversation*, 17–18.

10. Ibid., 438.

11. Blanchot, "Literature and the Right to Death," in *The Station Hill Blanchot Reader*, 359–99.

12. Emmanuel Lévinas, *Sur Maurice Blanchot* (Montpellier: Fata Morgana, 1975), 53–74.

13. The personified law, is not, it would seem, one of these beautiful creatures, even if she does bring a feminine presence to oppressively masculine surroundings (198). Again, the serenity to which the narrator attests at the start of his narrative contrasts with the sovereign ecstasy he enjoys with the law.

14. I comment upon this phrase in my *Infant Figures* with reference to a thought of usage (Stanford: Stanford University Press, 2000), 127–28. I emphasize there that the narrator is asserting not simply that he will "fade" with the day, in dependence on it, in the sense that the day would be the condition of his own being. The narrator is asserting that with the effacement of the day, he will efface himself. In the narrator's certainty of that coming step, we have what Blanchot terms a "pouvoir mourir." Barely a reflection, and "certain" at least by inevitability, the assumption of "mortality" is nevertheless an act of freedom that is predicated on a prior "usage," a prior acquiescence to the exposure that is assumed.

15. This brief narrative account of Blanchot's experience of being placed before a firing squad in the Second World War is the object of lengthy commentary in Jacques Derrida's *Demeure* (Paris: Galilée, 1998).

16. The paragraphs from *L'instant de ma mort* to which I refer here are the following: "I know—do I know?—that the one the Germans had already in their sights, awaiting only the final order, experienced a feeling of extraordinary lightness, a kind of beatitude (nothing of a happiness, nevertheless)—a sovereign elation [*allégresse souveraine*]? The encounter of death and death? I will not seek to analyse this sentiment of lightness. He was perhaps suddenly invincible. Dead—immortal. Perhaps ecstasy" (10–11).

17. "L'instant de ma mort désormais toujours en instance"—the last lines of *L'instant de ma mort* (18).

18. Maurice Blanchot, *The Writing of the Disaster*, trans. Ann Smock (Lincoln: University of Nebraska Press, 1986), 116.

19. Ibid., 72.

20. Ibid., 71.

21. Ibid., 115.

22. Ibid., 65–66.

23. *The Infinite Conversation*, xxiii.

SEVEN

ON MINOR READING EVENTS

ORALITY AND SPACING IN THE OPENING OF
AU MOMENT VOULU

Christophe Bident

I would like here to examine two minor reading events, focused on the openings of some *récits* by Maurice Blanchot.[1] These events might seem secondary. The first, obsessively repeated, is the shock that has seized me as a reader for more than ten years, every time I read, every time I say, and every time I repeat this first, apparently simple sentence of a *récit* from 1951, *Au moment voulu:* "In the absence of the friend who lived with her, the door was opened by Judith."[2] The second, worked out and performed *in the world,* so to speak, is the paralysis that derails every reader or every actor who attempts to say this same sentence out loud. Let me explain: a theatre director, I gave myself the opportunity, several years ago, of directing a workshop on Maurice Blanchot with four actors. At the time, I was far from considering staging a performance; Blanchot's permission would have been necessary anyway, and we know today that, with only one exception, he always refused to grant the rights to perform his novels and stories. I wanted only to put to the test the repeated shock of my silent and solitary reading of *Au moment voulu*'s opening. I wanted to sense

196

what would be entailed for an actor who would have to recite or act this phrase. We spent many hours and many nights seeking the right balance between the text, the voice, the posture, and the body. We quickly moved to no longer simply speaking the text but to miming it, putting it into gestures, movements, traces, into a body, into space. I had always believed that Blanchot's stories offered an extraordinary challenge to the actor, imposing on him or her the search for the origin, the place, the spacing, the time, the rhythm, the approach, the address of all speech. I could, then, after this workshop work on more theatrical texts, notably those of Bernard-Marie Koltès. But the unique character of the questioning that Blanchot's texts present to the practice of the theatre, which is rarely attested to by well-known directors (I can only think of Claude Régy in France), merited further investigation. Thus, when Pierre-Antoine Villemaine, the only director to whom Blanchot gave the rights to stage a scene of his fiction, asked me to participate with him in some workshops and to read aloud Blanchot's texts for the Bibliothèque d'Information at the Centre Georges Pompidou in Beaubourg, I naturally accepted immediately, sure that I would find, with amateur readers this time and not professional actors, the same stakes and the same inexhaustible vein of questioning.[3] This is indeed what happened. Each reader found himself struck from the first lines, and especially in the first lines, for reasons that I want to turn or return to here and explore further.[4]

You will have already realized that I am taking up the aforementioned subject, "the openings of Maurice Blanchot's *récits*," in a perhaps unforeseen manner—not through a poetic reading, poeticized or semiological, which immediately would establish the text as an object of knowledge, but through a double perspective: that of the silent and solitary reading and that of the communal reading aloud, which first investigates the quality of an experience. It will nonetheless be a question of poetics, yet I would like to specify by this questioning a particular relation between poetics and philosophy (particularly phenomenology) that Blanchot's work affords us the opportunity to examine.

I must immediately clarify what I mean by "the work" of Blanchot. From this immense body of work, I will extract only a few sentences, which introduce the *récit*. And—a final confession—I will concentrate on one phrase (you have already guessed which one): the beginning of *Au moment voulu,* not without having in mind the beginnings of Blanchot's other works, of course. I would not say that this particular sentence is representative of the other openings of Blanchot's *récit*s. But I would say, despite the singularity of each *récit* and of each *récit*'s opening, that this sentence participates in a general movement and illustrates an insistent poetics specific to Blanchot's writing.

Now let me clarify the questions as well as their area of convergence. At what point can the inscription of the first sentence, reserving or preserving the void, be a factor for Blanchot in the crafting of a *récit*? At what point might the word's appearance, cleaving or displacing the silence, have an impact on readers, attempting to recite a *récit*? At what point might this transformation of space affect actors in the embodiment or the miming of a *récit*? From which origin do these words, voices, and bodies that transmit the beginning of the *récit* arise? Does the neutrality of the initial opening correspond to the darkness necessary to the look, the silence necessary to sound, the whiteness necessary to the page?

My hypothesis is that the opening of each *récit* may be read but also heard and seen as the bringing into play of an oralization and of a spacing of the *récit*, or rather, of an oralization of the narration and a spacing of the reading. It is a written verbalization, certainly, but one which, without lyricism or eloquence, affects the writing and thus the reading as well. It is also a written spacing, to be sure: one that, without theatricality or grandiloquence, affects the writing and therefore also the reading of the text. Might one say, nevertheless, that the paradigms of solitude and sharing, of void and of silence, of white and of black, of writing and of the voice, of page and body, and of book and space, intersect, join, are shrouded, sheltered, read, heard, understood, exactly?

Let us return therefore to the text. Let us reread, let us listen anew, to the opening of the *récit, Au moment voulu:* "In the absence of the friend who lived with her, the door was opened by Judith."

The uniqueness of this sentence seems to me to arise from three principles. The first is the curiosity of its referential functioning. A door opens—a metaphor, if you will, of the opening of the *récit* and even of the opening of the scene —but it is opened in the passive voice "by Judith," a Judith first identified by a pronoun "she," and the first to be named by the narrator. Yet the narrator-character is not yet named, specified, or identified by a pronoun; in short, he has not yet come forward, since the first to be named is not Judith (the Judith whom the narrator, we learn on the following page, knew well) but this "friend who lived with her," a person whom, this same narrator rapidly admits, he does not know. This is a strange order of presentation of facts and identities. The useless passes for the useful, the expected becomes surprising, clarity collapses into disorder, the subject of the exposition withdraws: we are at the limit of all referentiality, of all representation, of all possible correlation.

The second principle is the device of reflection. The "I" is not named, advanced, or shifted, but as readers we are immediately exposed, deposed, or even imposed on with respect to his gaze. We look with him without knowing who he is, we see with him the door open, we know even before he does that a friend lives with Judith. He must have knocked or rung—we did not see it or hear it—but we advance placidly toward the threshold of the door and that of the *récit:* placidly, yes, in the tranquil rhythm of the anapestic and nonetheless epic alexandrine verse ("In the absence / of the friend / who lived / with her"),[5] and of the decasyllabic, punctuated by the consonants ("the door was opened by Judith").[6] We are thus immediately ushered into the strangeness of a face-to-face meeting.

The third principle is that the enunciative structure, despite all appearances, is perhaps more discursive than narrative. It is oral, even oracular, insofar as Blanchot says elsewhere that prophecy does not so much give us a future as it takes the present away from us. Who is Judith? Who is the friend? Who is the "I"? The opacity of the enigma is delivered in two lines, incredibly quickly. Here, everything gives itself—the foyer, the look, the opening, the vision—but at the same time everything withdraws: the absence of the friend, the transparency of the narrator, the void of the framing of the door. Rather than the opening of a *récit,* we attend the opening of a scene: it is as if we are at the theatre, *we are* the theatre, we are the place *from which we see.* In this way, the narrator looks over us, but also we see with him, and still the *récit* regards itself. I would say it thus—and I will return to this point: a *voice* exceeds the *récit* and intercedes in the writing. In short, there is a true beginning, a beginning that encounters an obstacle, a beginning that begins by tripping, if we follow the etymology of *débuter.*[7] Should we not, indeed, see in this the mark of a theological and teleological hold, even a mystical hold? For to begin is never to begin *ex nihilo*.[8] From the first accounts of the verb, in the seventeenth century, "to begin" signified deflecting a ball from its position, that is, striking an initial hit or blow in order to know who will *then* really start the game.[9] The paradox demands that it should be, as Antoine Furetière explains in the *Dictionnaire Universel,* "an advantage to play the last ball because you 'begin' by displacing the opponent's ball." The narrator of *Au moment voulu* plays first and last at the same time: the first without us seeing it (that is the *récit*), and the last because he has *started* us playing (this is the reflection of the narration on the *récit*). We are not therefore dealing with so much a beginning *in medias res,* as we say, as with a beginning *in medias ludos.* A ludic beginning—specular, spectacular; oral, oracular; such is the hypothesis. (The door swings freely.) There is play: a new metaphor, if you will, no longer in the *récit* but in the discourse, play in the hinges of this opening door.

The beginning, we see, is always an excessive figure. It is indeed this excess that motivates us or frightens us, when we bring ourselves silently or orally to the act of reading. All beginnings are a culmination, since the goal of the beginning is, so to speak, to have a beginning. In this simple and unique sentence we would therefore have two beginnings for the price of one. This is precisely what accounts for its value; it lends it perhaps also a slight preciosity, but at the same time, it gives it a play and a movement.

Let me restate my hypothesis. The beginning of *Au moment voulu* opens with a strong structure: ludic, specular, spectacular, oral, oracular. Such a structure rests upon, respectively, the game, the mirror, the theatre, the voice, and the enigma, and, therefore, as their essence, on chance, reflection, space, the gift, and the secret. Finally, and as the condition of the preceding, it rests on time, the look, the body, the other, and the third person. Among these terms, the terms of the beginning but no doubt also of the end, of all beginnings and all endings—among these terms, the beginning of *Au moment voulu* establishes relations of attraction, of polarization, and of orientation (or of disorientation, depolarization, and repulsion). We who are reading, silently or aloud, or we who are acting or miming, or acting or "actuating," as Jerzy Grotowski writes, are caught in the magnetic field between the game, the mirror, the theatre, the voice, the enigma; between chance, the reflection, space, the gift, the secret; between time, the look, the body, the other, and the third person. In this situation there occurs, by turns, the peal of thunder, the suspense of the pause, and the hardness of reserve or of discretion. In a word, the field becomes charged, everything is posed, nothing is firmly placed, and it is this field that readers and actors confront every time that they must read or "actuate" Blanchot's text.

Let us return once more to the beginning of *Au moment voulu*. There we find some of the terms mentioned just now: the game, by the withdrawal of a narrator who envelops us in his presence; the mirror, at the least its framing, and the immediate height at which we are placed, which can only be that of Judith; the theatre, by the opening of the door as well as the opening of the first scene which we attend; the voice, by the substitution of a discursive beginning to its narrative beginning; the enigma, by the absence of identification of any character (save perhaps Judith, identified by her allegorical signification, "Jewess," or by her legendary reference to the biblical heroine who decapitated Holofernes—but both of these supposed references ultimately contribute to reinforcing the enigma). And, therefore, once again, we see the themes of chance, because the friend's absence seems unexpected, as the second sentence confirms; of reflection, by the use of the passive voice; of space, by the opening of the door and that which we can imagine it gives to our sight beyond Judith; of the gift, by the very gesture of welcome, as well as hospitality; of the secret, because who can say what, then, is the relationship that ties Judith to her friend; of time, because we cannot, from the first sentence, *not* think of the title "in the desired moment" (was it, precisely, the desired moment?); in addition, we see the themes of the look and the body, provoked by the face-to-face; of the other, Judith; and of the third person, Claudia, without our being able to suppose that the story might not end up reversing all of these roles.

If we read more carefully the lines and pages that follow the first sentence, we are able to perceive that all of these terms are amplified, questioned, or commented upon by the narrator. I have suggested as much in connection with the theme of chance, as the second sentence of *Au moment voulu* suggests: "My surprise was extreme, inextricable, much greater, assuredly, than if I had met her by chance." It is, in some way, the ultimate chance, which redoubles the enigma: because, in the end, how can one be this surprised to see someone whom one has gone to visit? The third sentence does not resolve the enigma but, on the contrary, further deepens it: "The astonishment was such that it expressed itself in me by these words: 'My God! Another face I know!'"[10] By this we understand that it is the face [*figure*] that gives rise to the surprise, but which face? Judith's? The image provided by memory? The trace or the specter of knowledge? The object of recognition? The vision of the scene? The word "face" returns immediately in the fourth sentence, a sentence placed in parentheses like an aside: "(Maybe my decision to walk right towards this face was so strong as to make it impossible)." *Impossible face* [*figure*]: this "impossible" does not clarify the sense of this beginning, of this initiative, of this reduction, of this decision—or instead, we might say, the sense of these beginnings, of these steps, of these decisions, since each applies both to the narrative utterance and to the discursive enunciation. The key words of the scene—"surprise," "me," "face"—are at first unexpected; however, once posed, they do not cease to be interpreted; but this commentary, rather than clarifying their appearance, their stakes and meaning, redoubles their enigmatic character.

If the three sentences that follow the first thus reinforce the enigma in thematizing the surprise and the element of chance, in attesting a face [*figure*] only immediately to suspend it, it is because they establish an enunciative strategy, in this case a discursive strategy, of syncopating the *récit*, opening its commentaries *ad infinitum*, unfolding them by paradoxical, disjointed sentences, and then refolding them by terse, intricate sentences, aligning, to the limits of parataxis, the quotation marks of interior monologue and the parenthesis of commentary within commentary. These dislocations, these oddities, these shocks, these clashes multiply the oral or orational procedures, if not, once again, the oracular ones. Alternately, the interior voice exclaims, in the time of the narrative, and then puts itself in reserve, in the time of the enunciation. This beginning has no purpose or function of narrative explanation. Its vocation—quite literally—or the complicated orality of its calls and counter-calls is to dissociate and to stratify the process of these strange encounters. In short, the door does not open so easily or so harmoniously; it lacks play in its hinges, and this play increases through its very lack.

I speak of strategy because it is a matter, at the outset of the narrative, of attaining the other, of placing or displacing the reader. This enunciative strategy of the double entry, both narrative and discursive, could refer to what Blanchot has called, in underscoring a distinction, the instantiating narrative voice and the neutral narrative voice.[11] Therefore, it is as if there were a hand that writes, that maintains, and maneuvers, that would call to the narrative voice to take down the narrating voice. But since, in the epoch of the *nouveau roman,* none of this is truly original, I cannot limit my analysis to this single marking of differentiations. For more on this subject, I refer to an invaluable study by Jean-Patrice Courtois, which takes up the poetics of Blanchot's *récits* where Jean Starobinski and Henri Meschonnic left off.[12] It is noteworthy that Courtois, a noted scholar of Montesquieu and of the Enlightenment, is also, first and foremost, a poet.

Courtois, starting from a parallel examination of "The Essential Solitude," the chapter that opens *The Space of Literature,* and of the *récit* entitled *The One Who Was Standing Apart from Me,* engages in a critical, poetic, and philosophical study of the elaboration of the narrative voice in Blanchot and its relation to the *neutre* and the murmur. The key words are there—the *neutre,* the murmur, the voice—and so too are the tone, the retreat, the articulation, and the interruption, which Courtois relates to various theories of Benveniste, for example, when he speaks of "the link between the neutralization of the properly linguistic conditions of the enunciation and the 'he,' the person who is not a person according to Benveniste, the neuter of the work which only exists in the discourse by the unweaving of the significant stitches of the enunciation" (553). It is to such an "unweaving of the significant stitches of enunciation" that I have also tried, thus far, to be attentive, and this is why I will recall here at least three important points.

The first point is the emphasis placed on orality and musicality. Courtois speaks of an enunciation "in the form of an accordion" (550).[13] Further on, he adds, "the exterior signs of fiction of the fiction [we are truly, as we see, in a reading that proceeds by double entry] return to the heart of language and modify the regime of the *récit,* to the point of resembling a recitative of thought" (558). It is with such a recitative that those reading aloud must grapple both vocally and physically, something which each time and for each reader complicates things to the extent that it is orality as such that is woven into the writing. (Courtois sees here "a thought and a type of speech that can appear only in writing" [571].)

The second point is the accent placed on the syntactic collision, in terms of "undressing" and "disappropriation": "the grammatical undressing of language, the disappropriation in the very place of the proper." "As a result," Courtois says, "the deconstruction of the linguistic conditions of the enunciation has itself, as its reverse side, the recomposition of the conditions of interlocution in another space, I / he designating a proper interlocutory geography" (557). This, equally, is just what happens when one attempts to read these texts aloud.

The third point is the accent placed on the indissociably abstract and perceptible part of this murmur articulated in language and withdrawing within it. If Blanchot's writing sets aside all representational facility, it does not, for all that, take refuge in "abstraction, the bad infinite of the murmur" (554). The murmur, perhaps the *neutre,* is always that of a voice or a body. I am grateful to Courtois for never using that all too easy expression "the body." If I use it, it is precisely because I have put it in question: the speaking voice in the murmur, and the exposed body in the non-identity of self or of every face [*figure*]. And so it is precisely here that questions are raised or raised again.

These incessant games between orality and literariness, between spacing and pagination, between disappropriation and appropriation, between perception and abstraction—*between* precisely because one never overcomes the other—none is ever undone by the other. These complications to which the reading of the text commits us are thus focused in *Au moment voulu* in a "surprising" rapport between a "me" and a "face" [*figure*]. If the fifteen terms that I have already identified (ludic, specular, spectacular, oral, oracular; the game, the mirror, the theatre, the voice, the enigma; chance, reflection, space, the gift, and the secret) return in the first three or four pages of the *récit,* it is precisely to question this surprising rapport between the me and the face: an "I" caught between personality and impersonality, authority and unraveling, injury and fascination, renunciation and resurrection; a face presenting itself by turns as outline, copy, resemblance, memory, forgetting, look, and melody, an aggregate of traits or of appearance. Thus, Judith's face does not simply appear in the *récit*. What Blanchot gives us to read, whether silently or orally, is the shock visited on a subject by a face that, thematically and recurrently, comes to fissure a *récit* that nonetheless moves forward, that progresses in conjunction with the narrator's movements in the apartment, and in conjunction with our own progress, along with the narrator, in that apartment.

No doubt there was no way of setting forth this play of the discourse with the *récit* other than by absence: the double absence that inaugurates the *récit,* the thematized absence of the friend, and the thematized absence, that of the narrator (a narrator "set a-part from his own part," says Courtois again [552], or an "I" always already *illéisé,* I might say). Let me be clear on this point: had Blanchot simply wanted to say that the narrator, several years after their break, returns to see his old friend, who henceforth lives with a woman, but that he is surprised to find her so little changed, he would have gone about it differently. What surprises the reader, in this beginning *in medias ludos,* is not the anxious awaiting of what will soon happen, as when Tchen lifts the mosquito netting in Malraux's *Man's Fate,* nor is it even the eagerness to know what has happened before, but it is how things can happen thus in a scene that must necessarily be called a *scene of recognition.* In other words, what happens in the beginning involves a phenomenology of recognition.

Must one then push aside the third person, the active voice, and presence, in order to begin to write what occurs in a scene of recognition? What is it that opens this scene so singularly and that paralyzes or dumbfounds both narrator and reader? What is it that makes it so difficult for a recitation and corporeal miming to betray something of this arrest, of this astonishment, of this gaping surprise? The silent reader can continue, even if he or she is stupefied, irritated, intrigued, or shocked; but how can someone reading aloud speak with his or her mouth agape? How can the actor or the mime act with a paralyzed body? How, therefore, can one write, read, speak, or play a scene of recognition? Does it even have a beginning, an end, a middle? And can one thus limit, spatialize, and clarify it? In the *récit* the first way out of our astonishment occurs three and a half pages after the beginning: this virtual end of the beginning expresses the sudden passage, in a devastating radiance, of a power without a face.

As always with Blanchot, the questions at issue are immense. Between an "inextricable surprise" and a "force without a face," between a look without force and a blinding clarity, between a beginning of a beginning and an end of a beginning, what has happened? What is the first event to occur in this *récit*? And to whom does it happen? Is it even a narrative event? Does this entire beginning, and all of the writing of this beginning, not signify the extent to which this event does not belong to the narrative order? From what language might it then derive? This is what I would at the least like to indicate in the rest of this essay. This event of recognition can result only from a poetic or fragmentary language. The play of discourse in the *récit* derives precisely from this dissonant and distended irruption, opening what had been enclosed, of the poetic or of the fragmentary within the narrative. This *or* itself, in the alternative poetic *or* fragmentary, must be investigated. If my hypothesis is correct, it allows us to understand why these texts simultaneously pose the difficulty and the enthusiasm of reading of which I have been speaking.

No phenomenology of recognition could begin without ascertaining the infinite character of the recognition. And it is precisely in this that the end of the beginning must be virtual, even if it actualizes an event. What it inscribes are the paradoxical conditions without which no instance of recognition could occur or even reconstitute itself: ignorance, interference, disagreement, strangeness, misunderstanding, and blindness. It is therefore an infinite process that is given in the finite moment of the *récit*'s opening. Blanchot, as we see, does not only let us view a scene of recognition, as would be the case of Julien Sorel and Madame de Rénal, but also opens up the narrative to what happens and to what contracts (or precipitates) in the recognition scene. Or rather, he gives it at the same time as he opens it, deferring it as he diffracts it, composes it, but immediately deconstructs it—whence, once again, this "inextricable surprise" of both the difficulty and the appeal of the reading.

Can a phenomenology of recognition even begin? Doesn't the writing of this scene pose the same question to phenomenology of the touch or of touching that Jacques Derrida approaches with the motif of the eyes that meet or touch: a "pre-phenomenological" or maybe "transphenomenal" question?[14] Let us note, in order to bring both the corpus and the questioning together, the appearance of this motif of the striking glance on the third page of *Au moment voulu:* "She was looking at me in a strange manner, spontaneous and lively, and yet sideways. This look, I don't know why, struck me in my very heart."[15] The look, the blow, the heart—these are all echoes of the book by Derrida that I have just cited, *Le Toucher, Jean-Luc Nancy.* Oddly, we might say, Blanchot is cited only once in this monumental book, in a note concerning the touch of reading *Thomas l'obscur!*[16] I will return to this point. What interests me first, by and through the theme of the touch, is the extent to which the phenomenological shock that he opens up to thought pertains to the question of recognition. And since we know what skillful readers of Blanchot both Derrida and Nancy are, what I wish to suggest here is that their reading of Blanchot has inflected their thinking of the touch and their questioning of phenomenology. Once again, the opening scene of *Au moment voulu* serves as an example or a benchmark.

We witness here, in effect, a movement of the subject's exteriorization in the sense that, as Nancy writes, this "does not signify that he wears on the outside the visible face of an invisible interiority. This signifies literally that the ego makes, and makes itself, an exteriority, the spacing of place, the opening and foreignness that make the site and therefore space itself, the first spatiality of a true tracing in which, and only in which, the ego can set itself up, trace itself, and think itself."[17] These lines seem written precisely *for* or *with* the first lines of Blanchot's *récit.* Let us recall Bataille's line, written in a 1947 article: "Levinas describes and Maurice Blanchot exclaims, in some way, the *there is.*"[18] Could we then say that Nancy describes and Blanchot exclaims the spacing, the displacing, and the foreignness that Nancy mentions? The oral metaphor, the cry, which could refer at once to the orality of the beginning, its stridence or its written striations, can describe Blanchot's text, as Bataille writes, "to a certain extent." What we hear emerge from a cry suppressed or smothered, what we see dawning from the depths, from a gaping mouth, an O that opens in the ego, is the arrival of a subject, of a possibility to say "I," to experience oneself and identify oneself in a scene of recognition. And this occurs through a process of figuration. Thus, Derrida says that this spacing does not happen without a "ghostly return [*phantasma*]."[19] "We know," he adds, "that it is not sufficient to recognize or to attribute a spatial dimension to something or to someone . . . in order to make of it a body or a tangible body."[20] This is exactly what the character tests, and it is also the gaping, faltering situation in which the narrator places the reader. The *récit* opens only upon space, and this does not yet compose a body, any tangible body, or any proper body, or even any subjectivity, any subjectness. The *récit* opens and initiates us by a scene of exposition, of "exposition": a "face" [*figure*] and a "me" (or an ego), are "ex-posed" in an open space, on the two edges of a threshold, posed and "ex-posed," the one to the other, confronted, expropriated, dissymmetrical (let us recall, moreover, the "sidelong" glance), and without assumption or common figuration. It is precisely the anticipated specter of an anterior figuration which is hinted at by the opening door, only manifestly to return on the following page: "Anyway, there had apparently been between us such an accumulation of events, of immoderate realities, of torments, of unbelievable thoughts and also such a depth of happy forgetting that she had hardly any trouble not being surprised by me." Such a remark by the narrator reinforces, moreover, the initial dissymmetry, since what is revealed as shocking in the surprise is ultimately that the one who ought to have been surprised by the arrival of the other, is not. Even this surprise is therefore not the locus of any possible assumption or of any common figuration. Everything in presence, in proximity, in propriety, in co-presence, in co-appearance [*com-parution*], is suspended: "the simultaneity of the separation and of contact," Nancy writes, "that is to say the most literal constitution of the *cum*—exposes itself as indetermination and as problem. There is not, in this logic, a common scale of the *with:* the *other* removes it from him, in the alternative or the dialectic of incommensurability and of shared intimacy. In an extreme paradox, the other is revealed to be *the other of the with.*"[21] This way there is, at the outset of this *récit*, neither being nor being *with,* but the negative incommensurability of an alterity or of alteration of the *with* in the spacing of the field of space. Putting recognition into question, as Derrida comments concerning the touch, manifests an experience always already "haunted," "constituitively haunted, by some hetero-affection tied to spacing, then to visible spatiality."[22] No recognition scene happens without this intrusion of a spectrality that displaces all possible figuration and delivers it over to spacing. The door's opening presides here *in medias res* over the reconstitution of a body, because the intrusion of the discourse into the *récit* indicates that this reconstitution is in reality a process *in medias ludos,* at once cyclical, fragmentary, and residual. This reconstitution happens by the expanse, the spacing, the other, the other of the *with,* the outside, the absence, the specter, the forgetting. No spacing of this sort is possible without the figure of an *"archi-espacement"* that makes possible the collapse into the initial spacing of the *récit.* Here also is what, at the limit of the ungraspable, seizes the reader and what, at the limit of the beginning, pushes him aside. It is in or upon this spacing that the variations and dislocations of figuration—of thought and memory—are going to inscribe themselves.

The beginning of *Au moment voulu* exposes, therefore, an interrupted relation, which established itself and reestablishes itself, experiences and reexperiences itself, in its very interruption. This is figured as well by the door, which must have been touched two times: it is knocked on, battered, hammered, or its bell rung, before being opened by the latch, the catch, or the handle—yet without any of these touches coinciding. This metonymic noncoincidence is discreetly silenced, displaced from the beginning, referred to the start of the *récit* which itself opens immediately onto the opening and the spacing: a door passively opened, an open field freed by the absence of Claudia, a threshold occupied by the strangeness of a face [*figure*]. That which is referred to at the opening of the *récit* is therefore the operation in a sensory certainty; thus an "I" and a face [*figure*] are gripped in their very absence, in a detachment that immediately, though divergently, disturbs the senses, penetrates the body, and suspends all certainties and identities.[23] At the outset, everything touches on not being touched: the two sides of the door, the two hands, the two faces [*visages*], the four eyes, the two bodies. The recognition scene is initiated by such a touch without touching. As to the rest of the *récit,* crisscrossed by interruptions to the point of the image of the character's disappearance, it will take place in a to-and-fro movement between the not touching and the touching too much.

In his *Corpus* one finds this sentence by Nancy: "The creator's power stems from the original deconstruction of any recognizable image."[24] One can see here what touches on "the deconstruction of Christianity" undertaken by Nancy. (Although I will not enter into this topic here, such a horizon is evoked both strangely and powerfully in Blanchot by the simple names of Thomas, Anne, and Judith, along with the lines that I analyzed above, the apostrophe, "My surprise was extreme, inextricable, much greater, assuredly, than if I had met her by chance. The astonishment was such that it expressed itself in me by these words: 'My God! Another face I know!'") Let me simply recall the phrase cited at the creation of the *récit:* the power of this opening results, in effect, from "the original deconstruction of every recognizable image." We see in this that the face [*figure*] comes long before the face [*visage*] and the opening, *before* every subject. It is this exposition of the nonrecognizable, or of the motif of recognition as impossible extraction, that grips both the character and the reader and which is paradoxically and solely that which grounds the scene of recognition. The event of recognition occurs only to the extent that it comes away from [*é-venir*], or comes out of [*ex-venir*], all that seems orchestrated so that it might not occur. In this sense, the recognition is, each time, a senseless event. Its strength is without sight, beyond sight, beyond even the look that touches. Its strength is the pure strength of all sensory faculty, but affected from its source [*archi-affectée*]—not affected by some object, but by a *face* [*figure*].

Such a spacing posed from the first sentence with unequalled power remains, then, to be written out [*s'ex-crire*]. The word, we know, occurs often in Nancy's writings, but it originates in Blanchot in *Le pas au-delà:* the "re" of *rewrite,* like "ex," "the opening of all exteriority," and, in general in this book, the writing, like exteriority, dislocation, demand, or exigency.[25] It is indeed a writing, as Derrida says concerning Lévinas, that "deliberately disorients the syntax of an onto-phenemenology, be it even dialectical."[26] This is all the more the case since we are precisely in the sphere or the space of the *neutre.* There is here a neutralization of the *récit,* expressed by its dismembered syntax and by its dislocated oralization—its oralization being written or written-out [*ex-crite*]. How can we read, then, otherwise than out of the apparent intuitionist and continuist flux which so often characterizes readings, both silent and aloud, caught in the written line, equally and placidly disposed on the book's page? Time, hours, days, nights are necessary. This is, moreover, what those passages of *Thomas l'obscur* devoted to the act of reading describe. We find there the power, the "mortal power" of the book; the touch, the touch of words by the look; a door that opens, empty corridors, already haunted; fascination, interruption, the privation of the senses or of sense; and an impossible recognition: "he recognized himself with distaste in the form of the text he was reading."[27] In this *récit,* in this condensed episode, an entire night is necessary.

If writing—writing out—traces, then we have to say with Courtois that the image of tracing does not suffice. This is why the image is negative here and always yields to a maneuver: "The *récit* is written not on the level of maneuver itself, about which one never knows whether it has truly begun, but on the level of a movement which engages that which must be the maneuver of which we gather the thrusts, the impulses, the back-and-forths, and of which the two hands, the one that writes and the one that does not write, the two hands of the 'essential solitude' are the critical unfolding" (565). These thrusts, impulses, see-saws, striae, slippages, fragmentation: they are the fragmentation of the *récit,* of a *récit* by a syntax which is through and through parataxical, and, paradoxically, they are what, in the writing-out, hold the récit together. *Au moment voulu* remains a *récit* because it dialectically connects the images, but it approaches the limit of the non-*récit* by incessantly opening the image to that which exceeds and undoes the image.[28]

There is doubt that Blanchot evinces, especially in these years (the only ones in which, if he didn't exactly write about art, he at least published in art journals), a concern for plastic arts and poetics. It is time to identify a *poetics* in Blanchot's writing. This writing—which becomes more and more dislocated, up to the fragments of *L'attente l'oubli* that disjoin speech, interspersed with one or two leitmotifs ("Do it in such a way that I might talk to you," "Make it so that I might speak to you"), and up to the fragments of *Le pas au-delà* and of *L'écriture du désastre*—will yield its constituent elements more and more resolutely to the grooves of the pen stroke, to the isolation of the block, to the resonance of the "inextricable surprise." Here again, in *Au moment voulu,* are collected, concatenated, coordinated, parataxic sentences, and blocks of sentences regarding one another, drawing aside, returning, touching, transforming, interpreting, recognizing each other, and disfiguring themselves. No elements of the skeletal structure are lost, but the vertebrae are jeopardized. It seems possible to say the following concerning such a poetics, which remains to be defined, analyzed, and yes, even schematized: it never ceases to expose the scene, the space, the spacing, the touch, and perhaps the reading of recognition.

I do not have much left to say, perhaps only something to read, some fragments of poems, the author of which will, I trust, forgive me for citing them here. They seem to me to correspond so fully to Blanchot's poetics, while obviously deviating from it, that I cannot resist citing them. Jean-Louis Giovannoni has, on occasion, presented these texts to me as an "attempt to be just a little in dis-adherence." It is to such an intention that I have attempted to yield here, and I read, perhaps inadequately, several passages from *L'absence réelle* and from *L'immobile est un geste* as a homage to Giovannoni. Don't forget to listen behind, far behind, for the sound of the door opened by Judith.

> "For us who are the place, the sensitive inner wall of that which forever withdrew from us: absence is perhaps the only form of presence that we might really touch; the only form we might feel in the least of our gestures; the only that might restore us to life's movement, displacing it within us at each instant."

> Perhaps the surface is only
> the incessant call of the interior?
> Every body holds on to the edge of itself, of all
> its strengths, as if it were waiting for a sign in order to
> overcome itself.

> A body always comes from afar.
> It does not start with the moment of its apparition.
> It begins, before, in that which calls it.

> For there to be a world, we must subtract much
> and above all add nothing. It is by subtracting
> something from this world that bodies may
> appear.

> A moving body is a body from which one takes away
> at each moment of its steps, not only the volume
> of its body, but also the weight-of-the-body.
> And if one finds the body in the following step,

> it is that there is such an insistence of the invisible
> in wishing to appear, that it cannot be denied a body
> to slip into the appearance of an instant.

A final excerpt, already so close, but so different, is from the "interior novel" that Jean-Louis Giovannoni published in 2005, *Le lai du solitaire*.[29]

> If everything would appear in the same instant: there would no
>   longer
> be an interior, everything would be interior.
> No body could begin.

It is, it seems to me, precisely because everything does not appear in the same instant, *au moment voulu,* that the body begins, begins again, and is recognizable, even in *real absence,* and that writing and reading pursue an endless exteriority.

—Translated by Marianne Peracchio

NOTES

1. Translator's Note: I retain the use of *récit* rather than translating it as "short story," since it expresses a form similar to the short story, but one characterized by a repetitive and fragmentary structure.

2. Translator's Note: I retain most of the French titles for Blanchot's works, since they contain an ambiguity and a double or triple meaning, which can be rendered only clumsily in English. *Au moment voulu* has been translated by Lydia Davis as *When the Time Comes,* in *The Station Hill Blanchot Reader: Fiction and Literary Essays* (Barrytown, NY: Station Hill Press, 1999). All translations from the French are mine unless otherwise noted. Translation of Jean-Louis Giovannoni, quoted toward the end of this essay, is also mine.

3. This 1987 staging by Villemaine gave rise to a debate in the review *Théâtre/Public* in 1988, notably with Jacques Derrida and Philippe Lacoue-Labarthe, who had attended a performance. See Maurice Attias, Jacques Derrida, Philippe Lacoue-Labarthe, and Pierre-Antoine Villemaine, "De l'écrit à la parole," a roundtable conducted by Jacques Munier, *Théâtre/Public,* no. 79, Théâtre de Gennevilliers (January–February 1988), 36, 41.

4. Between January and June of 2004, the Bibliothèque Publique d'Information du Centre Georges Pompidou in Paris organized a monthly get-together around the figure of Maurice Blanchot. Emmanuèle Payen had requested that Pierre-Antoine Villemaine direct a reading workshop that would assemble more than a dozen invitees to read the texts aloud. The workshops proper were followed by lectures. The present essay arose from a lecture given at the June meeting.

5. Translator's note: the rhythm and meter of the line are lost in the English translation. The French reads, "En l'absenc(e) / de l'ami(e) / qui vivait / avec elle."

6. Translator's Note: the rest of the line reads, "la porte fut ouverte par Judith."

7. Translator's Note: Here, the author's original phrasing reads, "un début qui bute, qui dé-bute, conformément à l'étymologie," in which *buter* means to stumble and is the etymological root of *débuter,* "to begin."

8. All mystics, I believe, would find themselves here. Consider, among other examples that today have inflected my readings, Yadollah Royaï, sur l'Azal, "the before the beginning," l'Avval, "the anti-beginning," and the It (see *Le Passé en je signature* [Tehran: Caravan Books, 2000], poem 36, pp. 77–78). Alain de Libera, speaking of Meister Eckhart, calls this "the detachment regarding time and space" or "the separation of the me from fiction," or what I would call the suspension of all resemblance to the created and the emptying of all representation (*La Mystique rhénane* [Paris: Seuil/Points, 1994], 262).

9. Translator's Note: Bident alludes here to the game of *boules* or *pétanque* (similar to the Italian game of bocce), in which the game begins in earnest only after the first throw. Since the object of the game is to throw the ball closest to a mark, the one who throws the first *boule* begins the game, only to wait to see if his ball is deflected by the one who throws the second ball.

10. Translator's Note: In French, the word translated here as "face" is "figure," a word which Blanchot played with for its double sense: both the face and the rhetorical or artistic figure. The term will return throughout the text, and its double meaning is vital for comprehension, but since no English word captures that meaning and Bident occasionally juxtaposes *figure* with *visage,* the original French will be given in brackets within the text when the reader should be aware of which word is being employed.

11. Blanchot, "La voix narrative (1964)," in *L'entretien infini* (Paris: Gallimard, 1969), 556–67. Translator's Note: Blanchot counterposes two "narrative voices" in *L'entretien infini,* the first the *voix narratrice* (here translated as narrating) and the second, the *voix narrative* (translated as narrative).

12. Jean-Patrice Courtois, "La grammaticalisation du *récit,*" in *Maurice Blanchot, récits critiques* (Tours: Farrago, 2003), 547–71. Henceforth, I refer to the excerpted portions of this article by citing the page numbers parenthetically in the body of the text.

13. Translator's Note: The original French reads "en 'accordéon.'"

14. Jacques Derrida, *Le Toucher, Jean-Luc Nancy* (Paris: Galilée, 2000), 11.

15. And also, further on in the *récit*, "She touched me by a glance" (Blanchot, *Au moment voulu* [Paris: Gallimard, 1951], 118). And in *L'espace littéraire:* "What happens when one sees, while at a distance, seeming to touch you by a gripping touch . . . ? When what is seen imposes itself on the gaze, as if the gaze itself is seized, touches, comes into contact with appearance?" (Paris: Gallimard, 1955).

16. Derrida, *Le Toucher,* 120.

17. Jean-Luc Nancy, *Ego sum,* 163 (as cited by Derrida in *Le Toucher,* 40).

18. Georges Bataille, "De l'existentialisme au primat de l'économie (1947)," in *Œuvres complètes,* vol. 9 (Paris: Gallimard, 1988), 292.

19. Derrida, *Le Toucher,* 48.

20. Ibid., 59.

21. Jean-Luc Nancy, *Être singulier pluriel* (Paris: Galilée, 1996), 105.

22. Derrida, *Le Toucher,* 205.

23. Here I am thinking of a passage in the recent *récit* by Sofiane Hadjadj, a sort of *Dernier homme* in Algeria at the end of the previous century: "As if a thing could happen without it having any proper reality, or on the contrary, that it might achieve its physical manifestation without one being able, for as much, to be certain of its happening" (*Ce n'est pas moi* [Alger: Barzakh, 2003], 69).

24. Jean-Luc Nancy, *Corpus* (Paris: A. M. Métailié, 2000), 56.

25. Blanchot, *Le Pas au-delà* (Paris: Gallimard, 1973), 49.

26. Derrida, *Le Toucher,* 97.

27. Blanchot, *Thomas l'obscur: Nouvelle version* (Paris: Gallimard, 1950), 27, 29.

28. We read elsewhere in Blanchot's "Vaste comme la nuit": "The image trembled, it is the trembling of the image, the frisson of that which oscillates and vacillates: it comes out of itself, it is that there is nothing where it itself may be, always already outside of it and always the inside of this outside, at the same time of a simplicity that renders it simpler than any other language and is in the language like the springs from which it "comes," but it is this spring that is the same force of the "coming," the stream of the outside in (by virtue of) writing" (in *L'entretien infini,* 476).

29. The first five excerpts from Jean-Louis Giovannoni appeared, respectively, in *L'Absence réelle* (Le Muy: Unes, 1986), 10–11; and *L'Immobile est un geste* (Le Muy: Unes, 1989), 115, 128, 130–31, 134. The excerpt from *Le lai du solitaire* is from its earlier appearance in *La Revue littéraire,* no. 2 (May 2004). These excerpts are translated and published here by permission of Jean-Louis Giovannoni.

EIGHT

THE IMPERATIVE OF TRANSPARENCY

CELUI QUI NE M'ACCOMPAGNAIT PAS

Rodolphe Gasché

To engage with a philosophical question already at work in a narrative, or rather, a *récit,* such as Maurice Blanchot's *Celui qui ne m'accompagnait pas (The One Who Was Standing Apart from Me),* or to engage with one that may illuminate it—does this not require a prior philosophical reading to first locate such a question, or to establish the narrative's philosophical credentials so that a specific philosophical question can shed light on it?[1] However, if such a reading implies the search for a thematic content that is philosophically significant, or that takes place in view of principles underpinning Blanchot's writings and thought, then his fictional texts may have little to offer. Though it is clear from both his essays and his more theoretical writings that Blanchot was familiar with phenomenology— with Hegelian and Husserlian phenomenology and with its subsequent developments in the works of Heidegger, Sartre, and Lévinas—the very lack of any explicit philosophical conceptuality, not to speak of the absence of any direct references in *The One Who Was Standing Apart from Me,* make it very hard to detect any reverberations of Blanchot's philosophical preoccupations.[2] But what if, in addition to these difficulties,

Blanchot presented us with more formidable ones? What if, for instance, philosophy represented nothing less than a retreat away from, or an attempt to wear out and neutralize, that which this narrative weaves and brings to light? And, even if the quest for knowledge that Blanchot associates with philosophy in *The Infinite Conversation* is given a significant place in the narrative in question, the transfiguration that it undergoes in being undermined by the *récit* makes it almost unrecognizable as anything philosophical.[3] Finally, one might ask, what if the narrative's subject matter, as a subject matter thoroughly alien to philosophical concern, unfolded itself and was staged in such a way that it remained at odds with the fundamental methodological concepts of philosophical inquiry, and with the methods of phenomenological investigation in particular?

Any philosophical approach must take *The One Who Was Standing Apart from Me* just as it offers itself—that is, in the extreme desolation and poverty of its setting and plot. And it must do so without trying to recuperate anything that Blanchot was himself clearly at pains to eradicate. Elsewhere, Blanchot provides sufficient hints for us to recognize the house in which the story is set. It is the house on the Mediterranean to which he moved in 1946—the house at Eze. And, it is in the "little room" of this house that he did most of his writing. That Blanchot provides this fact makes it possible to attribute an unmistakable biographical significance to the text.[4] But, does not such a gesture undo the "reduction" of all such references, to which the *récit* owes its very consistency and specificity?[5] However, deprived of all definite specificity, the space in which the *récit* is set is not therefore the ghostly essence of a place; rather, deprived of all concrete specificity, it is a no-place. It is no doubt a place without a specific location, but it is also one that is stripped of its very character as a place—a place that is barely a place anymore. It is a place where, moreover, "place" reverts unvariably into a no-place. Only as such can it be entered into by any reading worthy of its name. Even though one may recognize the voice of Blanchot in the narrative voice, the "I" in the narrative must be taken as "just" a "grammatical fold," as Foucault so accurately noted.[6]

Invoking the theory of grammatical pronouns alone, however, may not be sufficient to characterize the status of the "I" in this *récit*. The narrator's reference to himself as "I" and to his companion as "he" (*lui*, or *il*) suggests, of course, that their encounter takes place within the element of language. But, does that therefore make them mere grammatical folds? Although the "I," like the "he," as well as all the enunciations of "we," "you," and the occasionally mentioned "Thou (*tu*)" (including the "they [*ils*, or *elles*]" of "Company! People!" [9]), are pronouns, grammatically speaking, they are also much more than grammatical categories; in fact, they are also much more than grammatical categories that have come alive, as, for example, in Callias of Athens' *Grammarian's Tragedy*. Like the words that the narrator says he is tempted to hold as "beings much more real than I was myself" (70), the "pronouns" in question are undoubtedly the agents of the narrative. However, in advance of names and standing in where no names are available or where the names have been factored out, these anonymous and faceless "pronouns" (which may, at times, acquire something of a name and face), that is, the "I" and the "he," as well as all the other "pronouns," are perhaps better described as categories, or, more precisely, as "existentialia," or categories of Dasein that concern lived experience. More precisely, these "existentialia" pertain to that which seems to replace experience in Blanchot. Here it becomes a matter of the frightening and thoroughly impersonal ordeal or trial [*épreuve*] of selfhood and otherness that, paradoxically, is no longer truly lived by any subject, regardless of the subject's empirical or transcendental status. This ordeal, in which all these "existentialia" entertain relations with one another—constantly deferring the formation of any sovereign self, such as an Ego—therefore implies a narrative. And this narrative structure, in turn, entails a spacing temporality and a temporalized spacing in which events occur: on the one hand, a nondescript house with its various levels, spaces, and a garden visible through the bay windows, and on the other hand, the alternations of day and night and of winter and summer. These are the pruned spatial and temporal coordinates in which the narrative unfolds. One coordinate consists in a hollowed-out space in which "a place[is] reserved within a place" (24), while the other coordinate is a time that is "airless and rootless" (16).[7] Furthermore, we are dealing with a *récit*, not simply a narrative or fiction. More precisely, we are dealing with a "re-citation"—that is, a re-citing and an affirmation of the cited in which everything absences itself in order to return, and in which everything is characterized by repeatability—a fact that points to the ghostly immateriality or ideality of the piece in question. To restore those aspects that needed to be abstracted for this peculiar ideality to come into view would, paradoxically, undercut the very intelligibility or transparency that has been achieved through these efforts of abstraction. Of course, this is not to say that a philosophical approach or a discourse of a certain generality about this *récit* is possible only on condition that everything concrete is eliminated from it. Rather, it must be taken just as it is, in its very austerity and immateriality. Resistance to the fleshing out of the *récit*'s naked skeleton is necessary, if one is to read Blanchot's text—if one is to read it in all its nakedness, as one must, since its very readability and intelligibility are intrinsically tied to this bareness. This is also to argue that, independent of any context, the bare skeleton of the piece will and must remain intelligible. The transparency of *The One Who Was Standing Apart from Me* is grounded in its gesture of purging and exiling everything concrete.

This peculiar abstraction of Blanchot's *récit*—this "reduction"—is a first hint of the status of the *récit* and of how it could be approached philosophically. In light of Husserl's elaborations on the notion of "reduction," such an approach would take place with a view toward essential subject matters and ideal structural forms, offering themselves in full self-evidence in unmediated intuition. Yet, despite its immateriality and abstraction, it is far from evident that the intricate textual relations spun by the *récit* are in any way essential in the phenomenological sense. Not only is it the case that the narrator's gaze is not the familiar glance that fixes a single thing, focusing on the thing itself, but this glance is also always divided. Speaking of words, the narrator remarks: "I see them all, never one in particular, never one single one in the familiarity of an undivided gaze, and if, even so, I try to stare at one of them separately, what I'm looking at then is a terrible, impersonal presence, the frightening affirmation of something I don't understand, don't penetrate, that isn't here and that nevertheless conceals itself in the ignorance and emptiness of my own gaze" (75–76). According to Husserl, evidence denotes a universal and primal phenomenon of intentional life. It is the character of intuiting a thing as it shows itself, as it were, in flesh and blood, in its true presence, that is, as it gives itself *originaliter* to an Ego.[8] Yet what the narrator of *The One Who Was Standing Apart from Me* beholds is, much like his glance, divided to the extent that whatever he fixes instantly turns into its reverse. He is not blessed by an experience of truth, and no thing shows itself to his gaze as it is in its very essence. On the contrary, what he intuits is divided, thereby dividing his glance and emptying it of all self-evident insight. Taking this into consideration, then, in what sense is one to speak of "reduction" in Blanchot's *récit*?

In the exchange of words between the companion and the narrator, between "him" [*lui*] and "me" [*je*], the companion occasionally interjects the phrase, "I wonder" [*Je me le demande*]. As the narrator explains, this phrase is "a sort of parenthesis in which time circulate[s]" (19). "Je me le demande," literally, "I ask myself (it)," expresses a question one poses to oneself, particularly when one is faced with a puzzling situation. It is a question to which generally no answer is given, since it presupposes a negative answer. The expression can further point to something that I ask of myself, a demand that I make upon myself, such as when, for instance, the narrator remarks: "I don't think I should ask it of myself" [*je ne dois pas me le demander*] (38). In the context of the *récit*, however, the phrase "Je me le demande" functions as a parenthesis of sorts, performing some-thing like a phenomenological reduction, or *epochē*. Although it is neither a methodical doubt with the view of establishing with certainty the exis-tence of the thinking subject, nor a temporary putting-out-of-work of the assumptions of the natural attitude in order to be able to focus on ex-periencing life itself, the interjectival utterance "Je me le demande"—seemingly directed at oneself, and also thrown between oneself and oneself—interrupts and suspends, like Cartesian doubt or the Husserlian *epochē* ordinary consciousness and, in particular, natural time. However, unlike the phenomenological *epochē* (which renders natural time in-operative so that the structures of experience themselves become the-matic), the parenthetical remark—although it suspends the natural flow of time rather than enclosing it (thus neutralizing what it encloses)—opens up a space between its brackets; it is a space in which the circula-tion of time becomes manifest. The meaning of the formula in question thus suddenly becomes clear to the narrator when he realizes that his question about what the companion could have meant by "the foggy pres-ence of that remark" comes too late. In advance of all meaning, the paren-thetical remark, whose very presence has already freed the space in which meaning can circulate, and with which meaning can never hope to catch up, has already occurred.

The remark in question, which is triggered by the narrator's inquiry into what might have happened in the past for him not to have always been here (that is, in the kitchen, and the house in which the narrative is set), and by his having moved farther and farther away, is repeated and affirmed once more when the narrator asks, "Do you mean it hasn't happened yet?" (19), and the companion responds, "Yes, I wonder about that." At this point, the anteriority of a parenthetical space of circulation that is prior to all determinate meaning and time is evident. But, subsequent to the companion's foggy performative speech act, the narrator "trie[s], in turn, to wonder about it." For a moment, he thinks that he is succeeding and that "the place where [he] arrives was nothing less than that beautiful bright spot, the kitchen, for whose sake I had broken the silence and which I looked at now as though it had been the space open to the one who wondered about it. Was it here?" (19). The space opened up by the parenthetical remark, from which every concrete or determinate meaning, place, and time has been removed so that this space can manifest itself, is therefore also the space in which the narrator and companion circulate, exchange places, and, at times, even fuse into one another in advance of their own distinct voices. In posing a question to myself that is also posed to him who is me, the parenthetical remark "Je me le demande" is, perhaps, a locution that even opens up the space of the text of the *récit* itself. In its "foggy presence," this remark is of the order of an event: within this event an encounter with a companion takes place whose alterity is not the least diminished by the fact that, at times, he may be indistinguishable from the narrator's own reflection.

At the core of the narrative of *The One Who Was Standing Apart from Me,* suspended between inverted commas, are the words that make up the interchange between the "I" and the "he," between the narrator and his companion. This conversation or dialogue consists of extremely terse and, at times, even curt interventions: short questions, shorter replies, exclamations, and lapidary establishments of facts that are often followed by long silences. The terseness of the dialogue is all the more emphasized by the occasionally astonishing "flood of words" (14). More often than not, the language in which these exchanges take place is that of ordinary speech. Indeed, "the impression of naturalness that [according to the narrator] had always marked our relations" (87) stands in sharp contrast to the complexity and the fierce logical consistency of the running commentary and the reflections that accompany them, and within which, by way of quotation marks, their voices are embedded.[9] It is a dissymmetric interchange insofar as the narrator is the one who most often speaks first, although at rare moments, surprisingly, the companion is the one who initiates the dialogue. Among several inequities between the partners, this one in particular needs to be highlighted. Not only does "he" ask the narrator to speak, but frequently, "he" wants him to "describe things" (59). The companion, "incessantly, without stopping" asks the narrator to talk to him. He demands that the narrator describe things, despite the fact that, at one point, the narrator observes, "there's nothing to describe, there's almost nothing left" (59). And, though the narrator never thought that his companion "might reveal anything important to" him (59), the latter, at all moments, depends on the former to "see." "You mean that I should describe things to you as I see them?" the narrator asks repeatedly, to which the companion either replies, "As I would like to see them, as I would see them" (29), or, "as we are able to see them, as we will see them" (61), thereby drawing the narrator, against his will, as it were, into a "shared vision" (61), a communal vision. At one point, when the possibility of "a completely different perspective"—and thus the "possibility of describing" things from another angle—offers itself to him, the narrator is led to consider playing "a friendly trick . . . on [his] old companion" (31).

One reason for this incessant demand for description is that the companion is primarily "interested in facts" (1)—something that is established right from the beginning of the *récit*. "I had noticed that he liked facts, he had a strange curiosity, almost a passion for the simplest events and things, which he carried off 'to his side of things' with a surprising, painful voracity" (46). Furthermore, "when it was possible to speak to him in the language everyone spoke, and that language certainly seemed to be the language of facts" (1), this gluttonous, even "blind hunger in him" (59–60) for facts becomes all the more exacting. "Couldn't you describe to me what you're like?" the companion asks the narrator at one point (87). Of the two, only the narrator has eyes. And things need to be described to "him"—the companion—so that he too can "get it" and be able to say: "'Well, I see, I see,' as though really, for him something like a portrait had emerged from me" (89). The companion's "ferreting . . . sort of eagerness" for descriptions is "unilluminated [*sans lumière*]" (88), clearly indicating his lack of vision. It comes as no surprise that he inquires about the narrator's eyes. When told that the latter has a smile on his face, "he asked feverishly: 'Where is it? In the eyes?' 'In the eyes, too, I think'" (88). In contrast to the narrator, the companion is in his element especially when the narrator resorts to ordinary language, this language being the language that corresponds to his interest in facts. Unlike the narrator's eyes, which are torn open by the "fissure still infinitesimal" (91) of a smile, the companion's faceless face is, as it were, eyeless. But what kind of eyes are these that allow the narrator to see? What or who opened them up for him? Might his open eyes not be those same eyes that, according to Heidegger, Husserl opened up for him?[10]

This dissymmetry between the partners in dialogue is not limited to what we have seen thus far. In contrast to his companion, who above all is interested in facts, the narrator is involved in constant reflections, comments, and reminiscences. Indeed, the crisp interchanges between the two are embedded in the long flow of a kind of inner dialogue in which the narrator reflects on his relation to his companion, his movements within the house, and everything that occurs in the present, often by recalling similar events in the past. At the beginning of the story it is stated that the companion is "extraordinarily lacking in intentions" (6) and that his "fierce singleness of mind apparently did not want to lead to anything" (9–10). At first, this means only that he pursues no goals and has no aims to motivate his inquiries. The companion even goes so far as to declare that he has no particular interest in himself (6). But given his prime interest in facts, this also seems to suggest that, unlike the narrator, the companion does not engage in any acts of consciousness other than those directed toward facts; that is, he does not engage in acts directed *upon* his voracious appetite for facts. The narrator, by contrast, is not only incessantly engaged in a variety of intentional acts—reflections, evaluations, reminiscences, and so forth—but also relentlessly busy reflecting on what he seems to experience. He never fails to accompany his lived experiences with elaborate reflections and never stops to appraise them once they are put into brackets by the reflective attitude. He constantly inquires into how such experiences occur, seeking to come to terms with how their respective objects are given in such intentional acts.

At this point, let us recall that in phenomenological thought, "description" is not just any neutral concept. Instead, it is raised to the level of a fundamental methodological concept. For Husserl, "description" designates the specific intentionality of the kind of cognition that is concerned with the unmediated reality of lived experience and that, distinct from self-observation, consists in a "radical consideration of the world," in which the world is approached as it is lived by consciousness and explored as it is given to us in the flowing alterations of the different manners of its givenness.[11] Phenomenological description subtends and pervades the entirety of phenomenological thought. This is true not only because it applies to all things—to those given in sense perception as well as to things in a broad sense, including ideal objects. Rather, phenomenological description is crucial precisely because description is the necessary correlate of the phenomenological conception of the thing or the phenomenon, insofar as things *show* themselves *in themselves*. Phenomenological description is primarily a reflective attitude that becomes necessary at the very moment philosophical inquiry investigates the way things are given to consciouness. Indeed, saying that phenomenological description focuses on the things themselves is tantamount to saying that, paradoxically, its objects are not the objects in the sense of what is given in natural, everyday, or even scientific perception; at stake are the objects themselves as they show themselves in their essential phenomenal content. Indeed, if phenomena are what show themselves, it follows that their description is not so much concerned with objects in a naturalistic and positivistic sense as with the modalities in which they are given to an Ego. That is, description is concerned with how I live and experience these objects in the various intentional acts that are directed upon them. Consequently, phenomenological description is not merely a reflective attitude—one that becomes possible only after the things as they are beheld in the naturalistic attitude are (by way of a phenomenological reduction) put into brackets, with the effect that they can show themselves as they are *themselves* and thus become thematized as correlates of intentional acts of consciousness. More precisely, it is an attitude that glances at and intuits what shows itself and is experienced as such.[12]

As has already been pointed out, the dialogue between the narrator and his companion is inserted within an untiring flow of analyses, commentaries, and reflections, to which the former subjects everything that occurs to him. This is particularly (but not exclusively) the case with the words that circulate between the partners in their dialogue. In Blanchot's *récit*, however, description is not limited to purely internal description, on the basis of which the complex of meaning can become the object of intuition; description is also performed in response to the demand of an other, the narrator's companion. Even though the narrator occasionally asks his companion for a break, in order to reflect before answering the companion's demand for description—"Can I reflect on it?"(9)—and even though the companion, for his part, wants "to keep himself at a distance from 'reflection'"(9), only urging the narrator to describe things for him to be able to see them, nevertheless, the demand for description in fact rests on the narrator's own reflections on his lived experiences and ordeals. But if the descriptions offered to the companion allow the latter to see—to see what he wishes to see, namely, facts—then what do the narrator's reflections do for him (the narrator)? Thought or reflection is experienced by the narrator as a way of distancing himself from his companion. It is also a way of interrupting the movement "by which," according to the narrator, "what I said escaped me" (9). As he readily admits, "the tranquil delay, the suspension that I granted myself so often while 'reflecting'" (45) is, first of all, a "refuge" (10) from the too great proximity to his companion. Hence it is also a means of preventing the circle from closing. Even though phenomenological description of phenomena is concerned with things as they present themselves—thus not aiming beyond the phenomena at something that would be generalizable—description nonetheless aims at universality, or apriority. The aim of description is to exhibit the universal structures of the intentional acts by which the givenness of what shows itself occurs.

Yet, what does the description of and the reflection upon the narrator's experiences in *The One Who Was Standing Apart from Me* yield? If it is true that the companion sees things once the narrator has described them to him—seeing them as he would like to see them (presumably, as facts)—then the narrator's seeing is far from unproblematic. It is certainly not comparable to a phenomenological intuition, in which things are beheld in their originary givenness and evidence. Indeed, the narrator does not always enjoy the privilege of sight in the brightness of a light that "evokes the most certain moment of the day, a midday freed of the seasons and the hours" (18). More often than not, his sight is blurred, and he is compelled to admit that he can't see very clearly (15). He not only acknowledges that "there was no more day for me" (81) but, at one point, also admits that the description he has offered to his companion is not yet complete (93). Furthermore, whatever the narrator gazes at—for example, the troubling presence of the figure of someone else on the premises—not only becomes fixed, "riveted to a single point by the fact that I was riveting it with my gaze," but also gets emptied out: "It was no longer more than that point, then, an empty, silent point, an empty moment that had become tragically foreign to my gaze at the very moment when my gaze became the error of what rivets, and my gaze itself was empty, did not enter that zone, entered it without reaching it, encountered only the emptiness, the closed circle of its own vision" (38). Distinct from the figure's glance, which embraces the entire space without seeing the narrator, the narrator's gaze, precisely because it zooms in on him, is bereaved of all spatial and temporal coordinates. As a result, what he beholds shrivels up to become nothing less than a meaningless spot. By the same token, the very glance that fixed it itself gets emptied out. Though the narrator is endowed with sight, what he sees, in becoming fixed, gets emptied out to the point where he no longer sees anything. Everything he fixes upon turns into its opposite, and his gaze, in taking in something precise, devolves into its contrary to become a vacant staring into the void.

The companion, who, for his part, lacks sight and needs the narrator's descriptions in order to see, "sees," but only in the sense of getting it once things are described to him; he gets the facts straight, as it were. By contrast, the mysterious figure that the narrator first perceives through the large bay windows of the house, and later in the house itself, is endowed with vision. Somewhat like the narrator, who, when looking at the room as a whole, "does not see objects distinctly" (50), the figure in question sees with a view to the larger context: "without pausing where I was, [he] stared rapidly, with an intense but rapid gaze, at the whole expanse and depth of the room" (15). Vision, rather than being a function of a single Ego, is thus divided up and shared between at least three different protagonists. It is also seemingly divided up into its distinct functions: the fixing of distinct objects, versus the space within which they are located; a seeing of things that jumps from one determination to another, versus getting things straight as facts; and so forth. The shared vision that the companion demands is a "di-vision," a partitioning of vision. We should also pay attention to the narrator's eyes, divided as they are by the infinitesimal difference of a smile. Without pursuing further the strange community between the various protagonists in the narrative, I point out that the modalities within which the narrator's reflections, observations, and remarks take place cast light on how he sees and experiences. "Perhaps," "probably," and "apparently" are among the various adverbial locutions that repeatedly modulate all of his observations. Certitude is left to the narrator only "on condition that it be insignificant, yes, deprived of meaning and truth" (40).

At one point in the narrative, when the narrator is made to realize that everything that has been said has kept passing over the same point again—that the same thing has been eternally said again and again and has eternally remained lacking—he observes that "now, it will no longer be possible for me to reflect" (50). Yet, between parentheses, he remarks: "when I reflected, I did not reflect, properly speaking, it was like a prayer addressed to time, asking it please to do its work" (50). As the narrator admits, even in the past he never reflected properly. Reflection never gives rise to essential insights, then, insights into the essence of what, through description, is supposedly allowed to show itself as such. No eidetic is proposed here. At one point, the narrator's ability to describe is said to be impaired by a new light; it prevents him from describing what he perceives—"from maintaining it firmly in a description"—and thus makes him unable to grasp it (52). "It wasn't a questioning of remembering, and wasn't I really there, wasn't I in it, really, as he had suggested to me? I did not refuse to believe it, but my belief also lacked reality, so that I didn't really believe it" (52). This passage seems to suggests that, whatever the status of the narrator's reality or presence in the here and now, it is his very ability to experience that is at issue. The mere possibility of lacking presence or of not really being there thoroughly undermines the possibility of a firm, lived experience. And, if there is no lived experience, then there is no description or reflection, either. Yet did the narrator not already admit that even when he reflected in the past, this was not reflection, properly speaking? As a prayer addressed to time, it was "only" the demand that time do its work. What could this mean?

Speaking of his inability to describe, the narrator avers: "this had to do with my relations with him, with the solitude of that 'we' in which I had to hold myself, always distancing him [*l'écartant*] so that, in that distance [*écart*], he could express himself and I could understand him, in which I had to hold myself, but not withdraw . . . this was what I thought" (52–53). What is true of expression and understanding is true of vision as well. It requires the space and the time of a distancing or a keeping apart, for the parts (my part, his part) to fall into play. Seeing can only occur in this distancing. Reflection, as a means of creating distance and delay, rather than thematizing the "as such" of things, is thus precisely what creates this essential apartness without which no dialogue, no vision held in common, is conceivable. In Blanchot's *récit*, reflection distributes the parts that are necessary for a conversation and a shared vision to become possible. It is in this conversation that the narrator describes what he beholds to his companion so that the latter is able to see as well. Here, the experience of vision is, by definition, to be shared as a division. Reflection, then, to say it as succinctly as possible, is here no longer a phenomenological attitude by dint of which things as they are can themselves come into view. Rather, reflection is here involved in securing the dimension in which all the parts are carved out so that a dialogue and vision can occur in the first place. No light, no transparency, no clarity, no evidence, and, properly speaking, no certainty any longer characterize this "space" and "time." It is a space or a dimension where the only certainty the narrator possesses is perhaps only "the certainty of being at a turning point" (55). Here, the narrator is described as undergoing an "errant coming and going" (52) where he experiences the passing of one aspect of things into the other. If there is any certainty at all here, then it is that of a pivoting that invariably destabilizes any fixed position; it is a pivot like the one "around which what was threat turned immediately into hope" (72).

This space, this region in which everything without exception turns into its opposition, or its underside, is that of a "dissimulation," in which all determined meaning is erased and nothing firm remains. Blanchot designates it as the outside, or the night. And only by making every experience turn immediately into its opposite does this region reveal itself in all its alterity. Yet if every experience reverts always to its flipside, then there is no longer any experience of this or that particular thing, and, in one and the same breath, no pole of experience; there is no Ego anymore. For all these reasons, the reflection on what is described in Blanchot's narrative never arrives at essential insights—insights in which the things themselves offer themselves in their originary self-givenness and full self-evidence; whatever is beheld immediately faces its double, its opposite, or reveals an underside. Strictly speaking, in a situation where whatever is beheld reverts into its opposite, no description takes place. But if there can be no description, properly speaking, because whatever becomes the object of a description is something whose figure stands in contrast to the night from which it has arisen—and into which it is again always susceptible of dissolving since it belongs to it insofar as it has arisen from it and insofar as it immediately calls upon its opposite— then it is even more improbable that there could be a description and an eidetic characterization of the night itself, precisely because it is nothing but this milieu of dissimulation in which everything stops resembling itself. The milieu of the night has no figure, essence, or meaning.

This may also be the appropriate point to discuss the narrator's constant questioning of his own resources, his constant anxiety that he does not have the necessary strength to go on. From the very first page he tries to make his companion understand that he has "exhausted [his] resources" and is "at the end of [his] strength" (1); he is not managing the enterprise that has been entrusted to him. If he does not fight his companion like an adversary, it is because his forces are not up to it. But, if he "wasn't yielding either," it is especially because "yielding would have required more strength than [he] had" (2). On the other hand, when he reflects on the task with which he is confronted, he notes that, although he "might not have the strength to bear" its seriousness, at the moment he is about to collapse it gave him back "a superabundance of strength" (84). As a result, although exhausted by the task demanded of him, he also has "the strength to perform it, the two fit each other exactly, as a cut fits the knife blade that made it" (84). Yet as soon as the possibility presents itself of "receiv[ing] an increase in strength," this is more often than not a "strength to which [he] can't consent" (77). In any event, the *récit* does not simply stage an economy of forces, strength, or, more precisely, a pattern of the distribution of forces, since, as the narrator tells us, his "strength is divided up, spread out through the whole of [his] life" (84). Rather, the forces (and the lack thereof) in this play are also different in kind: they are powers [*pouvoir*], potences [*puissance*], strengths [*force*], and so forth. Now, what is it precisely that draws on the narrator's powers and, at times, provides him with strength? After noticing that his companion withdraws or exiles himself from his vicinity in order to address him, it occurs to the narrator that the companion not only faces "the fascinating need to distance himself under the pretext of coming close," but that he himself also "first had to distance him [that is, the companion], and the greater the distance was, the more profound and true the speech was, like everything that comes from far away" (44–45). It is precisely this need to open up an interval between the "I" and the "he" that explains why, as the narrator muses, "I had to expend such strength in these conversations" (49). The efforts that draw on the narrator's strengths, constantly threatening him with exhaustion, derive from this need to put a distance between oneself and the other. It is a distancing and a moving away from him so that a space and an interval within which an exchange can take place will open up. Repeatedly, the narrator remarks that he does not struggle with his companion; the latter is not an adversary, and what goes on between them is not on the order of a struggle. By contrast, the opening up of an interval to make dialogue possible is itself "a silent, powerful struggle" (45), which consumes the narrator's strengths to such a degree that, as he admits, "I had to deprive myself of life, abstain from myself" (45).

However uncertain the narrator may be about the precise reasons for the incessant demands that are made on his resources, it is clear that the extraordinary expense of force is demanded by the necessity of preventing the other from being here and present, for, in such a circumstance, no communication with him would be possible. The companion seems to indicate this when he responds to the narrator's claim that he is not alone: "Is it that you're not here?" (44). Hence, the companion draws attention to the fact that the narrator's presence must be hollowed out for there to be the space in which he can communicate with his partner. But the narrator's worry about his strengths is not simply a question about the distance of his companion; it is also a matter of the spacing and temporalizing of his own here or presence: without it being emptied out, no distribution of positions such as those of an "I" and a "he" can fall into place. And again, without this, no conversation could then occur. Is this not the task and the responsibility that is incumbent on the narrator from the beginning of the *récit*? Is this what demands all of his strengths? And, what about the narrator's repetition of his resolution: "I will continue to go in this direction, never in any other" (41)? If this way is, above all, toward his companion, then does this not also provide a clue for what it is that costs him so much strength? Additionally, let us not lose sight of the fact that, if it is necessary to put a distance between oneself and the other for communication to be possible, then a redoubled effort is necessary if such distancing also harbors the inevitable possibility of "forgetfulness" (85).

As we now turn back to the narrator's glance—and above all to the light within which it occurs—we should keep in mind what has been said thus far about the play of forces in the *récit*. *The One Who Was Standing Apart from Me* is pervaded by light. Everything occurs in the medium of light, or the lack thereof. And, everything has a light of its own. Light, as that within which phenomena appear, is a major thematic concern of the narrative, in contrast with much of phenomenology, in which light is merely presupposed. Not only are there the different qualities of daylight, depending on how much remains of it as the day progresses, but, at times, the narrator is struck by the "poverty of the day . . . the extraordinary thinness of the day, its tenuousness, its superficial brilliance." It is on that very same day that he admits that "it was certainly a very beautiful day, but terribly worn" (84). The day is also called "dreamy" when it hides the narrator from himself (63). There is also the light of the different seasons, which strike one with feelings that are opposed to what one may expect, such as when the summer light in the "little room" is said to be "not without coldness" (26). At one point, the narrator calls night "the brilliant light of the summer" (62). In addition, there is the light inside the house, where, when it becomes too dark, the lights are turned on (23), and the outside light, such as that of the little garden, which is a "reserve of space and light toward which I was still allowed to turn" (44). The light also varies from room to room—from the darkness or half-light in some rooms, to the dimly lit storeroom, to "the beautiful bright spot" (19) of the kitchen, into which, through a small window, "a brightness poured down which evoked the most certain moment of the day, a midday freed of the seasons and the hours," a "silent light" (18). In "the little room" in particular, there is a "shiver of a light so startling" that "it made [the narrator] enter the heart of summer" (26); it is in this brightness that he contemplates "the splendor of limitlessness . . . as the unique moment and sovereign intensity of the outside" (44), a light so bright indeed that he even compares it to the "strange, dreamy daylight [of the little garden], a daylight as luminous as I could have imagined" (53). This daylight pales in comparison to the light in this little room—that is, the light of the outside. In this case, light is not simply evocative of the day or the seasons, for they themselves have their particular brightness or darkness. Here, light *itself* undergoes qualitative changes: there is light that is somber, but also light that, independently of all contexts, is unusually bright. In addition, there is "a light that was not entirely light, that [only] resembled it" (53).

Words, too, have their own light. Sometimes they have "another sort of light" than the one hoped for (30); a figurative light endows some of them with a "cruel transparency" (13). Things and affects have their own light, such as pain that shines with "a tranquil light" (20). Furthermore, the narrator's perceptions are themselves endowed with light, as when he notices through the window, "in a flash—a flash that was the shining, tranquil light of summer," the figure of someone, an impression "so vivid that it was like a spasm of brightness, a shiver of cold light" (17). The same holds true with an insight whose "diffuse manifestness [*évidence*]" is characterized as "a tempting light toward which truth itself drove" the narrator (20). And, beyond all of these concerns, there is the narrator's need of light in order to see. There are moments when, unable to see clearly "in his own way, [he] was looking for the daylight, even if I had to be content with an errant, imprisoned gleam, the scintillation of an instant, which I sometimes almost preferred to the light of the world" (35). At other moments everything seems to him "illuminated with a new, blinding light" (80). But there are also moments when desire takes him to the night, and when he confides that "in my expectation of that night, I no longer saw anything of the day but its dreamy lightness, the light that seemed to have lost the edge of its manifestness [*évidence*] and in which I could not make out anything, not even that the day was not lacking to me" (85). However, when he is illuminated [*illuminé*], he also seeks to illuminate [*éclairer*] things to his companion. When it is revealed to him how difficult, how impossible it is for his companion to speak—"a revelation that became wedded to the day"—the narrator remarks that, afterward, "there was no more day for me" (81). But then, toward the very end of the *récit,* there is also the reference to "the work of another day," which "is also the smile of the day and this smile is only the more beautiful because of it, as though in this smile its protective envelope begins to dissolve and into this dissolution penetrates a light that is closer to me, more human" (92).

Light is not only multilayered and multifaceted. There is another difference that is perhaps more intriguing: the difference within light, namely, a difference between light and itself. It is the difference between light and "light" (39)—light in quotation marks and light without them. While strongly sensing at one point the presence of someone else besides himself and his companion, the narrator is "illuminated" to such a degree by the "shiver of his approach," that he is convinced that his companion had to believe in his presence as well. However, the quick question that the latter poses to him, "Do you see him at this moment?" makes him realize "that the light [he] had just traveled through wanted to illuminate something quite different," namely, "the very answer [he] gave him at that moment in all its 'light': 'Yes, I have seen him before'"(39). Having already encountered the crucial function of parenthesis in *The One Who Was Standing Apart from Me,* the suspension of a word, and in particular a word such as "light," when put between inverted commas, should not escape our attention. Suspended within quotes, "'light'" is no doubt a citation of, or the mentioning of, the word "light" that was used in the previous sentence. But, suspended in this way, it also becomes modulated in other fashions. Is it a light "that [is] not entirely light, that [only] resembles it" (53)? In the exchange that takes place, the narrator is said to be illuminated to such a degree by the conviction of the mysterious presence of an other that his response to the companion's question is given in the "'light'" of "something quite different" than what the latter's question called for. The narrator's response, "Yes, I have seen him before," not only fails to respond to the query of whether he sees the other at this moment, but also addresses the fact that, earlier in the narrative, the narrator had already seen him and gave the same answer to the companion's inquiry: "Have you ever seen him before?" (31). At that time, the response, "Yes, I have seen him before," "was suddenly torn from [him]" (31). Now, however, it is qualified as "a mad thing to say," one that suddenly "slipped out" (39). In light of the light that now illuminates him so powerfully regarding the imposing presence of this other someone, giving the response that he has already seen him before strikes the narrator as "the most somber thing that could happen to [himself]" (39, trans. modified). The light that characterizes the narrator's response is thus a qualified light. Compared to the light that illuminated the indubitable presence of someone other, the light that permeates the response and constitutes its intelligibility only resembles light; it is a somber light, a light that is not a light—a light suspended between quotation marks and bracketed, as it were. The difference that these quotation marks make is consequently one between light in all its uncompromising, overwhelming brightness and limitlessness and a light that "reject[s] such a light" (39).

As the events that directly precede the utterance of the phrase show, the narrator's sudden response, "Yes, I have seen him before," though it escaped him against his will or against his better insight, did not happen without good reason. When he is asked by his companion whether he is frightened by the presence of the other or not, he is startled by the word "frightening": "All of a sudden I saw it with a force that, in fact, did not leave me intact: what had been there was frightening [*effrayant*], was what I could not associate with [*avec quoi je ne pouvais frayer*], and in this slipping, it seemed to me that I myself could no longer associate [*frayer*] with anyone, not even with myself" (39). By changing the subject or, as the French original has it, the horizon, the companion's question of whether he is not frightened makes the narrator aware that the presence of the other and the light that makes his being there (or here) unquestionably evident is so overwhelming that it stifles the possibility of any relation between himself and this other—insofar as the latter is a presence of unbearable fullness—in addition to stifling the relations with all possible others, including himself as an other. Let us recall the importance of the motif of opening up, or of tracing paths, in the *récit*. From the beginning, the narrator is on his way, relentlessly journeying toward the companion on paths that he cuts. One of the dissymmetries that characterizes the relation between "I" and "him" is that "he had to content himself with the paths I drew for him" (8). It is the narrator who clears the paths on which "he" can approach him. Yet on occasion, "without waiting for me to clear a path for him" (82), "he showed he was capable of coming to me by a path I had not laid out" (43), that is, he comes "by unprepared paths" (70). What is so frightful about the presence of the other—what throws the narrator from a previously tranquil or peaceful state, as the etymology of the French verb *effrayer* would seem to suggest—is something that takes the form of a horizon. Rather than representing the Husserlian space for phenomena to come into a meaningful appearance, this horizon seems to foreclose, by way of the unmitigated presence of the other, all possible otherness and hence all relations. If the narrator realizes that he cannot associate with the overwhelming light of such a presence, then this is because it inhibits the tracing of the paths that are necessary in order to relate to others and oneself.

In the light of the uncompromising light, to acknowledge that he has already seen the other is, in the narrator's words, to follow "the cowardly impulse . . . to replace the disconcerting with the familiar, and, out of a desire to master the unknown, [to replace it] with the already known" (39). In the light of the light that so illuminated him (and in the context of the realization that such a light is frightful to the extent that it inhibits all association with others and oneself), the recourse to the "light" of recognition is undoubtedly of the order of a fall, since it represents an attempt to master the unknown and replace it with the already familiar. Nonetheless, the narrator asks: "And yet, could I reject such a light?" (39). By stating that he "will continue to go in this direction, never in any other" (41), he affirms unmistakably his commitment to light in all its infinity. Yet this merciless light is also one in which everything dissolves, in which all figures lose their contrasting difference. Paradoxically, this light is thus indistinguishable from the opaqueness of the night and the emptiness of the void. According to the narrator,

> For me, 'in this direction' no doubt indicated where he was, the interminable, the place where the moments led me back to such a point of

uncertainty and sterility that what had preceded them was obliterated, that they themselves were obliterated. Infinite moments, which
I could not master, and the most terrible thing was that, as a constant
pressure, I felt the duty to make myself their master, to orient them,
to transmit to them that pressure, which sought to make them slide
toward an end to which they could not consent. I could not entirely
resist this pressure, this imperious narration, it was inside me like an
order, an order that I was giving myself, that unsettled me, dragged
me along, obliged me to wonder. (41)

It is precisely because of this light, in whose pitiless brightness everything
becomes dissimilar and all certainties dissolve, that the pressure and the
duty to perform the impossible task of mastering in "light" the unknown
(and thus inevitably the possibility of erring) arise. While affirming light
in all its merciless intransigency and, with it, "the emptiness of the reflections [*reflets*]" into which everything dissolves in the blinding brightness of this light, the narrator also affirms "the transparent vision of the
day" (41), in which the unknown becomes known, the anonymous acquires a name, and the figureless gains a shape or a figure. Such an affirmation of "light" and its transparency can only take place in a struggle
with the inexorable light to which the narrator also remains committed.
This struggle consists in a bracketing, as it were, of the merciless light, so
that a narrower light—a light suspended between its quotation marks—
can come to the fore. It is a light that, however limited it may be, is itself the openness of natural light. "I had to fight against the interminable
and yet lift it up to the daylight" (42). The struggle with the interminable
thus consists in wrenching from it the light of the day, a "light" that, although it only resembles light, in its transparency enables things to acquire figures, thereby allowing them to resemble themselves and thus
be identifiable. The transparency of the day (and the possibility of erring
that concurs with its truth) is a clarity that, despite its narrowness, originates in the inexorable light insofar as it is won from it precisely by being
lifted up into the daylight. This struggle for transparency, which, in the
The One Who Was Standing Apart from Me, is also associated with "the will
to remain on my feet [*debout*]," "connected to myself" with "faithfulness
and seriousness" (42), and, more generally, with ordinary everydayness,

also causes "light" and what appears within it—the things that resemble themselves—no longer to be natural givens that have "the authority of obviousness (*évidence*)." Rather, "light" is "a prodigy," something almost "gratuitous, unjustified, incontestable, but not sure" (43). Since the transparency of the day—natural light—has to be won in a struggle against a pitilessly leveling light, the very fact that there is something as fragile as natural light is simply extraordinary. To be able to wrench it from a light that is so blindingly bright that it is inseparable from the night is nothing short of a miracle. Rather than being self-evident or something that is given in an originary intuition, such an existence is a "prodigious" fact, something so extraordinary that it gains prophetic significance, though it is "prophetic in the absence of time" (72).

As we have seen, the narrator feels pressured. He senses the duty to struggle for the transparency of "light" against the interminable and dissimulating light. In his words: "Go up, go down, but even in the shadows and as far as possible, one must fight for transparency" (42). "Lutter pour la transparence, il le faut."[13] One must struggle for transparency, it must be! This injunction draws its urgency from the contrast in which it stands to the other demand, the other demand coming from the interminable light that remains indistinguishable from the night. One must struggle for transparency! It is imperative!

In *The One Who Was Standing Apart from Me,* such transparency is that of "the little room" situated in the upper part of the house. This room is also the brightest room—"the floating fantasy of summer" (26). "With a clear, joyful knowledge," the narrator acknowledges the strong impression of life—of "a radiant life" (27)—that emanates from this little room, and to which he is attracted. "This is open space, I said to myself, the vast country: here I work" (27). The narrator feels himself powerfully connected to this room. And, even if the life, happiness, and radiance of the day that he associates with it is, at this stage in the *récit*, only a vision that rapidly "comsum[es] itself to the transparency of a single point" and one single instant, he still feels, in his words,

> under its domination, because of this my master, in the impression that here a sovereign event was taking place and that to live consisted for me in being eternally here and at the same time in revolving only

around here, in an incessant voyage, without discovery, obedient to myself and equal to sovereignty. Yes, this was the highest degree of life and even though, through this life, I had strayed into a deadly realm and deadly solitude, I could say: it must be, it must be—I draw you to myself in a powerful way. (27–28)

The transparency that is called for, the one that is concurrent with life, work, knowledge, reason, mastery, and sovereignty (and philosophy as well), remains an exigency, even though such a life of work and illuminating knowledge leads to the "cold thought" (27) of that deadly realm in which light is one and the same as the night. The deadly realm from which transparency must be wrested (which at the same time is therefore also the possibility of life), in a struggle that draws on the narrator's forces and exhausts him (at least) as much as the dissolution of his "I" in this region of dissemblance and sameness, and in light of which the transparency that is won inevitably shrivels to resembling, at best, only a single point of transparency, does not therefore make this vision, revelation, and prophecy any less imperative. It must be!

The pressure to bring about transparency is indivisible from the pressure and the imperious order to narrate. Although the direction to which the narrator is committed—"I will continue to go in this direction, never in any other"—is that of "the interminable, the place where the moments led me back to such a point of uncertainty and sterility that what had preceded them was obliterated, that they themselves were obliterated" (41), in short, to what he cannot master, yet he also feels "a constant pressure . . . the duty to make myself their master, to orient them, to transmit to them that pressure, which sought to make them slide toward an end to which they could not consent. I could not entirely resist this pressure, this imperious narration, it was inside me like an order, an order that I was giving myself, that unsettled me, dragged me along, obliged me to wander" (41). It is not possible to outline here, however roughly, what orients *The One Who Was Standing Apart from Me*, that is, the end to which Blanchot makes everything slide. As Foucault has remarked, toward the end of the narrative, "the appearance of a smile that lacks a face but which finally carries a silent name" announces something like the promise of a beginning.[14] On the *récit*'s last page, the narrator speaks to himself, inciting himself not to distance his companion: "draw him to you instead, lead him to you, clear the way for him, call him, call him softly by his name. By his name? But I mustn't call him, and at this moment I couldn't. You can't? at this moment? But it is the only moment, it is urgently necessary, you haven't said everything to him, the essential part is missing, the description must be completed, 'It must be. Now! Now!'" (93). The description must go on, it must be completed, it must be completed by filling in the essential part that is missing. Yet, in spite of the fact that "all the force of the day had to strain toward that end, rise toward it" (93), everything disappears; it disappears with the day at the moment the end comes, but the demand that "Now!" the description must be completed, that the vision which "alas [was] only a vision"—yet, "What a vision!" (27)—continues to resonate with the undiminished urgency that there must be transparency.

Notes

1. Maurice Blanchot, *The One Who Was Standing Apart from Me*, trans. Lydia Davis (Barrytown, NY: Station Hill Press, 1993). All page references in the text are to this edition.

2. For Blanchot's reception and his debate with phenomenology in his literary critical texts, see the superb and indispensable work by Marlène Zarader, *L'être et le neutre: Á partir de Maurice Blanchot* (Lagrasse: Éditions Verdier, 2001).

3. Maurice Blanchot, *The Infinite Conversation,* trans. Susan Hanson (Minneapolis: University of Minnesota Press, 1993), 50.

4. See for example, Maurice Blanchot, *Une voix venue d'ailleurs: Sur les poèmes de Louis-René des Forêts* (Plombières-les-Dijon: Ulysse Fin de Siècle, 1992), 13.

5. By successfully fleshing out a number of blank spaces in Blanchot's novels with biographical data, Christophe Bident has made it possible to situate Blanchot's work—*The One Who Was Standing Apart from Me,* among others—in historical, cultural, and political context. In this regard, Bident's *Maurice Blanchot: Partenaire invisible. Essai biographique* (Seyssel: Champ Vallon, 1998) is undoubtedly a major contribution to our understanding of this difficult writer. However, as I will argue, not only must the *récit* in question remain readable in the absence of all these references, but its very intelligibility must be established without the help of these data or facts.

6. Michel Foucault, *La pensée du dehors* (Montpellier: Fata Morgana, 1986), 56.

7. For a fine discussion of the temporality of *The One Who Was Standing Apart from Me*, see Hans-Jost Frey, *Maurice Blanchot: Das Ende der Sprache schreiben* (Basel/Weil am Rhein: Urs Engeler, 2007), 77–96.

8. Edmund Husserl, *Cartesian Meditations: An Introduction to Phenomenology*, trans. D. Cairns (The Hague: Martinus Nijhoff, 1977), 57.

9. Occasionally, in the French original, italics within the dialogue suspended between quotation marks produces an additional step toward the framing and the embedding of what counts in some of the sentences. Maurice Blanchot, *Celui qui ne m'accompagnait pas* (Paris: Gallimard, 1987; reprint of 1953 edition), 126, 130.

10. Martin Heidegger, *Ontology—The Hermeneutics of Facticity*, trans. J. van Buren (Bloomington: Indiana University Press, 1999), 4.

11. Edmund Husserl, *The Crisis of European Sciences and Transcendental Phenomenology*, trans. D. Carr (Evanston, IL: Northwestern University Press, 1970), 113.

12. Phenomenological description is not a form of naive portrayal or reproduction. It is intimately linked to reduction and reflection. For an elaborate discussion of the precise way that description, reflection, and reduction are interlinked in phenomenological thought, see Ernst Wolfgang Orth, "Beschreibung in der Phänomenologie Edmund Husserls," in *Phänomenologische Forschungen*, vol. 24/25 (Freiburg: K. Alber, 1991), 8–45.

13. Blanchot, *Celui qui ne m'accompagnait pas*, 81.

14. Foucault, *La pensée du dehors*, 57.

NINE

"As Though with a New Beginning"

Le dernier homme

Caroline Sheaffer-Jones

> *The law of the return supposing that "everything" would come again, seems to take time as completed: the circle out of circulation of all circles; but, in as much as it breaks the ring in its middle, it proposes a time not uncompleted, but, on the contrary, finite, except in the present point that alone we think we hold, and that, lacking, introduces rupture into infinity, making us live as in a state of perpetual death.*
>
> —Blanchot, *The Step Not Beyond*[1]

> *Who are you? You can't be what you are. But you are someone. Then, who? I ask this. I don't even ask it. But our words are so light that they keep opening out into questions.*
>
> —Blanchot, *The Last Man*[2]

Thinking Everything

Maurice Blanchot's *The Last Man* (1987), originally published as *Le dernier homme* (1957), addresses the philosophical question of the last man and, more broadly, life, death, and the limits of knowledge. Is Blanchot's last man simply an individual who comes at the end of the human species, or does he perhaps stand for all of the long history of civilization? Is he a replica of the last man who is described by Nietzsche in *Thus Spoke Zarathustra* and who clutches at life, refusing to die? In the course of his reflections, Blanchot has referred extensively to Nietzsche, notably in *The Infinite Conversation, The Step Not Beyond,* and *The Writing of the Disaster,* as well as in early articles.[3] While Blanchot later turned his attention closely to Emmanuel Lévinas's writings, Nietzsche's texts remained important to him, in particular, in his consideration of nihilism and the end of metaphysics.[4] Blanchot takes up the question of the last man and echoes Nietzsche in his narrative, but of course does not correlate his own conception exactly with Nietzsche's theories. In *The Last Man,* Blanchot returns to the major questions of writing and dying, broached from different perspectives in his work.[5] In short, does the notion of the last man mean that there is no future for man, Blanchot's figure simply occupying the place of the very last, or does it in fact indicate the last man in the sense of the last before the one to come, one who is unknown? Does Blanchot envisage the end of the old values and the possibility of overcoming man, as in Nietzsche's idea of the superman? Is *The Last Man* solely about death, or is it also about life?

In *The Order of Things,* Michel Foucault writes about the last man with reference to Nietzsche: "the last man is at the same time older and yet younger than the death of God; since he has killed God, it is he himself who must answer for his own finitude; but since it is in the death of God that he speaks, thinks, and exists, his murder itself is doomed to die; new gods, the same gods, are already swelling the future Ocean; man will disappear."[6] For Foucault, Nietzsche announces the end of God's murderer. Blanchot's conception of the last man must be seen within the context of this portrayal of man's disappearance, however it is surrounded with uncertainty; and thus what precisely man's finitude might signify in *The Last Man* must be considered more closely. Descartes's rational method inaugurating modernity is also brought into question in *The Last Man.* What is contested is the doubt of Cartesian metaphysics leading to the *cogito,* that is, self-consciousness as the point of certainty and the proof of the existence of God. In his writings, Blanchot exposes another side of man whose thought cannot be contained within the rational. The precarious relationship of the last man with himself and with others is a focus of *The Last Man;* consciousness and certainty are reexamined. Indeed, Blanchot approaches these issues from many different perspectives in writings that span over half a century, including in the early article "Literature and the Right to Death" in *The Work of Fire.*[7] This text, however, is grounded on the realization of absolute knowledge, with reference to Hegel's *Phenomenology of Mind,* more particularly as read by Alexandre Kojève in his *Introduction to the Reading of Hegel. The Last Man* puts forward a very different idea of consciousness, truth, and the end of man.

My reading of *The Last Man* draws on certain passages in Nietzsche's writings, sometimes discussed by Blanchot in other texts; however, it obviously does not provide an extensive elaboration of Nietzsche's complex theories or any detailed correlation of them with Blanchot's fictional story. *The Last Man* is a profound and complex text and only some aspects of it are developed in my reading. Blanchot uses poetic license to create a narrative in his own style and chooses philosophical elements eclectically. In this essay, I concentrate above all on the sketch of the last man. In the first section, I consider the notion of the last man predominantly with reference to Nietzsche's *Thus Spoke Zarathustra* and some writings by Blanchot on Nietzsche in *The Infinite Conversation.* In the second section, in a discussion of the limits of knowledge, I briefly examine a fragment by Nietzsche on Oedipus. I also analyze the way in which the characters in *The Last Man* might achieve wholeness through thoughts that would relate to themselves and indeed the world. What is at stake in the demise of the last man is the revelation of everything, or perhaps nothing. It is as if there were an instant eternally drawn out, as described in Blanchot's *The Instant of My Death:* "As if the death outside of him could only henceforth collide with the death in him. 'I am alive. No, you are dead.'"[8] Life and Death would be indistinguishable, the ultimate goal of death already pervading life. Finally, I consider whether Blanchot's idea of the last man signals the overcoming of man and in what sense any new conception of man may be affirmed.

In "Nietzsche and Fragmentary Writing" in *The Infinite Conversation,* Blanchot emphasizes that rather than passing, "man of the last rank" lingers on, not wanting to perish. Blanchot writes: "Man is always man of the decline, a decline that is not a degeneration but, on the contrary, a lack that one can love; a lack that, in separation and distance, makes 'human' truth one with the possibility of perishing. Man of the last rank is the man of permanence, of subsistence, the man who does not want to be the last man."[9] By not recognizing his finitude, by not being "a lack that one can love," the man of the last rank, who does not want to be the last, in fact fulfills the characteristics of the last man. "'Human' truth" is united above all with that which is finite; however, the last man believes in permanence. In "Crossing the Line" in *The Infinite Conversation*, Blanchot analyzes a view of Nietzsche concerning man who is of low character but who also has a power that surpasses him: "Present-day man is man of the lowest rank, but his power is that of a being who is already beyond man. How could this contradiction not harbor the greatest danger?"[10] Importantly, this idea of man of the lowest rank who does want to die—the last man—incorporates all humans today. However, in this reading of Nietzsche, Blanchot notes the power to exceed in the becoming of humanity, despite the fact that man is petty, believes himself to be permanent, and remains caught up in the spirit of vengeance. Does Blanchot's portrayal of the last man, indeed of "present-day man," provide any resolution to this contradiction between subsisting and a power to exceed inherent in man?

In "Zarathustra's Prologue," in *Thus Spoke Zarathustra*, Nietzsche's protagonist derides the last man or the Ultimate Man as "the most contemptible man":

Alas! The time is coming when man will give birth to no more stars. Alas! The time of the most contemptible man is coming, the man who can no longer despise himself.
Behold! I shall show you the *Ultimate Man*.
"What is love? What is creation? What is longing? What is a star?" thus asks the Ultimate Man and blinks.
The earth has become small, and upon it hops the Ultimate Man, who makes everything small. His race is as inexterminable as the flea; the Ultimate Man lives longest.[11]

The people in the crowd tell Zarathustra that they want the last man and would like to be made into the last man; he can retain the superman. The superman clearly stands in opposition to the last man, who is to be scorned, like the good and the just; they are unable to create new values and pose the greatest danger to the future of mankind. In characterizing the good, Zarathustra reminds his listeners precisely of what he said of the "Ultimate Man."[12] In a reading of "Why I am a Destiny," the final chapter of Nietzsche's *Ecce Homo,* Sarah Kofman highlights Zarathustra's aversion to the good man, who is the last of men, and moreover she states that the superhuman, which designates man's greatness, is conceived precisely with reference to this type, the last of men.[13]

In *Thus Spoke Zarathustra,* it is evident that the last man counters what is great in man. Instead of asserting decline and a movement beyond, the last man believes in living the longest, in permanence, and in the old values. In the prologue, Zarathustra addresses his thoughts on man to the people:

> Man is a rope, fastened between animal and Superman— a rope over an abyss.
>
> A dangerous going-across, a dangerous wayfaring, a dangerous looking-back, a dangerous shuddering and staying-still.
>
> What is great in man is that he is a bridge and not a goal; what can be loved in man is that he is a *going-across* and a *down-going.*
>
> I love those who do not know how to live except their lives be a down-going, for they are those who are going across.
>
> I love the great despisers, for they are the great venerators and arrows of longing for the other bank.[14]

Nietzsche describes man as "a bridge and not a goal"; it is in man's "down-going" that he might achieve a movement beyond. The "despisers" who pursue this direction are "arrows of longing for the other bank." Is Blanchot's *The Last Man* simply a depiction of the "Ultimate Man," lacking the power to step beyond, or is there also a sense of man as a "dangerous going-across"?

Blanchot focuses on the protagonist of the story at the very beginning of *The Last Man.* The narrator notes that almost nothing distinguished him from the others around him. "He" is the last man, also referred to as the professor, and yet, for the "I" who speaks, he is barely different from the other people. It is as if he were paradigmatic of man today. However, the narrator says: "Now I think that maybe he didn't always exist or that he didn't yet exist" (1; 8),[15] as if the last man's life were interrupted, intangible, or to come. Blanchot's narrative revolves around the last man, the narrator, and a female friend, who also spends time with the last man. They are depicted in a setting of rooms and corridors, where nameless people are ill and die. This alone is the world that unfolds in the story, as the narrator seems to withdraw more and more. What might characterize the anonymous figure as the last man, when he seems to resemble the others to the point that his identity is blurred? If he is the "Ultimate Man," who lingers on, the narrator is perhaps also in a sense the last man, just as another might follow—perhaps one of those shades in the corridor, or those whom the narrator sees wandering around incessantly toward the close of the story and who come and go endlessly.

The Last Man is divided into two sections, the first more than twice as long as the second. In the first section, the narrator speaks in the first person about the last man; about the woman, who also dies; and about himself. In the second section, the "I" of the narrator is more removed, speaking to what he calls motionless thought, addressing it, someone, himself, another, in a kind of monologue. The story tells of the last man's drawn-out suffering, the woman's demise, and the fading of the narrator. Early in the story, the narrator broaches the issue of whether the last man was indeed the last; that the last man would not be the last was a thought that he was spared. However, it is as if the last man were doubled by other figures, in particular, the narrator.[16]

Insofar as Blanchot's last man lingers on, as if at the end of the world, he would be in a position to think everything, synthesizing thought being one of the aspects that Blanchot emphasizes about Nietzsche's higher Man in his essay "Nietzsche and Fragmentary Writing" in *The Infinite Conversation*.[17] In *The Last Man*, the narrator states about the protagonist: "Surely he was capable of thinking everything, knowing everything, but he was also nothing" (16; 32).[18] At the brink of the earth, he might vanish; thinking would not guarantee the certitude of his existence. Living on as perhaps the last man, the narrator says: "If I had wanted to, I would have thought everything" (64; 108), and toward the end of the text: "I know everything, I know everything" (81;134).[19] It is as if in death, the figure of the last man might reveal all knowledge at the end of the human species.

If Nietzsche derides the last man and heralds the superman, Blanchot's last man, as considered in several texts in *The Infinite Conversation,* is also scorned. Yet is the figure that Blanchot describes in *The Last Man* a turning point, where man's power to exceed is apparent? At the point of death, thinking everything, he would be nothing. Does he represent in any way a "down-going" that might be a "going-across"? Does the last man accomplish in any way the extreme in man?

The Point

In a short fragment "from the history of posterity" entitled "Oedipus: Soliloquy of the Last Philosopher," Nietzsche calls Oedipus the last man. The monologue of Blanchot's narrator, especially in the final section of *The Last Man,* echoes the soliloquy described by Nietzsche where Oedipus converses "'as if I were two persons.'" The first words of the fragment are "'I call myself the last philosopher, because I am the last man. No one speaks with me but myself, and my voice comes to me like the voice of a dying man!'"[20] It is apparent that Oedipus is divided, as if his own voice were separate from him, and what he hears coming back to him is the voice of one who perishes, the voice of death. The fragment finishes with the following words: "'And yet, I still hear you, dear voice! *Something* else dies, something other than me, the last man in this universe. The last sigh, *your* sigh, dies with me. The drawn-out 'alas! alas!' sighed for me, Oedipus, the last miserable man.'"[21] An estranged sound dies that is not simply able to be subsumed into the consciousness of the last man. Detached from himself in that voice, Oedipus speaks as if he were two. Philippe Lacoue-Labarthe notes that Oedipus has been considered to epitomize the hero of Western philosophy and that, clearly, Nietzsche's dying Oedipus cannot be thought of in terms of the identity of the self. The text is about what is prior or beyond self-presence, not about the subject as the self-representation of identity, which opens the way to Freud.[22]

In "The Most Profound Question," originally published a few years after *The Last Man,* in 1960 and 1961, and then in 1969 in *The Infinite Conversation,* Blanchot discusses Oedipus, indicating that his response to the Sphinx's obscure, profound, and dangerous question rests with the human and the question of the whole.[23] Although Oedipus displays his knowledge, Blanchot also underlines an inescapable ignorance, explaining that Oedipus put out his eyes in his attempt to reconcile clarity and obscurity, knowledge and ignorance, the two conflicting parts of the question. For Blanchot, Oedipus ultimately uncovers a more profound question that lies beyond the human. In both Nietzsche's and Blanchot's texts, Oedipus is a tragic figure who represents the impossibility of the unified subject. Indeed, according to the narrator in *The Last Man*, self-consciousness would not even be a divine privilege: "Even God needs a witness. The divine incognito needs to be perceived down here" (10; 22).[24] The word "perceived" is used here to translate "percé," also meaning "pierced," as if the very perception of the divine incognito meant that a hole was put through it, that it lacked any completeness or that God was dead. In *The Last Man*, what is ultimately brought into question is the point at which the subject would think everything and see itself as whole. That decisive instant, like every instant, is pervaded by death and elusive. The presence and the possibility of self-consciousness of the last man are undermined at every point. How might the last man witness his own living and dying? For Bataille, Blanchot's text is above all about the world in which we die. Bataille underscores the fact that there is no immediate knowledge of death, which, without the subterfuge of the spectacle, would remain completely unknown.[25]

In *The Last Man*, Blanchot portrays characters whose unity is uncertain. Even the boundaries separating each from the other are not steadfast, and a figure might be drawn into using "we." Near the beginning of the text, the narrator says about the last man:

> And what if he hadn't said to me, one day, "I can't think about myself: there is something terrible there, a difficulty that slips away, an obstacle that can't be met"?
>
> And right afterward: "He says he can't think about himself: about others, still, about one other, but it's like an arrow coming from too far away that won't reach the target, and yet when it stops and falls, the target quivers in the distance and comes to meet it." (2; 8)[26]

The narrator initially quotes the last man speaking in the first person about his difficulty in thinking about himself. The words are then repeated in the third person. Neither "I" nor "he," the last man is a stranger to himself. He lacks identity, like the narrator, whose words also change into the third person at the very end of the text, when "he" wonders how "he" had entered into the calm, something he could not talk about with himself.[27] By using the third person instead of the first, in effect a neutral third person which is repeated, is the narrator then writing about another rather than himself? Does he perhaps see himself at a distance as the last man? The image of the arrow near the beginning of the text, as quoted above, shows how precarious it is for the last man to reach himself or others in his thoughts. Does the target actually join up, at some point, with the falling arrow in this encounter? That the narrator describes the sentences spoken by the last man at such moments as seemingly infinite, planetary, is significant. It is as if the words had no goal, or only a vast and distant one—as if the thoughts of the last man almost dissipated in space rather than reaching some designated point.

It is not simply the last man who experiences a problem in thinking about himself and others. Shortly after the passage quoted above from the beginning of the text, the narrator asks, in relation to what he had just heard:

> How to answer? Listening to it, who wouldn't have the feeling of being that target?
>
> He wasn't addressing anyone. I don't mean he wasn't speaking to me, but someone other than me was listening to him, someone who was perhaps richer, vaster, and yet more singular, almost too general, as though, confronting him, what had been "I" had strangely awakened into a "we," the presence and united force of the common spirit. I was a little more, a little less than myself: more, in any case, than all men. (2; 9)[28]

If the narrator thinks that listening to the last man one may indeed have felt that one was the target, he adds that the last man's communication was not directed at anyone. How, then, might the thoughts of the last man about himself or others arrive at their goal? It would seem that the sentences spoken to the narrator listening are an address directed at no one. It is as if the last man's sentences were too great for the listener alone to receive. Who might be there to listen to the last man or to the narrator's address?

Is the last man able to think about himself so that he relates to himself, to others as a whole, his thoughts returning to him the impression of completeness? Is the narrator able to seize the sense of his own presence? What is the "united force" listening when no one is being addressed? What is this force into which the narrator has been transformed, the boundaries defining him dissolving into the presence of the "we"? In the vastness of the "we," in which there is earth, sky, calm, the last man now all but disappears, for the narrator states: "All of this is I before him, and he seems almost nothing at all" (2; 9).[29] Confronted with the spectacle of death, and not just at the end of the journey but at every instant, Blanchot's figures do not assert their identity, but rather the unknown. The narrator remarks that if he glanced profoundly at the last man rather than superficially at his person, he was aware that the last man was unattainable. There is a profound level at which the last man was untouchable, diffuse.

The characters in *The Last Man* are unable to fathom regions of themselves; they harbor within themselves an unknown center. The narrator writes about the woman: "Even for her, then, there were places [*points*] where she was no longer as secure and felt dangerously distanced from herself" (40; 69).[30] The figure of the circle or sphere recurs in the text in relation to the characters and the world, and the surface is often light, whereas a dark point is at the center.[31] The narrator also notes that the woman feared being distanced from herself at death: "She had always been afraid of dying outside herself; she would say: 'You have to hold me firmly. I must be struck at the point where you're holding me'" (60–61; 102).[32] She desired to be held, kept together, at the point of her undoing, as if her mortality might be overcome. It is significant that it is there, in death, that she would have a link to another. It is perhaps also in the affirmation of death that the last man might point beyond, toward the other bank.

THE JOY OF THE CIRCLE

In thinking through the extreme of the possible for man in *Inner Experience,* Bataille brings to attention the blind spot that is not absorbed into knowledge and into which knowledge itself is lost. He describes existence as a circle that includes the night, passing from the unknown to the known, and back to the unknown.[33] Bataille remarks in this text that Blanchot had suggested that he pursue the inner experience as though he were the last man. Bataille considers this briefly in relation to the subject of the inner experience which is consciousness of the other, like the antique chorus or the witness, and asks what would happen if the crowd were lost, if the possible that it represented were dead, the subject being the last. Bataille focuses on the unbearably anguished last man, perhaps himself, caught in the self as if interred. There are certain similarities between this portrayal and, in particular, Blanchot's figure walled up in his room in the last section of *The Last Man*. Death, meaninglessness, indeed an insoluble enigma are evoked in Bataille's thoughts about the last man.[34]

In the last section of Blanchot's text, the narrator addresses the motionless thought that envelops him. He comes up against the strangeness of the void. It would seem that the sky, that point of infinite blackness, pierces the narrator's distant memories, and supreme calm takes over. The narrator describes this moment as unique but beyond recollection: "And yet, I remember many things— everything, maybe, but not that moment, and as soon as I move toward it more boldly, I run up against that extremely fine and amazingly distant point: that black point we call the sky, that single changing point, ever blacker and sharper, which we find suddenly before us and which is there only to urge us to withdraw, go back inside the calm from which our lightness has also eternally made us go forth" (70; 116–17).[35] Remembering perhaps everything, the narrator nevertheless confronts the black point of nothingness, the forgetfulness that precedes memory. Does the narrator now merge into the void? Has he taken the place of the last man, whom he described at the beginning of the text in front of the vastness of the "we" and who all but disappears? To recount the story of the last man, the narrator can only indicate that which incessantly escapes him. At the end of the text, he wonders about death, his death, that of another, and "the extremely fine and amazingly distant point that always slips away" (88–9; 147).[36]

Alone and reduced to almost nothing, the last man might achieve communion in separation. In *The Last Man,* solitude is represented in terms of the sky that manifests that point as sharp as a needle. The narrator reflects that the sky sometimes becomes blacker, the impenetrable receding even further, and then he states: "Everything, it claims [*prétend-il*], is common to us, except the sky: our share of solitude passes through this point. But it [*il*] also says this share is the same for everyone and we are all united within this point even in our separation, united only here and not elsewhere: this would be the ultimate goal" (69; 115).[37] The goal would be in a paradoxically shared solitude in death. It is as if a point impossibly united human beings in their undoing, in a sense, like the absence of community described by Blanchot in writing on Bataille in *The Unavowable Community*.[38] The narrator could hear the "we" that sprang from him; he could hear himself in a chorus farther away, near the sea. It is as if death were, in a sense, a turning point insofar as the last man would distinguish a community in death, the eternal "we" associated with the calm returning to the calm. He would see clearly for an instant, through the one to whom he speaks. The narrator addresses himself more and more pressingly to one who is ill-defined. He states: "I know very well that you don't exist anyway, and that this is what reunites us" (82; 137).[39] However, while death might unite in separation, the narrator is intent on pursuing a vision of this visage on the horizon, where the one whom he addresses would materialize.

The presence of the visage is uncertain. "Sometimes it seems that certain faces [*figures*], by coming together, try to sketch out such a visage. It seems that they all eternally rise toward one another to cause it to be present. It seems that each would like to be the only one for all the others, wanting all to be the only one for it, and to be, for each, all the others. It seems that the emptiness is never empty enough" (87, trans. slightly modified; 144–45).[40] A visage would be outlined by the faces coming together, each eternally showing the others in a configuration where one and all reflect each other in different ways. The emptiness must intensify because what the narrator desires to see is paradoxically the face of the void. Toward the end of *The Last Man* he states: "Too beautiful troubled faces. A visage cannot be that. The very last visage, merely manifest, beyond waiting and beyond reach. Visage which is the emptiness, perhaps" (88, trans. slightly modified; 145–46).[41] What could appear at death, moreover the death of the last man? To the end, the narrator is engaged in a combat with the void that would show the nudity of the visage. There is the possibility that exteriority might be possessed in an instant, unlike the alterity in Lévinas's notion of the visage or the Stranger's voice from the other bank.[42] Who speaks, who is addressing whom, is not clear, the narrator and the one addressed somehow coming together: "Could it be that he is dying at this moment? Is it you who always die in him, near him?" (88; 147).[43] For the last man, this is the instant of death at which all of the faces of humanity might represent the visage; yet is it nothing but the void?

In "Nietzsche and Fragmentary Writing," Blanchot writes of the superman or overman: "In truth, what is the overman? We do not know and, properly speaking, Nietzsche does not know. We know only that the thought of the overman signifies: man disappears; an affirmation that is pushed furthest when it doubles into a question: does man disappear?"[44] This question resounds in *The Last Man*. At the beginning, the narrator writes that the last man gave him the "feeling of eternity." He asks: "Where does it come from that in the space where I am, where he has brought me, I constantly go back near the point where everything could start up again as though with a new beginning?" (5; 13).[45] The point that marks the end would also be the beginning. It is as if there were a life force that is renewed beyond death. In both sections of the text, the narrator writes about the happiness of saying "yes," of affirming endlessly. Saying "yes" to life in its eternal repetition and accepting the world as it is, after the death of God, are necessary for the coming of the superman. Blanchot's narrator states that there was a necessity to communicate to the last man "the life in us, the inexhaustible force of life" (31–32; 56).[46]

In *Thus Spoke Zarathustra,* Nietzsche writes about the thought of the eternal return. "'Everything goes, everything returns; the wheel of existence rolls for ever. Everything dies, everything blossoms anew; the year of existence runs on for ever. / Everything breaks, everything is joined anew; the same house of existence builds itself for ever. Everything departs, everything meets again; the ring of existence is true to itself for ever.'"[47] Zarathustra is the teacher of both the superman and the eternal return.[48] Blanchot maintains that Nietzsche's thought of the eternal return is supreme nihilism: "nihilism surpasses itself absolutely by making itself definitively unsurpassable."[49] In focusing on the infinite repetition of the eternal return in "Nietzsche and Fragmentary Writing," Blanchot emphasizes the repetition of that which has no beginning, the repetition that is not one and that is, to a certain extent, a parody and unrepresentable.[50]

Toward the end of *The Last Man,* the narrator addresses the figure in his thought, considering the visage that might emerge for him to see at death. To the partner with whom he struggles in this prosopopeia, the narrator says: "We must melt into each other. What is an end for you will surely be a beginning in me. Aren't you tempted by the joy of the circle? You go before me, a loving memory [*mémoire aimante*], a recollection [*souvenir*] of what hasn't taken place" (84, trans. modified; 140).[51] How might the visage be witnessed? Would it not be like perceiving God, or the death of God and man? Who is the "we" in "We must melt into each other"? In a sense, the final section of the text mirrors the first section, in which the "we" refers in particular to the narrator and the woman facing the last man. Is that "we" then also the one whom the narrator now addresses in the final section, namely, himself, the woman, and others? Or has that "we," previously facing the last man, now changed places with the last man, as if one had melted into the other? What, then, of the death of the last man and also the future of the "we"? What of the joy of the circle, if the "we" is annihilated in the obliteration of everything, nothing remaining in this spectacle but the infinite blackness of the point? Is this the visage of the void, the death of God and man? Such uncertainty is expressed by the woman, who says to the narrator at the end of the first section: "'Am I the one who's dying? Or is it you?'" (61; 103).[52] When they look at the last man, the narrator sees reflected on their faces perhaps that the future, our future and that of man, is dead.

However, it is as if, facing the last man, the "we" might also be transformed into something new. The narrator writes about the "temptation to allow ourselves to disappear, before his gaze, and be reborn as a nameless and faceless power" (32; 56–57).[53] Yet would this "faceless power" not be from the ruined vision of the last man? Would it not be that which is always at the brink of death, always risking disappearance, that visage of the void that the narrator confronts at the end of the text? The narrator writes about the "we" in the presence of the last man: "A movement of separation, but also of attraction, which seemed to cause faces to become attractive, attracted to one another as though to form, together, the future of a completely different figure, necessary and yet impossible to represent" (33; 58).[54] Does man disappear? Would man have reached the ultimate goal in this vision of man, perhaps the superman? It is apparent that the narrator has arrived at a point which is unknown, where his vision of the circle is not clear. Toward the end of the text, the meeting of the arrow and its target is again uncertain when the narrator asks: "Might the arrow I didn't hold back try to find you, a target that would grant it rest?" (78; 130).[55]

Whom does the last man address in the final section of the text? Who is this "you" to whom he speaks? Does it not indicate one who is beyond the present and who is that unrepresentable figure, the visage of the unknown? Is it not the evocation of faces of a community of the past or to come, which cannot be seen in the present? It is as if the future and the past had been confounded. In the first section, the narrator believes that he sees the last man turning back to them, to "us," "as though, at that moment, he was tempted by the illusion of a circle, coming back toward us as toward his real future, so that once again he could hope to die in advance of himself" (31; 54–55).[56] What this future or this past is, is not defined. In this circular movement, the last man moves toward "us." Is the future with us? Do we belong to the past? Do Blanchot's last man and the superman join together? Toward the end of the text, the narrator has a vision in his solitude, where each person is the reflection of universal reflection, eternally coming and going. Nietzsche writes: *"all joy wants—eternity!"*[57] The momentary vision of eternity, the source or the eternal heart that each person augments in dying in *The Last Man,* points to a community that would perdure. The one being addressed, those unknown figures of the future, as well as the one speaking, would belong to the eternal "we." In the eternal circle that the narrator describes, the figures are distanced from themselves. Like Nietzsche's Oedipus, they are divided, without identity. The last man is doubled by the narrator, the woman, and other figures who lack presence. In considering the eternal return in *The Step Not Beyond,* Blanchot writes about the demand of the return: "What will come again? Everything, *save* the present, the possibility of a presence."[58] Perhaps it is less Nietzsche's contemptible character that Blanchot depicts in the last man than his lack of presence, the infinite point of the sky piercing him. Blanchot's figures are split from themselves, the "I" and the neutral "he" unidentifiable and unrepresentable. Where does the decline point? Is it the end as though it were a beginning?

It is death that the community shares and that would hold it together in separation. Unity with others, with oneself, through death, is perceived like an illusion of the circle. The last man is not only the last but also the last in a line, the one who precedes the last; it is as if the last man were the one who dies in advance of himself, separated from himself. Self-representation shows a lack of identity and of self-presence. In the story about the last man, in the vision of the narrator, does man disappear? In his essay "The Indestructible" in *The Infinite Conversation,* Blanchot describes man as "the indestructible that can be destroyed."[59] Man's relationship with death, the finitude of every man, is indestructible, and yet this means in effect that he can be eternally destroyed. Is the last man the coming of the great noontide, the overcoming of man? In writing about Bataille's *Inner Experience* in *Faux Pas,* Blanchot reminds us of the danger of this time of brilliant light: "for the man hungry to see, it is the time when, looking, he risks becoming blinder than a blind man, a kind of seer who remembers the sun as a gray spot, a burden."[60] Zarathustra says: "And this is the great noontide: it is when man stands at the middle of his course between animal and superman and celebrates his journey to the evening as his highest hope: for it is the journey to a new morning. / Then man, going under, will bless himself; for he will be going over to superman; and the sun of his knowledge will stand at noontide."[61] Blanchot's last man arrives once more at a point at which his own demise is reflected in the many faces before him. Does he see the visage of the void or another reflection of the community, "another, a stranger, close, gone, the shadow of the other shore, no one" (11, trans. slightly modified; 23)?[62]

NOTES

This essay was written with assistance from the Faculty Research Promotion Grants Program at the University of New South Wales, Sydney.

1. Maurice Blanchot, *The Step Not Beyond,* trans. and intro. Lycette Nelson (Albany: State University of New York Press, 1993), 12. "La loi du retour supposant que 'tout' reviendrait, semble poser le temps comme achevé: le cercle hors circulation de tous cercles; mais, pour autant qu'elle rompt l'anneau en son milieu, elle propose un temps non pas inaccompli, fini au contraire, sauf en ce point actuel que nous croyons détenir seul et qui, manquant, introduit la rupture

d'infinité, nous obligeant à vivre comme en état de mort perpétuelle." *Le pas au-delà* (Paris: Gallimard, 1973), 22.

2. Blanchot, *The Last Man,* trans. Lydia Davis (New York: Columbia University Press, 1987), 76–77. "Qui es-tu? Tu ne peux pas être ce que tu es. Mais tu es quelqu'un. Alors, qui? Je le demande. Je ne le demande même pas. Nos paroles sont seulement si légères qu'elles s'ouvrent sans cesse en question." *Le dernier homme* (Paris: Gallimard, 1957 [1977]), 127. Page references to the English text and then to the French text are given in parentheses after the English quotations. See also Geoffrey H. Hartman, "Maurice Blanchot: Philosopher-Novelist," in *Beyond Formalism: Literary Essays 1958–1970* (New Haven: Yale University Press, 1970), 93–110; Evelyne Londyn, *Maurice Blanchot romancier* (Paris: A.-G Nizet, 1976), 75–87; Hans-Jost Frey, "The Last Man and the Reader," *Yale French Studies* 93 (1998), "The Place of Maurice Blanchot," 252–79; Christophe Bident, *Maurice Blanchot: Partenaire invisible. Essai biographique* (Seyssel: Champ Vallon, 1998), 359–67; Éric Hoppenot, "Qui témoignera pour le témoin? ou le lecteur survivant," in *Maurice Blanchot, la singularité d'une écriture*, Études rassemblées et présentées par Arthur Cools et al. (Louvain-la-Neuve, Belgium: Les Lettres romanes, 2005), 191–204; Daniel Just, "Weakness as a Form of Engagement: Maurice Blanchot on the Figure of the Last Man," *Forum for Modern Language Studies* 44, no. 1 (2008): 40–52; Daniel Dobbels, "Le dernier geste du dernier homme," in *Blanchot dans son siècle,* Textes rassemblés par Monique Antelme [et al.] (Lyon: Paragon/Vs, 2009), 362–66.

3. See Blanchot, *Chroniques littéraires du "Journal des débats," avril 1941–août 1944,* textes choisis et établis par Christophe Bident (Paris: Gallimard, 2007), in particular, 14, 54, 210; and "On Nietzsche's Side," in *The Work of Fire,* trans. Charlotte Mandell (Stanford: Stanford University Press, 1995), 287–99; *La Part du feu* (Paris: Gallimard, 1949), 278–89.

4. See also Jacques Derrida, "The Ends of Man," in *Margins of Philosophy,* trans. Alan Bass (Chicago: University of Chicago Press, 1982), 109–36; *Marges de la philosophie* (Paris: Les Éditions de Minuit, 1972), 129–64.

5. See, in particular, "The Work and Death's Space," in *The Space of Literature,* trans. and intro. Ann Smock (Lincoln: University of Nebraska Press, 1982), 85–159; *L'espace littéraire* (Paris: Gallimard, 1955), 99–211; "Death of the Last Writer," in *The Book to Come,* trans. Charlotte Mandell (Stanford: Stanford University Press, 2003), 218–23; *Le livre à venir* (Paris: Gallimard, 1959), 318–25; "The Last to Speak," in *A Voice from Elsewhere,* trans. Charlotte Mandell (Albany: State University of New York Press, 2007), 53–93; "Le dernier à parler," in *Une voix venue d'ailleurs* (Paris: Gallimard, 2002), 69–107.

6. Michel Foucault, *The Order of Things: An Archaeology of the Human Sciences* (London: Tavistock, 1970), 385. "le dernier homme est à la fois plus vieux et plus jeune que la mort de Dieu; puisqu'il a tué Dieu, c'est lui-même qui doit répondre de sa propre finitude; mais puisque c'est dans la mort de Dieu qu'il parle, qu'il pense et existe, son meurtre lui-même est voué à mourir;

des dieux nouveaux, les mêmes, gonflent déjà l'Océan futur; l'homme va disparaître," *Les mots et les choses: Une archéologie des sciences humaines* (Paris:
Gallimard, 1966), 396.

7. Blanchot, *Work of Fire*, 300–344; *La part du feu*, 291–31.

8. Blanchot, *The Instant of My Death*, and Jacques Derrida, *Demeure: Fiction and Testimony*, trans. Elizabeth Rottenberg (Stanford: Stanford University
Press, 2000), 9. "Comme si la mort hors de lui ne pouvait désormais que se heur-
ter à la mort en lui. 'Je suis vivant. Non, tu es mort.'" *L'instant de ma mort* (Montpellier: Fata Morgana, 1994), 17.

9. Blanchot, *The Infinite Conversation*, trans. and foreword Susan Hanson
(Minneapolis: University of Minnesota Press, 1993), 155, translation slightly
modified. "L'homme est toujours l'homme du déclin, déclin qui n'est pas dégé-
nérescence, mais au contraire le manque que l'on peut aimer, qui unit, dans la
séparation et la distance, la vérité 'humaine' à la possibilité de périr. L'homme
de dernier rang, c'est l'homme de la permanence, de la subsistance, celui qui
ne veut pas être le dernier homme." *L'entretien infini* (Paris: Gallimard, 1969),
232–33.

10. Blanchot, *Infinite Conversation*, 147. "L'homme actuel est l'homme de
dernier rang, mais son pouvoir est celui d'un être qui est déjà au-delà de l'homme:
comment cette contradiction ne recèlerait-elle pas le plus grand danger?"
L'entretien infini, 221.

11. Friedrich Nietzsche, *Thus Spoke Zarathustra: A Book for Everyone and
No One*, trans. and intro. R. J. Hollingdale (London: Penguin, 2003), 46, original
emphasis.

12. Ibid., 229–30.

13. Sarah Kofman, *Explosion II. Les enfants de Nietzsche* (Paris: Galilée,
1993), 356–57, and Nietzsche, *Ecce homo: How One Becomes What One Is*, trans.
and intro. R. J. Hollingdale (Harmondsworth, Penguin, 1979), 130. See also
Blanchot, *The Writing of the Disaster*, trans. Ann Smock (Lincoln: University of
Nebraska Press, 1995), 105–6; *L'écriture du désastre* (Paris: Gallimard, 1980),
163–64; and Nietzsche, *Daybreak: Thoughts on the Prejudices of Morality*, trans.
R. J. Hollingdale, intro. Michael Tanner (Cambridge: Cambridge University
Press, 1982), 47.

14. Nietzsche, *Zarathustra*, 43–44, original emphasis. See also Nietzsche,
The Gay Science, with a Prelude in Rhymes and an Appendix of Songs, trans. Walter
Kaufmann (New York: Random House, 1974), 274–75.

15. "Je pense aujourd'hui que peut-être il n'existait pas toujours ou bien
qu'il n'existait pas encore."

16. See also Roger Laporte's perspective in *A l'extrême pointe: Proust, Bataille, Blanchot* (Paris: P.O.L. éditeur, 1998), 79.

17. Blanchot, *Infinite Conversation*, 155; *L'entretien infini*, 233. In Blanchot's
conception of the last man, there are perhaps also elements of the higher man.

Nietzsche's Zarathustra searched for him in preference to the mob of people. The higher man is far from the superman and must learn to dance— "to dance beyond yourselves"; Nietzsche, *Zarathustra,* 306. Importantly, Gilles Deleuze emphasizes that Zarathustra treats the higher man in two different ways: "sometimes as the enemy who will consider any trap, any infamy, in order to divert Zarathustra from his path and sometimes as a host, almost a companion who is engaged in an enterprise close to that of Zarathustra himself," *Nietzsche and Philosophy,* trans. Hugh Tomlinson (London: Athlone Press, 1983), 166; "tantôt comme l'ennemi qui ne recule devant aucun piège, aucune infamie, pour détourner Zarathoustra de son chemin; tantôt comme un hôte, presque un compagnon qui se lance dans une entreprise proche de celle de Zarathoustra lui-même," *Nietzsche et la philosophie* (Paris: Presses Universitaires de France, 1962), 191.

18. "Sûrement, il était capable de penser tout, de savoir tout, mais, en outre, il n'était rien."

19. "Si je l'avais voulu, j'aurais pensé tout." "Je sais tout, je sais tout."

20. Nietzsche, *Philosophy and Truth: Selections from Nietzsche's Notebooks of the early 1870's,* ed. and trans. Daniel Breazeale (Atlantic Highlands, NJ: Humanities Press, 1979), 33. See also Jacques Derrida, "Living On: Border Lines," trans. James Hulbert, in *Deconstruction and Criticism* by Harold Bloom et al. (New York: Seabury Press, 1979), 132–35; Derrida, "Survivre," in *Parages* (Paris: Galilée, 1986, 2003), 164–67; Derrida, "Of an Apocalyptic Tone Newly Adopted in Philosophy," trans. John P. Leavey, Jr., in *Derrida and Negative Theology,* ed. Harold Coward and Toby Foshay (New York: State University of New York, 1992), 25–71; Derrida, *D'un ton apocalyptique adopté naguère en philosophie* (Paris: Galilée, 1983).

21. Nietzsche, *Philosophy and Truth,* 33–34, original emphasis.

22. Philippe Lacoue-Labarthe, *L'imitation des modernes. Typographies 2* (Paris: Galilée, 1986), 206, 219–20. See also René Major, "De 'l'Œdipe' de Freud à 'l'Œdipe' de Lacan ou De la métaphore au néologisme," *Au commencement: La vie la mort* (Paris: Galilée, 1999), 91–106.

23. Blanchot, *Infinite Conversation,* 17–18. *L'entretien infini,* 21–22. On Oedipus, the tragic spectacle and catharsis, see Nietzsche, *The Birth of Tragedy and The Case of Wagner,* trans. Walter Kaufmann (New York: Random House, 1967), 67–69, 132. See also G. W. F. Hegel, *Hegel on Tragedy,* ed. and intro. Anne Paolucci and Henry Paolucci (Garden City, NY: Doubleday & Company, 1962), 69.

24. "Un Dieu lui-même a besoin d'un témoin. L'incognito divin, il faut qu'il soit percé ici-bas."

25. Georges Bataille, "Ce monde où nous mourons," *Critique* 123–24 (1957): 675–84. See also "Hegel, Death and Sacrifice," in *The Bataille Reader,* ed. Fred Botting and Scott Wilson (Oxford: Blackwell, 1997), 279–95, previously published in *Deucalion* 5, no. 40 (1955): 21–43; and Jacques Derrida, "From Restricted

to General Economy," in *Writing and Difference,* trans. Alan Bass (London and New York: Routledge, 1978), 317–50; *L'écriture et la différence* (Paris: Éditions du Seuil, 1967), 369–407.

26. "Et s'il ne m'avait dit un jour: 'Je ne puis penser à moi: il y a là quelque chose de terrible, une difficulté qui échappe, un obstacle qui ne se rencontre pas'? Et tout de suite après: 'Il dit qu'il ne peut penser à lui-même: aux autres encore, à tel autre, mais c'est comme une flèche, partie de trop loin, qui n'atteindrait pas son but, et pourtant quand elle s'arrête et tombe, le but, dans le lointain, frémit et vient à sa rencontre.'"

27. "Later, he asked himself how he had entered the calm. He couldn't talk about it with himself. Only joy at feeling he was in harmony with the words: 'Later, he . . .'" "Plus tard, il se demanda comment il était entré dans le calme. Il ne pouvait en parler avec lui-même. Seulement joie à se sentir en rapport avec les mots: 'Plus tard, il . . .'" (89; 147).

28. "Comment répondre? Qui n'aurait, écoutant cela, le sentiment d'être ce but? / Il ne s'adressait à personne. Je ne veux pas dire qu'il ne m'ait pas parlé à moi-même, mais l'écoutait un autre que moi, un être peut-être plus riche, plus vaste et cependant plus singulier, presque trop général, comme si, en face de lui, ce qui avait été moi se fût étrangement éveillé en 'nous,' présence et force unie de l'esprit commun. J'étais un peu plus, un peu moins que moi: plus, en tout cas, que tous les hommes."

29. "Tout cela est moi devant lui, et lui ne paraît presque rien."

30. "Il y avait donc, même pour elle, des points où elle n'était plus aussi sûre et où elle se sentait dangereusement éloignée d'elle-même."

31. On the sphere, see, in particular, "Joubert and Space," in *The Book to Come,* 49–65; *Le livre à venir,* 75–98.

32. "Elle avait toujours eu la crainte de mourir hors d'elle; elle disait: 'Vous me tiendrez fermement. Il faut que je sois atteinte au point où vous me tiendrez.'"

33. Georges Bataille, *Inner Experience,* trans. and intro. Leslie Anne Boldt (Albany: State University of New York, 1988), 110–11. *L'expérience intérieure, Œuvres complètes* 5 (Paris: Gallimard, 1973), 129.

34. Bataille, *Inner Experience,* 61; *L'expérience intérieure,* 76. See also Michael Holland, "Bataille, Blanchot and the 'Last Man,'" *Paragraph* 27, no. 1 (2004): 50–63; Leslie Anne Boldt-Irons, "Blanchot and Bataille on *The Last Man,*" *Angelaki* 11, no. 2 (2006): 3–17.

35. "Pourtant, je me souviens de beaucoup de choses— de tout peut-être, mais non pas de ce moment, et dès que je me porte vers lui, par un mouvement plus audacieux, je me heurte à cette pointe extrêmement fine et prodigieusement lointaine: ce point noir que nous appelons le ciel, cet unique point changeant, toujours plus noir et plus aigu, qu'on trouve tout à coup devant soi et qui ne serait là que pour nous inviter à reculer, à rentrer au sein du calme d'où notre légèreté nous a aussi éternellement fait sortir."

36. "la pointe extrêmement fine et prodigieusement lointaine qui toujours se dérobe."

37. "Tout, prétend-il, nous serait commun, sauf le ciel: par ce point passe notre part de solitude. Mais il dit aussi que cette part est la même pour tous et qu'en ce point nous sommes tous unis jusque dans notre séparation, unis là seulement et non ailleurs: ce serait le but ultime."

38. In "The Negative Community," Blanchot states: "The absence of community is not the failure of community: absence belongs to community as its extreme moment or as the ordeal that exposes it to its necessary disappearance." *The Unavowable Community,* trans. Pierre Joris (Barrytown, NY: Station Hill Press, 1988), 15. "L'absence de communauté n'est pas l'échec de la communauté: elle lui appartient comme à son moment extrême ou comme à l'épreuve qui l'expose à sa disparition nécessaire." *La communauté inavouable* (Paris: Minuit, 1983), 31.

39. "Je sais bien que de toute manière tu n'existes pas, et que c'est là ce qui nous réunit."

40. "Parfois il semble que certaines figures, en se réunissant, essaient d'ébaucher un tel visage. Il semble que toutes éternellement s'élèvent les unes vers les autres pour le rendre présent. Il semble que chacune voudrait être l'unique pour toutes les autres, voulant que toutes soient l'unique pour elle et être pour chacune toutes les autres. Il semble que le vide ne soit jamais assez vide."

41. "Trop belles figures troublées. Un visage ne peut pas être cela. Le visage ultime, seulement manifeste, hors d'attente et hors d'atteinte. Visage qui est le vide peut-être."

42. See Emmanuel Lévinas, *Totality and Infinity: An Essay on Exteriority,* trans. Alphonso Lingis (The Hague: Martinus Nijhoff, 1979); *Totalité et Infini: Essai sur l'extériorité* (The Hague: Martinus Nijhoff, 1961); Blanchot, "Knowledge of the Unknown," in *Infinite Conversation,* 49–58; "Connaissance de l'inconnu," in *L'entretien infini,* 70–83. For another perspective, see Gerald L. Bruns, *Maurice Blanchot: The Refusal of Philosophy* (Baltimore: Johns Hopkins University Press, 1997), 131–35.

43. "Est-ce qu'il mourrait en ce moment? Est-ce toi qui toujours meurs en lui, auprès de lui?"

44. *Infinite Conversation,* 158; "En vérité, qu'est-ce que le surhomme? Nous ne le savons pas et Nietzsche, à proprement parler, ne le sait pas. Nous savons seulement que la pensée du surhomme signifie: l'homme disparaît, affirmation qui est poussée au plus loin, lorsqu'elle se redouble en question: l'homme disparaît-il?" *L'entretien infini,* 236–37.

45. "le sentiment de l'éternité." "D'où vient que dans l'espace où je suis, où il m'a entraîné, je repasse constamment près du point où tout pourrait reprendre comme avec un autre commencement?"

46. "la vie en nous, la force inépuisable de la vie."

47. Nietzsche, *Zarathustra,* 234.

48. Heidegger develops the idea that these "doctrines are conjoined in a circle." Martin Heidegger, "Who is Nietzsche's Zarathustra?" in *Nietzsche,* vols. 1 and 2 (combined), *The Will to Power as Art* and *The Eternal Recurrence of the Same,* trans. David Farrell Krell (San Francisco: Harper Collins, 1991), 227–28.

49. Blanchot, "Crossing the Line," in *Infinite Conversation,* 148; "le nihilisme se dépasse absolument en se rendant définitivement indépassable," *L'entretien infini,* 223.

50. Blanchot, *Infinite Conversation,* 159; *L'entretien infini,* 238.

51. "Il nous faut fondre l'un dans l'autre. Ce qui est fin pour toi sera sûrement commencement en moi. N'es-tu pas tentée par le bonheur du cercle? Tu me précèdes, mémoire aimante, souvenir de ce qui n'a pas eu lieu."

52. "'Est-ce moi qui suis en train de mourir? est-ce vous?'"

53. "Tentation de nous laisser, sous son regard, disparaître et renaître en une puissance sans nom et sans visage."

54. "Mouvement de séparation, mais d'attrait, par lequel les visages semblaient rendus attirants, attirés les uns par les autres comme pour former, ensemble, l'avenir d'une tout autre figure, nécessaire et impossible à figurer."

55. "Est-ce que la flèche que je n'ai pas retenue voudrait trouver en toi le but qui lui accorderait le repos?"

56. "comme si, à cet instant, il était tenté par l'illusion du cercle, revenant vers nous comme vers son véritable avenir pour qu'à nouveau il pût espérer mourir en avant de lui-même."

57. Nietzsche, *Zarathustra,* 332, original emphasis.

58. Blanchot, *Step Not Beyond,* 16, original emphasis. "Qu'est-ce qui reviendra? Tout, *sauf* le présent, la possibilité d'une présence," *La pas au-delà,* 27.

59. Blanchot, *Infinite Conversation,* 135; "l'indestructible qui peut être détruit," *L'entretien infini,* 200.

60. Blanchot, *Faux Pas,* trans. Charlotte Mandell (Stanford: Stanford University Press, 2001), 37; "pour l'homme avide de voir, c'est le moment où, regardant, il risque de devenir plus aveugle qu'un aveugle, une sorte de voyant qui se souvient du soleil comme d'une tache grise, importune," *Faux pas* (Paris: Gallimard, 1943), 47.

61. Nietzsche, *Zarathustra,* 104.

62. "un autre, étranger, proche, disparu, l'ombre de l'autre rive, personne."

TEN

Space and Beyond

L'attente l'oubli

Michael Holland

> *Et ceux-là seuls en surent quelque chose, dont la mémoire est incertaine et*
> *le récit est aberrant.*
>
> —Saint-John Perse, *Neiges*

L'attente l'oubli (*Awaiting Oblivion*)[1] occupies a singular place in Blanchot's oeuvre. The way it begins suggests that it is the next in a series of narrative works that he had been writing since 1941. But unlike every other work in that series, it appeared without a generic marker. Its relation to the broad movement from *roman* to *récit* that Blanchot's narrative writing displays is thus exceptional. Whereas all the other works are the site, over time, of what might be called a struggle over genre, *Awaiting Oblivion* appears to have left genre behind.

To understand the full significance of this change, it is important to observe that the order of Blanchot's narratives is not merely chronological. Each succeeding work is concerned exclusively with a moment lying outside of time, a moment that is essentially impossible, and which recurs like an obsession throughout all of Blanchot's work: the moment following my death, when I am dead yet able somehow to look back on my final moment, and which Blanchot sums up in the words, "we have forgotten to die."[2] From his first novel, *Thomas the Obscure*, whose hero digs a grave only to find that he is already in it,[3] to what is probably his last published text,[4] to be dead yet conscious, like Jean-Paul's dreamer, Poe's M. Waldemar, or Kafka's Gracchus, is the experience that haunts Blanchot's writing from the outset. And from one narrative to the next, a single intention prevails: to bring that experience into language, to make its futurity coincide with the present of narrative, to say the end by saying "the end."

Seen in this light, Blanchot's narratives do not consist simply of a set of discrete instances of the same project. Rather, each work doubles back on the preceding one, treating the relation this latter can only fail to establish between past, present, and future as entirely past, and fictionalizing that failed relation as a drama of non-coincidence and incomprehension. Through narrative, Blanchot remains perpetually at the same threshold moment, where what is always future in relation to any attempt to speak it in the present is configured with each backward loop of narrative as a relation between present and past. In the process, narrative is progressively drained of all fictional content. Increasingly, his works exist as no more than the act of language in which the fractured moment of experience defies reduction to the status of an event in time.

From this perspective, Blanchot's narrative works fall into three groups: the novels (1941–1948); the triptych[5] of *récits* (1948–1953) inaugurated by *Death Sentence;* and what I will argue is a diptych formed by *The Last Man* and *Awaiting Oblivion* (1957–1962). Within the diptych, the development I have outlined becomes even more complex. Despite a break of four years, this governing pattern in Blanchot's narratives clearly determines the way that *The Last Man* follows on from *The One Who Was Standing Apart from Me*. When the anonymous "he" of the latter work says, "you know there must be no name between us," the narrator observes: "perhaps . . . without my knowing it, at this very moment I was giving him one" (*OSA*, 57). At the beginning of *The Last Man*, it is precisely to "this very moment" that the narrator returns, revealing that "without knowing it," he has never left it: "As soon as I was able to use that word, I said what I must always have thought of him: that he was the last man."[6] In its turn, therefore, *The Last Man* pursues the task in which every preceding work of fiction has failed: to make language coincide with the fractured moment of consciousness as "already dead," which the *récit* initially represents as follows: "I became convinced that I had first known him when he was dead, then when he was dying" (*LM*, 4).

When *The Last Man* reaches its conclusion, however, something new has happened, which will affect the way that *Awaiting Oblivion* will follow on from it: "Later, he asked himself how he had entered the calm. He could not talk about it with himself. Only joy at feeling in relation with the words 'Later, he . . .'" (*LM*, 89). Once again, language offers no help to thought, as it seeks to inquire into how it has entered the calm (of death) while remaining itself ("He could not talk about it with himself"). Yet something has changed. In every previous work, the narrative doubled back on itself, dramatizing as past its failed attempt to capture what is always future in relation to its own present. Each time, it fell short: the work's last word excluded that moment from the work. But in the brief section that concludes *The Last Man,* the abortive attempt to render the future moment present—"Later, he asked himself . . ."—is not simply left hanging in the form of a question. The doubling back to which each failed attempt necessarily gives rise is here harnessed into a potentially endless narrative loop. The closing words of *When The Time Comes* (1951) are the following: "And yet, even though the circle is already drawing me along, and even if I had to write this eternally, I would write it in order to obliterate eternity: Now, the end."[7] In *The Last Man,* the circle is the same, but it is now no longer in conflict with writing. Its circularity *is* writing, writing which is no longer identified with saying but rather silently inscribed, traced out in such a way that the "now" of the end is elided by the endlessly repeated circle of narrative. At the end of *The Last Man,* the silent "voice" of calm is thus allowed to "speak." The work effectively narrates the future in and as an infinite present, riding out the end in a euphoric transport ("joy at feeling in relation") that both traverses and embraces the repetitive temporality of narrative.

With *The Last Man,* Blanchot's narrative thus reaches a turning point. It seems at last to be about to achieve its goal. It is therefore no surprise that Blanchot seems eager to go on narrating. In 1958, the year following the appearance of *The Last Man,* he published "L'attente" ("Waiting").[8] In this piece things appear to have slipped back, however. Once again, the setting is one of rooms, corridors, and balconies. A man is listening to a woman and writing down what he hears. No "I" is in evidence: the "he" of *The Last Man* appears to have returned. But the movement which, in that work, seemed destined henceforth to transport writing silently back and forth between time and what lies beyond it has come to a halt: "Here. . . he was obliged to stop" (*AO,* 1) are its opening words. Things then resume: "He decided to begin again from there" (*AO,* 2). But between each of these points in the loop of recurrence ("he . . . he . . ."), instead of joy at "feeling in relation," there is a woman's sadness at being misunderstood—"She sadly pushed away all the pages" (*AO,* 1)—and a man's inquiry into that sadness—"Why did she repudiate so sadly what she had said?" (*AO,* 2). The relation between the euphoric "voice" of writing and the words "Later, he . . ." has been replaced by one in which writing has once again become the failed attempt to record a voice, immobilized in an insuperable present moment in which "he" is now confined: "But later? He must not concern himself with later, he would not seek guarantees for another time" (*AO,* 2). This is a clear rebuttal of the relation of silent recurrence into which "his" reflection on his own end is transformed at the end of *The Last Man.* In the very next loop of that recurrence, the process is brought to a halt. Something is still not right. The relation, like that between every one of Blanchot's narratives and the one that follows it, is one of return. But, unlike in previous stages, what *Awaiting Oblivion* returns to did not present itself as another failure of narrative: it appeared to overcome that failure by inscribing the movement of return *within* the language of narrative. What has happened?

At the end of *The Last Man,* questioning as voice ("he asked himself") is suspended ("He could not talk about it"), giving way to the joyous, silent "voice" of calm. In *Awaiting Oblivion,* that silent voice dispels euphoria by materializing as the sad and disappointed partner of a writer who admits on reflection that "he had questioned her too brutally. . . . he had questioned her in a more urgent manner by his silence, his waiting, and the signs he had made to her. He had induced her to say the truth too openly, a truth that was direct, disarmed, irrevocable [*sans retour*]" (*AO,* 2).

What happened at the end of *The Last Man,* however silent, was clearly not silent enough. The transports of joy required language in which to happen. *Awaiting Oblivion* would thus seem destined to continue the endless series of ultimately abortive attempts at saying the end, and its protagonist seems to acquiesce in this: "Perhaps he did not want to push her into other confidential relations: perhaps, on the contrary he secretly desired to keep her on this very tack." He acknowledges that he has what in French are *des arrière-pensées:* "other motives" in the translation, but literally "thoughts that hang back," and which prevent writing from completing the itinerary traced out for it by narrative. He sees clearly what his task is: "To take hold of this slightly cold hand that would lead him, by way of unusual meanders, to a place where she would disappear and leave him alone." But he knows he must be unfaithful to it: "it was difficult for him not to wonder to whom this hand belonged. He had always been like this. He thought about the hand, and about the person who had held it out to him, and not about the itinerary. Therein without a doubt lay his mistake [*faute*]" (*AO,* 2–3).

Looking back in 1983, Blanchot recalls that his original ambition was "to begin writing only so as to get immediately to the end (the encounter with the last word)," in the hope of "finding the quickest way to have done with it right from the start."[9] At the same time, he acknowledges, he was writing *Thomas the Obscure,* "which was perhaps about the same thing, but precisely would not have done and, on the contrary, encountered in the search for annihilation the unhappy demand of an endlessness within dying itself" (*VC,* 64). As "an attempt to short circuit the other book that was being written" (*VC,* 64), "The Last Word" manifestly failed. However, what Blanchot calls "the paradox of such a story," instead of simply making it appear impossible or absurd, may have concealed a more original project: "unless it claimed to be a prophetic work, announcing as past a future that had already arrived" (*VC,* 65). That is the future to which *Death Sentence* refers at its close: "To it eternally I say 'Come', and eternally, it is there."[10] It is the future in which thought encounters the truth of, and as, its own extinction. It is the moment that each succeeding *récit* falls short of, until *The Last Man* appears at last to inscribe it, as a loop of euphoric silence, in language. It is a future project about which the "he" of *Awaiting Oblivion* is in no doubt: "It is the voice that is entrusted to you, not what it says. What it says, the extraordinary secrets that you receive and transcribe so as to give them their due, you must lead them gently, in spite of their attempt to seduce, towards the silence that you first drew out of them" (*AO*, 3). But, as Blanchot indicates in 1983, if narrative is capable of announcing as past a future which is already there, in that very process it prevents that future from ever taking place (being "there" here and now) once and for all. It is thus what he calls "an interminable process whose end [*terme*] is repetition [*ressassement*] and eternity" (*VC*, 65).

In retrospect, Blanchot thus seems resigned to seeing the process at work in his narratives as a sterile and exhausting repetitiveness. The way in which *Awaiting Oblivion* follows on from *The Last Man* would seem to anticipate that view. The silent union between thought and truth is held back as a fruitless exchange between a man and a woman. At the threshold of their "clandestine encounter," Aminadab inevitably appears.[11] Something happens in *Awaiting Oblivion*, however, which Blanchot's reminiscence leaves out of account, and to which a passing observation, present in the *récit* but not in "L'attente," alludes: "It slowly, suddenly, dawned on him: from then on he would look for a way out. He would find it" (*AO*, 13). The following section of the *récit* is laconic and lapidary: "And yet everything remained unchanged" (*AO*, 13). But, as is now apparent, in the endless cycle of narrative it is precisely in the nature of "everything" to remain unchanged: all is over. Within that perspective, however, change at another level has begun to occur.

In the second part of *The Last Man*, the first-person narrative is interrupted on a number of occasions by the voice of a "we," emerging in the text in italicized sections and said by the narrating voice to come from "an opening onto a different region, one . . . we both dreaded in the same way" (*LM*, 65–66). Clearly, there are two "we's" at work here. The first corresponds to the narrator's relation to calm, in which he is perpetually "on the edge of the moment when I would have to be calm" (*LM*, 63). The second "we" is one to which the narrator relates totally differently. The space it occupies opens up *within* the space of calm. It is a dangerous space, "evasive, wily," perhaps without a center, "like a slope one had only to follow, a slope that started off from calm and ended in calm"; a space that resounds with "an endless din [*rumeur*]" (*LM*, 66), and of which the narrator says: "I could distinguish myself from it, only hear it, yet also hear myself in it, an immense speech [*parole*] which continuously says 'We'" (*LM,* 67). In short, the "we" that speaks in it, while distinct from the "we" with which the narrator reflects on his relation to the space of calm, nevertheless embraces the latter: it is "that 'We' which sprang from me and which, far beyond the room where space was beginning to enclose itself, obliged me to hear myself in that chorus whose base I situated over there, somewhere in the direction of the sea" (*LM,* 67).

This development brings to the fore the endless process out of which each of Blanchot's works of fiction arises. As language leads thought ever closer in the present to a silent encounter with the truth that has already put an end to it, this convergence has already failed to take place, and entered the endless cacophony that, as the reference to the sea would indicate,[12] embraces all of Blanchot's narratives. Through its use of "we," the narrative both hovers motionlessly at the brink of calm and endlessly intrudes upon it. The loop that *The Last Man* installs at its close, after a textual break, as what would appear at last to have broken the cycle of *ressassement,* does no more than elide the moment when the calm space of narrative opens onto the endless *rumeur* of a space without center or contour. In an attempt at reversing the relation that determines all of Blanchot's narrative works, *The Last Man* embraces *le ressassement* within a euphoric calm. The repetition of "Later, he . . ." is the only trace, in the language of *The Last Man* at its close, of the turbulent, vociferous space to which narrative belongs, the more it approaches silence.

In returning to that moment in *Awaiting Oblivion,* Blanchot is not just reversing this reversal. "There must be no turning back" (8), the work adds to "L'attente" in 1962. If it does turn back and renarrate the closing loop of *The Last Man,* this is the better to continue the work begun in that book, and to bring into writing that evasive and disorienting space which has always already embraced writing within its endless din. Thus, while from the writer's point of view the space to which the narrative returns initially is unchanging and identical—"her room was at the end of the same hallway . . . , at the place where the building began to turn" (*AO,* 2)—under the pressure of his questioning, space becomes something mobile and unpredictable for the female figure: "everything before her eyes was spinning [*tournait*]: she had lost the center from which events radiated and which she had held on to firmly until now" (*AO*, 1). From the outset, therefore, the two "spaces" that are briefly juxtaposed in *The Last Man*, then made to coexist at its close, recur in the situation onto which *Awaiting Oblivion* opens. He submits to her desire that he should describe to her the space they occupy (*AO*, 6). He discovers in doing so, however, that space becomes a void: "as soon as he wants to describe it, it is empty" (*AO*, 7). This void is a space of disorientation which "at times appeared to him as threatening, at times as joyous" (*AO*, 15). It is the "other" space, which the narrator of *The Last Man* described as "evasive, wily," yet also "light, joyous" (*DH*, 66), and to which, like the female protagonist in *Awaiting Oblivion*, he responded with a feeling of disorientation at its lack of a center. But though he retreated from it, he was not overcome by it: "But I, too, became wily . . . I had lost every habit, every path. The only firm thing I had was the motionless thought that enveloped us and perhaps protected us" (*LM*, 66). It is this motionless mobility that *The Last Man* harnessed into the endless loop on which it ended, but did not close, and whose two-fold space *Awaiting Oblivion* will seek to accommodate fully in a single act of writing.

The way it does so appears quite obvious on the surface. After a first burst of continuous third-person narrative, "L'attente" breaks up into discrete sections, each marked by a typographical symbol, and this is the form also adopted in *Awaiting Oblivion*. At the level of the story, continuity is not affected. The man and the woman are present to the very end, and indeed achieve a degree of intimacy rarely encountered in Blanchot's narratives: "He remembers that she is there, motionless, and while he helps her remove some of her clothing . . . he draws her towards him, takes hold of her, lets his gaze play over her face, as she lets herself slip, eyes calmly open"(*AO*, 81).[13] At the same time, the story is not all;[14] a fundamental break with narrative continuity is also at work. When "L'attente" is incorporated into *Awaiting Oblivion*, not only are its sections separated from each other by sections added for the book, but their original order is changed. The space of this work is thus not only discontinuous, it is also mobile, and would appear to conform to the space around which the narrator of *The Last Man* "tirelessly prowled" (*LM*, 66). But this mobility has also extended into the "space" of narrative voice, now deprived of the focus provided by an "I." At the end of "L'attente" we read: "There is no real dialogue between them. Only waiting maintains between what they say a certain relation, words spoken so as to wait, a waiting for words" (*AO*, 25), and within the discontinuous space of *Awaiting Oblivion*, voices speak which cannot fully be attributed to either the man or the woman of the story, and seem therefore to come from nowhere.

The significance of this can be seen in the repeated utterance of the words "Make it possible for me to speak to you," which in terms of the story are spoken by the woman. In "L'attente" (1958), they are couched in the familiar "tu" form and occur three times. The first time, they are part of a dialogue and are between inverted commas. The second time, they occur on their own in a separate section and have lost their inverted commas. The third time, still without inverted commas, they are now in italics and are followed by two sentences of unattributed speculation: "Is that what she really wanted? Was she sure she would not regret it?" (*AO*, 11).[15] Clearly, these words both do and do not belong to the story, and when "L'attente" is incorporated into *Awaiting Oblivion*, this duality deepens into discontinuity. The section containing the first appearance of the words is moved to the very end of Part I of the work (*AO*, 43–44) and replaced by a new one, in which the words "Make it possible for me to speak to you" are spoken by the woman in the "vous" form, which is and remains the mode in which the two characters address each other (*AO*, 5). Having initially responded to her demand in the "vous" form, the man goes on in the familiar "tu" mode: "Well then, begin, speak to me." She is surprised at this: "Why this familiar form of address? You never address anyone that way." The section is followed by one that reads: "And therefore, in a single language always allow a double speech [*parole*] to be heard," and over the course of the first part of *Awaiting Oblivion*, in five other places,[16] the words "Make it possible for me to speak to you" recur in such a way that, although originally part of a *je-vous* dialogue, they have broken free to become a vocative (*tu*) without identifiable voice.

This disjunctive doubling within the vocative mode is also found at the level of the third person. At a primary level, "he" and "she" interact as the story requires. In two ways, however, the stability of this mode is affected. First, "he"s and "she"s detach themselves and become the subject of discrete sections, sometimes just a sentence long. Second, there is a regular shift from the level of the personal to that of the analytical, where "il" and "elle" signify "it," rather than "he" or "she." In itself, this move is perfectly compatible with narrative. However, the analytical mode in *Awaiting Oblivion* also exists independently of the narrative, as in the following passage: "To wait, to make oneself attentive to that which makes waiting a neutral act, coiled in on itself in tight circles, the innermost and outermost of which coincide . . . Waiting, waiting that is the refusal to wait for anything, a calm expanse unfurled beneath each step" (*AO*, 8). Significantly, after "Make it possible for me to speak to you," this is the next section of "L'attente" to be removed from its original place when the text is incorporated into *Awaiting Oblivion*. In this work, both the second- and third-person modes are given their freedom, while remaining tied to the story.

Another order would thus seem to be governing the text: a second space, arising out of the homogeneous space of narrative, but opening up and doubling back so as to embrace narrative within it, and in the process, subjecting the unity afforded it by the first- and third-person modes to disruption and dispersal. But how "double" is that language in reality? Drawing, no doubt, on the experience of writing *Awaiting Oblivion*, Blanchot wrote the following in 1964:

> Within an interrelational space, I can seek to communicate with someone in a number of ways: first, by considering him as an objective possibility in the world . . . ; another time, by regarding him as another self, perhaps quite different, but whose difference passes by way of a primary identity, that of two beings each equally able to speak in the first person; and a third time, no longer by a mediating relation of impersonal knowledge or personal comprehension, but by attempting to achieve an immediate relation wherein the same and the other seek to lose themselves in one another or draw near to one another through the proximity of a familiar address that forgets or effaces distance.[17]

Transposed onto narrative, these three modes correspond to the third person (s/he or it), to dialogue, and to the direct address exemplified by the "tu"-mode in *Awaiting Oblivion*, each of which exists in that work both within the confines of the story and in what the material layout of the book would suggest is a free and open space. Blanchot continues his analysis as follows, however: "These relations have in common the fact that all three tend towards unity: the 'I' wants to annex the other (identify the other with itself) by making of it its own thing, or by studying it as a thing, or else it wants to find in the other another 'me', whether this be through free recognition or through an instantaneous union of the heart" (*IC*, 77). Simply to separate them out and allow them to become mobile does not of itself open up a second space, therefore. This space, which he calls *interruption*, "introduces the waiting that measures the distance between two interlocutors, a distance that is no longer reducible, but is the irreducible" (*IC*, 76). The strangeness that it introduces allows of no common space, because it is "a separation, fissure, or interval that leaves him [the other] infinitely outside of me" (*IC*, 77).

It seems important to bear these reflections in mind because, on two counts, it is plausible to argue that the space which allows *Awaiting Oblivion* to disrupt and disperse the space of its story is the space of analytical thought, of "philosophy." First, the two categories that give the work its title, *waiting, forgetting*, have a long history in Blanchot's thinking. As early as 1947 he writes: "for Baudelaire . . . [b]eauty is the unexpected [*l'inattendu*] and it is the expectation [*l'attente*] of rhythm."[18] Ten years later, in an article on Simone Weil, he writes: "Attention is the reception of what escapes attention, . . . a waiting that is the unawaited of all waiting [*l'inattendu de toute attente*]" (IC, 121). The next year he returns to the topic in an article on gambling, which he did not include in any subsequent volume: "Luck is never part of what we wait for: I can't wait for the number 22 to turn up, it is the unexpected. A gambler's waiting is linked to luck, as it is pure expectation [*attente*] . . . of the unexpected [*l'inattendu*] which cannot be waited for."[19]

Clearly, the category of waiting [*l'attente*] is deeply embedded in Blanchot's thought as it develops, and a closer study could also reveal that the same is true for oblivion or forgetting [*l'oubli*].[20] Furthermore, in the years leading up to the publication of *Awaiting Oblivion*, Blanchot transposes developments on the subject of waiting and forgetting from his critical texts into that work. The passage on Simone Weil just quoted turns up virtually identically in *Awaiting Oblivion* (*AO*, 21), as do numerous others from that study, sometimes by way of "L'attente."[21] Similarly, the opening section of Part II of *Awaiting Oblivion* repeats elements from the opening pages of a 1961 article on Foucault;[22] and a year earlier, an article on the poet Jules Supervielle contains passages which are also transposed, one on forgetting (*AO*, 77–78; *IC*, 316), the other on the subject of memory and the Greek poets that contains what will be the closing words of the book: "*the reserve of things in their latent state*" (*AO*, 85: *IC*, 315; the phrase only appears in the original article).

In the light of this widespread incorporation of material from Blanchot's critical writings into *Awaiting Oblivion,* there seems to be a strong case for arguing that the second space which coexists with that of narrative is the space of rational analysis, of philosophy. The disorienting, cacophonous space of rumor that narrative exposes at the heart of calm in *The Last Man* has here been accommodated within a hybrid space, where the endless proliferation of resurgent voices ("he . . . he . . .") can be distributed across a dynamic open space of writing, as thoughts on the subject of the very paradox out of which narrative arises, and which *The One Who Was Standing Apart from Me* has already characterized as "an interlacing of waiting and forgetting which was an invitation to uninterrupted agitation" (*OSA,* 49). "Dead," "I" thus live on not only as a "he" destined to interpose himself noisily between thought and calm for all eternity (*Aminadab*), but also as the "wily I" who emerges in *The Last Man,* a subject commensurate with the "wily" space onto which narrative opens, who can range as "it" [*il*] over this space of analysis and aphorism eternally, while never leaving "the motionless thought" ("I am dead") out of which the story arises. In short, each time Blanchot's text writes *il,* two spaces simultaneously open up: one which is the closed space of the story, where *il* as "he" remains confined with "I"; one where *il* is "it," which is the mobile space of philosophical analysis.

There is a second reason why this perspective seems plausible. The year after "L'attente" appeared in *Botteghe Oscure,* Blanchot published another piece bearing the same title in a very different place: a Festschrift offered to Martin Heidegger on his seventieth birthday.[23] This text, which, like its namesake, is in short sections, some narrative, some analytical, is in its turn incorporated into *Awaiting Oblivion* according to the same rule of redistribution. In addition, a significant proportion of the fragments that make up the 1958 text are to be found, in a different order, in the later one.[24] A prototype for the new space of writing that *Awaiting Oblivion* opens up would already appear to be in place.

In this account of what happens to space in *Awaiting Oblivion*, however, something has been left out. Coexisting with the "double speech" to which the pronoun *il* gives rise is a third *parole*. The brief, penultimate section of *The Last Man* provides an instance of this—"Thought, infinitesimal thought, calm thought, pain" (*LM*, 89). Its presence there throws into relief the fact that the key categories of waiting and forgetting, while entering this work in their usual guise as they had already done in *The One Who Was Standing Apart from Me*, emerge in the second part into another space where they are curiously free of the syntactic and semantic structures that have so far contained them: "First of all to forget. To remember only where nothing is remembered. To forget: to remember everything as if through forgetting" (*LM*, 85); "Face, face of waiting, yet withdrawn from what is expected, the unexpected of all expectation [*l'inattendu de toute attente*]" (*LM*, 88). When the end of *The Last Man* is renarrated, giving rise to *Awaiting Oblivion*, it turns out that both discrete sections that follow the main narrative have been included. But when the *parole* of the penultimate section is carried over into the second work, unlike the elements of the closing narrative loop, it remains identical to itself. More significantly, juxtaposed with the loop that closes *The Last Man*, it remains in the same relation of juxtaposition with the double space in which the second work in the diptych seeks to inscribe the "double speech" of the first. *The Last Man* thus passes on to *Awaiting Oblivion* a language that is neither narrative nor philosophical and that, as well as being irreducible to third-person discourse, emanates from no traceable source in an "I." Juxtaposed with what may be summed up as the unitary *descriptive-analytic* mode, which both narrative and philosophy share, there is thus a separate mode, which may be termed *vocative-invocative*.

This mode appears at first to have its source in the story. The move from *vous* to *tu* in the first occurrence of the words "Make it possible for me to speak to you" marks the emergence of an independent vocative mode, which provides a counterpart to the doubling of "he" as "it." This vocative allows the narrating voice to stray quite far beyond the confines of the story, sometimes as dialogue, sometimes as monologue. Yet the "I" it always presupposes and generally pronounces not only keeps it anchored within the story, it also brings to the light the fact that, however different the space of narrative and the space of philosophical analysis may be, they ultimately entertain a continuity with each other, which derives from the unbroken unity of self that the first-person pronoun guarantees. To find what Blanchot calls in 1964 "a separation, fissure, or interval" (*IC*, 77), in short, the radical *interruption* that allows the unitary descriptive-analytic mode in which both narrative and philosophy coexist to open onto a space that he will soon term *fragmentary*, the vocative-invocative mode of writing found in *Awaiting Oblivion* must be given its due. In it, not only has the vocative broken free of any subject in language, but it has summoned certain key abstractions out of their descriptive-analytic space into one where they float free, *invoked* in such a way that they yield up their significance in all its unresolvable complexity. This can be seen in the following passage, which occurs in both versions of "L'attente" as well as in *Awaiting Oblivion:*

> To wait, only to wait. Unfamiliar waiting, equal in all its moments, as is space in all its points; similar to space, exerting the same continuous pressure, not exerting it. Solitary waiting that was within us and has now gone outside, waiting for ourselves without ourselves, forcing us to wait outside our own waiting, leaving us nothing more to await. (*AO*, 14)[25]

There can be no question of elucidating this passage analytically or relating it to the story. *Awaiting Oblivion* itself repeatedly does just that, by anchoring passages like it either in philosophical developments or in narrative. The way that the passage continues in both the original *Botteghe Oscure* piece and in *Awaiting Oblivion* (but not in the 1959 Festschrift version of "L'attente") illustrates the latter option: "At first, intimacy; at first, the ignorance of intimacy; at first, instants unaware of each other existing side by side, touching and unconcerned with each other." But it is clear from these lines that if the story is reflected there, something is also distorting quite radically what the story entails: a perspective of temporal regress, of recurrent deferral ("at first... at first... at first...") within a time-scale that might be described as a rolling eternity, where the closed, *substantive* space of story ("intimacy") and of dialectical analysis ("intimacy"/"ignorance of intimacy") is embraced and traversed by a *participial*, quasi- *gerundive* space of nonrelation, of separation.

It seems clear, then, that when the work refers to "[t]wo languages [*paroles*] clinging tightly to each other, like two bodies but with indeterminate boundaries" (*AO*, 18), these languages correspond not simply to those of philosophy and narrative, but rather to the descriptive-analytic space that brings them together, on the one hand, and on the other, to the vocative-invocative mode that allows the subject of each to coincide in a space that is irreducible to both philosophy and fiction—a space of invocation which embraces them both, while remaining absolutely irreducible to either of them. But the question arises: from where does this space originate? Clearly it does not have its source in narrative itself. In *The Last Man*, waiting brought the narrator to the threshold of a hostile space, which is the obverse of the calm that he feels is imminent. But it is also a cacophonous space, exhilarating and versatile, a space in which reason enters a dimension of delirium. This is not a space that recurs in *Awaiting Oblivion*. Indeed, like the narrator of *The Last Man*, the "he" of the later work acknowledges that it is a space into which neither he nor the woman can go. Under the influence of this other space, he [*il*] moves between the space of the story (description) and the space of analysis. However, whatever his mobility, he never enters that other space, because from the perspective of the other two it has been reduced to nothing: "he knew, and it seemed to him that she knew, that somewhere here there was a kind of void" (*AO*, 15). The presence of another space in *Awaiting Oblivion* seems, therefore, to presuppose a totally different source, one which has hitherto not been present in the closely structured development of Blanchot's narratives.

What is its origin? As Timothy Clark has observed, Blanchot's category of waiting in *Awaiting Oblivion* "is often indistinguishable from the notion of the *wait*, or *waiting* in Heidegger's *Conversation on a Country Path*. . . . Some of the *récit*, indeed, is practically a French translation of fragments from Heidegger." How then, he asks, is *Awaiting Oblivion* anything other than "a French version of Heidegger's dialogue?"[26] The 1958 version of "L'attente" concludes with the following words: "In waiting, each word become slow and solitary" (*AO*, 25). As Clark points out, this echoes a line from Heidegger's "poetic" text "The Thinker as Poet": "In thinking, all things become solitary and slow."[27] In advance of writing for the Festschrift, Blanchot would appear to be giving a signal. And this is not the only gesture in the direction of poetry in "L'attente." Toward the beginning, a series of questions by the woman leads to the passage: "In a low voice to himself, in a lower voice to him . . . , murmur without trace that he follows, nowhere-straying, everywhere-dwelling" (AO, 4). This is the first appearance of the vocative-invocative mode that will come to govern the work, and its mode is distinctly "poetic." More significantly, it contains the unmistakable echo of the words of another poet, Saint-John Perse, in whose Anabasis we read: "In a lower voice for the dead, in a lower voice in the day,"[28] and in Exile: "And who then before dawn wanders at the limit of the world with this cry for me? . . . Everywhere-straying was her courtesan name among the priests."[29]

An answer to Clark's question would thus seem to come from within Awaiting Oblivion itself. The vocative-invocative mode by which its language distinguishes itself from both narrative and philosophy is the language of poetry. While appearing to engage with both the form and the subject of Heidegger's dialogues, Blanchot indicates that his dialogue is with what is poetic in Heidegger's philosophy. By altering the terms of Heidegger's formula, however, and by echoing another poet while also altering his words, Blanchot indicates, too, that poetry lies beyond the discourse in which both philosopher and poet seek to give it voice. In The Space of Literature he writes: "When Saint-John Perse names one of his poems Exile, he has named the poetic condition as well" (SL, 237). The link this sets up between that work and Awaiting Oblivion is not fortuitous, but rather points clearly to where the original space of poetry has its origin for him: in Hölderlin, the writer in whom a "categorical reversal" (SL, 272) opens onto "a hiatus, a void" (SL, 274). The waiting that Awaiting Oblivion takes as its subject is therefore not that to be found in Heidegger's philosophy at all. It is the waiting to which Hölderlin refers in "Bread and Wine": "Always waiting [so zu harren], and what to do or say in the meantime / I don't know" (SL, 245).[30] By gesturing to Heidegger as a poet rather than as a philosopher in 1958, Blanchot is not just signaling the importance of the poetic in Awaiting Oblivion. He is referring back to the work of his in which the relation between poetry and philosophy in Heidegger's thinking is thoroughly explored and radically overturned.

The Space of Literature is not *about* the space of literature: it presents itself *as* that space, a space in which philosophy in its relation to poetry is subjected to the "categoric reversal" that poetry enacts.

Seen in this way, *The Space of Literature* emerges as a "missing link" in the development of Blanchot's narrative writing. As a more detailed study would show, the space that emerges in *Awaiting Oblivion* as one that fundamentally fragments the descriptive-analytic space to which both narrative and philosophy belong is the space of "Orpheus's gaze," which, after completing the triptych, Blanchot had set about deploying within the language of critical analysis. After 1955 he is thus able, as a reader of poetry and a writer of narrative, to push the language of philosophical analysis to its limit from two separate directions. In *Awaiting Oblivion* it is at this disjunctive limit that his writing will move beyond space and turn toward the *fragmentary*.

NOTES

1. Maurice Blanchot, *Awaiting Oblivion,* trans. John Gregg (Lincoln: University of Nebraska Press, 1997). (Henceforth *AO*. Translations occasionally modified.) It is unfortunate that the translation of the original title introduces into what Blanchot in his *prière d'insérer* calls "the juxtaposed words" which give the work its title (*L'attente l'oubli*), a syntactic relation that is totally absent in the French.

2. Maurice Blanchot, *The Space of Literature,* trans. Ann Smock (Lincoln: University if Nebraska Press, 1982), 147. (Henceforth *SL*. Translations occasionally modified.) The essay dates originally from 1953.

3. Maurice Blanchot, *Thomas l'obscur* (Paris: Gallimard, 1941), chapter 5, 75–79. See also *Thomas the Obscure,* new version, trans. Robert Lamberton (New York: David Lewis, 1973), 35–37. (Henceforth *TO*. Translations occasionally modified.)

4. See "Claude Lucas's novel *Suerte* begins with the words '*In those days wasn't I already dead?*' That is a sentence worth lingering over: literature . . . begins with the end which alone makes understanding possible." Blanchot, "Writing, Between Life and Death," trans. Michael Holland, in "Blanchot's Epoch," edited by Leslie Hill and Michael Holland, *Paragraph* 30:3 (November 2007): 44–45. The text originally appeared in April 1998.

5. In the *prière d'insérer* for Blanchot, *The One Who Was Standing Apart from Me,* trans. Lydia Davis (Barrytown, NY: Station Hill Press, 1993) (henceforth *OSA;* translations occasionally modified), this work is described as "the third

panel of the triptych whose first two panels are formed by *Death Sentence* and *When the Time Comes*. They constitute three separate *récits*, however they all belong to the same experience."

6. Maurice Blanchot, *The Last Man*, trans. Lydia Davis (New York: Columbia University Press, 1987), 1. (Henceforth *LM*. Translations occasionally modified.)

7. Maurice Blanchot, *When The Time Comes*, trans. Lydia Davis (Barrytown, NY: Station Hill Press, 1985), 74. (Henceforth *WTC*.)

8. Blanchot, "L'attente," *Botteghe Oscure* 22 (August 1958): 22–33. All parenthetical citations following quotations, however, are to page numbers in *Awaiting Oblivion*.

9. Maurice Blanchot, *Vicious Circles: Two Fictions and "After the Fact,"* trans. Paul Auster (Barrytown, NY: Station Hill Press, 1985), 64. (Henceforth *VC*. Translations occasionally modified.)

10. Maurice Blanchot, *Death Sentence*, trans. Lydia Davis (Barrytown, NY: Station Hill Press, 1978), 80.

11. At the close of the "Spiritual Canticle" of St. John of the Cross, the union between the Bride and the Beloved is expressed as follows: "And nobody saw it / Nor did Aminadab appear." From the outset, Blanchot's narrative writing adopts the opposite view: Aminadab always appears. See Michael Holland, "Qui est l'Aminadab de Blanchot?" *Revue des sciences humaines* 253 (January–March 1999): 21–42.

12. *Thomas the Obscure* begins with an image of the sea and ends on "a prolonged cry [in which] all recognized the ocean" (*TO*, 116–17).

13. Could this be a gesture to a dying Bataille, who once wrote, "I think the way a whore takes off her dress" [*Je pense comme une fille enlève sa robe*]? Georges Bataille, "Methode of Meditation" (1947), in *Inner Experience*, trans. Leslie Anne Boldt (Albany: State University of New York Press, 1988), 200.

14. *Awaiting Oblivion* repeats, as "an almost faded memory" that haunts the male protagonist, the words of Claudia in *When the Time Comes*: "No one here wants to be tied to a story" (*AO*, 9; *WTC*, 47).

15. In the 1958 essay in *Botteghe Oscure* (see note 8 above), the three occurrences are on pp. 25, 27, and 28, respectively.

16. *AO*, 5, 10, 11 (twice), 28, 43.

17. Blanchot, "Interruption," in *The Infinite Conversation*, trans. Susan Hanson (Minneapolis: University of Minnesota Press, 1993), 76–77. (Henceforth *IC*. Translations occasionally modified.)

18. Blanchot, *The Work of Fire*, trans. Charlotte Mandell (Stanford: Stanford University Press, 1995), 140. (Henceforth *WF*. Translations occasionally modified.)

19. Blanchot, "L'attrait, l'horreur du jeu" [The attraction and the horror of gambling], *Nouvelle Revue française* 65 (May 1958): 864. Blanchot's birthday was on September 22.

20. In "Essential Solitude" (1953) he evokes "the very element of forgetting: writing" (*SL*, 29).

21. For example, the section beginning "Mystery: its essence is to be always on this side of attention" (*AO*, 21), is also in "L'attente" (1958; in *Botteghe Oscure*, p. 31), and *The Infinite Conversation* (*IC*, 21).

22. *AO*, 67; *IC*, 194.

23. "L'attente," in *Martin Heidegger zum siebzigsten Geburtstag* (Pfullingen: Neske, 1959), 217–24.

24. Twenty-three of the seventy-nine sections of the 1958 text reappear among the seventy-three sections of Festschrift text (1959). The sole difference between them of note is that in the fictional passages of the second there is no female figure.

25. See also "L'attente" (1958), 28; "L'attente" (1959), 219–20 (instead of "we" it has "he").

26. Timothy Clark, *Derrida, Heidegger, Blanchot: Sources of Derrida's Notion and Practice of Literature* (Cambridge: Cambridge University Press, 1992), 91.

27. Martin Heidegger, *Poetry, Language, Thought,* trans. Albert Hofstadter (New York: Harper & Row, 1971), 9.

28. Saint-John Perse, *Anabasis,* trans. T. S. Eliot (London: Faber 1959), 46. (Translation modified.)

29. Saint-John Perse, *Exile,* trans. Denis Devlin (New York: Pantheon Books, 1962), 99.

30. Friedrich Hölderlin, "Bread and Wine," in *Poems & Fragments,* trans. Michael Hamburger (London: Anvil Press, 1994), 271. See also *WF*, 117; *IC*, 39.

ELEVEN

WEARY WORDS

L'ENTRETIEN INFINI

Leslie Hill

±± . . . "It would seem that, however weary you are, you nevertheless still complete your task, exactly as you should. It could even be said not only that weariness does not prevent you from working, but that working requires you be weary beyond all measure."—"This does not apply only to me, in any case can it still be called weariness or unwearying indifference to weariness?"— "To be weary, to be indifferent, is no doubt the same thing."—"Indifference then might therefore be described as the meaning of weariness."—"Its truth."—"Its weary truth."

—Maurice Blanchot, L'entretien infini[1]

According to a letter of 13 February [1969] addressed to Dominique Aury, at the time general secretary of *La Nouvelle Revue française,* the influential literary journal in which many of his best-known essays and articles first appeared, Maurice Blanchot by autumn 1965, following *Faux pas* (1943), *Lautréamont et Sade* (1949), *La part du feu* (1949), *L'espace littéraire* (1955), and *Le livre à venir* (1959), was ready to bring out what would have been his sixth collection of literary, critical, philosophical essays. "Let me

282

say this," he told Aury: "several years ago—around 1965—*I completed a volume* containing quite a number of essays I published in the *NRF* (though not all) and various other unpublished texts in a sequence that seemed to me at the time not entirely strained."[2] Despondency had, however, set in. This was in part a consequence of the final unraveling of the project for the *Revue internationale* upon whose promise and failure the seal was simultaneously set, in August 1964, with the appearance of its first and only (zero) issue, published in exile, so to speak, under the auspices of *Il Menabò*.[3] It was in any case not by chance that, in an earlier letter to Aury dated Thursday 18 [July 1964], drawing attention to a misprint in the proofs for his forthcoming essay on "The Athenaeum," a piece in which Blanchot had cause to express his disappointment at the way fragmentary writing in Schlegel had reverted to a kind of "complacent self-indulgence" (*EI*, 526; 359)—a charge that Blanchot was minded to extend to others, more recently, particularly in the Federal Republic, who had similarly proven unresponsive to the urgency and exigency of the fragmentary—the writer took the opportunity to indicate to his correspondent his intention to limit the frequency of his contributions to *La Nouvelle Revue française*. The reasons he gave were "fatigue" and "saturation."[4] More than a year later, matters remained at a low ebb. Despite having an almost finished book on his hands, "by aversion to publication,"[5] Blanchot's weariness made him hesitate, postpone the volume, and interrupt his work, in a gesture that owed less to contingent personal circumstances than to abyssal necessity, for what it threw into jeopardy was nothing less than the very possibility of fulfilling philosophy's founding ambitions to contain writing and subordinate its interminable wanderings to the closure of a discourse on truth.

Blanchot's reluctance to publish was as a result surprisingly long-lasting, and it was not until November 1969 that this intended sixth collection of essays, still mainly based on work produced between 1954 and 1965, finally appeared. Until a relatively late stage, according to another letter to Aury, dated 8 December [1967], the working title for this new book—both tacit acknowledgement and covert prognosis—remained *The Absence of Book* [*L'absence de livre*], an expression the future volume shared with an essay Blanchot first enclosed in his letter, but then, in a subsequent communication of 13 January [1968], having decided "*to suspend* [*suspendre*]" the piece, asked Aury to return to him in exchange for the promise of an article on Kafka's recently published correspondence with his fiancée Felice Bauer.[6] This the journal duly published some months later, under the doubly valedictory title, "The Very Last Word [*Le tout dernier mot*]," discreetly marking, by serendipity or by design, the imminent conclusion of Blanchot's fifteen-year involvement with the journal and the impending exhaustion of the philosophical-critical discourse he had so authoritatively represented in its pages. From now on, what would follow would be interventions of an increasingly occasional character and that other discourse Blanchot called the fragmentary. As far as the forthcoming book was concerned, as his letter to Aury indicates, by early February of the following year Blanchot had again revised his plans, opting to relegate his original title, *L'absence de livre* —henceforth qualified with the unpunctuated, parenthetic rider "(the neuter the fragmentary)"— to the status of a subtitle announcing the third and final section in the volume, containing essays on an eclectic series of modern authors, together with a version of the eponymous essay "L'absence de livre," ironically bringing the book to a provisional or absent conclusion. As for the volume as a whole, this assumed the less emphatic, now canonic title: *L'entretien infini.*

Between 1965, when work on the volume was initially completed, and 1969, when the book eventually came out, several things had come to pass, each affecting the status of Blanchot's critical discourse and its claims to exhaustivity. First, through 1966 and 1967, notwithstanding illness and fatigue, though at a slower rate than before, Blanchot nevertheless continued publishing in *La Nouvelle Revue française,* contributing alongside "Le tout dernier mot" (May 1968) such compelling new work as the essays "Nietzsche et l'écriture fragmentaire" ("Nietzsche and Fragmentary Writing," December 1966 and January 1967), "Le demain joueur" ("Tomorrow At Stake," April 1967), and "L'athéisme et l'écriture: L'humanisme et le cri" ("Atheism and Writing: Humanism and the Cry," October and November 1967). The essay "L'absence de livre," retrieved from Aury in January 1968, likewise also finally appeared in print, albeit only the following year, in April 1969, in *L'Éphémère,* a journal that proved as short-lived as its title promised.[7]

Second, even as Blanchot's book continued to wait in abeyance, the writer's literary critical and other activities were further interrupted by something that Blanchot, like numerous others, could not be expected to have foreseen, namely, the *événements* of May 1968, to the actuality of which, barely a year later, *L'entretien infini* would end up explicitly paying homage. In turn, Blanchot's uncompromising commitment to the struggle against the Fifth Republic had one additional consequence, announced in a letter to Aury dated 7 October [1968] and sent two days before the death of Jean Paulhan, the long-serving—staunchly Gaullist—editor of *La Nouvelle Revue française,* in which Blanchot discreetly gave notice of his decision to withdraw entirely from the journal, explaining that "the position of *refusal* which I have maintained since 1958 [i.e. since de Gaulle's return to power], not only towards the regime itself, but also towards all institutions connected with it, has become so powerful in me that I find it impossible to continue to exist liberally and honourably here, whereas I would be negating myself elsewhere, in struggling in anonymity with my comrades."[8]

Informing and informed by these broader personal, professional, and political factors was a third set of changes, dividing Blanchot's book from itself and problematizing its status as an apparent summation of Blanchot's philosophical and critical thinking as a whole. For when his sixth volume of essays finally appeared, some four years after it was first mooted, it did so, as we have seen, under a new title. This change of heading was no mere afterthought; it was part of a concerted effort of re-presentation and reframing. For the book now entitled *L'entretien infini* opened with two epigraphs (printed in italics) attributed to the presiding figures of Mallarmé and Nietzsche, one of which was quoted later in the book several times over, while the other, not mentioned within the book but added only at proof stage, was instead given the task of overstepping and thus exceeding its physical boundaries. These two epigraphs, in turn, like a pair of epochal parentheses, bracketed three unsourced quotations from Blanchot's own work (printed in roman), and all five were followed by a two-page prefatory note bearing the initials "M. B."—to which the book itself would later reply by way of a brief postscript recalling the figure of the absence of book and insisting on the virtual anonymity of the preceding, by now already posthumous, texts.[9]

These were not the only framing effects put to work in the book, thereby problematizing its limits, fraying its edges, and erasing its boundaries. The volume also "began" (began without beginning) with an untitled, eighteen-page narration, printed in italics and numbered in roman, staging or recounting a fictional dialogue between two (or more) male voices, and broken into twenty-eight fragments, each prefaced with a mathematical double neuter symbol: ±±.[10] This liminal *récit* was most likely the same as the narrative fragment ("fragment de récit," in Blanchot's words) sent to Aury in a letter dated 12 November [1965], which, when it first appeared in *La Nouvelle Revue française* four months later, did so under the still unassigned heading "L'entretien infini."[11] In the first instance, then, Blanchot's title belonged not to the 1969 book but to this 1966 *récit*. Accordingly, when "L'entretien infini" (the *récit*) reappeared on the threshold of *L'entretien infini* (the book), cited or re-cited from beginning to end, albeit with a dozen minor, relatively insignificant revisions affecting some of the punctuation and a small number of individual words (not forgetting that, like an illustrative or abyssal quotation, it was now printed entirely in italics), it found itself not only separated and detached from itself as its own ghostly double but also, having relinquished its former title, anonymized and delegitimized too, left to feature not as an autonomous narrative but a series of unfinished exchanges at once inside and outside Blanchot's collection, whose discursive economy found itself displaced and set aside, exposed to a writing no longer answerable to any conceptual authority.

These transformations affecting Blanchot's 1965 project were far-reaching. Here, now, was a volume of essays that was somehow completed and yet had chosen to carry on, beyond exhaustion and overload, in response to a demand outstripping all teleological reason and capable of being neither stilled nor satisfied. Here, too, was a collection of texts seeking to bring to a close a philosophical-critical discourse that belonged to the past, a task it was able to fulfill only insofar as the texts testifying to that end simultaneously marked and exceeded that border, in much the same way as the political and other events toward which the book gestured, and which likewise partook in history precisely to the extent that they challenged the possibility of its closure. And here, finally, was a title, "L'entretien infini," initially attributed to a finite, fragmentary *récit*, which now designated an infinitely garrulous, weighty tome some thirty-five times its length. Moreover, while there was little prospect of the one text being mistaken for the other, Blanchot's dual use of the same six-syllable

(3 + 3) titular formula, now remembering an excessively short story, now announcing an excessively long collection of essays incorporating that story, created between the two a dizzying relationship of mutual inclusion. For if *L'entretien infini* (the book) now contained "L'entretien infini" (the *récit*), it was also true that, having bequeathed its name to the book, the *récit* itself already implicitly contained the collection.[12] The actuality of the inclusion of the story within the collection was supplemented by the virtuality of the inclusion of the collection within the story, with neither microcosm nor macrocosm being in a position to take precedence over the other. If the book framed the story, then, it was only insofar as the story already framed the book—with the result that, even as each of the two texts might be thought to comprehend (in the sense of both surrounding and understanding) the other, so it followed that the act of comprehension fell victim to a kind of infinite regress: even as the one sought to comprehend the other entirely, so the movement of comprehension itself escaped all comprehension. The understanding of one text by another could not be other than forcibly partial, intermittent, and interrupted, and the relation between them could only be a relation of non-relation. The one text found itself in the predicament of commenting exhaustively on the other only insofar as what it encountered in the other was proof of its paradoxical inexhaustibility.

Between the one and the other, between *L'entretien infini* (the book) and "L'entretien infini" (the *récit*), between the totalizing ambition of critical or philosophical discourse to comprehend literary narrative and the infinite potential of literary narrative to exceed critical or philosophical discourse, if only by (re)citing it in its entirety, there was therefore continuity but also interruption; reciprocity but also dissymmetry; understanding but also exposure to the unknown—in a word, or rather two words, what a reader might be prompted to call an infinite conversation, or, perhaps better, more in tune with the resources of French idiom, an infinite holding-between,[13] such that, even as each text was differentiated from the other, it was no longer apparent where the one might end and the other begin. The distance between the philosophical and the literary in *L'entretien infini* was not, however, effaced because of the story's inclusion within the collection; yet nor was the difference between them guaranteed. On the contrary, by dint of its exposure to the other and the suspension of the opposition between them, each was impelled to with-draw from itself, testifying not to the inclusive dialectic of the book but to their proliferating exposure to what two years before, in *De la grammatolo-gie*, Derrida called "the end of the book and the beginning of writing," i.e., the insidious reinscription of all that traverses and exceeds the logic of the book—which *L'entretien infini*, for its part, as mentioned earlier, would call: "The Absence of Book (the neuter the fragmentary)." As a result, even as it drew on any number of philosophical sources, from Heraclitus to Hegel, from Nietzsche to Lévinas, *L'entretien infini*, by dint of the non-coincidence of that title's referent, exposed those philosophical discourses, insofar as they belonged to philosophy, to the non-identity of an otherness that questioned their power, competence, or authority.

The interferences between Blanchot's liminal *récit* and the essays contained in *L'entretien infini* are both varied and persistent. In the body of the collection itself, many are the exchanges between interlocutors that recall the opening narrative, for instance, printed now in italics, now in roman, surfacing in the dialogue form of several later articles (notably those on Lévinas, Antelme, or Beckett) or in such fragmentary supple-ments as that added in 1969 to the 1960 discussion "On a Change of Epoch," or in the parenthetic, at times fragmentary, at times polyphonic interludes that (ir)regularly interrupt Blanchot's critical discourse to pro-pose a thesis—yet only insofar as, under pressure from the neuter, as Blanchot puts it, all such theses are only ever parentheses, like so much else in the volume, which itself is arguably no more and no less than a se-ries of epochal parentheses suspending the world "as such," putting it at a distance from itself in order to give voice to the otherwise of writing that precedes and exceeds the founding of any world. And if many of the es-says in the volume may be thought to prolong remarks made in the story, the reverse is equally the case, and on several occasions it is the turn of the *récit* to expand on arguments put forward in the subsequent essays. It is telling in this regard that the third of Blanchot's opening epigraphs— "The neuter, the neuter, how strangely that sounds for *me*" (*EI,* xxii, 102; xxi, 71)[14]—weaves its way not only through "L'entretien infini" (the *récit*) but also through at least one of the essays (notably, "Le rapport du troi-sième genre: Homme sans horizon" [The Relation of the Third Kind: Man without Horizon]), passing as it does so from margin to center, testifying to writing as a kind of impersonal nomadic event that is impossible to fix in any one location and constantly in breach of any phenomenological horizon of intention or expectation. Indeed, such is the effect of the neuter (Blanchot calls it the "effect of a non-effect" [*EI*, 447; 303], a status without status which it owes to the fact that, being neither visible nor invisible, it is irreducible to all phenomenality) that any writing, whatever its supposed discursive or generic affiliation, insofar as it is attributable to a discourse or genre at all, and for that reason reliant on the necessary possibility of repetition and citation, cannot do other than pay secret homage to its own exteriority to itself. For this is the radical thought countersigned by Blanchot's text: that all writing, prior to any legislation, positionality, or thematic intention, by virtue of the always possible application of visible or invisible, explicit or implicit quotation marks, which are therefore always already present even when they are absent, is necessarily inscribed within a never-ending holding-between, resistant to all final philosophical or critical authority—which is why, for Blanchot, as performed by the book's title, referring undecidably now to a so-called nonfictional sequence, now to a so-called fictional work, the neuter names nothing less than the possibility of literature "as such."

But literature "as such," the neuter also implies, is never given "as such" but always suspended in the very act. It is no sooner posited than postponed, emptied of all positionality. The possibility of literature, in other words, from the perspective of the neuter, is nothing other than the deferral or difference inherent in all words and irreducible to meaning (and the absence of meaning). In its modesty and discretion, what the neuter therefore affirms in Blanchot (like Derridean *différance*, from which it however also differs) is that there is no essential literariness or literarity, and therefore no autonomous literary or poetic discourse, as claimed by Formalist and post-Formalist literary theory. For if it is made possible by the suspension worked or, better, unworked by the neuter, literature is also inseparable, like language in general, from the possibility of a suspension of that suspension. What seems literary at one moment, then, will turn out to be anything but literary at another, and vice versa. Admittedly, literature at any given historical moment will be equated with its various institutionalized forms, from pulp fiction to high modernism, but these are only ever provisional, historically contingent manifestations of what is never given "as such." As far as the event of literature is concerned, there are no bounds except those of language (and its shadowy companion, silence), which, insofar as they are finite, are also thereby infinite. The one condition, paradoxically enough, always implies the other. As Blanchot phrases it in *La communauté inavouable,* there is "no finality where finitude reigns [*Pas de fin là où règne la finitude*]."[15] At the limit the only encounter that occurs (or does not occur) is with that which is without limit. Literature, in other words, is nothing other than this chance of the outside. Wherever it happens, as *récit* or as essay, writing never coincides with itself but, traversed by the otherness it contains but cannot contain, always returns to itself as different from what it was: as a ghostly presence—or clandestine encounter. "Neuter," proposes one of Blanchot's anonymous interlocutors, in one of several parenthetic asides,

> might be a word for the act of literature, which belongs neither to affirmation nor to negation, and (in the first instance) releases meaning only as the phantom, obsession, or simulacrum of itself, as though what were proper to literature were its spectral quality, not because it might be thought to be haunted by itself, but because it might be said to carry with it that prior condition of all meaning which is its obsessive return, or, put more simply, because it might then be reduced to concerning itself with nothing other than *simulating the reduction of the reduction,* whether or not in the phenomenological sense, and thus, far from abolishing it (even if it sometimes gives the impression of doing so), augmenting it, interminably, with everything that exacerbates it, and pushes it to breaking point (*EI,* 448–49; 304).[16]

"— But why two? Why two voices to say one and the same thing?" rejoins another speaker, more than a hundred pages later, glossing that moment's hesitation—like an interruption inscribing the name without name of the neuter itself—during which K., on the threshold of Kafka's *Castle,* "linger[s] on the wooden bridge leading from the main road to the village and gaze[s] upwards into the apparent emptiness." The answer that comes, given earlier but by dint of repetition always other than what it was, and thus reiterating the nomadic displacement that is but another name for the refusal of writing to pose itself "as such," is seemingly familiar yet forever different: "Because whoever says it—is always the other"(*EI*, 582; 396).[17]

In these circumstances, it comes perhaps as no surprise that, as it begins, the *récit* formerly known as "L'entretien infini" speaks of a beginning that, lost in the distance and perpetually preceding itself, is no longer accessible as such. Advancing under the auspices of the repeated neuter symbol already employed in 1966, memorializing as it does so any number of previous opening sentences (including those of, say, *Aminadab, Au moment voulu, Le dernier homme,* or *L'attente l'oubli,* not to mention the numerous other beginnings without beginning of literature in general), Blanchot's now untitled, unmarked *récit* starts with a double gesture, both a description and an enactment, both the telling and the staging of a writing and a reading: "±± The feeling he has, each time he enters, and becomes aware of the man, robust and courteous, already advanced in years, who tells him to enter, rising and opening the door as he does so, is that the conversation has been underway for a long time" (*EI*, ix; xiii).[18] Beginning without beginning, describing a scene occurring elsewhere only insofar as it produces it here, producing it here only insofar as it is described as occurring elsewhere, Blanchot's text is irresistibly caught in a detour less of self-presentation than of spectral self-withdrawal. What the text affirms, it also suspends; what it inscribes, it also effaces; and what lingers as the fragile testimony of the text's occurrence is the silent, unpronounceable double neuter mark (±±) preceding each of the irregular movements of the text as a kind of abyssal memory of presence and absence, poverty and excess, inscription and erasure.

Grounding itself in repetition, Blanchot's *récit* perforce ungrounds itself. It offers no present or presence that is not already past, and no inside that is not already an outside. To cross the threshold of the text as a reader is to encounter something, mirroring the vacant room and exhausted temporality of the story, that is bereft of all temporal or spatial actuality. This results, however, not in the timeless ubiquity of fiction but in the singular inscription of an event that, in equal measure, demands yet refuses narrative. "Slightly later," the reader is given to understand, just like the visitor in the *récit*—on the unimpeachable if uncertain authority of Blanchot's narrating voice—that "this conversation will be the last" (*EI,* ix;

xiii).[19] Imminent finality nevertheless implies a future, albeit a future without present, and for the uncertain duration of their conversation, Blanchot's twin protagonists find themselves bound by the promise to evoke, here and now, the mysterious event to which reference is made in the opening paragraphs of the story and which, by dint of its very secrecy, cannot but be synonymous—provisionally, perpetually, with its whole mystery intact—with the event of the conversation itself. To evoke the event is to be exposed to the event of its evocation. As Blanchot argues in Le livre à venir, the story of the event, before all else, is the event of that story.[20] And the event, in turn, insofar as it belongs to the future, rather than bringing matters to any meaningful close, can but bear witness to its own deferral, to the realization, so to speak, that what is proper to it as an event is an absence of all properness. When or if it comes, in other words, it both interrupts and is interrupted. But this inaccessibility of the event "as such" only reinforces its intractable hold on the protagonist, to whom it speaks without speaking, not as a fundamental existential or ontological question—as care, concern, or Sorge, for instance—but precisely insofar as, like the neuter, it resists the question of being or nonbeing, and, not concerning it, does not concern him either. There is, however, nothing negative about what, pushing French syntax to the limit, Blanchot is drawn to call "the non-concerning," that is, as he writes, "not only what does not concern him, but also does not concern itself" (EI, xxiii; xxi).[21] The "non-concerning" is in this sense a radical limit, with which no relation (positive or negative) is possible. "±± Everything begins for him," the reader was told shortly before, "— and at that moment everything seemed to have come to an end—with an event from which he cannot be released, because the event does not concern him." "An event," Blanchot's text explains, quickly reaching by dint of its own idiom the limit of (un)translatability: "that which however does not happen, the arena of non-happening and, at the same time, that which, happening, happens without gathering itself at some definite or determinable point—the occurring of what does not take place as any single or overall possibility" (EI, xviii–xix; xviii–xix).[22]

But what is it that occurs, then, by dint of this holding-between that is an event, or this event that is a holding-between? Something like a common commitment to shared discourse has mysteriously brought Blanchot's two interlocutors together, not for the first time, it seems, but for one last time, nonetheless, in order to entertain what is both a memory (of the past) and a promise (for the future). The relation without relation between the two is vouchsafed, however, by no explicit agreement. It nevertheless has the status of an accord, suggests Blanchot's text, a kind of tone or tuning that, like language itself, constitutes the withdrawn and inaccessible condition of their exchanges, from which it follows that although the conversation between the older man and his visitor is the site of an encounter, it remains obstinately irreducible to maieutic completion. Their discourse, it seems, is interrupted by the silent intervention of a supernumerary futural presence (or absence) which it cannot assimilate, essential to understanding but irreducible to it. The gap or interval between the pair, the reader is told—appropriately enough, since what is evoked here is the part played by this always anonymous other, the singular reader—is "wide enough for another person to consider himself their true interlocutor, the one to whom they would be speaking, if they were to address him" (*EI*, x; xiii–xiv).[23] The motive or occasion of the protagonists' meeting remains, however, secret. The guest seems to have come to visit, if not out of mere friendship, then in response to a request, reiterated in various epistolary or telephone messages by the resident, who believed— fatigue, however, prevents him from being more specific—that he had things to say to the other about the event beyond his power occurring without occurring in or by virtue of the story. Dim necessity in this case is also uncertain fortune: "[t]hat's right," says the one, "speaking is the last chance we have left, speaking is our chance" (*EI*, xvi; xvii).[24]

If so, then time, at least, somehow still remains: premised on its ending but perpetually deferred, exhausted, so to speak, but forever inexhaustible. Throughout Blanchot's *récit*, this is how time is spent, that is, both given and taken. No longer the time of conceptual progress, it is the time of writing: withdrawn, recursive, suspended. Its emblem, repeatedly, as in Kafka's *Castle,* as Blanchot expertly argues elsewhere,[25] is weariness, tiredness, lassitude, fatigue. Weariness, as all commentators know, is what occurs only at the limit. No limit, however, entirely coincides with itself, and what may be thought to unfold in Blanchot's *récit* is an attempt to reach to the limit of weariness in order to apprehend it as what it is— only for it then to be discovered that what stands at the limit is anything but a finite, self-identical object: rather the fleeting trace of its absence. "I had not realised," remarks a voice, "that what weariness makes possible, weariness also makes difficult" (EI, x; xiv).[26] Without limitlessness, it seems, no limit can ever be traced; but if the limit is but an acknowledgement of the limitless, so it follows that the limit is barely a limit at all. The only true limit is limitlessness, in the same way, Blanchot's narrative insists, that the only truth of weariness is the weariness of truth. Conceptuality, in other words, is riven by what it cannot contain. What occurs at the limit is an encounter with the limit, but also an encounter with the limitlessness of that limit that makes that limit both possible and impossible. Enough, in other words, is never enough, and can only be enough because it is simultaneously not enough, and is always exceeded by what it cannot assimilate. As the one asks the other, "in a low, but distinct voice," in the room filled to bursting with books, yet without touching any volume, referring perhaps to an impending demise consigned in words: "How will we manage to disappear?" And the text continues, repeating part of what was said a sentence before: "In a low but distinct voice, as if night, with its distant murmur, falling around them—it is broad daylight, he could easily notice—obliged him to reply: 'Well, it would be enough for us . . .'—'No, it would not be enough.'" And then, across an interval on Blanchot's page, writing a story of ending that is an ending of story (and vice versa): "±± From the moment this word—a word or phrase— came between them, something changed, a story came to an end" (EI, xi–xii; xiv).[27]

Though it is named several times over in Blanchot's story, weariness cannot properly be described as a philosophical or even as a literary theme. It is neither an intending, nor a positing, nor a positioning of meaning. Nor is it a physical or even psychological state, identifiable and attributable as such to some self-present subjectivity capable of apprehending it in and for itself. And though too originary to be a theme, this is not to say it can be described as some primary ontological Grundstimmung, "that which gives Dasein," as Heidegger puts it, "subsistence and possibility [Bestand und Möglichkeit] in its very foundations"[28]—not least because weariness necessarily pushes all stable foundations to the point of collapse, and beyond. Whoever experiences weariness is by that token already weary, and cannot apprehend weariness as an object other than self; but no self is left intact by weariness, which cannot do otherwise than dissipate the self in turn. Belonging properly neither to a subject nor to an object, but exceeding the powers of both, weariness names, then, not only an experience of exhaustion but an exhaustion of experience. Weariness is not, however, negativity. True, it disables; but it also alludes to an encounter with the infinite, with that which lies beyond possibility: inaccessible, irreducible, interminable. Weariness exhausts—but it is also experience without experience of the inexhaustible. "When he speaks of weariness," Blanchot's narrating voice observes of one of the protagonists, "it is difficult to know of what he is speaking" (*EI,* xxi; xx).[29] "Weariness," the narrator put it earlier, "is what he calls it, but weariness does not allow him the resources that make it possible for him legitimately to call it that" (*EI,* xxi; xx).[30] Weariness, then, is both more and less than words can say, a poverty and a profusion at once inside and outside language, dual testimony to extreme possibility and radical impossibility alike. This double responsiveness (and responsibility) is why weariness features in Blanchot's story as a figure without figure of the neuter, as one of the neuter's most understated manifestations—precisely because it is in truth neither a statement nor a manifestation. Blanchot's writing continues, some two-thirds of the way into its task, wearying now of storytelling in its turn, abandoning the use of superfluous speech marks, and, though still exposed to discontinuity, no longer mediating its words through the pretence of different voices passing themselves off as distinct characters: "Weariness is the most modest of misfortunes, that most neuter of neuters, an experience that, if one were in a position to choose, no one would choose out of vanity. Oh neuter, release me from my weariness, lead me towards that which, though preoccupying me to the point of occupying the whole space, does not concern me.—But that's what weariness is, a state which is not possessive, which absorbs without challenging" (*EI,* xxi; xx).[31]

Weariness divides in and against itself. Just like the tired, exhausted volume to which it belongs, it is a passage to the limit and an exposure to what exceeds the limit. It is that to which philosophy, thought, knowledge, work, writing, all must tend as their only, sufficient end; but it is also what mocks and defeats the possibility of all sufficiency. "It is all quite derisory, rightly so," says one voice to another. "You keep on working, but to no purpose. I'll leave you to work, then, since it is the only way for you to realise that you are incapable of working" (*EI,* xxii; xx).[32] On the one hand, weariness confirms power, authority, strength of purpose. Not for nothing is it suggested that the man in the room "gives the impression, because of his powerful frame, of being not so much weary as powerful, and also of giving weariness the imposing scale of his power" (*EI*, xi; xiv).[33] It is also inseparable from the exhaustive, encyclopaedic knowledge that comes from books, which explains why the vacant space of the room in which the two men are speaking nevertheless contains a vast library. But on the other hand, none of this is entirely true: for weariness is also proof of physical frailty, impending death, ignorance. Books, too, are not without their severe limitations, yet so often relegated to their margins. And however solemn or serious it may appear, weariness is an irrepressible source of affirmation and gaiety, which leaves the pair laughing together in the empty room, too weary to do otherwise. For such is the paradoxical logic that weariness shares with the neuter. It is never one, but always double, never coinciding with itself, but always differing and deferring: finite yet infinite, limited yet limitless, vacant yet full, neither visible nor invisible, everywhere in evidence but never present as such. "Thinking weary," says Blanchot's text at one stage, in a sentence (and paragraph) whose syntax teeters on the brink of exhaustion. The passage continues:

> Weariness increases imperceptibly; it is imperceptible; no proof, no evidence that is entirely certain; at every moment, it seems to have reached its high point—but this is of course a lure, a promise that is not kept. As though weariness was what kept him alive. For how much longer? There is no end in sight.
>
> Weariness having become his only livelihood, with the difference that the more weary he is, the less alive he is, and yet alive only by dint of weariness (*EI*, xx; xix).[34]

Testifying to the future as both persistence and interruption, then, weariness is inseparable from living and from dying. For that reason, and others too, perhaps, it is the condition of possibility and impossibility of all books, including the book entitled *L'entretien infini*, with its numerous exhaustive developments on philosophy, literature, criticism, and so much else besides, but which remains forcibly exposed to the outside (the neuter, the fragmentary, the absence of book), to that which it cannot claim as its own, raise up, or assimilate, not least because books themselves always come second. The paradox is that of the supplement, articulated by Derrida in *De la grammatologie* in 1967, only two years before *L'entretien infini* and in secret conversation with it, a logic that Blanchot, in his turn, also reaching a limit, and undecidably in his own name as a critic and in that of an unnamed fictional other, sums up thus:

> ±± There comes a moment in human life—consequently everyone's life—when everything is completed, the books written, the universe quiet, beings at rest. Only the task of announcing it remains: nothing is easier. But as this supplementary word risks upsetting the balance—and where to find the strength to say it? where still to find room for it?—it is left unsaid, and the task remains incomplete. All that gets written is what I have just said, but in the end does not get written either (*EI*, xii; xv).[35]

Ending, like dying, is therefore impossible. The same applies to Blanchot's liminal story, too, these weary words formerly known as "L'entretien infini." Weariness, the story suggests, anticipating what Blanchot argues apropos Kafka in a subsequent essay (*EI*, 556–58; 379–80), is like an unending circle surrounding, extenuating, and neutralizing the imperious diurnal and nocturnal logic of philosophical sense, whose authority it exceeds, suspends, interrupts.[36] Such a circle, then, is also an absence of circle, a circle without exteriority—not because it represents imperturbable transcendence or tranquil immanence, but because, neither present nor absent, it is already its own outside, a figure of that radical exteriority which, without interruption, leaves a blank trail of interruption: exhausting, yet inexhaustible. "It is an uninterrupted line," says Blanchot's *récit*, "that is drawn by dint of being interrupted" (*EI*, xvii; xviii).[37] "What he had wanted," the *récit* says in closing, referring to the same unnamed protagonist, "was quite different, a chill interruption, the breach of the circle. And straightaway it had happened: the heart stopping beating, the eternal drive to language coming to a halt" (*EI*, xxvi; xxiii).[38]

Countersigning their endless finitude, these weary words contain, however, both a paradox and a quotation. The quotation is from Novalis, who in a famous fragment entitled "Monolog" (1798) likewise wondered whether, rather than any human desire to communicate, it might not be the "drive to language [*Sprachtrieb*]" that was proof of the inspiration and effectiveness of words.[39] The passage is one that Blanchot explicitly cites later in *L'entretien infini*, in the course of the 1964 essay on "The Athaeneum" (*EI*, 523; 357), albeit in a French translation by Armel Guerne that secretly obscures the original coinage, and which, retranslating it for himself, the writer uses again, some months later in his 1965 essay on Sade (*EI*, 336; 226), as a name for that constituted political and discursive power interrupted and called to account by the epochal caesura effected (yet without being effected) by writing and revolution. And this is the paradox: that the interruption of words can only be evoked by a detour, by way of the infinite (re)citation of words themselves, those very words that, in announcing the end, also defer it and thereby pay tribute to the unending silence that inhabits all speech, interrupting the conversation yet demanding that it endure. Philosophy, literature: both are delivered to the promise or to the threat that divorces each from itself, leaving it exhausted yet inexhaustible, finite but futural.

Weary words: mortal interruption: speech without end.

NOTES

1. Blanchot, *L'entretien infini* (Paris: Gallimard, 1969), xvi–xvii; *The Infinite Conversation*, trans. Susan Hanson (Minneapolis: University of Minnesota Press, 1993), xvii; translation modified. Further references to the book will be given in the text, preceded by the abbreviation *EI*. The first numeral indicates the page of the Gallimard edition, the second that of Hanson's translation. For the purposes of this discussion, the existing English translation has often been modified. "±± . . . 'Il semble que, si fatigué que vous soyez, vous n'en accomplissiez pas moins votre tâche, exactement comme il faut. On dirait que non seulement la fatigue ne gêne pas le travail, mais que le travail exige cela, être fatigué sans mesure.' — 'Cela n'est pas vrai seulement de moi, et est-ce encore de la fatigue ou l'infatigable indifférence à la fatigue?' — 'Être fatigué, être indifférent, c'est sans doute la même chose.' — 'L'indifférence serait donc comme le sens de la fatigue.' — 'Sa vérité.' — 'Sa vérité fatiguée.'" For an alternative reading that intersects with my own, see Christopher Fynsk, "Un simple changement," in *Blanchot dans son siècle* (Lyon: Éditions Parangon, 2009), 228–36.

2. Angie David, *Dominique Aury* (Paris: Léo Scheer, 2006), 379–80. "Je voudrais ajouter ceci: il y a plusieurs années — vers 1965 — *j'ai terminé un volume*

où se retrouvent, dans un agencement qui alors ne me semblait pas tout à fait forcé, bon nombre de textes que j'ai publiés à la nrf (pas tous, cependant) et quelques autres non publiés" (author's emphasis). In her biography, David cites a significant number of letters from Blanchot mainly concerned with his relations with *La Nouvelle Revue française*. The writer's standard practice is to indicate the date and month, sometimes the day of the week, but rarely the year. In several cases, the content of the letters is at odds with David's proposed datings, which I have corrected accordingly.

3. For a detailed account of the project for the *Revue internationale,* see Christophe Bident, *Maurice Blanchot: Partenaire invisible. Essai biographique* (Seyssel: Champ Vallon, 1998), 403–17.

4. David, *Dominique Aury,* 368.

5. Ibid., 380.

6. Ibid., 365, 377. David suggests that these two letters were written in December and January 1959, respectively. In the second of the two, however, Blanchot refers explicitly to the essay entitled "L'absence de livre," sent to Aury with the previous letter (clearly indicating that the second letter cannot belong to the same calendar year as the first), while also mentioning the 1967 German publication of Kafka's letters to Felice (whose family name is mistranscribed as Barns!), which Blanchot subsequently reviewed for the *NRF.*

7. For these texts, see Blanchot, *L'entretien infini,* 227–55, 367–93, 597–619, 620–36; *The Infinite Conversation,* 151–70, 246–63, 407–21, 422–34. For the essay on Kafka, see Blanchot, *L'amitié* (Paris: Gallimard, 1971), 300–325; *Friendship,* trans. Elizabeth Rottenberg (Stanford: Stanford University Press, 1997), 265–88. On *L'Éphémère* and the writers associated with it, see James Petterson, *Postwar Figures of L'Ephémère: Yves Bonnefoy, Louis-René Des Forêts, Jacques Dupin, André Du Bouchet* (Lewisburg, PA: Bucknell University Press, 2000).

8. David, *Dominique Aury,* 378. "J'ajoute que le *refus* que, depuis 1958, j'ai exprimé non seulement à l'égard du régime, mais de toutes les institutions qui y sont liées, a pris corps de telle sorte qu'il m'est impossible de continuer à exister libéralement et honorablement ici, tandis que je me supprimerais ailleurs, en luttant anonymement avec mes camarades" (author's emphasis).

9. For the epigraph by Mallarmé ("Ce jeu insensé d'écrire"; "This senseless game [or wager] of writing"), see Mallarmé, *Œuvres complètes,* ed. Bertrand Marchal, 2 vols. (Paris: Gallimard, 1998–2003), 2:23; for that by Nietzsche ("C'est une belle folie: parler. Avec cela, l'homme danse sur et par-dessus toutes choses"; "Speaking is a fine madness; with it man dances upon and beyond all things"; "Es ist eine schöne Narrethei, das Sprechen: damit tanzt der Mensch über alle Dinge"), see Nietzsche, "Also sprach Zarathustra," in *Kritische Studienausgabe,* ed. Giorgio Colli and Mazzino Montinari, 15 vols., 2nd ed. (Berlin: de Gruyer/ dtv, 1988), 4:272 (with thanks to Duncan Large for assistance in identifying the quotation, and to John McKeane for information about the page proofs for *L'entretien infini* held in the Houghton Library, Harvard University, MS Fr 497).

Blanchot re-cites the Mallarmé in *EI*, vii, 620, 627, 630; xii, 422, 428, 429. The wording of the translation from *Zarathustra* is most likely Blanchot's own; the redundancy of the double rendering of *über* as both *upon* and *beyond* is abyssal: it affirms the extent to which language in general, in so far as it springs over all things and (un)founds all "world" (one of the issues in Nietzsche addressed by Blanchot later [*EI*, 245; 163–64]), is excessively and joyously parenthetic—as the epigraph itself testifies by dint of its liminal position and "over"-translation. It is no surprise to learn that the chapter from which Nietzsche's words are taken (*Zarathustra* III, §13: "Der Genesende," 2) is largely concerned with the proclamation of the over-man and eternal return. Of the three unattributed quotations from Blanchot's own work, the first two recur later in the volume (*EI*, 582, xxii, 102; 396, xxi, 71), while the third is from *Thomas l'obscur, nouvelle version* (Paris: Gallimard, 1950), 94; *Thomas the Obscure*, trans. Robert Lamberton, in *The Station Hill Blanchot Reader*, ed. George Quasha (Barrytown, NY: Station Hill Press, 1998), 105. A passage similar to this last, though it arises at a different stage in the narrative and apropos a different character, appears in the first *Thomas l'obscur* (Paris: Gallimard, 1941), 131, where Blanchot writes: "L'attitude d'Irène était celle d'un être pour lequel au sein du jour va apparaître quelque chose qui dans une atmosphère de limpidité et de lumière représente le frisson d'effroi d'où le jour est sorti." (Thanks to Parham Shahrjerdi and Michael Holland for assistance in locating this quotation.) For the postscript countersigning, that is, both confirming and inverting the introductory note, see *EI*, 637; 435.

10. See *EI*, v–xxvi; ix–xxiii. Bizarrely, the English version undoes Blanchot's careful framing by inserting Susan Hanson's foreword and translator's acknowledgements *between* the narrative and the opening essay in the volume!

11. See Blanchot, "L'entretien infini," *La Nouvelle Revue française*, 159 (March 1966): 385–401. For Blanchot's letter of 12 November, see David, *Dominique Aury*, 377. Oddly, however, David dates the letter itself to 1966, implying that Blanchot was referring to a different narrative fragment, which is hardly likely in the circumstances.

12. On such topographical disturbances in Blanchot's writing in general, see Jacques Derrida, *Parages* (Paris: Galilée, [1986] 2003).

13. English has little alternative to rendering Blanchot's *entretien* as *conversation*. The third segment of Blanchot's *récit* (*EI*, x; xiii), however, emphasizes that the two protagonists are "not turned towards one another [*non pas tournés l'un vers l'autre*]." Strictly speaking, therefore, if only on etymological grounds, the scene described in the story is anything but a *con -vers -ation*.

14. "Le neutre, le neutre, comme cela sonne étrangement pour *moi*." *Neutre*, in Blanchot, is a grammatico-syntactic rather than ideologico-political category; there are consequently strong reasons for preferring English *neuter* to *neutral* (adopted by Susan Hanson).

15. Blanchot, *La communauté inavouable* (Paris: Minuit, 1983), 38; *The Unavowable Community*, trans. Pierre Joris (Barrytown, NY: Station Hill Press, 1988), 20; translation modified.

16. "Neutre serait l'acte littéraire qui n'est ni d'affirmation ni de négation et (en un premier temps) libère le sens comme fantôme, hantise, simulacre de sens, comme si le propre de la littérature était d'être spectrale, non pas hantée d'elle-même, mais parce qu'elle porterait ce préalable de tout sens qui serait sa hantise, ou plus facilement parce qu'elle se réduirait à ne s'occuper de rien d'autre qu'à *simuler la réduction de la réduction*, que celle-ci soit ou non phénoménologique et ainsi, loin de l'annuler (même s'il lui arrive de s'en donner l'apparence), l'accroissant, selon l'interminable, de tout ce qui la creuse et la rompt" (author's emphasis).

17. "— Mais pourquoi deux? Pourquoi deux paroles pour dire une même chose?—C'est que celui qui la dit, c'est toujours l'autre."

18. "±± Le sentiment qu'il a, chaque fois qu'il entre et lorsqu'il prend connaissance de l'homme déjà âgé, robuste et courtois, qui lui dit d'entrer, se levant et lui ouvrant la porte, c'est que l'entretien est commencé depuis longtemps."

19. "Un peu plus tard, il se rend compte que cet entretien sera le dernier."

20. See Blanchot, *Le livre à venir* (Paris: Gallimard, 1959), 13; *The Book to Come*, trans. Charlotte Mandell (Stanford: Stanford University Press, 2003), 6.

21. "±± Le non-concernant. Non seulement ce qui ne le concerne pas, mais ce qui ne se concerne pas."

22. "±± Tout commence pour lui — et à ce moment tout semblait avoir pris fin — par un événement dont il ne peut se libérer, parce que cet événement ne le concerne pas. / Un événement: cela qui pourtant n'arrive pas, le champ de l'inarrivée [on first publication Blanchot's text read: le champ de l'inarrivé] et, en même temps, ce qui, arrivant, arrive sans se rassembler en quelque point défini ou déterminable — la survenue de ce qui n'a pas lieu comme possibilité une ou d'ensemble."

23. "±± Ils prennent place, séparés par une table, non pas tournés l'un vers l'autre, mais dégageant [in 1966 Blanchot had: *maintenant*], autour de la table qui les sépare, un assez large intervalle pour qu'une autre personne puisse se considérer comme leur véritable interlocuteur, celui pour lequel ils parleraient, s'ils s'adressaient à lui."

24. "C'est juste, parler est la dernière chance qui nous reste, parler est notre chance."

25. See Blanchot, *L'écriture du désastre* (Paris: Gallimard, 1980), 214; *The Writing of the Disaster*, trans. Ann Smock (Lincoln: University of Nebraska Press, 1986), 141.

26. "Seulement, je ne m'étais pas rendu compte que ce que la fatigue rend possible, la fatigue le rend difficile."

27. "Il ne touche à aucun volume, il reste là, le dos tourné, et prononce à voix basse, mais distincte: 'Comment ferons-nous pour disparaître?' / A voix basse, mais distincte, comme si la nuit, avec sa rumeur, s'établissant autour d'eux — il fait grand jour, il pourrait s'en rendre compte—, l'obligeait à répondre: 'Eh bien, il nous suffirait . . .' — 'Non, il ne suffirait pas . . .' / ±± Dès l'instant où ce mot — un mot, une phrase—s'est glissé entre eux, quelque chose a changé, une histoire a pris fin."

28. See Martin Heidegger, *Die Grundbegriffe der Metaphysik: Welt — Endlichkeit — Einsamkeit*, in *Gesamtausgabe*, vols. 29/30 (Frankfurt: Klostermann, 1983), 101; *The Fundamental Concepts of Metaphysics: World, Finitude, Solitude*, trans. William McNeill and Nicholas Walker (Bloomington: Indiana University Press, 1995), 67.

29. "±± Quand il parle de fatigue, il est difficile de savoir de quoi il parle."

30. "La fatigue, il l'appelle ainsi, mais la fatigue ne lui laisse pas les ressources qui lui permettraient de l'appeler légitimement ainsi."

31. "La fatigue est le plus modeste des malheurs, le plus neutre des neutres, une expérience que, si l'on pouvait choisir, personne ne choisirait par vanité. O neutre, libère-moi de ma fatigue, conduis-moi vers cela qui, quoique me préoccupant au point d'occuper toute la place, ne me concerne pas. — Mais c'est cela, la fatigue, un état qui n'est pas possessif, qui absorbe sans mettre en question." For Roland Barthes, too, weariness was an important signature effect of the neuter, and in his lecture course at the Collège de France given in 1977–78, Barthes cites Blanchot on several occasions to this effect. See Roland Barthes, *Le Neutre*, ed. Thomas Clerc (Paris: Seuil, 2002), 47–48; *The Neutral*, trans. Rosalind E. Krauss and Denis Hollier (New York: Columbia University Press, 2005), 20. For more detailed discussion of the differences between the neuter in Blanchot and Barthes, see my *Radical Indecision: Barthes, Blanchot, Derrida, and the Future of Criticism* (Notre Dame, IN: University of Notre Dame Press, 2010).

32. "Tout cela est dérisoire, c'est juste. Tu travailles, mais dans le dérisoire. Je te laisse donc travailler puisque c'est le seul moyen de te rendre compte que tu es incapable de travailler."

33. "Son interlocuteur incline la tête, comme s'il s'appesantissait et se préparait à dormir — il est vrai qu'il donne l'impression, à cause de sa puissante carrure, d'être, non pas fatigué, mais puissant, et aussi de donner à la fatigue l'envergure de sa puissance."

34. "Pensant fatigué. / La fatigue monte insensiblement; c'est insensible; nulle preuve, nul signe tout à fait sûr; à chaque instant, elle semble avoir atteint son point le plus haut — mais, bien entendu, c'est un leurre, une promesse qui n'est pas tenue. Comme si la fatigue le maintenait en vie. Encore combien de temps? C'est sans fin. / La fatigue étant devenue son seul moyen de vivre, avec cette différence que plus il est fatigué moins il vit, et cependant ne vivant que par la fatigue."

35. "±± Il y a un moment dans la vie d'un homme — par conséquent des hommes — où tout est achevé, les livres écrits, l'univers silencieux, les êtres en repos. Il ne reste plus que la tâche de l'annoncer: c'est facile. Mais comme cette parole supplémentaire risque de rompre l'équilibre — et où trouver la force pour la dire? où trouver encore une place pour elle? —, on ne la prononce pas, et la tâche reste inachevée. On écrit seulement ce que je viens de dire, finalement on ne l'écrit pas non plus." In writing *homme,* Blanchot means *homo,* not *vir.*

36. On Blanchot's reading of the neuter in Kafka, see my *Bataille, Klossowski, Blanchot: Writing at the Limit* (Oxford: Oxford University Press, 2001), 206–26.

37. "C'est une ligne ininterrompue et qui s'inscrit en s'interrompant."

38. "Ce qu'il avait voulu était tout autre, une interruption froide, la rupture du cercle. Et aussitôt cela était arrivé: le cœur cessant de battre, l'éternelle pulsion parlante s'arrêtant."

39. See Novalis, *Werke,* ed. Gerhard Schulz (Munich: Verlag C. H. Beck, 1981), 426.

TWELVE

NEUTRAL WAR

L'INSTANT DE MA MORT

Thomas S. Davis

How does art approach the experience of death? Perhaps no other question underwrites Maurice Blanchot's narratives and critical writings with such consistency and urgency. Blanchot's final *récit*, *The Instant of My Death*, punctuates a long career devoted to thinking of death outside of Hegel's negativity and Heidegger's being-toward-death; neither dialectical possibility nor ontological affirmation, Blanchot's philosophy of death-as-dying points us toward impossibility. This is the very idea at work in literary texts such as *Death Sentence*, *The Madness of the Day*, and *The Step Not Beyond*, and it also underwrites his critical evaluations of Rilke, Woolf, Antelme, Mallarmé, and several other writers. In many ways, *The Instant of My Death* repeats the same themes from these earlier works: there is a distinction between death and dying, the assertion of nonhistorical time, and a loss of the power to say "I."[1] Even the death scene at the heart of the last *récit* is not particularly new. Like the young man in *The Instant of My Death*, the protagonist in *The Madness of the Day* also faces a firing squad.[2]

The Instant of My Death, however, approaches death in a decidedly singular way because the death is Blanchot's own. With so few autobiographical writings, the publication of such a text is an event in and of itself.[3] And it is precisely this autobiographical dimension that has generated commentary from Philippe Lacoue-Labarthe and Jacques Derrida. Both have attended patiently to the movements of Blanchot's text in and out of those various genres of life-writing to which it is the closest— philosophical autobiography, autothanatography, the testimony.[4] But *The Instant of My Death* is also singular because it recounts a near execution during wartime, a death that would have been a purely political one. Although their central concerns lie elsewhere, Derrida and Lacoue-Labarthe gesture toward the thanato-political dimension of Blanchot's *récit:* Derrida briefly raises the question of law and, via Carl Schmitt, the status of the partisan, while Lacoue-Labarthe locates *The Instant of My Death* within the "war story" genre.[5] When we acknowledge both the political nature of the *récit* and its relationship to the Second World War, it becomes increasingly difficult to pursue only the autobiographical dimension of the text. Following Blanchot's unforgettable essay on Marx, we might discern three voices that speak in *The Instant of My Death:* the autobiographical, the historical, and the literary. And, as with Marx, these three are "necessary, but separated and more than opposed, as if they were juxtaposed. The disparity which holds them together designates a plurality of demands."[6] The analytic task, then, is to identify these voices and their relation to one another. As I hope to show below, how we assess these relationships goes a long way toward answering the two most extraordinary questions Blanchot's final text poses. First, on a more general level, how does *The Instant of My Death* extend the question of literature and death into the equally vexed relationship between aesthetic form and historical content, or, in more properly Blanchovian terms, between writing and the event? Second, where does *The Instant of My Death* fit within the larger debates over Blanchot's politics and, even more importantly, how might *The Instant of My Death*'s formal operations be read politically? What I would like to suggest here is that the text's problems of genre and form encode a concept of the political, a concept that adheres closely to Blanchot's idea of literature as pure contestation.

Before moving too far, I want to address one of the ways in which *The Instant of My Death* responds to this second question. It is perhaps impossible, even irresponsible, to neglect *The Instant of My Death*'s role in the ongoing debates over Blanchot's writings and affiliations during the 1930s and 1940s. The charges levied against Blanchot are well documented, and I will not rehearse them (or the varied responses to them) all here.[7] It is important, however, to understand why critics like Jeffery Mehlman and Richard Wolin assert that Blanchot was on "the wrong side" of politics during these years.[8] We know that Blanchot was an extraordinarily prolific writer for right-wing, and sometimes openly anti-Semitic, journals, such as *Combat, Journal des débats, L'Insurgé*, and *Le Rempart*. He penned violent antirepublican articles and cast his lot with the Falangists in Spain, among other things. As the story goes, Blanchot abandoned all political activity after 1945 and retreated from public life.[9] Yet, contrary to identifications of Blanchot as a "*littérateur* and aesthete . . . in the postwar period," he did not cease political activity and, by all appearances, underwent a sort of political apostasy.[10] His politics shifted from "the wrong side" to the right side (that is to say, the far left), and we find him engaging very publicly in the most heated and partisan conflicts of the latter half of the twentieth century; he openly supported the Algerian resistance in the late 1950s, participated in street demonstrations and on committees during May 1968, and, as a last gesture, joined the "Not In Our Name!" movement that protested the United States' perpetual "war on terror."[11] None of Blanchot's late writings openly discuss this dramatic shift, but *The Instant of My Death* may explain what Kevin Hart calls Blanchot's transition "from right-wing monarchism to left-wing radicalism."[12]

On one level, then, *The Instant of My Death* acts as a kind of personal disclosure of Blanchot's political leanings during the Occupation. Lacoue-Labarthe sees it as a "defense" or a "redemption": this last work, then, is also a closing statement in the endless trial of his political past.[13] Of course, as Derrida has reminded us, the literary quality of *The Instant of My Death* makes this text something more and something less than a testimony. Still, it does account for some of Blanchot's activities and whereabouts during the closing days of the Second World War, even if in an extremely elusive manner. As readers will recall, *The Instant of My Death* features a brief death scene in which a young man, presumably the young

Blanchot, is nearly executed by a Nazi firing squad. Although he escapes the execution, he undergoes an "unanalyzable" experience of death.[14] We know from Derrida that the date of this incident was July 20, 1944, the very date of the failed "July Plot," a late German attempt to assassinate Hitler.[15] The war in France was quickly coming to an end, and the Germans were in retreat. The Allies had landed on Normandy the previous month and swept through towns including St. Lô, Cherbourg, and Caen. *The Instant of My Death* appears to place Blanchot squarely on the side of the Resistance during these pivotal months. There are three particular moments in the story that function as evidence of his political alignment. The first is the young man's response to a knock on the door of his château. The external narrator (or at least it appears to be an external narrator at this point in the narrative) tells us that the young man interprets the "timid" knock to be from "guests who were presumably asking for help" (*IM*, 3; 2). The young man's château, it seems, had hosted other "guests," perhaps *maquisards* or other fighters, before. This knock, however, is not from insurgents of any kind. It is from a Nazi lieutenant. "This time" (*IM*, 3; 2) a Nazi howls and pulls the man from his château; "this time" distinguishes this moment from others when the château accepted "guests" looking for refuge. Blanchot's account here is highly suggestive, but it does receive some corroboration in the remarkable trial scene that follows:

> The lieutenant shook him, showed him the casings, bullets; there had obviously been fighting; the soil was a war soil.
> The lieutenant choked in a bizarre language. And putting the casings, the bullets, a grenade under the nose of the man already less young (one ages quickly) he distinctly shouted: "This is what you have come to." (*IM*, 3 and 5; 2 and 4)

At this point, "French soil" (*IM*, 3; 2) has become "a war soil." The Occupation is virtually over, but there is no sovereign power in France and no rule of law. While the trial bears all the characteristics of a juridical procedure, its primary work is paradoxically to indict and then exempt all enemies from the law. The young man is not a French soldier and, like the *maquisards* and Resistance fighters, he is not an identifiable enemy, what

Carl Schmitt calls a *justus hostis* or just enemy.[16] His status is beyond law: he is a brigand, a partisan, a friend and companion of the Resistance, and is subject to any and all forms of violence. The young man is lined against the wall before a firing squad. Although he narrowly escapes, others do not. When the young man returns to the village, he finds that "three young men, sons of farmers—truly strangers to all combat, whose only fault was their youth—had been slaughtered" (*IM*, 3; 2). If "slaughtered" highlights the senselessness of their killing, Blanchot's definition of war, "life for some, for others, the cruelty of assassination" (*IM*, 7; 6), accentuates the political nature of all killing, be it of combatants, noncombatants, or those partisans who fit neither category. Neither wanton murder (slaughter) nor legal death (execution), assassination refers to purely political killing.

The guilty verdict passed by the Nazi lieutenant, then, underscores the extralegal status of war, its remove from all international law. Like the killing of the farmhands, the "trial" exposes the lawlessness of war and the dissolution of legal (and moral) categories like innocence and guilt. What it does establish, however, are the political lines of friend and enemy. If the Nazi's verdict had not drawn those lines between friend and enemy clearly enough, the young man's death is prevented by the sounds of "comrades from the maquis" (*IM*, 5; 4) coming to the aid of "one they knew to be in danger" (*IM*, 5; 4). If nothing else, "comrade" aligns the young man politically with the Resistance fighters, confirming the Nazi's guilty verdict and, by extension, confirming the young man's (the young Blanchot's) political affiliation with the Resistance, an affiliation that nearly cost him his life. The timid knock, the refuse from battle, and the death sentence levied on Blanchot by the Nazis serve to establish the friend/enemy (Resistance/Nazi) divide and locate Blanchot on the more favorable end of it.

Are these formal maneuvers all a way of saying that Blanchot's guilt in the eyes of the Nazis should be enough to dismiss some of the more extravagant charges brought by his critics? *The Instant of My Death* may never settle the score on Blanchot's past. If Derrida is right to suggest that *The Instant of My Death* turns on a "disturbing complicity between fiction and testimony," its truth claims remain forever under suspicion.[17] But it may very well be the case that the text is not responding to, or not only responding to, questions of innocence and guilt, complicity and resistance. Could it be that *The Instant of My Death* is putting these questions themselves on trial? Are there other conclusions or implications to be drawn from the formal operations of the text? Is it possible to read *The Instant of My Death* as neither a confession nor an apology (two of the most predominant modes of philosophical autobiography), but as a meditation on the changes to the very concept of the political in the wake of the Second World War? To answer this question entails a methodological shift away from indicting or acquitting Blanchot—the purely autobiographical voice—to a closer consideration of the aesthetic or literary treatment of this incident. What *The Instant of My Death* requires us to do is to specify how art approaches historical violence and to discern the politics of aesthetically rendering such violence.

DEATH SENTENCES: BATAILLE AND BLANCHOT

I return, then, to Blanchot's death scene: a firing squad, a political execution, an enemy "awaiting the final order" (*IM,* 5; 4). This harrowing scene has predecessors in Blanchot's own work and in the works of those whom Blanchot admired. Fyodor Dostoevsky and André Malraux's near-death experiences are well documented, and Blanchot certainly knew them.[18] One cannot help but recall Francisco de Goya's *Shootings of May Third* and Édouard Manet's *Execution of Maximilian*. These paintings were the objects of considerable scrutiny by Blanchot's friends Malraux and Bataille at the same time that Blanchot was working out his own ideas on death and writing. Malraux's *Saturn: An Essay on Goya* appeared in 1950, and Bataille's *Manet: A Biographical and Critical Study* was published by Skira in 1955, the same year Gallimard published *The Space of Literature*. While Malraux and Bataille were exploring art's power to negate or to remain indifferent to subject matter, Blanchot was pursuing the powerlessness of writing and the movements of the neutral. In a way, *The Instant of My Death* reiterates ideas of worklessness (*désoeuvrement*), the neutral, aesthetic impotence, pure passivity, and so on. But the political nature of death in this *récit* lends those ideas a different inflection. A different category of experience raises different questions. What does it mean to be exposed to death? What turns of aesthetic form are required to render such an experience? These questions are what place Blanchot's text much closer to the canvases of Goya and Manet than the likes of Rilke, Kafka, and Mallarmé, whose works spurred so much of his thinking on death. I want to recall Bataille's comments on Manet and pay particular attention to his extension of Malraux's notion of aesthetic indifference. Bataille's analysis of the *Execution of Maximilian* is especially important because it turns on the relation of aesthetic violence and historical violence; that is, it articulates one way in which art might treat political death. This is one of the fundamental problems posed to us by *The Instant of My Death*, and the distance between Bataille and Blanchot's aesthetics begs for our attention.

Bataille adopts Malraux's claim that Goya's *Shootings of May Third* opened the way to an aesthetics of indifference that eventually reaches its summit in Manet. He quotes frequently and approvingly from Malraux's *Saturn*, but he only follows Malraux's philosophy of art up to a certain point. With a quote from Malraux doing much of the work, Bataille argues that Manet's task was to evacuate painting of the "metaphysical passion that ravaged Goya; it had to become *an end in itself*" [Bataille's italics].[19] Bataille's emphasis marks his agreement with Malraux, but also marks the limit of that agreement. Bataille is primarily interested in the mediation of violence in both paintings. "On the face of it," he writes, "death, coldly, methodically dealt out by a firing squad precludes an indifferent treatment; such a subject is nothing if not charged with meaning for each one of us" (*M,* 52; 133). His explanation of the *Shootings of May Third* praises Goya for aptly rendering the violence of the execution, of fitting the depiction to the thing depicted:[20]

> In that vision of a man about to die, flinging up his arms with a shriek, which we call *The Shootings of May Third,* we have the very image of death, such as a man can hardly ever know it, since the event itself wipes out all consciousness of it. In this picture Goya caught the blinding, instantaneous flash of death, a thunderbolt of sight-destroying intensity, brighter than any known light. The eloquence, the rhetoric of painting has never been carried further, but here its effect is that of definitive silence, an outcry smothered before it can arise. (*M,* 51;132)

Bataille's description of death as an event that "wipes out all consciousness of it" aligns quite well with the non-experience of death in *The Instant of My Death,* even though Blanchot's young man displays nothing of the terror or shock of Goya's peasant. What incites Bataille's critical interest here is not just the limit-experience of death, but the fact that Goya carries painting to its absolute limit in order to render that experience. The rhetoric of painting nearly turns itself inside out (smothering its own outcries) in order to create a fit between the representation and the experience. But if Goya brought painting to its limit in terms of representation, Manet enacted another sort of violence by transgressing that limit. Manet had seen Goya's painting in Madrid in 1865, and he began his own series of execution paintings two years later. It is difficult to say how much of a model Goya provided for Manet, but, in Bataille's account, such a comparison allows us to see how Manet displaces the violence of the painting. Manet's aesthetic is not one that amplifies the horror of its content; there are no shrieking peasants, no smothered outcries. The soldiers coldly fire on three victims who are rendered as flat, almost expressionless figures; the onlookers blur seamlessly into the landscape, imparting none of the horror of the witnesses in *Shootings of May Third.* Whereas Goya's painting is anchored to the terror of its content and to the Peninsular War to which it refers, Manet's painting, at least for Bataille, seems unmoored from the extreme demands of the depicted incident: "Manet deliberately rendered the condemned man's death with the same indifference as if he had chosen a fish or a flower for his subject. True, the picture relates an incident, no less than Goya's does, but—and this is what counts—without the least concern for the incident itself" (*M,* 52; 132). On the face of it, Bataille seems to reiterate Malraux. For Malraux, from whom Bataille quotes yet again, Manet's canvas is "Goya's *Shootings of May Third* minus what the latter picture signifies" (*M,* 50; 131). But Bataille is not simply telling us that aesthetic indifference has reached its full development or that Manet's painting is detached from the demands of representation; if that were the case, Bataille's thesis would have been more at home with abstract expressionists like Jackson Pollock, Willem de Kooning, and Barnett Newman, who were producing their signature works by the early to mid 1950s. Bataille departs from Malraux by heralding the power of aesthetic negation. In Bataille's account, Manet's primary achievement in the *Execution of Maximilian* is not indifference at all; rather, it is the transference of the violence of the execution to the violence of the painting's form.

Whereas Goya signals the end of the rhetoric of painting, of the deployment of paint, light, and color to depict history's grim episodes, Manet uses form to negate the content. But, as Bataille is careful to note, the content is "not altogether absent" (M, 52; 133); to modify Samuel Beckett's remark about James Joyce, form has not become content and content has not become form. This is why it is important that viewers can identify the historical incident. The cold treatment of political execution transforms the event into a mere occasion for formal experimentation. Manet's canvas announces the sovereignty of art, and this is why Bataille sees this painting as the inauguration of modernism. Because Manet's painting does not adhere to painterly conventions, it draws our attention to the lack of fit between the execution and its treatment; this is precisely what commands the viewer's eye and sparks the experience of the painting. Bataille thinks that this exemplifies the vocation of modern art, which, in his own words, is "to suppress and destroy the subject" (M, 52; 133) and to render titles and content as "mere pretexts for the painting" (M, 52; 133). In the end, "the meaning of the picture [both Olympia and Execution of Maximilian] is not in the text behind it but in the obliteration of that text" (M, 67; 142). It is not Maximilian who is executed in Manet's painting; it is history itself.

Unlike Bataille, Blanchot does not oppose aesthetics to history, and this is where his approach becomes most distinctive. His is neither the indifference of Malraux nor the negativity of Bataille. Blanchot's treatment of historical events, be it through the complex allegory of Death Sentence or the more fragmentary, dispersed meditations in The Writing of the Disaster, proceeds otherwise. His writing does not turn away from the force of history, but turns toward those moments and events that are forever without redemption, reconciliation, and meaning. This is what goes by the name of the neutral, the un-manifest, and the disaster in Blanchot's oeuvre. In this way, the disastrous events of history—the Second World War, the Holocaust, the Reign of Terror, the French Revolution—do not readily lend themselves to representation for him, but neither are they simply occasions or pretexts. There is a sustained fidelity to historical events in Blanchot, and that fidelity is one that exceeds personal obligation. This is why Blanchot asserts that "there must always be at least two languages, or two requirements: one dialectical, the other not; one where negativity is the task, the other where the neutral remains apart, cut off both from being and from not-being."[21] The relation of these two languages (or exigencies) constitutes Blanchot's theory of how writing attends to the historical event. It is not the case that one language is directed to what is available to representation and the other moves toward the un-manifest: "Write in order that the negative and the neutral, in their always concealed difference—in the most dangerous of proximities—might recall to each other the respective specificity, the one working, the other un-working" (WD, 37; 41). Thus, we do not grasp the un-manifest in history any more than we turn away from it. Instead, the un-manifest, the disasters of history, "keep watch" over us, extending from their incipient moment into the present without ever manifesting. I will have more to say about Blanchot's strange notion of vigilance (or is it surveillance?) and responsibility below. For now, though, I want to hold on to Blanchot's rather eccentric idea that writing bears the traces of historical events without ever acquiring the power to give them meaning.

"Nocturnal Signals, Silent Warnings"

Blanchot offers one way to conceive writing's relationship to history in an occasional essay entitled "War and Literature."[22] A Polish magazine had solicited replies to what was, by all appearances, a fairly straightforward question: "In your opinion, what is the influence that the war has had on literature after 1945?" (F, 297; 128). Blanchot answered briefly, but his response is hardly straightforward. The first section of his reply is worth quoting at length:

> The change undergone by the concept of literature—which those attempts marked by the names "the new novel," "new criticism," "structuralism," have helped to render spectacular in France—is not in immediate relation to the "Second World War," having been in the process of becoming long before; however, it found the accelerated confirmation of the fundamental crisis in the war, the change of an

era that we do not yet know how to measure for lack of a language. Which amounts to saying, In the crisis that keeps getting deeper and that literature also conveys according to its mode, war is always present and, in some ways, pursued. Which also amounts to saying, The war (the Second World War) was not only a war, a historical event like any other, circumscribed and limited with its causes, its turns, its results. It was an absolute. The *absolute* is named when one utters the names of Auschwitz, Warsaw (the ghetto and the struggle for liberation of the city), Treblinka, Dachau, Buchenwald, Neuengamme, Oranienburg, Belsen, Mauthausen, Ravensbrück, and so many others. (*F*, 109; 128)

Blanchot is careful to eliminate certain kinds of relations that one might establish between a particular historical event and literary innovation. First and foremost, there is no "immediate relation" between the two; that is, there is no causal relation.[23] As evidence, he points to the significant changes in literature that began prior to the war.[24] Furthermore, we also know that Blanchot sees literature's interrogation of its own conditions of possibility as a key feature of literature itself; contesting its own concept is fundamental to the very concept of literature, and any changes or developments that follow are not a direct effect of any historical event, be it the Second World War or anything else.[25] Because the initial question asks only about a causal relation, Blanchot deems it unanswerable. Of course, he does not dismiss the possibility of a relation between war and literature, nor does he diminish the importance of thinking through that relation. Leaving causal logic and theories of influence to the side, Blanchot recurs to his common formula for a relation of the third kind; that is, a relation without relation, X without X.[26] In order to open the way for this other relation, he first recasts the Second World War's place in history.

Blanchot's claim here is that the narration of the Second World War may misconstrue its status as an event. When first mentioned, the Second World War is set off in quotation marks, as are the names—*nouveau roman*, structuralism, new criticism—used to conceptualize the changes in literature. These names designate a set of characteristics or identifiable principles that describe a kind of novel or a particular mode of reading. In theory, we could move from the general features of the *nouveau roman* and locate them in a novel by someone like Alain Robbe-Grillet; the same could be done with any critical work adhering to the tenets of structuralism or the new criticism. If the "Second World War" operates like these others, it would be the general name for a series of causes and effects, provocations and reactions, victories and defeats. But this is not how Blanchot conceives it. "The war (the Second World War) is not only a war, a historical event like any other, circumscribed and limited with its causes, its turns, and its results" (*F*, 109; 128). The war exceeds the categories and concepts that would allow us to narrate it as another historical event. Blanchot's word choice here should not be overlooked: "circumscribed" and "limited" point us directly to the capacities (or incapacities) of writing to record or represent such an event. At the very moment that the Second World War exceeds historical narrative, it also disables the power of language. In this regard, the syntax of the above passage deserves special attention because it appears to enact part of Blanchot's argument.

When Blanchot describes his understanding of the war, he switches the syntax from quotation marks to parentheses. What has occurred in this shift of syntax? It seems that Blanchot is more interested in what escapes the narration of the Second World War. He brackets this idea of the war, literally placing it in parentheses, in order to address the abiding force of that event rather than its place within some Hegelian unfolding of History. Blanchot dubs the Second World War "an *absolute*" (and importantly, not *the* absolute). An absolute, of course, has no name itself, and, like those other corrosive ideas in Blanchot—the neutral, disaster, the Outside—it designates the place where meaning and understanding reach their limits; we might say it is the point where conditions of possibility turn into conditions of impossibility. The absolute names what occurred in such places as Auschwitz, Buchenwald, Warsaw, and Dachau. Such experiences are not so easily available to understanding, to narration, or even to memory itself; they reconstruct how we learn "to remember and to forget" (*F*, 109; 128), and, moreover, they enjoin us to never forget what we can never know.[27] It is this absolute, that which exceeds articulation, to which literature bears an impossible but inescapable relation, a relation without relation. We are back, then, to Blanchot's demand that writing must always speak in two languages, the negative and the neutral, the historical and the un-manifest. Blanchot wants writing to send us on a detour from knowledge and to turn us toward another temporality of the war, one that does not begin with a first battle nor end with a formal cessation of hostilities. Instead, this writing attends to what Blanchot would call the "nonhistorical time" of the war; that is, its peculiar duration and its effects on knowledge and memory.

Time, knowledge, memory: to write of the Second World War would mean addressing how the war put all of these into question. If the Second World War is not just another context for literature, then narrating the experiences of it may require another kind of writing, and, for Blanchot, another sort of narrative voice. He found this to be done in a remarkable way in Robert Antelme's *The Human Race,* and it is with reference to this text that he concludes "War and Literature": "This is also why the books stemming from the experience of which the camps were the place forever without place, have kept their dark radiance: not read and consumed in the same way as other books, important though they may be, but present as nocturnal signals, as silent warnings. I will cite only one, which for me is the simplest, the purest, and the closest to this absolute that it makes us remember: Robert Antelme's *L'Espèce humaine"* (F, 110; 129). The cold horror of Antelme's book never left Blanchot, and, like *The Instant of My Death,* it marks an attempt to write of the experience of living and dying in a concrete state of exception—one in the camps and the other in a war zone. More than this shared situation, both books also display a marked departure from autobiography. In "Humankind," his longer essay on *The Human Race,* Blanchot points to the peculiar status of Antelme's text and the problems it causes for any sort of generic classification. "It is not, as I have said, simply a witness's testimony to the reality of the camps or a historical reporting, nor is it an autobiographical narrative."[28] Neither testimony nor reporting nor autobiography: as we have seen, this same description applies equally to *The Instant of My Death.* All of these genres require the speaking subject to have the capacity to say "I," to command the narrative, and to speak with authority. Both *The Human Race* and *The Instant of My Death* deploy another kind of narrative voice, one that speaks not from the "I," but from what Blanchot calls the afflicted voice, or, the voice of one who has been deprived of "the power to say 'I'" (IC, 131; 193). In Blanchot's account, this narrative voice is a being deprived of subjectivity; it is the voice of one without "personal identity . . . a being without horizon" (*IC*, 131; 193). What, or who, speaks in these narratives? And further, how do we assess such narratives that speak in an afflicted voice, stripped of all individual sovereignty, all manner of subjectivity, and, for *The Instant of My Death,* even the certitude of memory?[29] What sort of autobiographical writing disperses, rather than consolidates, the narrative "I"?

Part of the problem with *The Instant of My Death* is that it opens with a clear division between an external narrator, the "I," and the object of narration, the young man: "I remember a young man—a man still young—prevented from dying by death itself—and perhaps the error of injustice" (*IM*, 3; 2). So much is open to question in this single sentence: the division of dying and death, the modality of "perhaps" that runs through so much of the *récit*, and "the error of injustice" (is there a correct or proper form of injustice?). This pivotal moment the narrator recalls is precisely the moment that inaugurates the split between the first and third person, making any certain knowledge impossible. Many critics have offered elaborate descriptions of the implications of this split for the narrator's knowledge of an experience that seems to be simultaneously his own and someone else's.[30] This passage from "I" to he is also the condition for literature in Blanchot, and it disables the epistemological certainty that should follow statements like "I remember" and "I know" (*je sais*). Three times the external narrator begins a part of his story with "I know," and each succeeding time the narrative's epistemological claims lose their hold. In the first occurrence, the narrator leaves the "I know" unqualified; "I know that the young man came to open the door to guests who were presumably asking for help" (*IM*, 3; 2). The statement offers no reason to doubt its veracity. The next two are noticeably different in appearance and function. "I know—do I know it—" (*IM*, 5; 4) and "I know, I imagine" (*IM*, 9; 8) bear their qualifiers alongside them, leaving all that follows uncertain. As Derrida points out, the "do I know it" (*IM*, 5; 4) operates as a question, threatening to turn the "I know" into its opposite. The "I imagine" works in similar fashion, but it also sketches out a series of juxtapositions: knowledge/imagination, testimony/fiction, and so on. All the same, the narrator's account proceeds in a speculative manner, leaving us with as many questions as answers.

Though we may not be able to verify exactly what the narrator knows, we can pinpoint when knowledge and memory part company: it is the instant of death when the "I" splits. What is the time of this instant? Blanchot had already considered the instant as a way to measure the strange, impossible time of death. Writing of Mallarmé's *Igitur,* he tells us of "the very instant of death, which is never present, which is the celebration of the absolute future, the instant at which one might say that, in a time without present, what has been will be."[31] Although the death in this case is "never present" (*SL,* 114; 142) because it is a suicide, the instant still names an experience that cannot be explained in terms of past, present, or future. Absolute future refers to a temporality wholly severed from the present, but it also has always been occurring and continues to occur without any resolution. Instant-time in Blanchot is not an alternate temporal order, but a kind of time that disperses linear, developmental time. In his remarks on instant-time in Blanchot's final *récit,* Hent de Vries writes that "the text of *L'instant de ma mort* can be read as an exploration of the untemporality, or atemporality, or countertemporality, of the instant, that is to say, of the instant of death, or, as we shall soon see, of the very *instance* and instantiation of this instant."[32] The sheer proliferation of prefixes to conceptualize the time of the instant indicates the corrosive effect this "instant" has on its own conceptualization. As de Vries points out, there are many variations of "instant"—instant, *instance,* instantiation. What do we make of the many instants in the *récit* that may or may not be part of the "instant" announced in the title?

This is a conceptual problem that migrates into the narrative form of *The Instant of My Death.* The first occurrence of the instant announces two simultaneous events: "At that instant, an abrupt return to the world, the considerable noise of a nearby battle exploded. Comrades from the maquis wanted to bring help to one they knew to be in danger. The lieutenant moved away to assess the situation. The Germans stayed in order, prepared to remain thus in an immobility that arrested time" (*IM,* 5; 4). In terms of the narrative, the instant sequences two moments at the level of the story: the moment before the Nazis receive the order to fire and the approach of the *maquisards.* What precedes this paragraph in the narrative discourse, though, is a slight interruption of the story. The external narrator intrudes and briefly suspends the time of the story to comment on the impossibility of analyzing or describing the experience of death. That experience may evade any firm description, but it introduces another temporal marker that accompanies both occurrences of the instant: "henceforth [*désormais*], he was bound to death by a surreptitious friendship" (*IM*, 5; 4). Death has been deferred, but not exactly escaped; henceforth, or from now on, the young man will forever be exposed to death. What these movements between story and narrative discourse encode is the operation of instant-time, which appears as a conjunction of two temporal orders: it is an irruption and a recurrence, a point (at that instant) and a duration (henceforth). The second occurrence of the instant draws these two temporalities much closer together. It also marks the first moment in the narrative when the narrator and the young man appear as the same person: "All that remains is the feeling of lightness that is death itself or, to put it more precisely, the instant of my death henceforth always in abeyance" (*IM*, 11; 10). The instant, the moment, endures into the present. Death deferred is reformulated as an endless exposure to death, where the instant is protracted into an endless, perhaps timeless, duration of death. That the narrator and the young man coalesce into the same person here should not be read as the consolidation of the split subject. Again, we refer back to the time of death, or, instant-time; the conjuncture of the instantaneous and the durational severs the "I" irreparably, and death slips outside of any dialectical movement or any ontological affirmation. "My death" is not the mark of a unified subject but the signature of an afflicted and dispersed "I," whose movements are evident everywhere in the formal operations of the *récit*. Encoded deftly in the movements between the third and first persons throughout the *récit*, the past and present will never be assembled into any sort of unity; they are forever disassembled and unworked.

OTHER VOICES

The exposure to death and that surreptitious friendship that follows open history onto the neutral. Even though this indescribable experience exists within nonhistorical time, the infinite exposure to death also designates far more than one person's confrontation with death. An extraordinary responsibility for those "assassinated" farmhands weighs over the young man (and the older Blanchot): "No doubt what then began for the young man was the torment of injustice. No more ecstasy; the feeling that he was only living because, even in the eyes of the Russians, he belonged to a noble class" (*IM*, 7; 6). "What then began" operates as another iteration of "henceforth" and suggests that the young man and the older Blanchot abide under two exposures to death: the young man's deferred death and those deaths handed out to the young farmhands. We would do well to recall Blanchot's strange, yet powerful, meditations on history and vigilance from *The Writing of the Disaster*. He tells us that it is not in the subject's power to keep watch over the past. In Blanchot's mind, no one has a hold over the disasters of history. Leslie Hill reminds us that Blanchot's philosophy of history, far from abdicating responsibility to the past, directs itself not toward "the meaning of history, but to the limits of historical understanding, not to the teleology and so-called objectivity of history, but to the burden of responsibility that history imposes, willingly or not, on those who are its actors or protagonists."[33] The responsibility toward the vanquished of history is not an active duty, nor is it in the subject's power to choose to keep watch. "It is not a power," Blanchot writes, "but the touch of the powerless infinite, exposure to the other of the night, where thought renounces the vigor of vigilance, gives up worldly clear-sightedness, perspicacious mastery" (*WD*, 49; 82). The vanquished do not require our vigilance, but instead *they* keep watch over us in the form of an unavoidable injunction (almost as a kind of surveillance or a haunting). It is not in the power of the subject to redeem those lost to history, nor will any form of writing answer their demand. For Blanchot, writing should exhibit the "passive pressure" (*WD*, 41; 71) of that demand by drawing the negative and the neutral into "the most dangerous of proximities" (*WD*, 37; 65). As we have seen with *The Instant of My Death* the working and unworking of history resurfaces in the writing itself, in the movements of the fragmentary, and in the dissolution of narrative form. For Blanchot, this is the only way for writing to maintain any fidelity to these disasters.

I have argued throughout that the crossing of the three voices that speak in *The Instant of My Death*—the autobiographical, the historical, the literary—both enable and interfere with one another. I close by asking what concept of the political emerges from *The Instant of My Death*. On the one hand, Blanchot's essays from the late 1930s and early 1940s set up a direct relation between writing and politics. If we are to believe that literary space serves as a postwar retreat, then the debates over Blanchot's politics will continue to turn on his activism and his other writings that display a direct relation to politics. On the other hand, Blanchot tells us that writing never knows "what will become of it politically: this is its intransitivity, its necessarily indirect relation to the political" (*WD*, 78; 126). This kind of writing can never be directly related to politics, and it can never pass as *littérature engagé*. Still, this is far from a defense of aesthetic autonomy. In the words of Jacques Rancière, this is precisely where literature "'does' politics."[34] If writing is to bear witness to the violence of history, its vocation is not to make sense of that violence or to explain it through cause and effect or, perhaps, even to seek reconciliation or redemption. If literature's singular power is its capacity to say anything, to speak without authority, its political work resides in its fidelity to those people and experiences that are impossible to account for. The detours of writing, its endless contestation of making knowledge possible, preserves the demands of the past on the present and ensures that they remain unavoidable and unanswerable. The concept of the political enciphered within *The Instant of My Death* is not a concept at all, but an incessant questioning. We might ask if the notion of the political as pure contestation of all concepts and all commitments is enough. For Blanchot, a recurring and unanswerable "is it enough?" might be the only properly political question.

Notes

Thanks to Nathan Hensley for our numerous conversations about this essay. It is all the better for those conversations, and any shortcomings or oversights are entirely mine.

    1. See chapter 4 of Kevin Hart's *The Dark Gaze: Maurice Blanchot and the Sacred* (Chicago: University of Chicago Press, 2004), 105–32. Hart shows how the "I" never fully disappears in Blanchot's writing. The "I" may lose its sovereignty, but it is not altogether abandoned or even superseded.

    2. See Maurice Blanchot, *The Madness of the Day*, in *The Station Hill Blanchot Reader: Fiction and Literary Essays*, trans. Lydia Davis, Paul Auster, and Robert

Lamberton, ed. George Quasha (Barrytown, NY: Station Hill Press, 1999); *La folie du jour* (Paris: Gallimard, 2002). "I was made to stand against the wall like many others. Why? For no reason. The guns did not go off. I said to myself, God, what are you doing? At that point I stopped being insane. The world hesitated, then regained its equilibrium" (191–92; 11). The page numbers in the translation are followed by the page of the French edition.

3. Many of Blanchot's texts bear an autobiographical mark. In addition to the aforementioned scene from *The Madness of the Day,* see also "Les rencontres," in *Le Nouvel Observateur* 1045 (November 1984): 84; "Notre compagne clandestine," in *Textes pour Emmanuel Lévinas,* ed. Françoise Laruelle (Paris: J-M Place, 1980), 79–87.

4. See Jacques Derrida, *Demeure: Fiction and Testimony,* trans. Elizabeth Rottenberg, bound with Maurice Blanchot, *The Instant of My Death* (Stanford: Stanford University Press, 2000); Philippe Lacoue-Labarthe, "The Contestation of Death" in *The Power of Contestation: Perspectives on Maurice Blanchot,* ed. Kevin Hart and Geoffrey Hartmann (Baltimore: Johns Hopkins University Press, 2004), 141–55; Lacoue-Labarthe, "Fidelities," in *Oxford Literary Review* 22 (2000): 132–51.

5. See Leslie Hill, "'Not In Our Name': Blanchot, Politics, the Neuter," *Paragraph* 30, no. 3 (2007): 141–59. Hill also considers Blanchot's writings as "political," and not merely as evidence of his politics. His essay puts Blanchot's thought into dialogue with current discussions of law, sovereignty, and the political.

6. Maurice Blanchot, "Marx's Three Voices," in *Friendship,* trans. Elizabeth Rottenberg (Stanford: Stanford University Press, 1997), 98; *L'amitié* (Paris: Gallimard, 1971), 115.

7. See Steven Ungar, *Scandal and Aftereffect: Blanchot and France since 1930* (Minneapolis: University of Minnesota Press, 1995); Jeffrey Mehlman, *Legacies of Anti-Semitism in France* (Minneapolis: University of Minnesota Press, 1983) and *Genealogies of the Text: Literature, Psychoanalysis, and Politics in Modern France* (Cambridge: Cambridge University Press, 1995); Richard Wolin, *The Seduction of Unreason: The Intellectual Romance with Fascism from Nietzsche to Postmodernism* (Princeton: Princeton University Press, 2004). All these writers have investigated the questionable work from Blanchot's political past, while Leslie Hill, Christopher Fynsk, and Michael Holland have been especially vigilant in reminding us of the scope and range of Blanchot's political writings over his entire career. Christophe Bident's recent edition of all of Blanchot's essays for *Journal des débats* will certainly enrich the current debate. See *Chroniques littéraires du "Journal des débats": Avril 1941–août 1944* (Paris: Gallimard, 2007).

8. Wolin, *The Seduction of Unreason,* 190. Wolin's analysis is rich in its exploration of those essays of Blanchot's that his admirers find so disconcerting, but his chapter on Blanchot is remarkably myopic. Any analysis of Blanchot's

politics that does not address writings such as *The Step Not Beyond, The Writing of the Disaster, The Instant of My Death,* or the important essays on politics and war in *Friendship* and *The Infinite Conversation* seems lacking and even a bit reckless. Wolin serves up two propositions that are of great concern (and would be of greater concern if they were historically accurate): first, Blanchot moves from being an engaged intellectual in the 1930s and 1940s to being an aesthete as far removed from public life as one could imagine; second, Wolin asserts that Blanchot's alignment with the Resistance during the Occupation is a "fable" and that any such stories to the contrary are "apocryphal," 201–2. Regarding the first claim, one need only point to Blanchot's political activities listed above to dismiss such a characterization. As for the second, such an aggressive claim would seem impossible to defend without first passing through *The Instant of My Death* and those accounts of Blanchot's relationship with (and assistance to) Paul Lévy, as well as contemporary accounts by scholars such as Leslie Hill, Michael Holland, and Gerald L. Bruns, all of whom reach very different conclusions. Given that all of these works preceded the publication of *The Seduction of Unreason,* one wonders if motive has not trumped method in this case.

    9. Philip Watts repeats this story in "Blanchot: Rebuttals," in his *Allegories of the Purge: How Literature Responded to the Postwar Trials of Writers and Intellectuals in France* (Stanford: Stanford University Press, 1998). He draws a comparison between Paul de Man and Blanchot: "Both authors followed a startlingly similar path from an engagement with fascist politics in their youth to the radical disengagement of literature from political reality," 84.

    10. Wolin, *The Seduction of Unreason,* 190.

    11. See the dossier in Blanchot's "Responses and Interventions (1946–1998)," *Paragraph* 30, no. 3 (2007): 5–45, trans. Leslie Hill and Michael Holland.

    12. Hart, *The Dark Gaze,* 74.

    13. Lacoue-Labarthe, "The Contestation of Death," 152.

    14. Maurice Blanchot, *The Instant of My Death,* trans. Elizabeth Rottenberg, bound with Derrida, *Demeure: Fiction and Testimony* (Stanford: Stanford University Press, 2000), 9; *L'instant de ma mort* in the same work (a dual language edition with facing French-English), 8. Hereafter cited in the text as *IM.* Throughout, abbreviations of works by Blanchot and Bataille in main text are followed by the page number of the English translation and the page number of the French.

    15. In the course of his lecture, Derrida quotes from a letter he received on July 20 from Blanchot that summarized what we would eventually all learn from *The Instant of My Death:* "July 20. Fifty years ago, I knew the happiness of nearly being shot to death." Derrida, *Demeure,* 52.

    16. See Carl Schmitt,*The Nomos of the Earth in the International Law of the Jus Publicum Europaeum,* trans. G. L. Ulmen (New York: Telos Press, 2003).

This book contains Schmitt's most developed discussion of just and unjust enemies. Schmitt identifies the just enemy as the "beginning of all international law," 52.

17. Derrida, *Demeure*, 43.

18. See Fyodor Dostoevsky *The Idiot,* trans. Anna Brailovsky et al. (New York: Modern Library, 2003); André Malraux, *Anti-Memoirs,* trans. Terence Kilmartin (New York: Holt, Rinehart, and Winston, 1968), 147; *Antimèmoires* (Paris: Gallimard, 1967), 217–18.

19. Georges Bataille, *Manet: A Biographical and Critical Study,* trans. Austryn Wainhouse and James Emmons (New York: Skira, 1955), 49; vol. 9 of *Oeuvres completes,* 12 vols. (Paris: Gallimard, 1970–88), 130. Hereafter cited in the text as *M.*

20. Although he does not deal explicitly with Manet or Goya, J. M. Bernstein's thoughts on the fitness of world to representation and painterly realism are among the most insightful to have appeared in recent years. See his *Against Voluptuous Bodies: Late Modernism and the Meaning of Painting* (Stanford: Stanford University Press, 2006).

21. Blanchot, *The Writing of the Disaster,* trans. Ann Smock (Lincoln: University of Nebraska Press, 1995), 20; *L'écriture du désastre* (Paris: Gallimard, 1980), 38. Hereafter cited in the text as *WD.* Also see the essay "Traces," where Blanchot writes this of the neuter: "The entire history of philosophy could be seen as an effort to domesticate the neuter or to impugn it—thus it is constantly repressed from our language and our truths. How does one think the neuter? Is there a time, a historical time, a time without history, in which speaking is the exigency to speak the neuter? What would happen, supposing the neuter were essentially that which speaks (does not speak) when we speak?" In Blanchot, *Friendship,* 220; *L'amitié,* 249.

22. Blanchot, "War and Literature," in *Friendship,* 109–10; *L'amitié,* 128–29. Hereafter, this essay in *Friendship* is cited in the text with the abbreviation *F.*

23. While Blanchot will inevitably propose a third relation, I do not think that "immediate relation" here carries the same conceptual weight as it does in "The Relation of the Third Kind (Man without Horizon)," in *The Infinite Conversation* (Minneapolis: University of Minnesota Press, 1993), 66–74; *L'entretien infini* (Paris: Gallimard, 1969), 94–105. In that essay, Blanchot distinguishes the immediate relation from the mediated, dialectical relations of Hegel and others. An immediate relation is one where the "I" loses its sovereignty to the Other and the two fuse immediately and absolutely into the One (as opposed to the Same in Hegelian dialectics). In "War and Literature," "immediate relation" refers to a causal relation.

24. To think of literature and history as beyond influence or cause and effect poses serious methodological questions to literary criticism, particularly the subtle empiricism that certain brands of historicism and archival studies have

advanced as of late. One possible retort to Blanchot would be from Theodor W. Adorno. His theory of aesthetic mediation shares Blanchot's refusal of the Hegelian logic of identity, but poses a different relationship to the social world. Given the deep admiration of Blanchot and Adorno for writers such as Kafka and Beckett, their writings on the Holocaust, and their critiques of Hegel, it is surprising that there is not more attention to the aesthetic theories of Adorno and Blanchot. A welcome exception to this is Vivian Liska, "Two Sirens Singing: Literature as Contestation in Maurice Blanchot and Theodor W. Adorno," in *The Power of Contestation*, 80–100.

25. This accounts for Blanchot's theory of writing as an event in Heidegger's sense of the term. It is not, as it is for Theodor W. Adorno and most Marxist critics, a form of mediation. I thank Jerry Bruns for our weekly conversations on Heidegger, Adorno, and Walter Benjamin some years ago, which taught me the importance and weight of such a distinction and, later on, its importance for coming to terms with Blanchot. For more on Blanchot, Heidegger, and art as event, see Gerald L. Bruns, *Maurice Blanchot: The Refusal of Philosophy* (Baltimore: Johns Hopkins University Press, 1997).

26. For one of Blanchot's more methodical articulations of this type of relation, see "The Relation of the Third Kind."

27. "We read books on Auschwitz," Blanchot writes. "The wish of all, in the camps, the last wish: know what has happened, do not forget, and at the same time never will you know." *Writing of the Disaster*, 82; *L'écriture du désastre*, 131.

28. Blanchot, "Humankind," in "The Indestructible" (one essay composed of two smaller essays, "Humankind" and "Being Jewish"), in *The Infinite Conversation*, 130; *L'entretien infini*, 193. Hereafter, "Humankind" is cited in the text with the abbreviation *IC*. For an insightful and provocative reading of both "Humankind" and "Being Jewish," see Christopher Fynsk, "Blanchot's 'The Indestructible,'" in *After Blanchot: Literature, Criticism, Philosophy*, ed. Leslie Hill, Brian Nelson, and Dimitris Vardoulakis (Newark: University of Delaware Press, 2005),100–122.

29. One thinks here of Blanchot's comments on Jean Paulhan in "The Ease of Dying": "Too easily did I tell myself that we need the great void where war displaces us, depriving us of ourselves and according us only private happiness and unhappiness as privation, so that it should be possible for us then to speak of it, that is, really not to speak of it." In *Friendship*, 150; *L'amitié*, 173.

30. See Derrida, *Demeure;* Lacoue-Labarthe "The Contestation of Death"; Hart, *The Dark Gaze*, especially 70–75.

31. Blanchot, *The Space of Literature*, trans. Ann Smock (Lincoln: University of Nebraska Press, 1982), 114; *L'éspace littéraire* (Paris: Gallimard, 1955), 142. Hereafter cited in the text as *SL*.

32. Hent de Vries, "'Lapsus Absolu': Notes on Maurice Blanchot's *The Instant of My Death*," *Yale French Studies* no. 93 (1998): 37.

33. Leslie Hill, *Blanchot: Extreme Contemporary* (London: Routledge, 1997), 7.

34. Jacques Rancière opens a way for thinking of how literature does politics. His analysis takes us far from literature as subjective expression or as a mode of representation. Literary texts should not be read as encoded messages of their author's political leanings, nor can their political value be gleaned from the ways they transcribe this or that event. For Rancière, as for Blanchot in a slightly different way, literature's political force resides in its endless contestation of what he calls "the partition of the visible and the sayable," those mechanisms that determine who and what counts. Rancière, "The Politics of Literature," *SubStance* 33, no. 1 (2004): 10. See also his *The Politics of Aesthetics: The Distribution of the Sensible* (New York: Continuum, 2004).

Bibliography of Writings by Maurice Blanchot

French Publications

Thomas l'obscur. Paris: Gallimard, 1941. Rpt. 2005, *Thomas l'obscur: Première version, 1941,* intro. Pierre Madaule.

Comment la littérature est-elle possible? Paris: Corti, 1942.

Aminadab. Paris: Gallimard, 1942.

Faux pas. Paris: Gallimard, 1943.

Le Très-Haut. Paris: Gallimard, 1948.

L'arrêt de mort. Paris: Gallimard, 1948.

La part du feu. Paris: Gallimard, 1949.

Lautréamont et Sade. Paris: Minuit, 1949.

Thomas l'obscur, nouvelle version. Paris: Gallimard, 1950.

Au moment voulu. Paris: Gallimard, 1951.

Le ressassement éternal. Paris: Minuit, 1951.

Celui qui ne m'accompagnait pas. Paris: Gallimard, 1953.

L'espace littéraire. Paris: Gallimard, 1955.

Le dernier homme. Paris: Gallimard, 1957.

La bête de Lascaux. Paris: G. L. M., 1958.

Le livre à venir. Paris: Gallimard, 1959.

L'attente l'oubli. Paris: Gallimard, 1962.

L'entretien infini. Paris: Gallimard, 1969.

L'amitié. Paris: Gallimard, 1971.

La folie du jour. Montpellier: Fata Morgana, 1973.

Le pas au-delà. Paris: Gallimard, 1973.

L'écriture du désastre. Paris: Gallimard, 1980.

De Kafka à Kafka. Paris: Gallimard, 1981.

Après coup, précédé par "Le ressassement éternal." Paris: Minuit, 1983.

Le nom de Berlin. Berlin: Merve, 1983.

La communauté inavouable. Paris: Minuit, 1983.

Le dernier à parler. Montpellier: Fata Morgana, 1984.

Michel Foucault tel que je l'imagine. Montpellier: Fata Morgana, 1986.

Sade et Restif de la Bretonne. Bruxelles: Complexe, 1986.

Sur Lautréamont. Bruxelles: Complexe, 1987.

Joë Bousquet. Montpellier: Fata Morgana, 1987.

Une voix venue d'ailleurs: Sur les poèmes de Louis-René des Forêts. Plombières-les-Dijon: Ulysse Fin de Siècle, 1992.

L'instant de ma mort. Montpellier: Fata Morgana, 1994.

Les intellectuels en question. Paris: Fourbis, 1996.

Pour l'amitié. Paris: Fourbis, 1996.

Henri Michaux ou le refus de l'enfermement. Tours: Farrago, 1999.

Écrits politiques: Guerre d'Algérie, Mai 68 etc, 1958–1993. Paris: Lignes / Éditions Léo Scheer, 2003.

Chroniques littéraires du "Journal des débats": Avril 1941–août 1944, ed. Christophe Bident. Paris: Gallimard, 2007.

Lettres à Vadim Kozovoï suivi de "La parole ascendante," ed. Denis Aucouturier. Houilles: Éditions Manucius, 2009.

La Condition critique: Articles 1945–1988, ed. Christophe Bident. Paris: Gallimard, 2010.

ENGLISH TRANSLATIONS

The following translations are listed in the order of the original French publications.

Thomas the Obscure, trans. Robert Lamberton. New York: David Lewis, 1973. A translation of the "new version." Rpt., Barrytown, NY: Station Hill Press, 1995.

"How Is Literature Possible?" trans. Michael Syrotinski. In *The Blanchot Reader*, ed. Michael Holland, 49–60. Oxford: Basil Blackwell, 1995.

Aminadab, trans. Jeff Fort. Lincoln: University of Nebraska Press, 2002.

Faux Pas, trans. Charlotte Mandell. Stanford: Stanford University Press, 2001.

The Most High, trans. Allan Stoekl. Lincoln: University of Nebraska Press, 1996.

Death Sentence, trans. Lydia Davis. Barrytown, NY: Station Hill Press, 1978.

The Work of Fire, trans. Charlotte Mandell. Stanford: Stanford University Press, 1995.

Lautréamont and Sade, trans. Stuart Kendall and Michelle Kendall. Stanford: Stanford University Press, 2004.

When the Time Comes, trans. Lydia Davis. Barrytown, NY: Station Hill Press, 1985.

Vicious Circles: Two Fictions and "After the Fact," trans. Paul Auster. Barrytown, NY: Station Hill Press, 1985.

The One Who Was Standing Apart from Me, trans. Lydia Davis. Barrytown, NY: Station Hill Press, 1993.

The Space of Literature, trans. Ann Smock. Lincoln: University of Nebraska Press, 1982.

The Last Man, trans. Lydia Davis. New York: Columbia University Press, 1987.

"The Beast of Lascaux," trans. Leslie Hill. *Oxford Literary Review* 22 (2000): 9–18.

The Book to Come, trans. Charlotte Mandell. Stanford: Stanford University Press, 2003.

Awaiting Oblivion, trans. John Gregg. Lincoln: University of Nebraska Press, 1997.

The Infinite Conversation, trans. Susan Hanson. Minneapolis: University of Minnesota Press, 1993.

Friendship, trans. Elizabeth Rottenberg. Stanford: Stanford University Press, 1997.

The Madness of the Day, trans. Lydia Davis. Barrytown, NY: Station Hill Press, 1981.

The Step Not Beyond, trans. Lycette Nelson. Albany: State University of New York Press, 1992.

The Writing of the Disaster, trans. Ann Smock. Lincoln: University of Nebraska Press, 1986.

"The Name Berlin," trans. Michael Holland. In *The Blanchot Reader,* ed. Michael Holland, 266–68. Oxford: Basil Blackwell, 1995.

The Unavowable Community, trans. Pierre Joris. Barrytown, NY: Station Hill Press, 1988.

Michel Foucault as I Imagine Him, trans. Jeffrey Mehlmann, bound with Michel Foucault, *Maurice Blanchot: The Thought from Outside,* trans. Brian Massumi. New York: Zone Books, 1990.

A Voice from Elsewhere, trans. Charlotte Mandell. Albany: State University of New York Press, 2007.

The Instant of My Death, bound with Jacques Derrida, *Demeure: Fiction and Testimony,* trans. Elizabeth Rottenberg. Stanford: Stanford University Press, 2000.

"Intellectuals under Scrutiny," trans. Michael Holland. In *The Blanchot Reader,* ed. Michael Holland, 206–27. Oxford: Basil Blackwell, 1995.

"For Friendship," trans. Leslie Hill. *Oxford Literary Review* 22 (2000): 25–38.

Also see the following anthologies of Blanchot's writings in English translation:

The Gaze of Orpheus and Other Literary Essays, preface by Geoffrey Hartman, trans. Lydia Davis, ed. P. Adams Sitney. Barrytown, NY: Station Hill Press, 1981.

The Siren's Song: Selected Essays, ed. Gabriel Josipovici, trans. Sacha Rabinovitch. Brighton: Harvester Press, 1982.

The Blanchot Reader, ed. Michael Holland. Oxford: Basil Blackwell, 1995.

The Station Hill Blanchot Reader: Fiction and Literary Essays, ed. George Quasha, trans. Lydia Davis et al. Barrytown, NY: Station Hill Press, 1999.

"Responses and Interventions (1946–98)," trans. Leslie Hill and Michael Holland. *Paragraph* 30, no. 1 (2007): 5–45.

Notes on Contributors

Christophe Bident is Maître de Conférences at the University of Paris 7—Denis Diderot. He is the author of *Maurice Blanchot: Partenaire invisible* (Champ Vallon, 1998); *Bernard-Marie Koltès, Généalogies* (Farrago, 2000); and *Reconnaissances: Antelme, Blanchot, Deleuze* (Calmann-Lévy, 2003). He has edited a volume of early literary reviews by Maurice Blanchot, *Chroniques littéraires du "Journal des débats," Avril 1941–Août 1944* (Gallimard, 2007), along with a collection of essays from the 2007 colloquium at Cerisy that was devoted to Blanchot, *Blanchot dans son siècle* (Parangon, 2009), and has co-edited, with Pierre Vilar, *Maurice Blanchot: Récits critiques* (Farrago, 2003). He recently edited another volume of literary essays by Blanchot, *La Condition critique: Articles 1945–1998* (Gallimard, 2010).

Arthur Cools is Associate Professor in the Philosophy Department of the University of Antwerp where he teaches Contemporary Philosophy, Philosophy of Culture, and Philosophy of Art. He is the author of *Langage et subjectivité: Vers une approche du différend entre Maurice Blanchot et Emmanuel Lévinas* (Peeters, 2007). He is co-editor of *Maurice Blanchot: La singularité d'une écriture* (Les Lettres romanes, special issue, 2005); *The Locus of Tragedy*, Series in Contemporary Philosophy (Brill, 2008); and *Debating Levinas' Legacy* (Brill, forthcoming).

THOMAS S. DAVIS is an Assistant Professor of English at Ohio State University. His essay on Henri Lefebvre and modernist aesthetics appears in *Modernism and Theory: A Critical Debate*, ed. Stephen Ross (Routledge, 2009). He is currently working on a manuscript entitled *The Extinct Scene: Late Modernism and Everyday Life*.

CHRISTOPHER FYNSK is Professor of Modern Thought and Comparative Literature at the University of Aberdeen, and Director of the Centre for Modern Thought at Aberdeen. His publications include *Heidegger: Thought and Historicity* (Cornell University Press, 1993); *Language and Relation: . . . That There Is Language* (Stanford University Press, 1996); *Infant Figures: The Death of the Infans and Other Scenes of Origin* (Stanford University Press, 2000); and *The Claim of Language: A Case for the Humanities* (University of Minnesota Press, 2004).

RODOLPHE GASCHÉ is SUNY Distinguished Professor and Eugenio Donato Professor of Comparative Literature at the State University of New York at Buffalo. His numerous books include *Inventions of Difference: On Jacques Derrida* (Harvard University Press, 1994); *The Wild Card of Reading: On Paul de Man* (Harvard University Press, 1998); *Of Minimal Things: Studies on the Notion of Relation* (Stanford University Press, 1999); *The Idea of Form: Rethinking Kant's Aesthetic* (Stanford University Press, 2003); *Views and Interviews: On "Deconstruction" in America* (The Davies Group, 2006); *The Honor of Thinking: Critique, Theory, Philosophy* (Stanford University Press, 2007); and *Europe, or the Infinite Task: A Study of a Philosophical Concept* (Stanford University Press, 2009). Currently he is completing two book-length studies, one entitled *The Stelliferous Fold: Essays on Literature and Literary Criticism*, and the other, *Rhetoric, Hermeneutics, and Deconstruction*.

KEVIN HART is Edwin B. Kyle Professor of Christian Studies at the University of Virginia, where he teaches in the departments of Religious Studies, English, and French. He is the author of several books, including *The Trespass of the Sign: Deconstruction, Theology, and Philosophy* (Cambridge University Press, 1989; expanded ed., Fordham University Press, 2000), and *The Dark Gaze: Maurice Blanchot and the Sacred* (University of Chicago Press, 2004). He is the editor of *Counter-Experiences: Reading Jean-Luc Marion* (University of Notre Dame Press, 2007), and the co-editor of *Derrida and Religion: Other Testaments* (Routledge, 2004); *The Power of Contestation: Perspectives on Maurice Blanchot* (Johns Hopkins University Press, 2004); and *The Exorbitant: Emmanuel Levinas between Jews and Christians* (Fordham University Press, 2009). His most recent collections of poetry are *Flame Tree: Selected Poems* (Bloodaxe, 2004) and *Young Rain* (University of Notre Dame Press, 2009). He is currently editing *Jean-Luc Marion: The Essential Writings* for Fordham University Press, and has recently completed a new collection of poems, *Morning Knowledge*.

LESLIE HILL is Professor of French Studies at the University of Warwick and the author of *Beckett's Fiction: In Different Words* (Cambridge University Press, [1990] 2009); *Marguerite Duras: Apocalyptic Desires* (Routledge, 1993); *Blanchot: Extreme Contemporary* (Routledge, 1997); *Bataille, Klossowski, Blanchot: Writing at the Limit* (Oxford University Press, 2001); *The Cambridge Introduction to Jacques Derrida* (Cambridge University Press, 2007); and *Radical Indecision: Barthes, Blanchot, Derrida, and the Future of Criticism* (University of Notre Dame Press, 2010). He is also co-editor (with Brian Nelson and Dimitris Vardoulakis) of *After Blanchot: Literature, Philosophy, Criticism* (University of Delaware Press, 2005), and is currently completing a book on fragmentary writing in Blanchot.

MICHAEL HOLLAND is a Fellow of St Hugh's College, Oxford, where he teaches French literature. He is the editor of *The Blanchot Reader* (Blackwell, 1995) and the author of numerous essays on Blanchot's work in both journals and collected volumes. He is a founding editor of *Paragraph: A Journal of Modern Literary Theory*, and jointly with Leslie Hill he recently edited a special number of the journal entitled *Blanchot's Epoch* (November 2007). He is currently working on a book about narrative and time in Blanchot's writing.

STEPHEN E. LEWIS is Associate Professor of English at the Franciscan University of Steubenville. He has published several translations of contemporary French philosophy, including Jean-Louis Chrétien, *Hand to Hand: Listening to the Work of Art* (Fordham University Press, 2003); Jean-Luc Marion, *Prolegomena to Charity* (Fordham University Press, 2002); Jean-Luc Marion, *The Erotic Phenomenon* (University of Chicago Press, 2007); and Claude Romano, *Event and Time* (Fordham University Press, forthcoming). He is at work on a critical history of French Christian thought since World War II.

VIVIAN LISKA is Professor of German Literature and Director of the Institute of Jewish Studies at the University of Antwerp, Belgium, where she teaches modern German literature and literary theory. Her publications include *Die Nacht der Hymnen: Paul Celans Gedichte, 1938–1944* (Peter Lang, 1993); *Die Dichterin und das schelmische Erhabene: Else Lasker-Schülers Die Nächte Tino von Bagdads* (Franke, 1997); *"Die Moderne, ein Weib": Am Beispiel von Romanen Ricarda Huchs und Annette Kolbs* (Francke, 2000); *Girogio Agambens leerer Messianismus* (Schlebruegge, 2008); and *When Kafka Says We: Uncommon Communities in German-Jewish Literature* (Indiana University Press, 2009). She has co-edited, with Astradur Eysteinsson, *Modernism* (John Benjamins, 2007), with Thomas Nolden, *Contemporary Jewish Writing in Europe: A Guide* (Indiana University Press, 2007), and with Eva Meyer, *What Does the Veil Know?* (Voldemeer, 2009).

CAROLINE SHEAFFER-JONES teaches French literature at the University of New South Wales, Sydney. She has published widely on Blanchot, as well as on Camus, Derrida, Kofman, and Lévinas. Recent articles include "La parole du détour," in *Emmanuel Lévinas–Maurice Blanchot, penser la différence*, sous la direction d'Éric Hoppenot et Alain Milon (Presses Universitaires de Paris 10, 2008); "The Point of the Story: Levinas, Blanchot and *The Madness of the Day*," *Modern Fiction Studies* 54, no. 1 (2008); "Configurations of a Heritage: Élisabeth Roudinesco's *Philosophes dans la tourmente*," *Contemporary French Civilization* 33, no. 1 (2009); and "'Pardon for not meaning': Remarks on Derrida, Blanchot and Kafka," *Derrida Today* 2, no. 2 (2009).

CHRISTOPHER A. STRATHMAN teaches writing and humanities in the English Department at Case Western Reserve University in Cleveland, Ohio. His publications include *Romantic Poetry and the Fragmentary Imperative: Schegel, Byron, Joyce, Blanchot* (State University of New York Press, 2006), as well as articles on British romanticism, American romanticism, Victorian poetry, and literary theory. He has been a Golda Meir Postdoctoral Fellow in the Humanities at the Hebrew University of Jerusalem.

ALAIN TOUMAYAN teaches nineteenth- and twentieth-century French literature, literary criticism, and philosophy and literature at the University of Notre Dame. He is the author of *La Littérature et la hantise du mal: Lectures de Barbey d'Aurevilly, Huysmans et Baudelaire* (French Forum, 1987) and *Encountering the Other: The Artwork and the Problem of Difference in Blanchot and Levinas* (Duquesne University Press, 2004). He has edited *Literary Generations* (French Forum, 1992) and published various articles, most recently on Blanchot and Lévinas. He is currently working on Lévinas and the problem of human rights.

Index